I0824651

AVID
READER
PRESS

How the
DECLARATION
of
INDEPENDENCE
MADE AMERICA

National Treasure

MICHAEL AUSLIN

AVID READER PRESS
New York Amsterdam/Antwerp London
Toronto Sydney/Melbourne New Delhi

Avid Reader Press
An Imprint of Simon & Schuster, LLC
1230 Avenue of the Americas
New York, NY 10020

First Avid Reader Press hardcover edition May 2026

Interior design by Lewelin Polanco

Manufactured in the United States of America

1 3 5 7 9 10 8 6 4 2

Library of Congress Control Number: 2025949992

ISBN 978-1-6682-1454-1
ISBN 978-1-6682-1456-5 (ebook)

To my grandparents and great-grandparents,
who were inspired by the Declaration's
promises to cross an ocean

. . . this was the object of the Declaration of Independance. not to find out new principles, or new arguments, never before thought of, not merely to say things which had never been said before; but to place before mankind the common sense of the subject; . . . it was intended to be an expression of the american mind . . .

—**THOMAS JEFFERSON to Henry Lee, May 8, 1825**

Now, my countrymen, . . . if you have been inclined to believe that all men are not created equal in those inalienable rights enumerated by our chart of liberty, let me entreat you to come back. Return to the fountain whose waters spring close by the blood of the Revolution . . . *do not destroy that immortal emblem of Humanity—the Declaration of American Independence.*

—**ABRAHAM LINCOLN, "Speech at Lewiston, Illinois," August 17, 1858**

The Declaration is the Polaris of our political order—the fixed star of freedom. It is impervious to change because it states moral truths that are eternal.

—**GERALD R. FORD, "Remarks at a Bicentennial Ceremony at the National Archives," July 2, 1976**

CONTENTS

INTRODUCTION

I was six when I first saw the Declaration of Independence. There, in its old marble shrine in the Rotunda of the National Archives, it seemed as powerful to me as the Ten Commandments. Around me, people of all ages stood transfixed, straining to make out the faint words and signatures. Once I had stared in awe at the dim parchment, my parents took me to the gift shop and bought me an "antiqued" copy, printed on golden-brown, crinkly paper. I pinned it up on my bedroom wall and can still remember its sweet-sour aroma. When I looked up at it over the following years, it symbolized to me the basic ideals of America.

Though I didn't understand it at the time, my encounter with the Declaration—one that tens of millions of people have shared—reflected its three lives: as America's most revered relic, as a symbol of our most deeply held principles, and as an ever-present part of American culture. This book tells the story of how those three lives came together to create one nation.

The "official" engrossed parchment has survived two hundred and fifty years, overcoming neglect and abuse, heroically saved in times of war, and preserved by ingenious technology. Though it was nearly forgotten for a time when the Constitution seemed the more important founding document, for most of its existence it has been a priceless relic, protected by custodians, conservators, and armed guards. It has been displayed in bright sunlight and locked in dark cabinets, rescued from the flames, hidden in a cellar, carried in carts, moved secretly by train, and secured by the world's most sophisticated security systems. The scroll is a time machine, drawing visitors in a never-ending stream to gaze in wonder at the very parchment touched and signed by the larger-than-life men who founded America.

The Declaration's second life is as a noble ideal, making it the central expression of the American experience. This is the basis for Abraham Lincoln's claim, at Gettysburg, that ours is a nation "conceived in liberty and dedicated to the proposition that all men are created equal." Every major political program and piece of legislation, and so many of our most memorable speeches, refer to, build upon, or argue with the Declaration. It envisions a common destiny for the "one people" who chose to separate from the King of England and his Parliament. If the Constitution tells us how to live together as a political community, the Declaration tells us how we should *want* to live. How the Declaration came to be the supreme symbol of our national ideal is the story of America over two and a half centuries.

These two lives are linked together by a third: the transformation of this statement of lofty principles into a central element of American culture. The story of this third life is largely untold, though in many ways it is the one that has brought the Declaration closest to Americans. The Declaration has inspired heroic paintings and mass advertising, as well as melodramatic movies and a high-minded musical. It has been commodified to sell posters, T-shirts, hats, and scarves. We have carried the Declaration into our homes, schools, and offices, hanging that crinkly fake parchment on our walls or displaying a commemorative plate or medallion. In 2025, a limited-edition printing of the Declaration on calfskin parchment was marketed for well over one thousand dollars. While writing this book, I visited the National Park Service's Franklin Court Printing Office in Philadelphia and bought paper copies of the two earliest typeset Declarations fresh off a reproduction eighteenth-century printing press. The frames I bought to hang them in were more than ten times as expensive as the prints, but as Lincoln observed, what is inside the frame is worth its weight in gold. As an object and commodity, the Declaration has for over two centuries been part of our culture, linking us deliberately and tangibly to our founding moment.

Yet although the Declaration seems everywhere, its history and our relationship to it remain less known. Some persistent myths remain, such as the belief that the document was signed on July 4. Other questions are more intriguing. What explains its power to guide settlers on the banks of the Mississippi in the early 1800s and, nearly a century later, inspire my immigrant ancestors arriving in Chicago to assimilate and embrace American values? More difficult is understanding how the same document was used both by those fighting for equality throughout American history and by those who sought to separate from the United States to "preserve" their liberty. How could it contain eternal truths and yet be repeatedly reimagined to fit the needs of the time?

As a child I didn't know that John Locke's philosophy, or any other, had influenced Thomas Jefferson. Growing up in the North, I wasn't aware that Southerners had justified secession by appealing to the Declaration's claim that the governed could withdraw their consent, or that, a century later, Black Panthers and separatist militias alike would invoke its language to justify violent resistance to the federal government. For my friends and me, it was enough simply to hang the Declaration on our bedroom walls, as Americans had done in the 1820s, and 1880s, and 1940s, tying us just as powerfully to a shared national history.

The country we live in today came into focus roughly a century ago, when massive numbers of people flocked to our shores, radically transforming the fabric of a society that was industrializing and urbanizing. We went from being an agricultural, Anglo-Saxon Protestant nation of a few million souls in 1776 to a nation of immigrants from around the globe. How would these newcomers—poor, often illiterate, few of whom spoke English—become American? When the Librarian of Congress Herbert Putnam decided to enshrine the Declaration in 1924, it was part of a deliberate effort at civic education: our founding document taught people like my grandparents that they had as much a right to be considered American as the generation of '76, but that they had an equal responsibility to embrace the principles and values that gave rise to the Nation's founding and shaped our society afterward.

Throughout our history, new citizens have eagerly embraced both these new rights and new responsibilities, proudly joining those whose families have been here for generations and thinking of themselves as nothing other than Americans. In my family, the Declaration was a living document, always contrasted to the oppression of the old country. When my uncles shipped off to Europe and the Pacific in World War II to fight for freedom, they carried its values with them. This would link them, just a few decades later, to those at home who invoked the document in the Civil Rights Movement.

I am a historian of the nineteenth century by training and spent most of my career writing about America's relations with Asia. Living in Japan, where the government designates the country's most important historical artifacts as "national treasures," brought home to me how unique it is that

America has a founding document that expresses its values and principles. The Declaration is undeniably our National Treasure. But only recently have I come to understand why the Declaration is just as important to us now as it was to John Adams and Thomas Jefferson. While usually interpreted as either a passionate assertion of equality or a searing call for liberty (including rebellion), it is only by telling the whole story of the Declaration—from its inception to today—that we can recognize its vital role as an enduring symbol of unity and civic assimilation. Hence this book was conceived, in which the overlapping lives of the Declaration—as relic, symbol, and cultural object—are dug up, dusted off, explored, debunked, celebrated, critiqued, and woven into a single fabric for the first time.

Three decades ago, Pauline Maier's *American Scripture* revealed the deep and broad seams of colonial thought that informed Jefferson's immortal draft. More recently, Danielle Allen's *Our Declaration* brought the document's philosophy of equality to life for a modern audience by connecting her own experience in the classroom and her family's history to make a case for taking seriously its claim of equality for all. Fifty years earlier, the influential conservative political philosopher Harry Jaffa insisted that Lincoln's reading of the Declaration contained a powerful argument against moral relativism. Gordon Wood showed how the Declaration's philosophy was expanded by Americans almost as soon as the country was founded. In our fractured times we can take solace in the fact that people across the political spectrum find inspiration and meaning in the Declaration.[1]

A constitutional republic is a fragile creation, for only the people's adherence to its principles and rules preserves it. It is easy to undermine belief in democracy, and since the founding of the Republic, claims that either mob rule or shadowy cabals are destroying the people's sovereignty have been prevalent. Just as damagingly, moments of social dissension and political partisanship have flared throughout American history, most tragically in the Civil War and again in the 1960s and 1970s.

Against such views, our founding document remains a powerful statement of unity, as much today as two hundred and fifty years ago. It has as much to teach us about the bonds that tied generations of Americans together as it does about liberty and equality. The unity it creates is expressed not just in abstract philosophical ideas but also in common hopes and shared beliefs of what life is meant to be in America, of what we have long called "the American Dream." The Declaration speaks of *one* people in its opening line. The representatives adopted their document for the "united States," even as they believed in state sovereignty. And the Signers set an enduring example by pledging *to each other* "our Lives, our Fortunes, and our sacred Honor." They shared a similar set of values and assumptions—biblically inspired, steeped in natural law, and drawn from England's constitutional traditions. The new country they created embraced pluralism, but it saw individual liberty and political responsibility as tightly bound together. Equality was important, and its meaning would expand over time, but so were those sacred bonds.

It is the spirit of the Declaration that called forth the great defenses of national unity expressed by George Washington in his Farewell Address and by Daniel Webster's famous reply to Hayne and that animated Abraham Lincoln's entire political philosophy. Union was imposed by force, it is true, during the Civil War, but the Declaration's appeal has more often worked through persuasion and inspiration, by providing a cohesive, if evolving, set of beliefs that define the American ideal. Unity meant something different to Americans in 1776 than it did in 1789, let alone in 1861 or 1924. Yet even as our definition of unity has changed, the Declaration remains the bedrock upon which each generation has built its beliefs.

Unity and Union are no less important today in a vastly more multiethnic and multicultural America than the one that came into being in the 1770s and was torn apart and patched together in the 1860s. The Declaration, I believe, remains the starting point for defending that precious achievement. We can only do so by embracing the principles and preserving the traditions that gave rise to the world's first durably self-governing and self-correcting nation.

This is not a cynical or angry book—we have far too many of those already—but neither is it naive. It is an optimistic and hopeful book, celebrating America's successes and acknowledging our shortcomings. The story of the Declaration is an unfinished one, as we seek together to build a happier, more just, and more prosperous society, one "constantly labored for . . . even though never perfectly attained," as Lincoln put it in 1857. Each generation becomes part of a chain stretching back to 1776. What we learn from the history of the Declaration of Independence is our own history, ever evolving, ever striving.

National Treasure

Prologue

Declaration

On the morning of Thursday, July 4, 1776, Thomas Jefferson rose at dawn and measured the temperature in Philadelphia. It was a comfortable 68 degrees at six a.m. Later that morning, Jefferson, tall, retiring, with a shock of sandy hair, walked two blocks from his rooms on the southwest corner of Seventh and High Streets to the Pennsylvania State House. There, on the ground floor of a redbrick building with a prominent bell tower, he took his seat as a delegate to the Second Continental Congress.

Inside the wood-paneled Assembly Room, where the Pennsylvania legislature usually met, the members sat grouped by colony behind tables arranged in rows. On most days, the three tall windows on either side of the room were opened to relieve the heat, only to be closed again to block the noise coming from the carts and horses on cobblestone Chestnut Street in front of the State House and the horseflies buzzing in from a nearby stable. But this day was thankfully unseasonably cool, with temperatures topping out at 76 degrees Fahrenheit.

Until recently, the thirty-three-year-old Virginian had not made much of an impression on the Congress. Alone among the delegates he had taken detailed private notes of the debates, but he said little throughout the proceedings. In fact, he was rumored not to have made a single speech since his arrival in Philadelphia in June of the previous year. His pamphlet *A Summary View of the Rights of British America*, an eloquent case for self-government widely circulated in 1774, had won him some renown but Jefferson was overshadowed by many of his fellow delegates. The Congress was filled with some of the most influential leaders of the colonies, such as the printer and inventor Benjamin Franklin of Philadelphia, the passionate and irascible lawyer John Adams of Massachusetts, and the eloquent Pennsylvania farmer John Dickinson, whose popular *Letters from a Farmer in Pennsylvania* in the late 1760s vehemently denounced taxes and tariffs imposed by Parliament. Today, however, it was the quiet Jefferson and his written words that would define the moment.

For the roughly fifty men who walked into the State House in Philadelphia that morning, the day represented the end of the world they knew and the beginning of a new, uncertain one. Their original plan had been to convene "in Congress" in May 1775 to seek redress for a litany of grievances that had been festering with King George III and Parliament for more than a decade. But even before they could meet, tensions exploded into conflict in April 1775, as British Redcoats fired on militiamen at Lexington and Concord.

The British sent thousands of troops across the Atlantic to crush the rebellion. In response, the gathering in Philadelphia had quickly become a war congress, raising an army and navy and appointing the forty-three-year-old George Washington of Virginia commander of the Continental Army. After more than a year of fighting, things were not going well for Washington and his forces. They had driven the British out of Boston in March, but now General William Howe and his Redcoats were moving on New York City and Washington was severely outnumbered. The Congress had concluded that it was only with foreign support, in the form of money and arms, that the colonies could hope to prevail—and that conclusion had brought them to this day.

For most of the delegates, the Fourth of July was an anticlimax, a necessary finish to their great action of two days earlier. On July 2, 1776, Congress had taken the unprecedented step of voting to approve a resolution proposed by Richard Henry Lee of Virginia, to become "free and independent states." Having overcome strong opposition to Independence from delegates such as Dickinson, John Adams wrote to his wife, Abigail, back in Massachusetts that July 2 "will be the most memorable Epocha, in the History of America."[1] That was the day most delegates thought would be considered the dawn of a new era.

Now, two days later, the delegates had gathered once again to finish off what they considered to be an administrative job. A "decent respect to the opinions of mankind," as Jefferson would put it so memorably, required them to explain to their fellow citizens and the world why they had made this fateful decision.

John Hancock gaveled the session to order, sitting in his high-backed chair that legend recounts was emblazoned with a rising sun. At thirty-nine, the merchant Hancock was one of the richest men in Massachusetts, possibly even in the colonies. Years before, he had opposed British trade restrictions and tangled with customs officials over the Stamp and Townshend Acts, at the risk of losing his fortune. For these reasons and for his considerable political skill, he had been elected president of the Second Continental Congress.

Sitting just below Hancock and to his right, facing the delegates, was forty-six-year-old Charles Thomson, the powerful secretary of the Congress, who was carefully keeping overlapping journals of Congress's doings, including a handwritten daily *Rough Journal* and another *Secret Journal.* Single-handedly acting as the administrative staff of the Congress, Thomson recorded the body's decisions, responded to communications, jotted down notes, and collected and preserved all documents used in deliberations, including the slips of paper on which were written resolutions and other business.[2]

But on this most important of days, Thomson took no notes, not even in the *Secret Journal.* Future generations would not know exactly what was said in favor or against publicly declaring Independence. They would not even know how many men were in attendance on July 4, how long they debated, or the tally of the vote. Ever since, mystery has surrounded the earliest moments of the existence of the United States of America.

Before the delegates lay a draft statement declaring the colonies' separation from Great Britain. The words were almost entirely Jefferson's, composed over a few days in June. Though the Congress never formally labeled it a "declaration of independence," the document was an inspiring philosophical defense of freedom and a legal argument justifying the unprecedented step of asserting sovereignty. It was an essential element in becoming a country, but few in Congress saw it as more than a much-needed instrument. Other issues were even more pressing.

For two days Jefferson had watched with dismay as Congress tore into his draft, cutting almost a quarter of the document. Fatefully, it deleted the draft's most impassioned paragraph, a ringing denunciation of the British slave trade. At the very founding of the United States, the poisonous issue of slavery could only be dealt with by pushing the day of reckoning into the future. By the end, a total of eighty-six changes were made by various hands to Jefferson's draft, changes he later called "depredations" and "mutilations."[3]

By midmorning on the Fourth, it was done. Most of Jefferson's stirring phrases survived and the Declaration, now with a capital "D," was adopted. The *Rough Journal* of the Congress recorded events in as simple terms as possible: "The Declaration being again read was agreed to as follows." Here the rest of the page was left blank, for in the rush of business Charles Thomson had failed to copy down the actual text of what soon would be titled "A Declaration By the Representatives of the United States of America, In General Congress Assembled."[4]

After this final, irrevocable step . . . nothing happened. Work did not stop. No celebration was held, nor was there even a public reading, despite later claims to the contrary. The delegates turned to other business, meeting on their various committees or heading off on personal errands. When Caesar Rodney of Delaware sat down to write his brother, he noted simply that "the Declaration has laid the foundation," and then went on to talk about buying shoes for his sisters and about the coming harvest.[5] And Thomas Jefferson himself? He walked out of the State House and over to a merchant's shop, where he paid for seven pairs of women's gloves to be sent home to Monticello.[6]

Only in the full course of time would Jefferson's document come to be seen as the foundational statement of the principles binding together what was now the United States. Yet even two hundred and fifty years later, much of the Declaration's history remains unknown or shrouded in myth and misunderstanding. The date of its adoption would be misunderstood as the day of Independence, and for a half century almost no one knew that the document was not actually signed on July 4. When the Declaration was finally written on parchment and signed later that summer, the scroll was kept secret and then quickly forgotten. Just as surprisingly, it was not until well into the twentieth century that anyone knew the name of the scribe whose iconic script is now so familiar to Americans.

Though Thomas Jefferson and his colleagues had no doubt as to the importance of the document they had produced, and no little pride in it, they would have been astonished to learn that a quarter of a millennium later, the parchment they signed would still exist and that millions of people would patiently wait hours in line to view its faded script. To understand how this document became America's national treasure and the supreme expression of the Nation's ideals, we need to back up and retravel the road to July Fourth.

Chapter 1
The Road to July Fourth

When John Hancock gaveled in the Continental Congress on the morning of July 4, 1776, he may well have reflected on the road that England and the colonies had traveled over the past decade, one neither side expected to lead to this moment. This entire business had in fact started because of another war, one in which Great Britain and her American colonies had won a glorious victory.

Sparked in a secluded glen in the Pennsylvania colony in May 1754, when a twenty-two-year-old Virginian militia officer by the name of George Washington and his Indian allies had attacked a French detachment in territory contested by the two great powers, the French and Indian War had drawn the American colonies into a larger global struggle known as the Seven Years' War. Shepherded by the brilliant William Pitt, who as Prime Minister had championed the idea that the French should be confronted overseas rather than in mainland Europe, Britain had by 1763 defeated its mortal enemy and a coalition of European powers and secured control over the eastern part of North America, becoming the most powerful empire in the world.[1]

But the victory had come dearly, costing as much as £100 million and plunging Britain deeper into debt. The parsimonious government of King George III, who had ascended to the throne in 1760, decided that since British troops had saved the American colonies from French domination, the grateful colonists should pay to offset the expenses of the war and help defray the cost of the thousands of troops garrisoned in America to defend the greatly enlarged territory won by Britain. It would turn out to be one of the costliest miscalculations in world history.[2]

Starting with the hated Stamp Act, in 1765, officials in far-off London began imposing taxes for the first time to raise revenue from the colonists. The new policies spelled the end of the "salutary neglect," as the great political thinker Edmund Burke termed it, that had long marked English relations with the colonies. Over the next nine years, taxes were levied, abandoned, and levied again, on daily items such as paper, sugar, glass, and tea. American appeals were ignored, then listened to, then once again ignored. Most provocatively, Parliament formally asserted its right to legislate for the colonies in all cases whatsoever, raising the question whether Parliament's authority over the colonies was limited or absolute.

The colonists felt their rights as Englishmen were being trampled. They fundamentally objected to being taxed not by their own assemblies, but by Parliament, without consent or representation. It was one thing for Parliament to regulate trade within the empire, but something entirely different for lawmakers across an ocean to override local assemblies and extract revenue from people with no say in the matter. British arguments that the colonies were represented virtually in Parliament were as offensive to American sensibilities as claims of an inherent right to pass binding legislation.

The great danger thus went beyond taxes. London was destroying the colonists' indigenous mechanisms for governing themselves, their unwritten constitutions. Many of the emerging colonial leaders, men like John Adams, James Wilson, and Benjamin Rush, were steeped in the history of the ancient Roman Republic, and their reading of Cicero and Tacitus taught them to fear conspiracies against liberty. They and their fellow colonists now came to believe they faced just such a great conspiracy, spearheaded by a cabal of corrupt ministers who controlled the King and Parliament.[3]

Firebrands like Samuel Adams whipped up anti-British feeling, while secret groups like the Sons of Liberty formed in various colonies to agitate for greater freedom from British control. Riots and resistance to revenue collectors in Boston led the Crown to send British regulars to garrison the city in 1768, enraging the residents who saw the stationing of a standing army on their soil as a direct threat to their liberty. Two years later, on a snowy night in March 1770, a platoon of Redcoats fired on a crowd of jeering citizens pelting them with rocks and ice balls, killing five. The melee was quickly branded the "Boston Massacre" and memorialized in a famous print by Boston artisan Paul Revere that was widely publicized throughout the colonies.[4]

When London imposed the Tea Act of 1773, many colonists were ready to resist. The act was adopted to save the deeply indebted East India Company, which had over three million pounds sterling of overpriced leaves sitting unsold in its warehouses in England. It gave the Company a monopoly over tea sales in the colonies and allowed it to drop its prices by lifting most duties, making its imports more affordable than even smuggled tea.[5] Determined to assert its political authority over the colonies, Parliament retained the three-pence tax on tea first levied by the Townshend Act of 1767. Though tea was now cheaper, the real issue was political authority, and the Bostonians retaliated with their famous "Tea Party."

For over two weeks in December, tensions were brewing over the latest shipment of tea, brought into Boston Harbor by three British vessels. In public meetings, Bostonians demanded that the tea be returned and refused to unload the chests. Governor Thomas Hutchinson ordered the ships to stay docked in preparation for seizing the tea and forcing the town to pay the import duty. On the night of December 16, several dozen members of the Sons of Liberty dressed as Mohawk Indians boarded the three ships, broke into the holds, and dumped 340 chests of newly arrived Chinese leaves into the harbor, valued at more than £10,000.

The response, which arrived the next spring, was harsh. Parliament imposed a series of punitive measures called the Coercive Acts, which the colonists took to calling the Intolerable Acts, shutting down Boston's port, quartering British troops in American homes, and putting Massachusetts under direct British control.[6] As news spread, resolutions of sympathy were passed throughout the colonies and a shared feeling emerged that a crisis had arrived.

The more vigorously Parliament acted, the more the thirteen very different colonies were pushed together as key civic leaders became radicalized. For over 150 years, the colonies had been independent from one another, with little sense of common interest. Begun as private, for-profit endeavors organized by joint-stock companies or given as royal grants, they now stretched twelve hundred miles along the Atlantic seaboard, from New Hampshire in the north to Georgia, bordering Spanish Florida, in the south.[7] On the eve of Independence, there were approximately two million colonists and five hundred thousand Blacks held in bondage, while the number of American Indians, most of whom lived and hunted outside of the thirteen colonies, remains unknown.[8]

Tens of thousands of colonists lived in a scattering of port cities, from Boston and New York to Philadelphia, Baltimore, and Charleston. Though connected to England and the Caribbean, Parliament's Navigation Acts of 1651 and 1660 prevented them from engaging freely with the wider world. The overwhelming majority of the population settled in towns, villages, and isolated farmsteads stretching into the backcountry. The vast extent of the rest of the landmass, revealed with each new push westward, remained in their eyes a "hideous and desolate wilderness," as Pilgrim leader William Bradford had put it in his classic 1651 account *Of Plimouth Plantation.*

The thirteen colonies presented a geographical, religious, and social kaleidoscope. Approximately half the population was of English descent, with Scots, Irish, and Welsh making up another sixth. German immigrants clustered in Pennsylvania, Maryland, and New Jersey; Swedes maintained their residences in Delaware; French dotted the colonies and Dutch continued to live in New York long after losing New Amsterdam to the English in 1664.

In the north, small farmers worked the stony New England soil, while seafaring Bostonians depended on the trans-Atlantic trade in cod to buy manufactured goods from Britain. In the mid-Atlantic, Germans reaped wheat from Pennsylvania's rolling hills and both they and the Scotch-Irish hungered to open rich farming land in the Ohio Valley. Farther south, the Tidewater tobacco fields along the innumerable creeks and rivers of Virginia and Maryland gave way to rice and cotton plantations in the Carolinas and Georgia. Besides the farmers and merchants, there were thousands of self-made men, such as the inventor and printer Benjamin Franklin, who dirtied his hands in ways that the Dutch patroons along the Hudson River in New York or the aristocratic Fairfaxes of Virginia never did.

The Puritans of Massachusetts were as different in their faith from the Quakers of Pennsylvania and Anglicans of Virginia as they were from the Catholic Spanish and French, while Africans brought local beliefs from their homelands. The madness of the Salem witch trials of the 1690s would have astounded the cavaliers of Virginia, whose plantation system was odious to Massachusetts's moral sensibilities. Yet for all of that disapproval, slavery could be found throughout the colonies, both north and south, as it could in English and French colonies around the world.

By the 1760s, the colonists were overwhelmingly middle and lower class. Many families whose ancestors arrived as indentured servants now owned land and practiced a trade. A strong streak of egalitarianism remained, even as some became great landowners, merchants, and shippers. The abject poverty that engulfed the peasant class in the Old World was largely unknown in America, and pauperism was rare beyond pockets in the rapidly growing cities.[9] Such opportunity, of course, was denied to the vast majority of Africans held in bondage, though there were thousands of freedmen who owned land and houses and engaged in trade.[10]

Each colony was independent, ruled differently, produced different goods, and charted its own path. These "folkways," as David Hackett Fischer termed them, were deep and rich, yet underneath the differences, the customs and beliefs undergirding English culture would provide a bedrock upon which to build an independent nation.[11]

The growing crisis pushed the colonies into cooperation that only a few decades before would have been unimaginable. King George's obstinance and Parliament's blunders enflamed radical polemicists like Samuel Adams and Patrick Henry and led others to believe that some coordination of action was required. To show support for Massachusetts after the Intolerable Acts, all of the colonies but Georgia sent delegates to a "continental congress" that met in Philadelphia in 1774. There they formed a "Continental Association" and agreed not to import British goods, though full implementation of the plan was delayed by merchants' concerns. They also dispatched a so-called Olive Branch petition to the King, asking him to recognize their grievances and effect a reconciliation with Parliament. The delegates agreed to meet again the following spring if their petitions failed to bring about relief.[12] In the meantime, they set up committees of correspondence to maintain communication among themselves, began forming committees of safety, and started organizing militias and stockpiling arms and munitions.

Massachusetts was the most obstreperous colony. In January 1775, King George had maneuvered Parliament into declaring the colony in rebellion. This allowed his government to send thousands of British regulars to squelch resistance, hoping to make an example to the rest of the colonies. The move spurred more determined resistance, both physical and rhetorical. In a March lecture to a convention of committees for the county of Worcester, Massachusetts, a clergyman named Elisha Fish encapsulated in one sentence the entire philosophy that Thomas Jefferson would draft more than a year later. "The right each individual hath," asserted Fish, "to enjoy his own life, liberty, and property, or his own earnings, as a privilege of a reasonable creature, given him with his being from God the creator, evidently stampt on the human soul, which stamp gave birth to government, as a means to preserve and enjoy this right."[13] British actions aimed at destroying this right, the colonists believed, and they were prepared to defend their liberties.

Late on the night of April 18, British Redcoats in Boston set out to seize rebel arms and gunpowder and to arrest John Hancock, Samuel Adams, and other leaders of the rebellion. They marched toward Concord, about twenty miles from Boston. At dawn on the nineteenth on Lexington Green they clashed with the local militia and then engaged hundreds more militiamen at Concord later in the morning. After a bloody retreat back to Boston, the British found themselves encircled by thousands of American militiamen, who settled in for a long siege. The next month, the Second Continental Congress convened in Philadelphia. It was now a war congress, charged with raising funds to create a Continental Army, whose command had quickly been given to George Washington, at the urging of John Adams.[14]

Over the next year, news from the front lines was not good. Though he forced the British out of Boston in March, Washington was perpetually undersupplied and faced with short enlistments and desertions. By the spring of 1776, it was becoming clear that the Americans could not hold out without the financial and material support of France, Great Britain's main geopolitical adversary, and Spain. Congress would be forced to consider its most radical move yet.

All told, about eighty-six men gathered at various times in Philadelphia during the Second Continental Congress. Around them in the State House resonated the din of the colony's main administrative center. Across from Congress's Assembly Room on the first floor the Supreme Court continued to meet to dispense the King's justice until April 1776, with judges, lawyers, plaintiffs, defendants, and bailiffs all jostling and talking in the entrance hall. Meanwhile, the colony's legislative assembly met up on the second floor until mid-June, creating yet more noise and bustle as members trudged up and down the large staircase that circled the base of the clock tower.

Some of the Congress's delegates showed up for just a few days, others arrived months after it started. A good number, like Thomas Jefferson, left for long stretches and returned later, while some like John Adams participated regularly. They were great minds with petty jealousies, crafty politicians, and far-seeing philosophers. Stout John Adams was known for his prickliness and Roger Sherman for his Puritan simplicity. The shrewd and avuncular Ben Franklin was always ready with an anecdote or witticism. Many did not like the vanity and caprice of their president, deriding him as "King" Hancock and accusing him of calculating opportunism. Yet despite their failings and foibles, their shifting alliances and bitter battles, collectively they achieved something great and unprecedented.

The necessity of securing foreign support for their war forced them to face the fundamental question: What were they fighting for? Their "Olive Branch" petition proposing reconciliation had been rejected—indeed King George had refused even to receive it. But if returning to the British fold under more amenable terms was their goal, they could hardly ask for or expect foreign support. Could the thirteen colonies survive independently from Great Britain? There were tens of thousands of Loyalists in the colonies, many of whom were leading citizens. Eventually, between 60,000 and 80,000 Loyalists would leave the colonies, going to England, Canada, and other imperial possessions, a number five times greater than the exiles of the French Revolution. After a year of fighting, those who branded themselves as Patriots had yet to answer what the war was ultimately about.[15]

As the conflict raged and the British advanced, the colonies slowly but inexorably moved toward Independence. Despite the strong Loyalist feelings of many and the lack of any major battlefield victories, radical voices such as Samuel Adams continued to insist that the colonies take the ultimate step. Looming in the background was the very real possibility of military defeat.[16]

The cause of Independence was given an immeasurable boost in January 1776 with the publication of *Common Sense*, a fiery pamphlet by a thirty-nine-year-old English Quaker named Thomas Paine. Thin and ruddy-faced with blazing eyes, Paine had failed in every vocation he had attempted. His life was changed by a serendipitous introduction in London to Benjamin Franklin, then serving as the colonial agent representing the interests of Pennsylvania and several other colonies. By the end of November 1774, Paine had left London for Philadelphia, where he quickly became a polemicist.

Within a year of his arrival, Paine produced the most influential, and incendiary, political tract ever published in America. *Common Sense* was both a summation of previous arguments and a new, almost religious vision of the future, not only for America but for the world. Though far from the first to advocate separation from England, he was the most effective agitator on paper, the counterpart to Samuel Adams in the streets. In unforgettable language, he condemned the monarchy as "the most prosperous invention the Devil ever set on foot for the promotion of idolatry," dismissing lingering calls for reconciliation. "We have it in our power to begin the world over again," Paine assured his readers, using language that would soon become familiar among the radical revolutionaries in France. It was discussed in taverns, churches, village greens, and assembly halls throughout the colonies. By the spring, over one hundred thousand copies had been sold.[17]

Common Sense raised the political debate to a new level. Over two intense months, from May to July, radicals in Congress like John Adams and the Virginian Richard Henry Lee chipped away at the restraining influence of men like the Pennsylvanian Joseph Galloway, who proposed an ingenious yet utterly impractical plan of union between the colonies and Great Britain.

Yet Congress was not the only player. Each colony's elected assembly passed resolutions, sent petitions, and gave instructions to its delegates in Philadelphia. Some, like Pennsylvania and South Carolina, were more skeptical of Independence. Others, like Virginia, took concrete steps to separate from Britain. Political sparring took place in both Philadelphia's State House and the colonial assemblies.

By the middle of May, the radicals were gaining the upper hand. On May 10, 1776, Congress passed a resolution proposed by Richard Henry Lee, of Virginia, recommending that each colony "adopt such government as shall in the opinions of the representatives of the people best conduce to the happiness and safety of their constituents." This all but declared an end of British rule and would have made each colony a sovereign state. Upon acceptance of the resolution, John Adams wrote in his diary, "I thought it was independence itself, but we must have it with more formality yet."

Adams then forced through a more radical, even confrontational, preamble to the resolution advocating that "the exercise of every kind of authority under the said crown should be totally suppressed." A formal breach was now all but inevitable.[18]

Though Massachusetts radicals had long led in the vanguard of independence, it was the courtly yet passionate Virginians who opened the final act of the political drama. On May 15, the Virginia Convention, which had replaced the colony's House of Burgesses after its dissolution by the royal governor, passed a resolution declaring the "United Colonies" free and independent states and ordered its delegates to lay the resolution on the table in Congress. By mid-May, seven other colonies had aligned with Virginia to support Independence. Maryland, Pennsylvania, Delaware, New Jersey, and New York were as yet undecided. Debates over separation continued alongside the equally urgent business of fighting the war.[19]

The formal act of severance sought by John Adams came the next month. Once again, it was Richard Henry Lee who proposed the fateful step. On Friday, June 7, the tall, aristocratic-looking planter whose left hand, mangled by a musket accident, was covered in black silk, introduced three resolutions, all interconnected, each depending on the others to be successful.

> **Resolved:** That these United Colonies are, and of right ought to be, free and independent States, that they are absolved from all allegiance to the British Crown, and that all political connection between them and the State of Great Britain, is, and ought to be, totally dissolved.
>
> That it is expedient forthwith to take the most effectual measures for forming foreign Alliances.
>
> That a plan of confederation be prepared and transmitted to the respective Colonies for their consideration and approbation.[20]

The final break was at last on the table. Independence was the most dramatic proposal in Lee's resolutions, but it was an instrumental act, necessary to carry through the following two motions. The American colonies had to become independent so they could conduct foreign relations and create a new governing structure. And those steps had to be taken to win the war.

To be successful, the vote on the resolutions had to be unanimous; otherwise, the British would certainly try to drive a wedge between the colonies. But Adams, Lee, and the other pro-Independence leaders were not certain they could pull off unanimity. Most of the middle colonies, as Thomas Jefferson noted in his private record of the debate, were "not yet ripe for bidding adieu to British connection, but . . . they were fast ripening." The pro-Independence bloc hoped that the holdouts, especially Pennsylvania, South Carolina, and New York, would recall their anti-Independence delegates and send new ones with instructions to vote in favor of separation. So Congress voted on June 10 to postpone a decision on Lee's resolutions for nearly three weeks, until July 1.[21]

Fairly assured that the vote would go their way, and ready to seize the moment, the majority in Congress appointed three committees, each to start preparing the documents necessary to carry out the three resolutions of June 7: a public declaration, a "model treaty" for foreign alliances, and "articles of confederation" to govern the relations among the colonies. On June 11, a committee of five members was named to draft a declaration of independence: Benjamin Franklin, John Adams, Roger Sherman of Connecticut, New York's Robert R. Livingston, and Thomas Jefferson. With only a few weeks before the vote, the committee had little time to decide how it would handle its critical assignment.

The committee never seemed to consider jointly drafting the document, and instead soon narrowed down the candidates for authorship. Livingston agreed with men like Dickinson and Edward Rutledge that it was too soon to separate from England. He may have been included on the committee to give voice to the minority view.[22] Sherman, though a fervent supporter of Independence, also served on the committee to draft articles of confederation at the same time. Franklin was laid up with the gout and in any case commented that he'd never write anything that a committee would get its hands on.[23] That left Adams and Jefferson. Despite, or perhaps because of, Adams's position as leader of the pro-Independence faction, within days the young Jefferson had been given the task. Amid the rush of other business, Jefferson repaired to his rooms a few blocks away to focus on the declaration.

During those three weeks in June 1776, the colonies and Congress grappled with the looming decision on Independence. The Congress attracted attention far and wide and, though its members had adopted a resolution of secrecy "not to divulge, directly or indirectly, any matter or thing agitated or debated in Congress," Philadelphia newspapers reported on much of its business.[24] Some select groups were allowed to observe part of the proceedings, and on June 11, the day the Committee of Five was appointed to draft a declaration, a delegation of Indian *sachems* from the Iroquois Confederacy journeyed to the State House. There they met with the president of the Congress and bestowed upon him the name "Karanduawn," or "Great Tree," undoubtedly gratifying "King" Hancock's vanity.[25]

Such encounters did not amuse John Adams, who feared that the delays over the vote on Independence threatened the entire project. As he wrote to Samuel Chase of Maryland near the end of June, "it has been already so often postponed, that to postpone it again would hazard Convulsions, and dangerous Conspiracies." Other delegates laid some blame at the feet of the Karanduawn, later charging that Hancock "very much contributed to obstruct the Declaration of Independence . . . until it became inevitable, and [only then was] reluctantly drawn in with his vote it its favour."[26] Adams was typically overwrought, for despite his fears the pendulum was steadily swinging toward Independence.

Finally, on Monday, July 1, Congress reconvened to "take into consideration the resolution respecting independency." It resolved itself into a committee of the whole and John Hancock turned the gavel over to the portly Benjamin Harrison, of Virginia. No official notes were taken on any of the debates that week, not even in Thomson's *Secret Journal*, perhaps because the delegates knew they were committing treason and wanted no formal record of their words. Jefferson, however, kept a private account of the discussions, which became the most important record of the birth of the United States.[27]

Congress filed into the State House on July 1 for the last battle. For nine hours they clashed. While many may have spoken, it came down to John Dickinson on one side and John Adams on the other. Adams, then forty, was given the responsibility of making the final argument in favor of separating from England. Calling, as he said, on the "god of eloquence," his effort earned him the sobriquet the "Atlas of Independence." Though Jefferson noted that Adams "was not graceful nor elegant, nor remarkably fluent," his rhetoric that day "moved us from our seats." No one saw fit to record his precise words, but the lawyer from Massachusetts apparently masterfully summed up all the reasons for Independence. In the end, his case was based on what he had argued to Congress a month before, "that the question was not whether, by a declaration of independence, we should make ourselves what we are not; but whether we should

Congress Voting Independence, by Edward Savage, after Robert Edge Pine, was considered the most accurate image of the Assembly Room in Independence Hall during the Second Continental Congress. Begun in 1784 by Pine and completed after his death by Savage, the engraving did not appear until 1859.

declare a fact which already exists." Despite the praise, the ever-dyspeptic Adams had a far more negative view of the day, writing to Samuel Chase of Maryland that the debate was an "idle Mispence of Time for nothing was Said, but what had been repeated and hackneyed in that Room before an hundred Times for Six Months past."[28]

Yet after his performance Adams knew the resolutions would pass, at the least "by a great majority," as he wrote Chase.[29] The committee of the whole voted to move Richard Henry Lee's resolutions forward for a final decision. The three-week pause had played exactly the role he, Franklin, and Jefferson had hoped.

Independence was now all but assured, but three colonies remained opposed: a now-wavering South Carolina, influential Pennsylvania, and a split Delaware contingent. New York, meanwhile, had not yet received instructions to vote in favor. Even at this final moment, unanimity remained elusive. If Independence passed only by a majority vote and not by a unanimous one, Britain would take advantage of any division among the colonies. That could well prove fatal. At this most fragile pass, hope glimmered. The South Carolinians asked to postpone the final vote to the next day, indicating that for the sake of unity, they might cast their ballot in the affirmative.

Even with South Carolina's olive branch, none of the delegates could have expected that the next morning, July 2, the opposition would vanish, quite literally, and a savior would ride in on horseback. Yet that morning, both John Dickinson and Robert Morris, two of the most powerful voices against Independence, diplomatically absented themselves, allowing the Pennsylvanians to support the measure. Next, the South Carolinians held to their word and voted in favor. But unanimity still eluded the Congress.

And then, just as the vote was taking place, the cancer-stricken Caesar Rodney of Delaware galloped up to the State House. Summoned late the day before by his friend and fellow delegate Thomas McKean from his

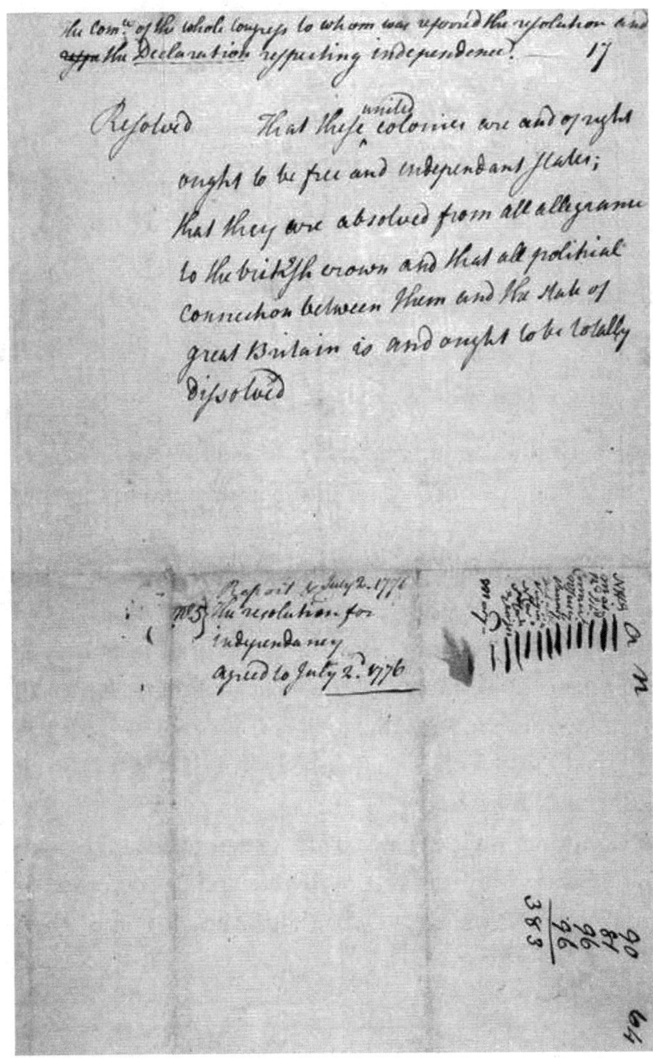
the Com.ee of the whole Congress to whom was referred the resolution and the Declaration respecting independence. 17

Resolved That these united colonies are and of right ought to be free and independant states; that they are absolved from all allegiance to the british crown and that all political connection between them and the state of great Britain is and ought to be totally dissolved

Report of July 2. 1776
No 5 The resolution for independancy agreed to July 2d 1776

The vote tally for Richard Henry Lee's Resolution for Independence, July 2, 1776.

home near Dover, eighty miles from Philadelphia, he had ridden the entire night through "thunder and rain." Booted, spurred, and mud-splattered, Rodney strode directly into the State House and cast his vote with McKean, thus giving Delaware a majority in favor. Twelve colonies had unanimously voted in favor of Independence. The delegates from New York, the last holdout, made it clear they would follow suit just as soon as new instructions arrived, which they did three days later.

For John Adams, it was the most important victory of his life. He had been away from his home and beloved family in Braintree for months, leading the charge for Independence. Above all, he missed his wife and closest confidante, Abigail, who had stayed back to manage the farm and look after the children while war raged only miles away.[30] With Independence at last achieved, he poured out his feelings to her in a letter the next day:

> Yesterday the greatest Question was decided; which ever was debated in America . . . The second Day of July 1776, will be the most memorable Epocha, in the History of America.—I am apt to believe that it will be celebrated, by succeeding Generations, as the great anniversary Festival . . . It ought to be solemnized with Pomp and Parade with Shews, Games, Sports, Guns, Bells, Bonfires and Illuminations from one End of this Continent to the other from this Time forward forever more.[31]

His emotion was both understandable and justified, for Adams knew best of all what they had gone through to reach this moment and the risks they were taking.

The first public announcement of Independence was far less dramatic than Adams's letter back home. Readers of the *Pennsylvania Evening Post* on July 2 could have been forgiven if they missed the brief note on the last page of the paper, next to a reward of three dollars for the return of a runaway slave and above an announcement of ships for sale: "This day the CONTINENTAL CONGRESS declared the UNITED COLONIES FREE and INDEPENDENT STATES."[32]

The great deed was done; the delegates had decided to separate from Great Britain. Now, it was time to explain to their fellow colonists—citizens of a new country—and the world what had happened, and why.

Chapter 2

"Our Lives, Our Fortunes, and Our Sacred Honor"

On the morning of June 12, 1776, Thomas Jefferson opened a portable wooden writing desk of his own design and began to draft a declaration of independence. Just over two weeks later, on June 28, he handed over the Committee of Five's draft statement to John Hancock. Four days after that, Congress voted to sever ties with the King and Parliament.

The members of the Continental Congress had been at war for over a year. Now they would have to become diplomats and create some kind of national government. But before that, they needed to inform the world of what they had done. They understood that Independence would become real only when others knew about it and supported it, and they knew that tens of thousands of colonists did not favor separation from England.

The Congress had picked some of its most distinguished members for the drafting committee, including John Adams and Benjamin Franklin. More than once, it would be asked why, if five well-known men were appointed to draft a declaration, it became the work largely of one. Thomas Jefferson was not considered a leader among the delegates. Nevertheless, his writings were admired, and he was known for a "happy talent at composition."[1] The young Virginian had been an early advocate of Independence, and it was to him that the committee entrusted the task.

In 1822, near the end of his long life, Adams claimed in a private letter that it was he who had thrust the pen into Jefferson's hands. According to this account, Jefferson balked at the suggestion and asked why him. Adams wrote that he replied,

"Reason 1st You are a Virginian and Virginia ought to appear at the head of this business.

"Reason 2d I am obnoxious, suspected and unpopular; You are very much otherwise.

"Reason 3d You can write ten times better than I can.

"'Well,' said Jefferson, 'if you are decided I will do as well as I can.'"

Jefferson remembered the exchange somewhat differently and less dramatically in a letter to James Madison the following year: "they unanimously pressed on myself alone to undertake the draught. I consented; I drew it . . ."[2]

Jefferson had rented the second floor of a narrow three-story house owned by a German bricklayer, Jacob Graff. Here, two blocks west of the State House, where the city gave way to undeveloped fields, he set to work.[3] Later artists would portray a somber Jefferson standing over a table strewn with crumpled pages, illuminated by candlelight, a heroic image of genius and toil. The reality was rather different. Like most delegates to Congress, he had been given multiple responsibilities, and even now he was on four other committees. The declaration was not the only item on his plate, and he worked in haste. Always a fluent writer, Jefferson composed quickly, and in a few days finished the draft, turning "to neither book or pamphlet while writing it," as he recalled decades later in his letter to Madison.[4]

What was the document Jefferson presented to the committee, which they revised with him before sending to the Congress?

To begin with, the Declaration was not a formal instrument of Independence—that would be accomplished by the vote that would take place on July 2. Its primary job was to lay out the causes that were forcing the colonies to separate from Great Britain and throw off allegiance to King George III. Further, while the Declaration's underlying philosophy was revolutionary, Jefferson's specific arguments were not original, nor were they meant to be. Decades later, John Adams tried to downplay Jefferson's intellectual contribution of so many years before: "there is not an idea in it, but what had been hackney'd in Congress for two years before.

The substance of it is contained in the Declaration of rights and the violation of those rights, in the Journals of Congress in 1774. Indeed, the essence of it is contained in a pamphlet, voted and printed by the Town of Boston before the first Congress met . . ."[5]

This was a judgment Jefferson himself agreed with. In his letter to James Madison in 1823, not long after learning of Adams's characterization, he admitted that "I did not consider it as any part of my charge to invent new ideas altogether & to offer no sentiment which had ever been expressed before."[6] Jefferson understood that to be accepted by the colonists in the summer of 1776, the Declaration had to include ideas that were widely shared and to enumerate injuries keenly felt. As he explained in a letter to Henry Lee in 1825, the Declaration "was intended to be an expression of the American mind."[7]

It was as difficult to define just what might be that American mind in 1776 as it would be 250 years later. To craft a declaration for this diverse yet interconnected society, Jefferson turned to the traditions that had shaped its culture, infusing his draft with ideas from a wide pool of sources, many of which were well known. He drew from the great example of Magna Carta, the source of Britain's constitutional order; from English common law; and, though a skeptic of organized religion, from Protestant Christianity broadly understood. He was particularly influenced by more abstract philosophical concepts that expressed largely Anglo ideas of freedom.[8]

Not surprisingly, Jefferson relied on his own writings that had brought him to the attention of men like John Adams. His draft reflected his powerful *Summary View of the Rights of British America*, published in 1774, which began by condemning the "unwarrantable encroachments . . . upon those rights which God and the laws have given equally and independently to all." The main section of his draft, which explained just how King George had violated the colonies, was largely reworked from his private thoughts on a model constitution for Virginia, written just a month earlier, in June 1776.[9]

Jefferson was one of the best-read men of his time, and he drew deeply from European philosophy and from the many writings of colonists defending their rights. Notable among these were the works of the seventeenth-century thinker John Locke, who insisted that all humans possess certain inherent or natural rights to life, liberty, and property, and thinkers of the Scottish Enlightenment like Francis Hutcheson.[10] Jefferson would also have been influenced by the 1689 English Bill of Rights, with its emphasis on political rights.

From the colonists' own arguments, Jefferson was undoubtedly familiar with the October 1774 "Declarations and Resolves" of the First Continental Congress (as John Adams would later charge), whose opening stated that the "inhabitants of the English colonies in North-America, by the immutable laws of nature, the principles of the English constitution . . . are entitled to life, liberty, and property . . ." He also likely had read what was known as the "Boston Pamphlet," printed in 1772 by the Boston Committee of Correspondence, which began by declaring that the "natural Rights of the Colonists are these: First, a Right to *Life*; secondly, to *Liberty*; thirdly, to *Property*."[11] Certainly as influential if not more so was the nearly contemporaneous Virginia Declaration of Rights, adopted on June 12, 1776, written largely by the planter and politician George Mason. Virginia's Declaration, which Jefferson probably read in the *Pennsylvania Gazette*, opened by claiming "That all men are by nature equally free and independent and have certain inherent rights."[12]

Such beliefs in natural rights were widely spread throughout the colonies. They were expressed in sermons and at local meetings and were debated in hundreds of pamphlets and newspapers. By 1776, local assemblies and gatherings throughout the colonies took such ideas and drafted dozens of their own declarations of what often was called "independency." The historian Pauline Maier would uncover at least ninety such declarations, all of which expressed some of the ideas Jefferson included in his draft. Reflecting the sentiments and arguments of sources both well known and locally produced made Jefferson's document both familiar and immediately acceptable to those who would soon hear or read it.[13]

Sitting alone in his rooms on High Street, Jefferson wrote his draft in his inimitable, elegant prose. The logic of his argument was simple: Man's God-given rights come before government, and government's only legitimate role is to secure those rights. Yet King George is attempting to deny those rights, thereby turning himself into a tyrant. Revolution to overthrow this budding tyranny is thus justified.[14]

Jefferson started off grandly: "When in the course of human events . . .", but immediately stumbled into an awkward phrase: " . . . it becomes necessary for a people to advance from that subordination in which they have hitherto remained . . ." Thankfully, this was soon changed, either by Jefferson himself or the committee, to the far more stirring "*When in the Course of human Events, it becomes necessary for one People to dissolve the Political Bands which have connected them with another* . . ." The power of this edit expressed a statement of a fact, explaining to the world a condition that already existed: the Americans did not have to appeal for their liberty; it was theirs by right, exercised through their long-standing constitutional mechanisms. The King's attempts to suppress this liberty invalidated any existing relations with Britain.

Just as critical is the phrase "one people." Jefferson originally had written "a people," but this was changed, likely by Benjamin Franklin. Franklin's edit made clear that though there were thirteen separate colonies declaring independence, they were a united people—a nation. This reflected the crisis of the moment, the need to make the colonists choose sides in a war that was close to being lost. It appealed to the native patriotism of Americans who now had to separate from the empire they had proudly been a part of in order to preserve their freedom.

Next came the preamble, in which Jefferson penned the first attempt at what would become the most famous lines of the Declaration. As ultimately worked over by Jefferson and the committee, these philosophical assertions justified the actions of the Americans on a universal, indeed heavenly level: "*We hold these truths to be self-evident, that all men are created equal, that they are endowed by their Creator with certain unalienable Rights, that among these are Life, Liberty and the pursuit of Happiness.*" Intended for a particular moment, it was a statement for all time.[15]

This soaring pronouncement was immediately followed by a theory of politics: "*That to secure these rights, Governments are instituted among Men, deriving their just powers from the consent of the governed.*" The following line was the crux of the political argument, implicitly defining what was a legitimate government and justifying the political act of rebellion: "*That whenever any Form of Government becomes destructive of these ends, it is the Right of the People to alter or to abolish it, and to institute new Government* . . . " To boil it down to its essence: all men are born equally free; to ensure this natural condition they form governments; if government fails to protect their liberty, it can and must be changed. The shift from the individual, in his freedom, to the community, in its self-governing form, is seamless.

Here is where most people today stop reading, but in 1776, what followed the preamble was most important. The body of the declaration laid out the critical facts of the colonists' case, as if presented in a court of law. Jefferson now vented the anger felt by so many Americans at King George and his unmentioned Parliament. Reworking the preamble of his recent draft constitution for Virginia, he unleashed a comprehensive, exaggerated, and in some cases even misleading review of the "long train of abuses and usurpations" that showed that liberty was in peril, the current government illegitimate, and rebellion justified. This was a critical part of Jefferson's approach, for he was not trying to prove that Americans deserved to be free, but that they *already* were a free people, defending their traditional rights against a conspiracy of tyranny.

Among the twenty-seven abuses and usurpations ultimately listed were acts of King George that obstructed the workings of the colonial assemblies and interfered with colonial courts, that quartered British troops in the colonies in times of peace and unleashed foreign mercenaries on American soil, that imposed taxes without consent and obstructed overseas trade, and committed aggression that "plundered our seas, ravaged our Coasts, burnt our towns, and destroyed the lives of our people." Also among them was a long, passionate condemnation of the slave trade imposed upon Americans by a British monarch who refused to stop the practice and at the same time sought to incite insurrection among the slaves, something deeply feared by slaveholders like Jefferson. In all, the King aimed at creating an "absolute tyranny" over the colonies, and this could not be accepted by a free people.

In the final paragraph, Jefferson turned from the past and looked to the colonies' future with confidence: "*as Free and Independent States, they have full Power to levy War, conclude Peace, contract Alliances, establish Commerce, and to do all other Acts and Things which Independent States may of right do.*" This, as the historian David Armitage notes, was a first in global history, "an assertion of sovereignty as independence."[16] In presenting the new country to the world and asking for recognition, the Declaration reflected just how critical foreign relations were to the colonies. They had been part of a large empire, and as they now formed an independent union, it was vital that they engage with that world from the very beginning of their Independence.

To support this Declaration, which Loyalists would have called treason, Jefferson concluded by making clear there was no turning back: "*we mutually pledge to each other our Lives, our Fortunes and our sacred Honor.*"

On "Friday morn.," likely June 21, Jefferson wrote Benjamin Franklin. The committee had "with some small alterations approved" his draft. Franklin, ill at the time, seemed not to have attended the committee's deliberations. Jefferson now diffidently approached the most famous man in America, asking "will Doct^r Franklyn be so good as to peruse it & suggest such alterations as his more enlarged view of the subject will dictate?" But the young politician did not give the good doctor much time, noting that he wanted to return the draft to the committee by the next morning.[17]

Nearly half a century later Jefferson told a different story to James Madison. He all but dismissed Sherman and Livingston, claiming that he first asked Adams and Franklin for their comments on the draft, that "their alterations were two or three only, and merely verbal," and that he then "wrote a fair copy, reported it to the Committee, and from them, unaltered to Congress."[18] However, Jefferson's letter to Franklin, now in the American Philosophical Society, bolsters later scholarly arguments that the drafting of the Declaration was far more of a joint effort than either Jefferson remembered, or which history credited. Not only did the committee review the draft multiple times, but some scholars also saw more of Franklin's hand in the rough draft that Jefferson kept. These alterations included the all-important *one people* in the very first sentence, and possibly the eternal *self-evident* in the line, "We hold these truths to be . . .", which Jefferson had originally written as "sacred & undeniable." Since the Committee of Five took no notes during its meetings, we have no idea how much revision came from members versus Jefferson himself, or which members suggested what changes ultimately made it into the fair copy presented to Congress. Jefferson also downplayed—or perhaps did not remember—differing views by other committee members. John Adams, for example, later recorded that he "never believed George to be a tyrant in disposition and nature . . . I thought the expression too passionate . . ."[19]

Jefferson's handwritten "rough draught" would be called "the most extraordinarily interesting document in American history" by the eminent scholar Julian Boyd (see insert).[20] Jefferson kept his revised draft, much later notating the edits supposedly inserted by Franklin and Adams. It survived among his papers and nearly a century and a half later would make its way to the Library of Congress, to become the crown jewel of the Library's collection. Just as importantly for posterity, John Adams made a copy for himself of the rough draft before the committee revised it, preserving perhaps the earliest version of Jefferson's document. This copy, too, survived, eventually being deposited in the Massachusetts Historical Society. Jefferson presented the "fair copy" for Congress's consideration on June 28, giving it to John Hancock or Charles Thomson in the State House. Three days later Congress reconvened to make its final decision on Independence.[21]

By the time the dramatic final vote took place on July 2, the Committee of Five's draft had lain on Charles Thomson's table for a week. It is possible that copies were made, so that delegates could peruse it and prepare suggested changes, but if so, no printing order exists, and no copies survived. In fact, the draft declaration was only one of the committee reports Congress had to deal with now that it was taking upon itself the governance of a new nation. All were working in haste getting the new nation on its feet.[22]

Immediately after voting for Independence on July 2, Congress resolved itself into another committee of the whole to consider Jefferson's draft declaration. "King" Hancock again surrendered the chair to Benjamin Harrison, who guided the debate. Thomson's daily *Rough Journal* contains no notes on the debate, so we do not know what was said over those two days when Congress took hold of Jefferson's soaring and impassioned prose and wrangled it into its final shape.[23]

Congress wisely limited its role to editing, not rewriting, and there is no record of who made which suggestions and edits to the final draft. Despite Jefferson's well-known reservations, most of the changes improved the document by polishing some of the awkward phrases, tempering Jefferson's more extreme language, and tightening the prose. Several references to God and divine Providence were added, bringing to Jefferson's prose a religious cast more appropriate for its times. Among the more significant changes was a decision to moderate Jefferson's virulent denunciation of the British people for being "deaf to the voice of justice & of consanguinity." Some of the charges against King George were clarified, as was Jefferson's claim that Britain was inciting slave insurrections and Indian attacks against the colonists.

The most important, and later most controversial, deletion was Jefferson's long condemnation of the slave trade. Jefferson had laid at King George's feet the entire sin of the trade, for denying the rights and liberties of a "distant people." This formulation meant that Africans in the colonies were not considered by Jefferson to be part of the "one people" forming a new government. Jefferson did not condemn the institution of slavery itself, though that may well have been read into his charge, but he made clear that those enslaved had rights as human beings.[24] Regardless, both Southern plantation and Northern mercantile interests in Congress combined to remove any mention of the practice, indeed, any reference to slavery in any form in the Declaration.

Finally, the delegates strengthened Jefferson's conclusion by directly inserting Richard Henry Lee's June 7 resolution, made more powerful by becoming the official statement of a people now bound together and sovereign. "*Appealing to the Supreme Judge of the World,*" the Representatives "*in the Name, and by the Authority of the good People of these Colonies, solemnly Publish and Declare That these United Colonies are, and of Right ought to be Free and Independent States; that they are Absolved from all Allegiance to the British Crown, and that all political connection between them and the State of Great-Britain, is and ought to be totally dissolved.*" In all, Congress made eighty-six alterations to Jefferson's draft and cut approximately one-quarter of his text.

This, then, was the Declaration of Independence championed by John Adams and Richard Henry Lee, written by Jefferson, revised by the Committee of Five, edited by the delegates, and ultimately adopted by the Continental Congress on the morning of July 4. Composed as it was primarily of an amalgamation of George Mason's Bill of Rights, Jefferson's draft Virginia Constitution, and Lee's resolution, one might say that the Declaration grew out of the Virginia soil, seeded by Massachusetts. The vote itself was not recorded, though historians assume it was unanimous (again, save for New York, which soon would ratify everything).

The members of Congress knew that their Declaration left much unsaid and unfinished. By design, it avoided any discussion, or even suggestion, of the type of government the colonies should establish. Formally, that was the responsibility of Roger Sherman's committee to draft articles of confederation, which ultimately created a uniquely weak central government. The more fundamental questions of governance were to be left to the States, eight of which would draft and adopt constitutions in 1776 alone. But in drawing up its list of twenty-seven charges against King George, Congress made clear how a just government should *not* act, and thus, by implication, how a government justly representing the consent of the governed *should* act. Only when a new, more centralized government was required would the echoes of Jefferson's charges inform the Constitution and especially the Bill of Rights.

The Declaration defined Americans as one people, but it did not declare a unitary "United States of America." It was issued in the name of thirteen united colonies, who were now "Free and Independent States." How these independent states would act in concert and what kind of nation they would form would consume their energies for the next twelve years, until the Articles of Confederation were set aside and the Constitution was ratified in 1788, giving a final form to the government of the now more fully United States.

Though the drafting committee had not specified which type of government was to be formed, all members assumed such liberties could only be guaranteed in a republic. Yet that was an audacious and risky undertaking. History had shown that the unrestrained exercise of liberty by equal men had brought ruin to all republics in the past, whether Athens and Rome or Venice and the Netherlands more recently. Over time, republics fell into corruption, licentiousness, and ultimately civil war.[25] Even the ancient Hebrew commonwealth, mandated by God and the most "perfect republic" balancing the powers of the one (the Judge), the few (the council of the Sanhedrin), and the many (the general assembly), had collapsed into monarchy.[26] Nor had any republic ever been as large as the United States, raising doubts as to its viability.

Jefferson and his colleagues did not envision trusting their liberties to a pure democracy, which John Adams later described as a form of government "arbitrary Tyrannical bloody cruel and intollera[nt]," and (as Aristotle warned) almost always leading to anarchy.[27] If America was to avoid the failures repeated throughout history, then a particular type of republican virtue would be required in its citizens and leaders. This was the virtue of public-spiritedness and service to preserve shared liberties. Ancient writers like Tacitus and Plutarch and the Bible inspired Jefferson and his contemporaries with their lessons on the lives of men both virtuous and immoral.[28]

To the delegates, the Declaration did not reflect abstract ideas. It was a covenant that invoked the Creator and identified a people, instituted to defend against tyranny and maintain a specific political community. Grounded in natural rights theory, English common law, classical thought, and Judeo-Christian theology, the Declaration expressed the specific kinds of liberty and equality understood by eighteenth-century men of property and learning. It eloquently asserted the traditional liberties of Englishmen, drawing the distinction between *positive* rights granted by governments and *natural* rights derived from God. This was a defense of man "in virtue of his nature," as later expressed by the political philosopher Harry Jaffa.[29] The Declaration described rights that could not be "alienated" or surrendered to any person or government, especially one failing to uphold its responsibilities to the people it sought to control.

A document so radical as to indict a king and declare all men equal was also extremely conservative. Liberty seemed a straightforward idea, but equality was a far more complicated concept than Jefferson's famous phrase expressed. Equality was not an end in itself but was a feature of liberty, in the sense that humans had equal rights. In the political sphere, equality was necessary to the preservation of those God-given liberties that were both individual and communal.[30]

The Declaration did not call for radical social equality or the leveling of all distinctions, however. As Gordon Wood has shown, Jefferson was a combination of visionary and backroom politician, and his text was similarly complex.[31] Neither he nor his fellow delegates supported social revolution. Instead, they implicitly presumed virtuous leadership by "a few of the most wise and good," as John Adams put it in his January 1776 pamphlet *Thoughts on Government*, selected freely by their fellow citizens to defend their common liberties.[32] In time, Jefferson would express more clearly his own views on a "natural aristocracy," but even in 1776 he believed in an idea of equality that freed a man from his family's background while assuming that the best and brightest would be the ones to use their talents on behalf of the broader body politic.[33]

Such arguments in favor of equality were not absolute especially when it came to the question of slavery. Chattel slavery was deplored as both a political and a moral evil by almost all the Founding Fathers, including slaveholders like George Mason, who in 1765 had written that it was the cause of the "destruction" of the Roman republic, being "an Evil very pathetically described by Roman historians."[34] Jefferson himself had written in his *Summary View of the Rights of British America* that "the abolition of domestic slavery is the great object of desire in those colonies where it was unhappily introduced in their infant state."[35] The hypocrisy of a slaveholding society demanding its own freedom had long been commented on in the colonies, often from the pulpit. It was well understood that holding fellow humans in bondage degraded both the enslaved and the enslaver, and Patrick Henry hoped for the time when the colonists would "abolish this lamentable evil."[36]

Up to now, political action to address slavery lay with the individual colonies, which not surprisingly took different paths. Massachusetts, Rhode Island, Connecticut, Delaware, and Pennsylvania had moved either to end slavery within their borders or to ban the slave trade. Congress saw Britain's dependence on the slave trade as a weakness, and in a tactical move to put pressure on London during the conflict, it had passed a resolution in April that "no slaves be imported into any of the thirteen United Colonies."[37] Yet when it came to authorizing a fundamental document that had to speak for all the colonies, one that was to express and create their identity as a nation, a decision was made to implicitly maintain the status quo.

In the eyes of many, the Americans' hypocrisy was too glaring to be passed over. The great English critic Samuel Johnson had earlier dismissed the colonists' demands for freedom by brusquely asking, "how is it that we hear the loudest yelps for liberty among the drivers of negroes?"[38] In cutting Jefferson's passionate condemnation of the slave trade, the Congress justified such critiques and revealed the moral failing that would bedevil the new nation and eventually threaten its very survival.

The Declaration was also silent on inequality among "Englishmen." Women in eighteenth-century colonial society could not vote or hold property and thus found themselves in a civilly subordinate position. Back in March, in anticipation of "independancy," Abigail Adams had written John, "in the new Code of Laws which I suppose it will be necessary for you to make I desire you would Remember the Ladies, and be more generous and favourable to them than your ancestors."[39] But it was not the intention of the Declaration to tackle the specific legal standing of any group. Such questions would be left to the States, the majority of which, like Virginia, were already sketching out their own constitutions. In the end, little change would be made to the legal inequality imposed on women.[40]

As for the list of charges against King George that Congress approved, the historian Andrew Roberts determined that only two were defensible: imposing taxes without the colonists' consent and Parliament illegitimately legislating for the colonies. Though these were perhaps the most common complaints of the colonists, the quartering of British troops during peacetime and the interruption of their local governing assemblies were decried just as much in pamphlets, petitions, and speeches. Yet the extremity of the charges did not match reality, Roberts concluded. "The Declaration of Independence," he summed up, "is simultaneously grotesquely hypocritical, illogical, mendacious and sublime."[41]

What later generations would see as the silences, errors, or hypocrisy of the Declaration cannot detract from its bold, indeed revolutionary, nature—its sublimity, according to Roberts. Jefferson's broad vision, largely unaltered by the Congress, pointed toward freedoms not entirely brought into focus, but never lost sight of. In condemning the King, the Declaration condemned any who would trample on the liberty of others, even if it did not—could not—yet follow its own logic to the inevitable end. It would later inspire movements to redress inequalities with which the Founders were not concerned or could not address in their struggle to conserve their traditional rights as eighteenth-century Englishmen.[42]

Seen in its totality, the Declaration was audacious yet prudent, visionary yet sober. It was infused with a "spirit of pragmatic idealism," to borrow the words of the historian Bernard Bailyn.[43] Though a compromise among different regions and interests, it was far from reflecting the lowest common denominator. It expressed the mind of a growing society more dynamic than the mother country, the moral certitude of those who refused to accept subordination, and the optimism of a people already eyeing the seemingly inexhaustible riches of a vast continent.

As far as can be reconstructed, forty-seven men were present at the vote in favor of the Declaration on Thursday, July 4. Yet while the vote of the colonies—now States—was unanimous, great opposition still remained to such an audacious step. The wealthy Robert Morris of Philadelphia felt that the move was premature and risked splitting the colonies. As he wrote that July, "I have uniformly voted against & opposed the declaration of Independance because in my poor opinion it was an improper time and will neither promote the interest or redound to the honor of America, for it has caused division when we wanted Union."[44]

But others were stout defenders, including the eminent Dr. Benjamin Rush of Philadelphia. "The declaration of independance was said to have divided & weakened the colonies—" he wrote in April 1777. "The contrary of this was the case. Nothing but the signing, & recognizing of the declaration of independance preserved the congress from dissolution in Decem' 1776 when Howe marched to the Delaware."[45] Most shared Rush's opinion. The die had been cast, and it was to the business of government—of forming alliances and crafting articles of confederation—that the Congress turned behind the closed doors of the State House, known to future generations as Independence Hall.

Out of doors, however, the Declaration would now take on a life of its own.

Chapter 3

Bringing the Declaration to the People

On his way to the State House on the morning of July 4, 1776, Thomas Jefferson would have walked along High (now Market) Street, Philadelphia's main thoroughfare. Four blocks down, past the open markets, on the southeast corner of Second Street was the printing shop of John Dunlap, an Irish immigrant and publisher of the *Pennsylvania Packet*, a weekly newspaper. In his shop at No. 48 High Street, Dunlap, then only twenty-nine, was about to play a key role in the first hours of American Independence.

Though Congress had adopted the Declaration in the name of the "good People" of the colonies, John Adams would later claim that only one-third of these good people had supported war with Great Britain, while another third had opposed it and a middle third remained undecided.[1] Americans needed to know that the colonies were now a new nation fighting for its existence, and they needed to be inspired to choose the right side. As soon as the delegates voted on the statement, they ordered "That the declaration be authenticated and printed" and "That the committee appointed to prepare the declaration superintend & correct the press."[2] After that, the record goes silent, and the questions begin.

Soon after the vote on July 4, John Dunlap was given the most important printing job in American history. Since the drafting committee was charged with overseeing the printing, Thomas Jefferson likely recommended Dunlap, who had printed his *Summary View of the Rights of British America* two years previously. Given that Philadelphia's most famous printer, the seventy-one-year-old Benjamin Franklin, was ill with gout, it is likely that Jefferson himself carried the approved copy of the Declaration the few blocks to Dunlap. He would most likely have arrived in the early afternoon, staying through the night to make sure that his words—harshly (to his mind) edited by Congress—were accurately typeset. Yet in his copious notes, Jefferson makes no mention of Dunlap or of the printing.

It is at this moment that one of the great mysteries of the Declaration began.

Given the need to print the Declaration as quickly as possible, it is unlikely that Charles Thomson took the time to rewrite the 1,320-word document as approved. Nor did Thomson write out the approved text into his *Rough Journal* on the Fourth, leaving instead a blank space to insert a printed copy later. In other words, Congress kept no official version of the Declaration's text. It would have to rely on what came back from the printer.[3]

If no clean copy was written out, Dunlap likely received the "fair copy" of the draft in Jefferson's hand, with lines crossed out and Congress's many edits written in. Someone intimately familiar with the changes made to the fair copy would have had to guide the printer as he deciphered the marked-up document for typesetting. Again, that person most likely would have been Jefferson himself. Whatever the truth, the piece of paper authenticated by Hancock, attested to by Thomson, and carried to Dunlap would have to be considered the official Declaration of Independence. And yet, almost inconceivably, this founding document of the United States disappeared from history the moment it left the State House.

One explanation for the disappearance is that Dunlap most likely did what many printers would do to save time on an urgent job. He would have cut up whatever official copy was brought him into sections and given them to different typesetters in his shop, a common practice in the printing process. If this is what happened, no one, not even Jefferson, thought to save the strips and restore the document once it had been typeset.

Like all printers, Dunlap would have first run off a "proof copy," to check the typesetting against the handwritten document. Someone from

IN CONGRESS, JULY 4, 1776.

A DECLARATION

BY THE REPRESENTATIVES OF THE

UNITED STATES OF AMERICA,

IN GENERAL CONGRESS ASSEMBLED.

WHEN in the Courſe of human Events, it becomes neceſſary for one People "to diſſolve the Political Bands which have connected them with another," and to aſſume among the Powers of the Earth, the ſeparate and equal Station "to which the Laws of Nature and of Nature's God entitle them," a decent Reſpect to the Opinions of Mankind requires "that they ſhould declare the cauſes which impel them to the Separation.

WE hold theſe Truths to be ſelf-evident, "that all Men are created equal," "that they are endowed by their Creator with certain unalienable Rights," that among theſe are Life, Liberty, and the Purſuit of Happineſs—That to ſecure theſe Rights, Governments are inſtituted among Men, "deriving their juſt Powers from the Conſent of the Governed," that whenever any Form of Government becomes deſtructive of theſe Ends, "it is the Right of the People to alter or to aboliſh it, and to inſtitute a new Government, laying its Foundation on ſuch Principles, and organizing its Powers in ſuch Form, as to them ſhall ſeem moſt likely to effect their Safety and Happineſs." Prudence, indeed, will dictate that Governments long eſtabliſhed ſhould not be changed for light and tranſient Cauſes; and accordingly all Experience hath ſhewn, that Mankind are more diſpoſed to ſuffer, while Evils are ſufferable, than to right themſelves by aboliſhing the Forms to which they are accuſtomed. But when a long Train of Abuſes and Uſurpations, purſuing invariably the ſame Object, evinces a Deſign to reduce them under abſolute Deſpotiſm, it is their Right, it is their Duty, to throw off ſuch Government, and to provide new Guards for their future Security." Such has been the patient Sufferance of theſe Colonies;" and ſuch is now the Neceſſity which conſtrains them to alter their former Syſtems of Government." The Hiſtory of the preſent King of Great-Britain is a Hiſtory of repeated Injuries and Uſurpations, all having in direct Object the Eſtabliſhment of an abſolute Tyranny over theſe States. To prove this, let Facts be ſubmitted to a candid World.

HE has refuſed his Aſſent to Laws, the moſt wholeſome and neceſſary for the public Good.

HE has forbidden his Governors to paſs Laws of immediate and preſſing Importance, unleſs ſuſpended in their Operation till his Aſſent ſhould be obtained; and when ſo ſuſpended, he has utterly neglected to attend to them.

HE has refuſed to paſs other Laws for the Accommodation of large Diſtricts of People, unleſs thoſe People would relinquiſh the Right of Repreſentation in the Legiſlature, a Right ineſtimable to them, and formidable to Tyrants only.

HE has called together Legiſlative Bodies at Places unuſual, uncomfortable, and diſtant from the Depoſitory of their public Records, for the ſole Purpoſe of fatiguing them into Compliance with his Meaſures.

HE has diſſolved Repreſentative Houſes repeatedly, for oppoſing with manly Firmneſs his Invaſions on the Rights of the People.

HE has refuſed for a long Time, after ſuch Diſſolutions, to cauſe others to be elected; whereby the Legiſlative Powers, incapable of Annihilation, have returned to the People at large for their exerciſe; the State remaining in the mean time expoſed to all the Dangers of Invaſion from without, and Convulſions within.

HE has endeavoured to prevent the Population of theſe States; for that Purpoſe obſtructing the Laws for Naturalization of Foreigners; refuſing to paſs others to encourage their Migrations hither, and raiſing the Conditions of new Appropriations of Lands.

Proof copy of the Dunlap Broadside, with unexplained quotation marks and the infamous "errant *a*" in the eighth line.

the committee, likely Jefferson, would have checked to make sure he got it right. As it turns out, whoever looked over the proof copy found some mistakes.

We know this because one printed Dunlap copy is different from all other surviving ones. It is now held by the Historical Society of Pennsylvania and is most likely Dunlap's proof sheet. Only part of this proof survived, but even so, we can see at least some of what was wrong with it. It contains multiple quotation marks around various phrases, like those Jefferson inserted in his surviving handwritten rough draft and in other documents he wrote. These quotation marks were probably used by Jefferson as guides for when the draft declaration was to be read aloud. He likely copied them from his rough draft onto the fair copy he presented to Congress, and from there, it went to the printer. However, Jefferson—or whoever looked over Dunlap's proof—realized these marks should be taken out of the printed document.[4]

The proofreader also caught a more serious mistake, most likely made by Dunlap. In line eight, the proof includes the phrase "institute **a** new government." All other copies of the Declaration, including the famous engrossed copy, omit the *a*. Inserting a single *a* may seem inconsequential, but it wasn't to Congress. What likely seemed grammatically correct to the typesetter was a potentially explosive error. The colonies had agreed to break from England as independent states, so their official proclamation could not refer to a unitary government. To assert otherwise could have wrecked the new nation before it got off the ground, given the fear smaller colonies had of domination by the larger ones. What later became known as the "errant *a*" was quickly removed.[5]

Working hastily throughout the evening and night, Dunlap and his assistants printed up what were known as "broadsides," single sheets of paper, generally 19½ by 15½ inches, on the shop's wooden presses. The broadsides were printed on several different types of high-quality cotton-fiber paper, many of which bore Dutch watermarks and some of which, ironically, included a crown and the initials "GR," Latin for King George and apparently made for the English market. At the top of the broadside, either Jefferson or Dunlap had decided to include the line "In Congress, July 4, 1776." The inclusion of this simple date would cause centuries of misunderstanding about when the Americans actually decided to separate from Great Britain. Then followed the title Congress likely approved: "A DECLARATION BY THE REPRESENTATIVES OF THE UNITED STATES OF AMERICA, IN GENERAL CONGRESS ASSEMBLED." Note that the document did not include the words *unanimous* or *thirteen*, since on July 4, the New York delegation had not yet been authorized to support Independence.

Without the officially approved copy from Congress, we don't know how much license Dunlap took with orthography, especially the frequent and unsystematic capitalization of nouns. For example, in Jefferson's rough draft, the famous triumvirate of "life, liberty, and the pursuit of happiness" is not capitalized, but it is in both John Adams's handwritten copy of the draft and the Dunlap broadside. Did Congress change Jefferson's draft? Did Adams pop by the print shop and instruct Dunlap to do so? Or was it a personal choice of Dunlap's? As was later quipped by the historian Carl Becker, the capitalization and punctuation in the Declaration followed "neither previous copies, nor reason, nor the custom of any age known to man."[6]

Something else was noticeable about the Dunlap broadside: the only names it contained were those of John Hancock, who "Signed by Order and in Behalf of the Congress," and Charles Thomson. The rest of the men who voted to adopt the Declaration kept themselves anonymous.

Neither ordinary Americans, nor the British, nor the rest of the world knew who had approved this audacious act. The Declaration was thus partially cloaked in the secrecy that marked all Congress's proceedings. It was, after all, treasonous, and perhaps discretion was the better part of "sacred honor."

Dunlap worked through the night and into the following morning. No record remains of how many copies he printed, though we know he ran off at least two batches, based on tiny stylistic differences between copies. In the rush, some were printed slightly askew, and some were folded before they were fully dry, leaving offset impressions. Perhaps unhappy with the haste of his work, Dunlap at some point reset the type and printed a single copy of the Declaration on durable animal parchment. This unique version is now held by the American Philosophical Society in Philadelphia, America's first learned society, founded by Benjamin Franklin in 1743, among whose members were fifteen of the Signers.[7]

Only twenty-six copies of Dunlap's broadsides would survive the ravages of time, making it one of the most sought-after artifacts in American history. By early morning on July 5, Dunlap had a batch ready for Congress. As soon as he received a copy, Charles Thomson affixed it with wax wafers in the space in the *Rough Journal* he had set aside the previous day (see insert).

It was now time to let the world know about American Independence.

On July 5 and 6, John Hancock and Charles Thomson dispatched express riders with copies of the Dunlap broadside, following Congress's order to send the Declaration to the State assemblies and local committees of safety, as well as to the Continental Army. Outside a few major cities, most roads were little more than tracks through the wilderness or rutted paths, sinking wagons in impassable mud pits or saturating travelers in dust. Only a few scattered stage lines operated, and a letter from Boston to Philadelphia would take the better part of a month.

Even as the riders started upon these abysmal roads, Heinrich Miller's widely read *Pennsylvanischer Staatsbote*, catering to the seventy thousand Germans concentrated in the fertile western part of Pennsylvania, became the first newspaper in the colonies to report that a Declaration of Independence had been adopted. Four days later, on July 9, the *Staatsbote* published a German translation of the Dunlap broadside.[8]

(335)

The PENNSYLVANIA EVENING POST.

Price only Two Coppers. Publiſhed every *Tueſday*, *Thurſday*, and *Saturday* Evenings.

Vol. II.] SATURDAY, JULY 6, 1776. [Num. 228.

In CONGRESS, July 4, 1776.

A Declaration by the Repreſentatives of the United States of America, in General Congreſs aſſembled.

WHEN, in the courſe of human events, it becomes neceſſary for one people to diſſolve the political bands which have connected them with another, and to aſſume, among the powers of the earth, the ſeparate and equal ſtation to which the laws of nature and of nature's God intitle them, a decent reſpect to the opinions of mankind requires that they ſhould declare the cauſes which impel them to the ſeparation.

We hold theſe truths to be ſelf-evident, That all men are created equal; that they are endowed, by their Creator, with certain unalienable rights; that among theſe are life, liberty, and the purſuit of happineſs. That to ſecure theſe rights, governments are inſtituted among men, deriving their juſt powers from the conſent of the governed; that whenever any form of government becomes deſtructive of theſe ends, it is the right of the people to alter or to aboliſh it, and to inſtitute new government, laying its foundation on ſuch principles, and organizing its powers in ſuch form, as to them ſhall ſeem moſt likely to effect their ſafety and happineſs. Prudence, indeed, will dictate that governments long eſtabliſhed ſhould not be changed for light and tranſient cauſes; and accordingly all experience hath ſhewn, that mankind are more diſpoſed to ſuffer, while evils are ſufferable, than to right themſelves by aboliſhing the forms to which they are accuſtomed. But when a long train of abuſes and uſurpations, purſuing invariably the ſame object, evinces a deſign to reduce them under abſolute deſpotiſm, it is their right, it is their duty, to throw off ſuch government, and to provide new guards for their future ſecurity. Such has been the patient ſufferance of theſe colonies, and ſuch is now the neceſſity which conſtrains them to alter their former ſyſtems of government. The hiſtory of the preſent King of Great-Britain is a hiſtory of repeated injuries and uſurpations, all having in direct object the eſtabliſhment of an abſolute tyranny over theſe ſtates. To prove this, let facts be ſubmitted to a candid world.

He has refuſed his aſſent to laws, the moſt wholeſome and neceſſary for the public good.

He has forbidden his Governors to paſs laws of immediate and preſſing importance, unleſs ſuſpended in their operation till his aſſent ſhould be obtained; and, when ſo ſuſpended, he has utterly neglected to attend to them.

He has refuſed to paſs other laws for the accommodation of large diſtricts of people, unleſs thoſe people would relinquiſh the right of repreſentation in the legiſlature, a right ineſtimable to them, and formidable to tyrants only.

He has called together legiſlative bodies at places unuſual, uncomfortable, and diſtant from the depoſitory of their public records, for the ſole purpoſe of fatiguing them into compliance with his meaſures.

He has diſſolved Repreſentative Houſes repeatedly, for oppoſing with manly firmneſs his invaſions on the rights of the people.

He has refuſed for a long time, after ſuch diſſolutions, to cauſe others to be elected; whereby the legiſlative powers, incapable of annihilation, have returned to the people at large for their exerciſe; the ſtate remaining in the mean time expoſed to all the dangers of invaſion from without, and convulſions within.

He has endeavoured to prevent the population of theſe ſtates; for that purpoſe obſtructing the laws for naturalization of foreigners; refuſing to paſs others to encourage their migrations hither, and raiſing the conditions of new appropriations of lands.

He has obſtructed the adminiſtration of juſtice, by refuſing his aſſent to laws for eſtabliſhing judiciary powers.

He has made Judges dependant on his will alone, for the tenure of their offices, and the amount and payment of their ſalaries.

He has erected a multitude of new offices, and ſent hither ſwarms of officers to harraſs our people, and eat out their ſubſtance.

He has kept among us, in times of peace, ſtanding armies, without the conſent of our legiſlatures.

He has affected to render the military independant of and ſuperior to the civil power.

He has combined with others to ſubject us to a juriſdiction foreign to our conſtitution, and unacknowledged by our laws; giving his aſſent to their acts of pretended legiſlation:

For quartering large bodies of armed troops among us:

For protecting them, by a mock trial, from puniſhment for any murders which they ſhould commit on the inhabitants of theſe ſtates:

For cutting off our trade with all parts of the world:

For impoſing taxes on us without our conſent:

For depriving us, in many caſes, of the benefits of trial by jury:

For tranſporting us beyond ſeas to be tried for pretended offences:

For aboliſhing the free ſyſtem of Engliſh laws in a neighbouring province, eſtabliſhing therein an arbitrary government, and enlarging its boundaries, ſo as to render it at once an example and fit inſtrument for introducing the ſame abſolute rule into theſe colonies:

For taking away our charters, aboliſhing our moſt valuable laws, and altering fundamentally the forms of our governments:

For ſuſpending our own legiſlatures, and declaring themſelves inveſted with power to legiſlate for us in all caſes whatſoever.

He has abdicated government here, by declaring us out of his protection and waging war againſt us.

He has plundered our ſeas, ravaged our coaſts, burnt our towns, and deſtroyed the lives of our people.

He is, at this time, tranſporting large armies of foreign mercenaries to complete the works of death, deſolation, and tyranny, already begun with circumſtances of cruelty and

The Pennsylvania Evening Post was the first paper to print the Declaration, on July 6, 1776.

The first unofficial printing of the Declaration appeared on July 6 in a Philadelphia newspaper. Surprisingly, it was not John Dunlap's own *Pennsylvania Packet* that brought the Declaration to the public, but his rival Benjamin Towne's *Pennsylvania Evening Post*. Towne's printing press was just a block from Dunlap's shop, at High and Front Streets, near the popular London Coffee House. No one knows how Towne got his hands on a copy of the Declaration. A spy in Dunlap's shop may have spirited a copy out or passed it surreptitiously in the coffeehouse. The news quickly made its way to other newspaper publishers up and down the seaboard. By the end of July, the Declaration had been reprinted in thirty newspapers, from New Hampshire down to Virginia. Americans farther south would have had to wait for the express riders to learn that they lived in a new country.[9]

As word of Independence spread, the new state assemblies printed their own official broadsides. Those north of Philadelphia were printed in New York, Massachusetts, and New Hampshire; none appear to have been published in the South. Some of these reprintings included State resolutions approving Congress's action while others told readers when the Declaration was to be read in public. Still others, addressed to local reverends, were intended to be read in church. In the public square and from the pulpit, Americans were learning about Independence.[10]

At noon on Monday, July 8, John Adams took a break from his duties and stepped outside the State House. A "great Crowd of People" were gathered in front of a viewing platform set up by the American Philosophical Society in 1769 to measure the Transit of Venus, the first great scientific endeavor undertaken in the colonies. From the platform, Colonel John Nixon, sheriff of Philadelphia, gave the first public reading of the Declaration.[11] Adams described the festive atmosphere in a letter to Samuel Chase, saying that the reading was followed by "Three Cheers . . . The Battalions paraded on the common and gave Us the Feu de Joy" (a rifle salute). After the ceremony, Adams told Chase, "The Bells rung all day, and almost all night."[12]

As Nixon finished reading the rousing pledge, a group of men rushed into the State House, took down the King's Arms, carried them outside to the common, placed them on a pile of wooden casks, and burned them. What seemed a spontaneous act of patriotism was a carefully choreographed action by eight members of the Pennsylvania Association, a volunteer military group. According to the Philadelphia druggist Christopher Marshall, who kept a detailed diary during those days, the plot was hatched on July 6 by members of the American Philosophical Society, of which Marshall was one. Designed to spark fervor among the listeners at the reading, it appears to have been the first instance of political theater after Independence.[13]

One would have expected Thomas Jefferson to be keenly interested in this first public reception of the Declaration, but he made no mention of the reading in his notes. Nor did Adams indicate that he was joined by Jefferson at the ceremony. It was an odd absence for someone so proud of his handiwork. Yet up and down the colonies, the Declaration was treated as a collective document, like the hundreds of resolutions passed in local committees over the past years. None of the accounts of the day, or the succeeding ones, include any mention of who, if anyone, was the primary author of the audacious document.

The next day, one of Hancock's express riders reached New York City, where George Washington was encamped with his troops, preparing for a British attack. Hancock had sent the broadside with a note requesting that Washington "have it proclaimed at the Head of the Army in the way, you shall think most proper."[14]

Washington was quick to write back:

> I perceive that Congress have been employed in deliberating on measures of the most Interesting nature. It is certain that It is not with us to determine in many Instances what consequences will flow from our Counsels, but yet It behoves us to adopt such, as under the smiles of a Gracious & All kind Providence will be most likely to promote our happiness; I trust the late decisive part they have taken is calculated for that end, and will secure us that freedom and those privileges which have been and are refused us, contrary to the voice of nature and the British Constitution.[15]

Washington understood the symbolic importance of this charter of freedom and hoped it would give material and moral support to his Continental Army. Just a week earlier, he had written to Hancock asking for flint, telling him that "an agreable spirit and willingness for Action seem to animate and pervade the whole of our Troops."[16] Yet at almost the same time, John Adams described the army as "an Object of Wretchedness . . . Disgraced, defeated, discontented, dispirited, diseased, naked, undisciplined, eaten up with Vermin . . ."[17]

Washington immediately ordered the Declaration "to be read with an audible voice" to the various brigades of the army throughout the country, reporting to Hancock that he hoped it would "serve as a free incentive to every officer, and soldier, to act with Fidelity and Courage." At his headquarters on Manhattan, where City Hall now stands, the reading took place at 6 p.m. that very day. The General sat on horseback at the head of the troops drawn up in ranks and later told Hancock that "the measure seemed to have their hearty assent." The cheers may well have been heard by British soldiers encamped on nearby Staten Island.[18]

That hearty assent soon turned into a mini-riot, as some of Washington's troops converged on the large equestrian statue of George III raised only six years earlier at the southern tip of Manhattan. John Adams had described it in his diary while on a visit to New York as "very large, of solid lead gilded with gold, standing on a pedestal of marble, very high." A colonial officer, Colonel Seymour, related its fate: the statue "was, by the sons of freedom, laid prostrate in the dirt" and melted down, the lead used for "bullets, to assimilate with the brain of our infatuated adversaries." Washington issued orders acknowledging the troops' "Zeal in the public cause," but fearing "riot and want of order," he directed that "in future these things shall be avoided by the Soldiery, and left to be executed by proper authority."[19]

Washington's men stopped toppling statues, but the General had less success controlling the citizens of New York. On July 18, when the Declaration was formally published by the New York State Convention, the

A fanciful contemporary print by Andre Basset of the pulling down of the statue of King George III in New York on July 9, 1776, after the reading of the Declaration of Independence.

British Arms over the seat of Justice in the Court House were taken down, torn to pieces, and burned. Those carved into the Court House pediment were likewise thrown down and smashed, while pictures of George III were burned to the cheers of the crowd. The Declaration released passions that American officials welcomed as proof of patriotism but also feared.

In Boston, cradle of the Revolution, the Declaration was read to a large crowd from the balcony of the State House on that same day. Abigail Adams had come in from the farm for the proclamation, and it was her turn to describe the festivities in a letter to her husband: "three cheers . . . bells rang, the privateers fired, the forts and batteries, the cannon were discharged, the platoons followed, and every face appeared joyful . . . Thus ends royall Authority in this State." As most Loyalists had left Boston with the British troops the previous March, passionate Patriots threw down the King's Arms and "every sign with a resemblance of it," and burned them in bonfires.[20]

The farther from Philadelphia, the longer it took for the news to spread. While some newspapers were reprinting the Declaration, most people learned the news of Independence from the official readings. The Declaration was proclaimed in Williamsburg, Virginia, on July 25, and in Charleston, South Carolina, in the beginning of August. The southernmost State, Georgia, was the last to receive notice. On August 10, nearly five weeks after Independence, a crowd in Savannah finally heard the Declaration read in public.[21]

On July 16, James Bowdoin, president of the Massachusetts Provincial Congress, was in Watertown, about twenty miles west of Boston, meeting with delegates from the St. John's and Mi'kmaq Indian Tribes of Nova Scotia. Long chafing under British control and resenting their expansion into tribal lands in Canada, the tribes were ripe for an alliance. Bowdoin had just received a copy of the Dunlap broadside, which he read and translated for the assembled Indians, emphasizing that the Americans had overthrown British rule and could help them do the same.

After hearing the Declaration, the Mi'kmaq leader, Ambrose Bear, said, "We like it well." He agreed to provide six hundred warriors to campaign with the Americans in Nova Scotia and defend the border of Maine. A week later, the parties signed the Treaty of Watertown, which directly quoted part of the Declaration's text, including the right to contract alliances.[22] The Indian tribes were most interested in protecting themselves from reprisals and reclaiming their lands. Had they known that

Washington had sent an expedition to destroy dozens of Iroquoian towns allied with the British along the northwest border of the colonies, their calculations may well have been different.[23]

A few months later, in November, the British defeated the Americans at the Battle of Fort Cumberland in Nova Scotia, ending the American threat to Canada. British pressure led the tribe to break its alliance in 1779 and sign a new treaty with the English. Trying to maintain a middle ground, the tribe continued to send ceremonial wampum belts to Congress as a sign of friendship, but no longer was there talk of a new partnership.[24]

On July 28, 1776, Vice Admiral Lord Richard Howe, commander of British naval forces and brother of General William Howe, sent a copy of the text of the Declaration to London. It arrived by mid-August and appeared in *The London Chronicle* on August 17. That same month, *The Gentleman's Magazine* also printed the Declaration, calling it a "desperate measure" and blithely dismissing Jefferson's charges by stating "whether those grievances were real or imaginary . . . we will not presume to decide."[25]

The British responses to the rebels were not long in coming. In the autumn John Lind, a London barrister, published *An Answer to the Declaration of the American Congress*, casting the conflict as an affront to national honor. The Americans had not just rebelled against the King, charged Lind: "the Declaration of the *American* Congress is an insult offered to everyone who bears the name of *Briton*." Among the more popular English critiques was James MacPherson's *The Rights of Great Britain Asserted against the Claims of America: Being an Answer to the Declaration of the General Congress*, which went through eight editions in 1776 alone. MacPherson dismissed the Declaration as a mere "paper" in which "the facts are either wilfully or ignorantly misrepresented."[26]

If anyone in England could be said to truly understand the Declaration, it was Thomas Hutchinson, who had been at the center of Massachusetts's politics for over three decades and had served as lieutenant governor from 1758 until he was named governor in 1771. An avowed Loyalist, despised for his support of the Stamp Act, Hutchinson had acted as the unofficial leader of the Massachusetts exiles in London since his flight in June of 1774.[27] In *Strictures upon the Declaration of the Congress in Philadelphia*, Hutchinson mocked the Declaration's claim that taxation without representation had driven the rebels to separation. If that issue had not appealed, he wrote, "other pretences would have been found for exception to the authority of Parliament."[28] Yet Hutchinson wrote as a man without any country, as unwanted in England as he was in Massachusetts. "We americans are plenty here and very cheap," he lamented. He would die in 1780, never setting foot back in his homeland.[29]

On October 31, in a speech opening the House of Peers, King George commented publicly on the rebels' action for the first time. "They have . . . presumed to set up their rebellious Confederacies for Independent States," he declared. "If their Treason be suffered to take Root, much Mischief must grow from it, to the Safety of my loyal Colonies, to the Commerce of my Kingdoms, and indeed to the present System of all Europe." Beyond this, the King was silent. As his biographer Andrew Roberts notes, George likely never read the Declaration and never referred to it in his extensive correspondence.[30]

Domestic political opposition to King George's government translated into muted support for the Americans. The Virginian diplomat William Lee, younger brother of Richard Henry Lee, who had lived in London for nearly twenty years and had been appointed a political agent of the Continental Congress, wrote on September 10 that the opposition party Whigs "do not say much, but rather seem to think the step a wise one . . . and what was an inevitable consequence of the measures taken by the British Ministry."[31] Another Whig, Edmund Burke, had long advocated for the colonists' rights as Englishmen, including in his famous 1775 "Speech on Conciliation with America." Burke was not sympathetic to the Declaration, however, just as he could not approve of outright revolution, lamenting the loss of "a large and noble part of our Empire."[32] As Burke and the King understood, the Americans had not just created a country, they had thrust Britain into a new era.

Chapter 4
The Signing

In the hectic weeks of early July 1776, Congress gave little thought to preserving its Declaration in permanent form. Not until July 19, after the New York delegation had voted to approve Independence, did Charles Thomson's *Rough Journal* record an order "That the Declaration passed on the 4th be fairly engrossed on parchment with the title and stile of 'The Unanimous Declaration of the thirteen United States of America' and that the same when engrossed be signed by every member of Congress." Then, two weeks later, the *Journal* noted that on August 2, "the declaration of independence being engrossed and compared at the table was signed."[1]

But compared to *what*? Was it the Dunlap broadside, itself only a copy of the final draft? Or could it have been the long-lost fair copy in Jefferson's hand, edited and approved by Congress? If the fair copy survived until August, what then happened to it? We are left tantalizingly ignorant. This is only one of the many mysteries surrounding the engrossed Declaration, leading to centuries of debate and controversy.

The first line of the faded parchment people crane to see in the dim light of the National Archives reads, "In CONGRESS, July 4, 1776." Yet it is almost certain, if the Congressional record is to be believed, that this most famous of American documents was not signed on July Fourth. But Congress's own record is contradicted by no less an authority than Thomas Jefferson himself, who, along with John Adams, Benjamin

Franklin, Charles Carroll, and others, indicated at various times that the Declaration was indeed signed on July Fourth. Jefferson's contemporaneous notes record that, on the Fourth, "The declaration was reported by the commee., agreed to by the house, and signed by every member present except Mr. Dickinson." Over thirty years later, Dr. Benjamin Rush dramatically remembered the vote and then "the pensive and awful silence which pervaded the house when we were called up, one after another, to the table of the President of Congress, to subscribe what was believed by many at that time to be our own death warrants."[2]

What Jefferson and Rush remembered was impossible, for at least eleven members who signed the scroll were not present in Philadelphia on that day. Strident denials by other members of Congress that any signing took place on the Fourth raise further doubts about Jefferson's notes and the claims made later by Rush and others. Given that there is reason to believe Jefferson later rewrote his notes from that period, the simplest explanation is that he and his colleagues misremembered what had happened during those hectic days of July 1776.[3]

Other anomalies have led to further suspicion. Most notable is the question of why the words *of the thirteen united* appear so abnormally small in the title. The scholar Wilfred Ritz suggested that the Declaration was in fact engrossed on July 4 with a different title, "The Unanimous Declaration of the Twelve States of America," acknowledging the fact that the New York delegation had not been authorized to sign. Once the New Yorkers were given the green light a new order was issued on July 19 and by August 2, the title was scraped and rewritten, ready for another round of signatures.[4]

This same scholar brings up the famous "errant *a*" inserted and then removed from the Dunlap broadside. Ritz points to an unusually large space between the words *institute* and *new government* in the fifth line of the engrossed copy, which leads him to conclude that the same mistake was made on parchment and broadside at the same time, and both were then corrected.

Despite some beguiling suggestions, the weight of the evidence leads most scholars to accept that there was no formal signing on the Fourth, and that the parchment now enshrined in the National Archives was in fact prepared in late July and signed by most, though not all, members in early August.

Sometime soon after July 19, John Hancock and Charles Thomson asked Timothy Matlack, Thomson's clerk who would soon see action in the Revolutionary War, to engross the Declaration.[5] Engrossing was a common practice in those days, when most official records were handwritten. It referred to the copying of a document in large, often ornate calligraphy, usually on a durable material, like parchment. John Dunlap's broadsides were printed on cotton-fiber paper, which was durable enough but prone to tearing. Parchment was treated animal skin, often goat or calf, preferred both for its permanence and because mistakes could be scraped off and overwritten. The ink used in Matlack's day for engrossing was usually "iron gall," made from combining oak galls, fungus-like growths produced by insects on oak trees, with iron shavings. As conservators have noted, iron gall ink darkens to purplish black as it oxidizes and then ages to a warm brown. Matlack wrote with a quill pen, as was the custom, sharpened by hand.[6]

To get the Declaration ready for signing while most members were still in Philadelphia, Matlack rushed his work. He chose a domestically produced parchment of average or poor quality, according to one longtime conservator in the Library of Congress, or a "rather crude vellum" of calfskin, in the words of another distinguished scholar.[7] Perhaps it was the only thing available on short notice in the markets of Philadelphia in the middle of the war; he certainly did not have time to prepare his own. Matlack cut the parchment down to roughly 29½ inches by 24 inches, though it would suffer more trimming through the years.

In a neat, controlled, and elegant script, Matlack wrote out the 1,337 words of the Declaration in forty-four ruler-straight lines. Flourishes and ornate lettering and frequent capitalization of nouns are scattered around the document. Under the dated heading, the title read

The unanimous Declaration of the thirteen united States of America

with its strangely small script in the middle. At the bottom of the parchment, Matlack left a large space and drew vertical lines to create columns for signatures.

Matlack's haste showed through in two places: in line sixteen, he wrote "Represtative," instead of "Representative," and in the thirty-fourth line he omitted the word *only*, in the charge "Our repeated Petitions have been answered [only] by repeated injury." In both cases, handwritten corrections were inserted above the line in question, still faintly visible today.

Matlack completed his work within two weeks and brought the final copy to Hancock, who, signing first as President of the Congress, famously wrote his name out in a large, bold script. When he finished, he was said to have proclaimed (though the story appears to be apocryphal), "There! John Bull can read my name without spectacles, and may now double his reward of £500 for my head. *That* is my defiance."[8]

Contrary to later myth, there was no single signing ceremony. Ultimately, fifty-six men would sign the parchment Declaration, ranging in age from the twenty-six-year-old Edward Rutledge of South Carolina to Benjamin Franklin, who was seventy. Those present in Philadelphia on August 2 presumably signed on that date or soon after, while others arranged with Thomson to sign when they returned or passed through on business. Some leading members of Congress, including Richard Henry Lee, the proposer of Independence, did not sign until after August 2. The most extreme case was that of Thomas McKean, who had voted for Independence on the Fourth, but by August was on active service and did not pen in his name until sometime in 1777, or possibly even as late as 1781.[9] Some names were notably absent, including John Dickinson and Robert Livingston, who had returned to New York and immersed himself in local defense.[10]

All signed underneath Hancock's outsize name, grouped by State, north to south, starting from the right with Josiah Bartlett of New Hampshire followed by the Massachusetts Adamses, Samuel and John. Near the middle came "Th. Jefferson" and "Benj[a] Franklin." George Walton, of Georgia, a twenty-seven-year-old self-educated carpenter and lawyer who later was captured by the British, signed last. Stephen Hopkins of Rhode Island wrote in a hand shaking with palsy, while Maryland's Charles Carroll, the only Roman Catholic Signer, added "of Carrollton," as he habitually did.

When the Signers pledged their sacred honor and affixed their names to the official statement severing the colonies from Britain, they were in deadly earnest. Once their names became known, the test of this pledge would come swiftly. Many saw no harm come to them for their boldness, but others suffered dreadfully. The merchant Francis Lewis's Long Island home was burned by the British and his wife, Elizabeth, imprisoned. Eventually exchanged for British prisoners, Elizabeth Lewis's health was ruined by her imprisonment, and she died in 1779. In New Jersey, John

Hart became a fugitive after his lands and property were ruined, hastening his death, and the distinguished lawyer Richard Stockton was held as a British prisoner for over a month in harsh conditions, leading him to an early death at the age of fifty. His home, like that of Francis Hopkinson, another New Jersey Signer, and William Hooper's in North Carolina, was pillaged by British troops. Three South Carolinians, Thomas Heyward, Jr., Arthur Middleton, and the young Edward Rutledge, were captured by the British and imprisoned in a dank fortress in St. Augustine, Florida, for nearly a year.

Even as new signatories added their names, knowing full well they would eventually be identified by the British, the infant United States now had its founding document. What Congress intended to do with the engrossed Declaration was never made clear, but for the duration of the war, it was kept among the papers held by Charles Thomson, the secretary of Congress.

We have no way of knowing how the Declaration was treated during these years. It was almost certainly rolled up and stored; only when another member of Congress came to add his name to the document was it unrolled. We do know the scroll was rolled from the top edge down, leaving the signatures at the bottom more exposed. Over time, the lower edge of the document became grimy as multiple hands rolled and unrolled the parchment. Ink does not penetrate parchment the way that it is absorbed by more porous paper; it has a tendency to stick to the surface of the scraped skin. Though Timothy Matlack undoubtedly gave his calligraphy time to dry, the more the document was handled, the greater the risk of ink flaking off. The signatures, inscribed on the parchment at different times with varying degrees of force and different types of inks, were the most vulnerable to wear and tear.

The Declaration was just one of many documents rolled up for safekeeping for the duration of the war. That might explain why, at some undetermined date, someone wrote on the back in a neat hand, "Original Declaration of Independence dated 4th July 1776." This was the equivalent of a crude filing tab, making identification easier for retrieval. It also had the unintended consequence of further cementing the belief that the Declaration was engrossed and signed on the day of its passing.

In fact, this formal parchment, with its elegant script and dozens of signatures, was a state secret, kept even from those fighting for the freedom it proclaimed. Secrecy had been the hallmark of the revolutionary movement, from the shadowy Sons of Liberty to Congressional debates and actions. For forty-five years, the true date of the signing was kept hidden, until 1821, when the *Secret Journals of the Acts and Proceedings of Congress* was published. By then, the myth that the Declaration was signed, and Independence decided, on July Fourth had become inscribed in the hearts of Americans.

Chapter 5
Success and Neglect

Members of the Continental Congress watched warily as George Washington and his men retreated into Pennsylvania in early December 1776. The month before, Washington had been driven from Manhattan and New Jersey. General William Howe and his subordinate, the thirty-eight-year-old Lord Charles Cornwallis, were hot on Washington's heels and aiming for Philadelphia. It was far from certain that the Revolution would survive into the New Year. These were, as Thomas Paine wrote in mid-December, "the times that try men's souls."

In a show of bravado, Charles Thomson had written to Washington, now encamped across the Delaware River from Trenton, on December 11, enclosing a resolution of Congress that read, in part, " . . . a false and malicious report hath been spread by the enemies of America that the Congress was about to disperse . . . Nor will they adjourn from the city of Philadelphia in the present state of affairs unless the last necessity shall direct it." Courage quickly gave way to prudence and the next day the "last necessity" apparently had come. The decision to flee Philadelphia, once arrived at, was quickly executed. Congress voted to abandon the city on December 12 and hastily retreated one hundred miles south to Baltimore.[1]

Charles Thomson packed up his records, including the Congressional journals and key papers of state, during the retreat. If captured, these would have revealed secret agreements, communications with military leaders, financial disbursements, attempts to form alliances with foreign powers, and other critical information. Among these papers was the newly engrossed parchment Declaration, including the still-secret signatures. On that cold December morning, the Declaration began the first of its many journeys.

Thomson left no clue as to how these state papers were handled. In the chaos of retreat, he and his clerks most likely rolled up the Declaration, put it in a large bag or wooden chest with other papers, and carted it away in a light wagon. It may have been crushed in transit, given the numerous creases and crimps still visible in the parchment today. It is possible the scroll was folded at some point, as both horizontal and vertical fold lines can be seen, though we'll never know whether that happened in the winter of 1776 or later.

For nearly three months, the Congress remained in Baltimore, a port city on the Chesapeake Bay of around six thousand inhabitants. By the New Year, welcome news had arrived of the first significant American victories of the war. On Christmas Night, in frigid conditions, General Washington had crossed the Delaware River and returned to New Jersey. The next day at Trenton, he defeated the German Hessian mercenaries hired by England, and a week later routed the British at Princeton.

As news from the shifting front raised hopes, Congress decided it was time to lift the veil of secrecy over its actions and to let Americans know who had voted for Independence. On January 18, 1777, it authorized a new broadside and provided that "an authenticated copy of the declaration of indepedency with the names of the members of Congress subscribing the same, be sent to each of the united states & that they be desired to have the same put upon the record."[2]

For the job, Thomson turned to a local Baltimore printer, Mary Katharine Goddard, who was the city's postmaster and the publisher of the *Maryland Journal.* A fervent patriot, the thirty-eight-year-old Goddard had printed Thomas Paine's wildly popular call to revolution, *Common Sense*, and was known as "an expert and correct compositor of types."[3]

Charles Thomson likely took the engrossed Declaration to Goddard's shop for the typesetting. Goddard's approach was significantly different from John Dunlap's. To begin with, she used the titling on the engrossed parchment as a model, which no one outside of Congress had yet seen. She also created a more aesthetically pleasing version of the document,

IN CONGRESS, JULY 4, 1776.

THE UNANIMOUS

DECLARATION

OF THE

THIRTEEN UNITED STATES OF AMERICA.

John Hancock.

IN CONGRESS, JANUARY 18, 1777.

By Order of CONGRESS,

JOHN HANCOCK, *President.*

Congress commissioned Mary Katherine Goddard to print this broadside in Baltimore in January 1777. It was the first to publicly reveal the names of the Signers.

spreading the text across two columns separated by a decorative divider, unlike Dunlap's single block. As instructed, Goddard included the names of the Signers (all but one, the missing Thomas McKean). Thus, for the first time the identities of the men who had pledged their lives, fortunes, and sacred honor to the cause of freedom were made public. For good measure, Goddard included at the bottom Congress's January 18, 1777, order to print the broadside. Like Dunlap, she included her own name and the place of publication.

This time, John Hancock and Charles Thomson personally signed Goddard's broadsides. This made Goddard's edition the first fully authenticated copy of the Declaration. Far fewer copies were printed, as their principal purpose was to be entered into the public record of each of the thirteen States. Only nine copies of the Goddard broadside exist today, making it almost as rare as the engrossed Declaration.

Hancock sent the new broadside to the State assemblies with a grandiloquent note:

> As there is not a more distinguished Event in the History of America, than the Declaration of her Independence—nor any, that, in all probability, will so much excite the Attention of future Ages, it is highly proper, that the Memory of that Transaction, together with the Causes that gave Rise to it, should be preserved in the most careful Manner that can be devised.[4]

Yet at the very moment he was calling for the careful preservation of the Declaration's origins, Hancock appeared to be party to a mysterious deception. When the States received Goddard's broadside, including for the first time the names of the Signers, it seemed to be an official acknowledgment that the Declaration was both adopted and signed on July 4. Hancock knew all too well that at least eleven Signers were absent from Philadelphia on that day. He also knew that the parchment's signing did not begin until August 2. Nonetheless, he authenticated Goddard's broadside with his distinct signature.

Later that year, Charles Thomson's journal of Congress's proceedings was published, giving further credence to July Fourth as the signing date. Thomson kept a daily *Rough Journal*, which he then supplemented with a fuller *Corrected Journal*, but the most sensitive items on Congress's agenda were recorded only in his *Secret Journal*. The public records in the *Corrected Journal* were published as the *Journals of Congress*, or the *Printed Journal*, but due to the exigencies of the war, the *Printed Journal* for 1776 did not appear until sometime in 1777. Its entry for July 4, 1776, reprinted the entire Declaration of Independence, adding that "The foregoing declaration was by order of Congress engrossed and signed by the following members." Then followed the list of signers for only the second time (still without Thomas McKean, who was serving in the army).

This printed record differed sharply from the original entry in Thomson's private *Rough Journal*, which did not include the text of the Declaration or any mention of engrossing and signing. Signers who were not in Philadelphia on the Fourth were again listed as having signed on that date. Neither Hancock nor anyone connected with the Declaration attempted to correct the mistake, other than the irrepressible Thomas McKean, who decades later swore to John Adams that the *Journal*'s entry for the Fourth was full of errors, hinting darkly that "false colours are certainly hung out; there is culpability somewhere."[5]

The new record had its effect. While John Adams had originally predicted that July 2 would be the date remembered in history, by the summer of 1777, even he had succumbed to the new legend of July Fourth. He wrote Abigail from Philadelphia that the Fourth, "being the anniversary of American Independence, was celebrated here with a festivity and ceremony becoming the occasion." By 1778, the Congress had abandoned July 2, holding a "grand festival" at Philadelphia's City Tavern on July 4 to celebrate the "glorious Anniversary of the INDEPENDENCE OF AMERICA," as John Dunlap's *Pennsylvania Packet* put it. George Washington ordered cannon salutes and double rations of rum for the troops on subsequent July Fourths throughout the war.[6]

In Paris, John Adams and Benjamin Franklin hosted an Independence Day banquet on July 4, 1778. Underscoring the importance of foreign alliances, Franklin had joined two other agents of Congress already in France to negotiate a treaty. Dissension among the three Americans led Congress to dispatch Adams, but two months before his arrival, to his chagrin, Franklin had successfully concluded an alliance. Now, though appalled by Franklin's extravagant and immoral lifestyle, he put on a unified front, hosting a joint celebration of their country's second birthday.[7] Yet as for the Declaration itself, after its prominent appearance in 1776, it began to fade into the background.

The engrossed parchment was kept by Charles Thomson and followed Congress over the next six years of war, when it was often feared that the delegates, and all their records, would be captured by the British. The Declaration returned to Philadelphia in March 1777, only to move around the state when the British occupied the capital city in September

1777. Congress stopped in Lancaster on September 27, then made a nine-month stay in York before heading back to Philadelphia.

The fighting ended in October 1781, with Washington's victory over Cornwallis at Yorktown, but in June 1783, when four hundred Continental Army soldiers mutinied over back pay and surrounded the State House, Congress hastily fled again, this time to Princeton, New Jersey. From then until December 1784 the Declaration was carted to Princeton, Annapolis, and Trenton. Each time the scroll was kept in whatever makeshift accommodations were arranged for Thomson and his clerks. No one knows how carefully it was stored or protected.

In March 1781, the Articles of Confederation came into effect, though the Congress remained essentially the same body.[8] Disagreement among the States, and concerns over whether larger States would cede their extensive territorial claims to Congress, had delayed the Articles' completion until November 15, 1777, and their ratification took another three years. There was no head of state under the new government. Congress itself was considered an executive body, and it established a handful of very small, specialized departments headed by members. One such was a Department of Foreign Affairs, initially led by Robert Livingston. Smoothing the transition to the new system was the fact that Charles Thomson remained the secretary of Congress.

The Declaration continued to move around with Thomson and the peripatetic Congress during the final years of war and first years of peace. Only with the dawn of 1785 did Congress and the scroll finally find some stability when the Confederation government moved to New York City. For the next five years, the Declaration was kept in Thomson's office on the second floor of the Old City Hall, on the corner of Wall and Nassau Streets. But physical stability did not mean political stability. The Confederation era, from 1781 through 1789, was a perilous time for the new Republic, as the Articles proved unequal to the demands of governing.

The first civic celebration of the independent nation was held in Boston in 1781, marked by cannon salutes and formal dinners at taverns attended by local notables. Slowly through the decade the practice caught on. One of the main groups behind these celebrations was the Society of the Cincinnati, formed by George Washington and Henry Knox in 1783 as a fraternal organization to honor the service of officers of the Continental Army. Though it was later accused of harboring aristocratic designs against democracy, the Society of the Cincinnati focused its attention on maintaining personal bonds among former officers and inculcating a reverence for the sacrifices of the Revolution. Holding its annual meetings on July Fourth in the main cities of each State, the Cincinnati published the orations delivered by distinguished speakers at local dinners. It pushed for a public commemoration of Independence Day in Philadelphia when no festivities were held in 1783 or 1784 and succeeded in getting an official ceremony sponsored in 1786, which soon became an annual tradition.[9]

While July Fourth gained in popularity as the date to celebrate America's founding, little attention was paid to the Declaration itself. When it was mentioned in orations or the press, it was remembered primarily as "that sacred Instrument" by which the colonies had secured Independence.[10] Some saw it as more, however. John Brooks, in an oration to the Society of the Cincinnati of Massachusetts in 1787, lauded the document as "an act which for conciseness and precision, for majesty of expression and loftiness of thought, stands unrivaled among the literary productions of this, or any former age—an act, it is but just to add, which does infinite honour to those bold and generous patriots who gave it their sanction."[11]

As far as ordinary Americans knew, five of those "generous patriots" had jointly written the Declaration. The veil of authorship was lifted by May 1783, during a sermon in Hartford, Connecticut, when the Reverend Ezra Stiles, president of Yale College in New Haven and America's leading Hebraist, lauded "Jefferson, who poured the soul of the continent into the monumental act of Independence." Stiles went on to praise the other Signers, "the illustrious band of heroes and compatriots, . . . who . . . resolutely and nobly dared, in the face of every danger, to sign the glorious act of Independence. May their names live, be preserved, and transmitted to posterity with deserved reputation and honor, through all American ages!" Perhaps more important than identifying Jefferson as the author, Stiles's invocation of "the soul of the continent" hinted at a larger meaning for the Declaration at a time when few paid much attention to it. Stiles may have been the first to tie the document to the emerging character of the new nation.[12]

Despite the patriotic efforts of groups like the Society of the Cincinnati, the nation was faltering. The Articles of Confederation had set up a government that was weak by design, as each State was considered sovereign and independent.[13] The impotence of the national government, such as it was, caused problems in the last year of the Revolutionary War and throughout the 1780s. The government could not tax, maintain a standing army, or establish permanent departments. The Articles proved unequal even to basic tasks like paying off the war debt. The Confederation government failed to respond to Shays's Rebellion, which rocked western Massachusetts in 1786 and 1787 when farmers and veterans of the War of Independence fought the government's attempts to collect taxes and personal debts. By the mid-1780s, the future of the Republic seemed in doubt.[14]

Efforts to reform the Confederation failed, and by 1787 it had become clear that the only hope was a second political founding. One of the prime movers was George Washington, now retired to Mount Vernon but increasingly frustrated by the inability of the States to cooperate on trade and canal-building, which he considered vital to the country's development. He was disturbed by the government's inability to raise troops during Shays's Rebellion, fearing anarchy in the future.[15]

Washington was also worried about the radicalization of politics, which threatened the individual freedom promised by the Declaration. This concern was shared by his brilliant fellow Virginian James Madison. In the 1770s, the danger to liberty had been identified as the tyranny of one man, the King. A decade later, it was the people and their representatives who appeared to pose a greater threat. The people had taken the Declaration's egalitarian message to heart, challenging all social distinctions and enabling, as one newspaper put it, "the most unfit men to shove themselves into stations of influence, where they soon gave way to the unrestrained inclination of bad habits."[16] Only a decade after Independence, the people's representatives were less motivated by republican virtue than by the allure of power over their fellow citizens, however short in duration. State legislatures were acting as capriciously as colonial rulers.[17] With the States becoming more radical, a more powerful central government seemed the only solution.

The thirty-six-year-old Madison and the equally brilliant Alexander Hamilton of New York maneuvered the States into gathering once again in Philadelphia. The call was ostensibly to revise the Articles of Confederation, but in reality, many of those converging on Philadelphia wanted to forge a federal constitution that would restrain the passions of the people and their legislatures. Washington presided over the Constitutional Convention, which opened in May 1787 and met in the same State House where the Declaration was signed. Under his guidance, with the careful planning of Madison, Hamilton, and James Wilson of Pennsylvania, the delegates over the next four months hammered out a new Constitution, which was adopted on September 17, 1787.

Though Madison's efforts earned him the sobriquet "The Father of the Constitution," the fight to ratify the document consumed domestic politics for the next year, pitting "Federalists" like Hamilton in favor of a strong central government against "Anti-Federalists" defending State and local autonomy.[18] In this great political battle, Hamilton, Madison, and John Jay poured their titanic energy into writing the newspaper articles that became the famed *The Federalist* (only later rechristened as *The Federalist Papers*). They argued for a powerful federal government, a bicameral legislature, and the establishment of executive and judicial branches. The core of their program was the separation and balancing of powers, with Hamilton focused primarily on fiscal issues while Madison sought robust protections of individual rights. There was only a single, indirect reference to the Declaration in the eighty-five *Federalist* articles, but its spirit infused the debates.[19]

The Anti-Federalists included some of the most powerful voices that had argued for Independence a decade earlier. Men like Patrick Henry charged that the Constitution was a direct threat to the spirit of freedom embodied by the Declaration and to the authority of State constitutions. They feared that the powerful central government proposed by the Federalists would bring taxes, debt, standing armies, and government intrusion into every nook and cranny of American life. The Virginia ratifying convention, in particular, witnessed a rancorous debate. George Mason, whose Virginia Declaration of Rights had so influenced Jefferson, laid out numerous objections, most notably that there was no similar set of guarantees in the Constitution. "The declarations of rights in the separate States are no security" against an overweening central government, he charged in the *Virginia Journal* in November 1787. "This government will commence in a moderate aristocracy," Mason warned, until it will eventually "produce a monarchy or a corrupt oppressive aristocracy."[20]

One great voice was absent from the entire process. Thomas Jefferson was in Paris, having been sent in 1784 to help negotiate a commercial treaty before succeeding Franklin as the American minister. Jefferson shipped James Madison books on constitutional theory and the history of republics, but for the most part he added little to the debates or to Madison's thinking. He initially sided with those seeking to preserve as much autonomy for the States as possible, opposing Madison's early proposal that the new federal government have the power of vetoing acts of the State legislatures. When he finally received the draft Constitution, Jefferson told acquaintances that he opposed about half of it. Like Madison, he supported the separation of powers into three branches, but he agreed with Mason that a Declaration of Rights should precede the articles of the Constitution. In general, Jefferson preferred a less energetic federal government but recognized the need for one more powerful than that provided by the Confederation.[21]

Jefferson downplayed the fear of anarchy that so animated Washington. Events like Shays's Rebellion are exceedingly rare, he told John Adams's son-in-law, William Smith, but one mustn't stamp out the spirit of resistance. "The tree of liberty," he famously and controversially wrote Smith, "must be refreshed from time to time with the blood of patriots and tyrants."[22] This letter was made public and used by Patrick Henry during the Virginia Convention. By then, however, Jefferson had largely swung his support behind Madison. They had exchanged many letters, and Madison had more fully explained the safeguards built into the Constitution. By now it was generally agreed that a separate Bill of Rights, which Madison initially had opposed, would be appended to the Constitution soon after its ratification.

The future shape of the American government was ultimately determined by Madison, Wilson, and the Federalists. Delaware was the first State to ratify, on December 7, 1787, and once New Hampshire became the ninth, on June 21, 1788, the Constitution went into effect. The spirit of the Declaration had carried Americans through the Revolutionary War, and the Federalists insisted that its basic principles infused the Constitution. As for the contentious Bill of Rights, it took three years to complete what Madison referred to as a "nauseous project." Anti-Federalist fears were only slightly allayed by the protections afforded by the Bill of Rights, which was ratified on December 15, 1791.

No one doubted that George Washington would be elected the first president of the new federal government in 1789. The next year, Washington and the new Congress returned to Philadelphia, where they would remain for a decade while a new capital was constructed on the Potomac River. In July, Congress created the first executive department under the

Constitution, the Department of Foreign Affairs. On September 15, 1789, this was reorganized as the Department of State and was given "the custody and charge . . . of all the books, records and papers, remaining in the office of the late Secretary of the United States in Congress assembled." That secretary was Charles Thomson, and his archive was the great treasure house of the Revolutionary era.[23]

No one had done more than Thomson to protect the important papers of state. Without the scraps of paper he had kept containing resolutions, minutes, and correspondence, and without his various journals, future historians would have almost no view into the months and years when the United States came into being. After fifteen years of dedicated service, Thomson had hoped for a position in the new federal government, such as Secretary of the Senate. His ambition and backing of the controversial Robert Morris had made him powerful enemies, however, and he was forced into retirement instead. Accepting his fate and turning to his interest in biblical translation, on July 23, 1789, Thomson relinquished to the new Department of State his journals, papers, and the cherished Declaration. Six months later, the first Secretary of State returned from his long sojourn in Paris to take up his new duties. That Secretary was Thomas Jefferson, and he was now custodian of his own creation.[24]

Twice disappointed in his desire to contribute to the framing of new constitutions, first for Virginia and then for the United States, Jefferson returned to America having witnessed the opening acts of one of the greatest national upheavals in European history. While the Americans were struggling to establish a new form of government, the centuries-old French monarchy was under assault. Jefferson, not surprisingly, was sympathetic to the so-called Third Estate, the lawyers and merchants demanding rights and reforms. Throughout May and June of 1789, he had traveled regularly to Versailles, where the Estates General, the French parliament, was meeting for the first time in over a century.[25] In July, Jefferson hosted an Independence Day banquet in Paris. One of his guests was Washington's old comrade the Marquis de Lafayette, a leader among the nobles trying to bridge King Louis XVI and the people. Ten days later, on July 14, the Bastille was stormed. Jefferson deplored the violence, but thought it inevitable given the reluctance of the King and nobles to accept meaningful reform.[26]

During these fraught months, Jefferson had spoken with Lafayette about drafting a declaration of rights for the French. The first French translation of the Declaration of Independence was printed as early as August 1776, in a journal published in the Netherlands. Multiple translations had appeared over the next few years until, in 1783, the Duc de La Rochefoucauld published the Declaration alongside constitutions of various American States, which members of the National Assembly consulted in their debates.[27]

Over the course of the summer, Lafayette sent Jefferson at least two drafts of a bill that the Virginian felt was too focused on economic and social equality. To Jefferson, the main concern should be equality before the law. Still, when the "Declaration of the Rights of Man and of the Citizen" was promulgated on August 26, 1789, he was largely supportive. Heavily influenced by Lafayette and issued by the Constituent Assembly, the successor to the National Assembly, the French Declaration of the Rights of Man was a summation of the ideals of the European Enlightenment, going well beyond the moderate British tradition expressed in the 1689 Bill of Rights, which had been so important to Jefferson and the framers of the Constitution.

The seventeen articles of the Declaration of the Rights of Man laid out the basis for a new compact between the French and their king.[28] Echoes of Jefferson's language permeate the document, beginning with the acknowledgment that "Men are born and remain free and equal in rights," among which are "liberty, property, security, and resistance to oppression." Jefferson had opposed the inclusion of the right to property, as he did not believe this was an "inalienable" right. He also felt there should be more protection for religious freedom.

In 1776, the American Declaration had been unique, but what seemed radical a decade before now appeared tame.

These next few years saw frenetic activity as President Washington set up the first Cabinet, focused on internal improvements, pursued commercial treaties with Great Britain and France, sought to gain full control of U.S. territory on which the British maintained forts, and worked hard to reduce British and Spanish connivance with Indian tribes.[29] During these years, the Department of State was housed in no fewer than six buildings in Philadelphia. Outbreaks of yellow fever forced the government to retreat to

Trenton for four-month stays in 1797, 1798, and 1799. Each time the key papers of state were carried along. The frequency of these moves took their toll on the Declaration, which remained rolled up in a chest or cabinet.

In 1796, Washington decided against running for a third term, removing any lingering fear that he might seek to remain in office for life, becoming a monarch in all but name. Jefferson unsuccessfully ran against Adams that year, and became Vice President instead, having garnered the second-highest number of Electoral College votes.[30] The two had become estranged and soon would break relations entirely. When Washington died in 1799 at the age of sixty-seven, the Revolutionary era began to recede into history. With the Constitution now guiding the government, the Declaration's urgency faded as rival political parties formed around the two men who had brought it into being.[31]

On May 31, 1800, Acting Secretary of State Charles Lee arrived in Washington City, on the banks of the Potomac River. Following an order from President John Adams, he had packed up all the government documents in his possession and brought them on a government sloop from Philadelphia. Stored somewhere among the hundreds of chests and boxes on board was the engrossed Declaration. In its only known journey by water, it had traveled down the Delaware River, briefly into the Atlantic Ocean, and then into Chesapeake Bay, before heading up the Potomac.

After three days aboard ship, Lee arrived at the site of what some called "The Capital of Miserable Huts." Although the new capital had been a work in progress for a decade, in May 1800 Washington was barely a functioning city. Unlike neighboring Georgetown, founded as a tobacco port in 1751, and which boasted a new college, the first Catholic institution of higher learning in the country, Washington City had only a few hundred structures of varying size and quality.[32]

At George Washington's behest, Pierre Charles L'Enfant, a French engineer, had come up with a grand plan for the capital city in 1790.[33] The temperamental Frenchman was soon dismissed for his confrontational behavior, and the building of the capital proceeded in fits and starts. As President Adams arrived to take up residence, the new capital's few streets were little more than dirt paths. Shrubs, trees, and swamp grass filled much of the city center and extended along Pennsylvania Avenue, the main thoroughfare. The Potomac nearly reached the grounds of the still-unfinished

President's House and Treasury Department, while marshes bordered the river to the west. Across town, up on Jenkins Hill, only one wing of the planned Capitol Building had been erected, housing the Senate, House of Representatives, and Supreme Court. In this city-in-the-making, the State Department was initially forced to share rooms in the Treasury Building, the only government structure ready for occupancy.

Within a few months, the Declaration moved with the State Department from the Treasury Building to one of the "Six Buildings," on Pennsylvania Avenue, and then finally to an unnamed public building just west of the President's House in May 1801, two months after Thomas Jefferson finally became President. Here, on the current site of the ornate Eisenhower Executive Office Building, the State, War, and Navy Departments, the Patent and Post Offices, and several other government bureaus were crowded into a simple two-story structure. That same month, James Madison became Jefferson's Secretary of State. Madison had only one Chief Clerk and seven assistant clerks and little in the way of space or manpower. At this point, the Declaration was most likely boxed up with other records in the building's small attic.[34] But if the physical parchment lay in the dark, partisan warfare was dragging it back into the limelight.

Political unity had all but evaporated by the time Thomas Jefferson became the third president of the United States in March 1801, after a bitter campaign pitting him against his former friend and colleague John Adams. The Declaration was soon sucked into the political maelstrom, and celebrations of July Fourth became ersatz political battles. Federalists tried to shift attention to July 2 as the true date of Independence, highlighting Adams's role, and their newspapers refused to republish the Declaration to mark the day. The Federalist *Gazette of the United States* could write on July 10, 1801, that "The American, if he is a real American does not consist in . . . publishing declarations. Mr. Jefferson has taught us that declarations and actions are widely different." In response, the Jeffersonian newspaper *Aurora* noted that Republicans enthusiastically celebrated the reading of the Declaration "in a manner distinct and energetic," while drinking toasts to Jefferson, "whose political creed is on record in the Declaration of our National Independence."[35]

In this fevered atmosphere, the Declaration was used as a cudgel by the political and intellectual classes. Few argued that it contained timeless principles that belonged to all Americans, if not the world. Such radicalism was anathema to the conservative Federalists, who were eager to distance themselves from the French Revolution, which had descended into a bloody Terror, paving the way for the Corsican General Napoleon Bonaparte's audacious coup d'etat. Meanwhile, Jeffersonians largely celebrated their man and not his most famous piece of writing.

Almost standing alone was the poet Mercy Otis Warren, who had been an active pamphleteer in Boston during the Revolution. Warren came from a prominent family: her brother James Otis had led opposition to the Stamp Act before descending into mental illness, while her husband, James Warren, had been president of the Massachusetts Provincial Congress during the Revolution. In 1805, at the age of seventy-seven, she penned a *History of the Rise, Progress and Termination of the American Revolution.* Though she was a Bostonian and had been close to John and Abigail Adams, she was an avowed supporter of Thomas Jefferson. In her history she extolled the Declaration, "drawn by the elegant and energetic pen of Jefferson . . . the language, the principles, and the spirit of which, were equally honorable to themselves and their country." She declared that it "ought to be frequently read by the rising youth of the American states, as a palladium of which they should never lose sight, so long as they wish to continue a free and independent people."[36]

Such impassioned praise was rare. The Declaration, when remembered, had become more divisive than it was unifying. Older citizens may have seen one of the many broadsides printed during the Revolution, but two decades on, the "Declaration" risked becoming a vestige of the past. It would take another war for a new generation to look to the founding document for unity and inspiration.

Chapter 6

The Declaration Escapes the Flames

The clattering of enemy troops echoed through the streets of Washington. Earlier that day, British forces had routed a ragtag group of American soldiers at Bladensburg, Maryland, just outside the city. Now, as the Americans retreated in disarray, the Redcoats were approaching the Capitol Building. President James Madison had fled the city to join Congress and organize resistance. Inside the sandstone-colored President's House, his wife, Dolley, was frantically packing up the most valuable items she could find. It was August 14, 1814, and the capital of the young nation was about to be torched.

Dolley Madison was forty-six years old, a vivacious companion to her short, dour, but brilliant husband, who had done so much to shape and secure the passage of the Constitution. As the British drew nearer, she raced through the mansion, briefly pausing to instruct her steward to save the magnificent full-length Gilbert Stuart portrait of George Washington by any means possible. Then, as the British prepared to set Washington aflame, "snatching up the precious parchment on which was written the Declaration of Independence and the autographs of the signers, which she had resolved to save also, she hastened to the carriage with her sister and her husband, and two servants, and was borne away to a place of safety beyond the Potomac."[1]

Or so wrote Benson J. Lossing, a popular historian of the mid-nineteenth century, in his account of the War of 1812. The book, published in 1869, thrillingly told how Dolley Madison had saved the Declaration from certain destruction. Only it wasn't true. The Declaration was indeed saved from the British in 1814, but not by the heroics of the First Lady as flames licked the walls of the President's House. Another myth had wrapped itself about the Declaration, adding to its mystique.

Long before Lossing's imaginative tale of derring-do, the very real rescue of the Declaration from a burning Washington had given it an aura of sanctity. Though few had ever seen the engrossed parchment, the grave threat it had faced inspired a new era of esteem, bonding Americans more firmly to their founding document.

In 1789, the eruption of the French Revolution had cheered liberals like Thomas Jefferson while horrifying Alexander Hamilton and his fellow conservatives. The 1778 Franco-American alliance persisted, however, and initially the United States was Revolutionary France's only diplomatic partner. As the radical Jacobins, led by Robespierre, took power, the French Revolution threatened to spread beyond France's borders, possibly even to America. George Washington's fears were confirmed in 1793 when the French representative in America, Edmond-Charles Genêt, maneuvered to bring the United States directly into France's confrontation with Great Britain and Spain.[2] Struggling with his instinctive sympathy for Republican France, Jefferson's ardor waned as the Terror gripped Paris in 1793. The execution of Louis XVI and his Austrian queen, Marie Antoinette, inflamed European monarchies and war broke out with England and Spain in 1793. By the time Napoleon seized power in 1799, most of Europe and Russia were at war with Revolutionary France. This proved to be a generational conflict that was to last until 1815. As in the French and Indian War, the Americans found themselves dragged into a global conflict they had hoped to stay out of.

It was the question of freedom on the high seas that most threatened the Americans. The same ocean that shielded them from the land battles convulsing Europe made their vessels prey to British and French ships. The question of neutrality bedeviled Americans, who wanted to carry non-contraband trade to all ports, claiming that "free ships make free goods." When Britain attempted to block American trade with France in the early 1790s, war cries arose in the United States. Washington sent John Jay to London to negotiate a treaty, which was ratified in 1794. The French began hunting American merchant ships, particularly in the Caribbean. In response, John Adams repudiated the alliance with France and built up the U.S. Navy, which notched a few victories in the so-called Quasi-War, from 1798 to 1800. Adams eventually negotiated a treaty with Napoleon's representatives, at great personal political cost, to keep America out of war.[3]

Desperately in need of sailors for their never-ending sea battles with the French, the British Royal Navy began to stop and board American ships, ostensibly to find sailors it claimed had deserted British naval vessels. This "impressment" swept up both guilty Englishmen and innocent Americans. Through his two terms as President, Thomas Jefferson was powerless to stop Americans from being kidnapped and forced into British service, infuriating both the American government and its citizens.

Even before impressment bedeviled Anglo-American relations, various issues had festered since the Peace of Paris in 1783. The British had violated the terms of the treaty by retaining their forts in the Northwest Territory, beyond the Ohio River. Americans blamed British intrigue with Indian tribes around the Great Lakes for the massive uprising of the Shawnee chief Tecumseh in 1811. Relations were further soured by disputes over the boundaries between British North America (Canada) and the United States and over trade.[4]

By 1812, tensions with Britain had reached a boiling point. A new generation had come to Congress, including "war hawks" like Henry Clay of Kentucky and John C. Calhoun of South Carolina, who hoped to take Canada from the British. Influenced by these voices, a deeply divided U.S. Congress declared war on Britain in June 1812. Five days later, Britain revoked its orders allowing American vessels to be boarded, but news did not cross the Atlantic in time to prevent hostilities. What Americans were to call the Second War of Independence had begun.

It was a war the young nation was completely unprepared to fight. Political paralysis gripped Washington, and Congress all but abandoned its responsibilities, including funding the Army and Navy. The country was essentially bankrupt. Madison had succeeded Jefferson in 1809 and his Cabinet was deeply divided. His incompetent Secretary of War, John Armstrong, was hated both by the Army and by his fellow Cabinet colleagues.[5] For two years, hostilities raged along the border between Canada and the United States, mostly to the detriment of the Americans. Detroit was captured and Buffalo, New York, burned. The single victory of note was won on Lake Erie, in September 1813, by Captain Oliver Hazard Perry, who rallied his outnumbered naval forces to defeat the British, famously reporting to his superiors, "We have met the enemy, and they are ours."

Then, in July 1814, with Napoleon seemingly finally defeated in Europe, the British decided on what they hoped would be a knockout blow to the Americans: capture the upstart country's capital city and put its government to flight. A small detachment of the Royal Navy operating in Chesapeake Bay was supplemented by a much larger force and on August 16, two dozen ships carrying four thousand men sailed into the Bay and headed north, to the Patuxent River. While a diversionary flotilla sailed up the Potomac to threaten the capital by water, the main force made their way to Benedict, Maryland, forty miles from the city. On August 20, a Saturday, Major General Robert Ross began the march on Washington.

While the obstreperous Armstrong did nothing to gather intelligence, James Monroe, the Secretary of State, offered to ride out to see where the British were likely to go. There were three possibilities: Baltimore, Annapolis, or Washington. The fifty-six-year-old Revolutionary War hero rode off in such haste he left his spyglass at home. For two days, he shadowed the British, watching as they moved north. When they swung west the question was settled. Washington was the target.

Early on the morning of August 22, as Monroe saw the British moving westward, he shot off a note to the State Department. "The enemy are in full march for Washington," he wrote. "Have the materials prepared to destroy the bridges." Almost as an afterthought, he added: "You had better remove the records."[6]

Monroe's note reached a capital in panic, its eight thousand inhabitants unprepared to defend the city. Yet President Madison and his government were not taken completely by surprise. For several months, they had been receiving bits of news and intelligence from England that a larger invasion was coming. In early July, Madison had established the Tenth Military District, to protect the District of Columbia, northern Virginia, and Maryland, and asked for three thousand soldiers to be positioned between the capital and the Chesapeake.

Yet such defense existed only on paper. The Secretary of War refused to take seriously reports that the British were coming for the city. Armstrong's commanding general, William Winder, was an inexperienced political appointee, and John Van Ness, who was in charge of the District

Militia, found himself competing with the Army for supplies. Both men and their troops were scouring the city and surrounding area for wagons, carts, and horses, moving supplies across the river or to scattered military units. Washingtonians who could flee did so while a ragtag force of Americans began to gather at Bladensburg, ten miles outside the capital, in a desperate effort to stop the British advance.

All around Washington, government clerks were frantically attempting to save records: in the Senate and House of Representatives, the Treasury, the Patent Office, and the War and Navy Departments. Clerks in the Capitol Building bitterly complained about having to leave behind the entire Library of Congress. But John Graham, a seasoned diplomat who was now the State Department's chief clerk, had under his care the country's most priceless documents.[7]

The Declaration, unbeknownst to most, had already escaped destruction once in its short time in Washington. Back in January 1801, a few months after the State Department had moved out of the Treasury Building, a fire had destroyed part of the structure, consuming many historical documents. Now, with British forces less than twelve miles away, a new threat loomed.[8]

According to his own account, written three decades later, responsibility for saving the Declaration fell on Stephen Pleasonton, Graham's assistant. Somehow, amid the commotion and panic, he "proceeded to purchase coarse linen, and cause it to be made into bags of convenient size," into which he unceremoniously shoved the Declaration, Constitution, Journals of the Continental Congress, Washington's wartime correspondence, and "all the laws, treaties, and correspondence of the Department of State since the adoption of the Constitution."[9] If ever there was a time when the Declaration was crushed, this was probably it.

Pleasonton somehow found carts at a time when almost all had been commandeered by the Army. Carrying the bags in which he had bundled America's founding documents, Pleasonton ran into none other than Secretary of War Armstrong, who told him that he was "under unnecessary alarm." Even then, Armstrong thought the British move toward Washington was just a diversion. Pleasonton, "under a different belief," as he put it, ignored the useless Secretary and loaded his bags into the carts.

It was August 23, and Pleasonton rode up Pennsylvania Avenue toward Georgetown in the stifling heat and humidity as fast as horse and cart would allow. He could have crossed the Long Bridge into Virginia, but he had in mind the gristmill of Edgar Patterson as a hiding place, and that was a few miles farther up the Potomac. He crossed the old bridge over Rock Creek, built in 1788, and headed into Georgetown.

Pleasonton drove the short mile through Georgetown, many of whose five thousand residents had fled. He continued along Bridge Street and then headed onto the difficult road—a path, really—leading to the Chain Bridge just below Little Falls. This iron bridge was fairly new, having been built around 1810 to replace two that had been washed away by the river's occasional but violent freshets. Pleasonton crossed the river and rode up into the rugged territory where the rocky Piedmont Plateau succeeds the gentle Coastal Plain. On the Virginia side of the Potomac, two miles above Georgetown, lay Patterson's gristmill, where an exhausted Pleasonton stopped sometime on the afternoon of the twenty-third.

As he rested, Pleasonton began to worry that the Declaration and other documents were not yet safe. Just across the Potomac was the largest foundry in the country for making cannon. It almost certainly would be a target of the British. Pleasonton thought an "evil disposed person" who had seen a cart full of bags being carried across the river might inform the Redcoats. He decided that he had to move again, and soon.

Events reached a climax on August 24. At Bladensburg, in the brutal summer heat, over six thousand untested American troops cobbled together from various units and militias were about to face forty-five hundred well-trained British forces who had fought and defeated Napoleon. President Madison, armed with a brace of pistols, Secretary of State Monroe, and other senior officials had ridden out to oversee the defensive effort. The Americans outnumbered the British and occupied the high ground looking down on the Eastern Branch of the Potomac River, also known as the Anacostia, which the British would have to cross.

Around 12:30 p.m., the long-awaited battle began. The British, led by Major General Ross, charged across the bridge and immediately began driving the Americans back. While some units, particularly the Marines under the command of Commodore Joshua Barney, performed heroically, most collapsed and fled in the face of enemy fire. The battle was all but over within an hour. By midafternoon, the Americans were in full rout, fleeing pell-mell back to Washington, pursued by the British. The capital was now defenseless before the advancing enemy.

It was exactly the scenario Stephen Pleasonton had feared. Without knowing the scale of the defeat about to unfold, that same morning he rode deeper into Virginia, likely up the Georgetown Pike. At some point, he found wagons at a farmhouse and switched from the smaller carts, transferring the Declaration and other documents. As the battle erupted in Bladensburg, Pleasonton was pressing deeper into Virginia, moving north and west toward the town of Leesburg.

Meanwhile, the government of the United States was nearing collapse. Disorganized units of militiamen and soldiers were streaming into Washington and quickly scurrying on in an effort to escape the British. In the President's House, First Lady Dolley Madison was warned of the approaching enemy and began securing the mansion's valuables. Throughout, she was adamant that the full-length Gilbert Stuart portrait of George Washington be saved or destroyed: under no circumstances could it fall into British hands. In the end, it was cut from its heavy frame and carried out of town, where it lodged with a farmer for several days. The First Lady fled to safety, missing her husband, who returned briefly after leaving Bladensburg.

During the whole of the Revolutionary War, the Declaration had never left the Continental Congress. Now, with the capital about to fall, parchment and politicians parted ways. Congress all but dispersed and President Madison, accompanied by a few officials, rode to the Georgetown Ferry, taking the pull-chain boats to Mason's Island (now Theodore Roosevelt Island) and then to the Virginia Shore. His plan was to meet up with General Winder at the small town of Brookeville, in Maryland. Meanwhile, rattling along Leesburg and Alexandria Turnpike in a wagon driven by Stephen Pleasonton, the Declaration was being carried to safety.

It took most of the day to cover the three-dozen miles, but eventually Pleasonton reached the outskirts of Leesburg, in Loudon County. Secretary of State Monroe lived at Oak Hill, a few miles away from the city, and likely knew about the Rokeby Mansion, located two miles south of Leesburg and currently vacant, which had a brick vault in the cellar that may have been used to store county documents. Whether Monroe suggested Rokeby or not, Pleasonton headed to the house and found the Reverend Mr. Littlejohn, the county collector of revenue. Into the roughly ten-by-six brick vault "the papers were safely placed, the doors locked, and the keys given" to the good reverend. The Declaration, Constitution, and other priceless documents lay unprotected and, hopefully, unnoticed. When the "fatigued" Pleasonton finally went to bed early in the evening

The Rokeby Mansion's cellar vault, where Stephen Pleasonton hid the Declaration during the British invasion.

of the twenty-fourth, he missed the denouement of the crisis in which he was so intimately involved.

When the British entered Washington that evening, they encountered only token resistance. Both sides then set into motion the destruction of the city. As evening fell, the Americans set fuses throughout the Navy Yard to blow up ships, storehouses, docks, and maritime equipment, to prevent them from falling into British hands. Meanwhile, the British descended on government buildings with a vengeance. They reached the Capitol around 9 p.m., its two richly decorated wings soaring sixty-seven feet high. Carrying torches, the Redcoats spread throughout the building. Soon, the citadel of American democracy was engulfed in flames, a bonfire that shot up into the night sky, fueled by the tons of carved wood, miles of drapery and upholstery, and the thousands of records, state papers, and books in the Library of Congress. Rumors that the Redcoats had kindled the Capitol fire using the Library's collection were false, but its loss was a particular blow, as collecting its three thousand volumes had been a particular focus of Thomas Jefferson during his presidency.[10]

A contemporary painting by George Munger of the burned-out White House in 1814.

Led by Ross, the British marched up Pennsylvania Avenue and quickly reached the dark and abandoned President's House. In recent years Dolley Madison had tastefully decorated the mansion, adding to Thomas Jefferson's furnishings. Now, all went up in flames. The building was entirely gutted and the Madisons' personal belongings incinerated along with state gifts and treasures. But the mansion's thick sandstone walls, insisted upon by George Washington, withstood the flames, leaving a shell standing once the fire had burned out.[11]

The Redcoats torched the buildings around the President's House. The State Department burned to the ground, along with the Treasury, War, and Navy Departments and their archives. It is uncertain if Ross and his men knew that the Declaration and Constitution had been kept in the State Department, but had the documents stayed there, they would have been reduced to ashes.

Throughout that awful night the city burned. Attorney General Richard Rush, the son of Signer Benjamin Rush, remembered four decades later the "columns of flame and smoke ascending from the Capitol, the President's House, and other public edifices, as the whole were on fire, some burning slowly, others with bursts of flame and sparks mounting high up in the dark horizon."[12] The conflagration was visible for dozens of miles, all the way to Chesapeake Bay in the east and Leesburg in the west. Stephen Pleasonton, exhausted and sleeping, did not join the residents of Leesburg who gathered to view the fire-reddened sky.

For two days President Madison wandered about Northern Virginia, his reunion with Dolley delayed by a massive thunderstorm that providentially ripped through the region, helping to quench the flames. He finally made his way past the Great Falls to Conn's Ferry, the site of today's Riverbend Park, where on August 26, he crossed the Potomac and journeyed on to Brookeville.

That same day, Stephen Pleasonton returned to Washington. As it turned out, the British had occupied the city for barely a day and had left residential buildings mostly untouched. Ross led his men toward Baltimore, a more strategically important city than Washington. In mid-September, he would lose his life to an American sniper while on the march to Baltimore. A few days later, a lawyer from Frederick, Maryland, named Francis Scott Key would watch through the night as British bombs burst over Fort McHenry, failing to dislodge the Americans or to knock down their flag, inspiring a poem that soon became a new anthem for the bruised nation. After losing the Battle of Baltimore, the British withdrew from the capital region, though the war would drag on the rest of the year, until the young nation had again defeated the King of England and his troops. A peace treaty was finally signed in Belgium on the day before Christmas.

The British left a devastated capital in their wake. For weeks, Madison tried to bring back some semblance of governing normalcy while Congress trickled back into town to survey the damage. Meanwhile, the Declaration lay hidden in the cellar at Rokeby. Today, when the scroll is protected by sophisticated security systems and handled with utmost care in atmosphere-controlled rooms by trained professionals in advanced protective gear, it is difficult to imagine the parchment lying unguarded for weeks in a coarse linen sack on the floor of a humid cellar, keeping company with rats and bugs.

Until the Americans could be sure the British had left the area for good, it was thought too dangerous to bring the state papers back to Washington. Many years later, Pleasonton remembered that Secretary of State Monroe had sent him on occasion back to the hiding place "for particular papers." Finally, sometime in September, the Declaration joined the State Department in its temporary offices in a house on G Street, where it would remain for the next eighteen months while the government buildings were rebuilt.

Defeating the world's greatest power for the second time in a generation inaugurated a new era at home and abroad. Foreign respect for the young country soared, as did fears of its potential power. Since Independence, America had been growing at a pace unknown in world history. With high birth rates and seemingly endless immigration, Americans were filling up old cities and building new towns. Thanks to the Northwest Ordinance of 1787, thousands of settlers had poured across the Appalachian Mountains, pushing back Indians and leveling forests. The prospect of new states being carved out of the territory ensured that American democracy would follow the frontier.[13] Once Thomas Jefferson purchased the Louisiana Territory from France in 1803, adding 828,000 square miles, the United States burst across the Mississippi and spread across roughly two-thirds of the North American continent south of Canada, a democratic empire in all but name.[14]

In the first decades of the nineteenth century, more land was cleared, settlements thrown up, and new territories claimed. Frontiersmen pushed farther into the wilderness, crossing the Great Plains and taking over Indian hunting lands, displacing them farther westward. They were followed by farmers, often poor families like the Lincolns, who moved west from Massachusetts into Kentucky, where a boy named Abraham was born in 1809, just a month before James Madison became President.

The victory over Britain combined with the growth and expansion to fuel a surge of patriotism. The Declaration was swept up in the celebratory mood. Throughout the country, July Fourth celebrations began to highlight the Declaration as they boasted about America's uniqueness. On July 4, 1815, a dinner was held at McLeod's Hotel on Capitol Hill, in Washington, "to celebrate the glorious anniversary of American Independence." Such fetes had of course taken place before the War of 1812, but the toasts during this first postvictory dinner revealed the new confidence of a proud and more united nation. The Declaration was described as "sacred to the western world," expressing a growing confidence that the American example would soon cascade throughout the hemisphere and even Europe. The point was emphasized in a toast championing Independence as "the natural right of every community that can govern and protect itself."[15] On the same day, *The Albany Register* reprinted "the GLORIOUS DECLARATION, which we hope may be forever engraved on the heart of every legitimate descendant of the brave, magnanimous, and immortal whigs and heroes of '76!" These were sentiments reflecting a new and more profound appreciation of the American experiment, whose influence was becoming global.[16]

Later in 1815, the *Weekly Aurora*, a leading Republican newspaper in Philadelphia, wrote that the American creed "is professedly founded on the Declaration of Independence, . . . which declares, that *all men are equal*, that there should be neither exclusive orders nor privileged sects; that the people have in fact the sovereignty." If the Jeffersonian paper slightly misquoted the document for political purposes, it nonetheless revealed a belief that the ideas championed by the Declaration were becoming universal. Over the previous two decades, the American experiment in democratic governance had become meaningful beyond the country's shores. A recognition of this fact became a common theme in the postwar years. As an 1818 item in the *New-York Daily Advertiser* put it, "the lessons of freedom and just government, which were taught the nations of the earth by the Declaration and War of Independence in the United States, will never be lost or forgotten."[17]

This invocation of the Declaration's global influence was not just patriotic braggadocio. Jefferson's words had inspired others seeking to topple governments and change the world. Yet the Terror in France had revealed how radical democracy could quickly spiral into unrestrained despotism, with its guillotine paving the way for Napoleon. Why had the same not occurred in America?

Several factors contributed to this, foremost among them the fact that the Declaration reflected the more moderate philosophical tradition of the British Enlightenment, which remained rooted in individual liberty, and the influence of the Bible, which the radical secularists in France had sought to dethrone.[18] Mob actions that threatened individual life and property had occurred in the American past, from the Salem witch trials to the burning of Thomas Hutchinson's house in 1765. But a sustained assault on the rights of individuals by an oppressive government had been hammered into the American consciousness as the cause of the Revolution and a thing to be avoided at all costs. In addition, the lesser extremes of wealth and seemingly inexhaustible open land offered endless opportunity, dispersing the population and turning its attention to hard work and self-fulfillment. For all their rambunctiousness, Americans seemed to be immune from the excesses in France. This stability and moderation accounted for much of the Declaration's global influence.

By the time of the *New-York Daily Advertiser*'s 1818 article, eight foreign nations had promulgated their own declarations of independence, with dozens more to follow. The first, in January 1790, was Flanders, issuing a manifesto of independence from Austria and Emperor Joseph II, who had failed in his constitutional duties, or so it was argued, and whose rule was thus illegitimate. Though the small state was reabsorbed by Austria later that year, the Flemish manifesto foreshadowed appeals to the decent opinions of mankind by revolutionary bands seeking freedom from imperial control. In Europe, succeeding declarations of rights and national constitutions resembled the American Declaration mostly in their assertions of sovereignty in a world of nation-states.[19] The American example of throwing off the chains of oppression remained vivid even if most more closely resembled the radical French declaration of 1789 (and its successors of 1791 and 1795).[20]

Starting in 1804 a wave of revolutions swept through the Caribbean and Latin America, followed by declarations of independence. Haiti, in its bloody uprising against the French, went first, but soon Spain's possessions were shaken, from Colombia (1810) and Venezuela (1811) to Mexico's abortive first attempt at independence in 1813, followed by Argentina (1816), and Chile (1818). In the great year of 1821, Peru, Guatemala, El Salvador, Mexico for a second time, Nicaragua, Costa Rica, and Panama all announced to the world that they were throwing off their colonial chains.

In December 1821, four months after the Treaty of Córdoba formalized Mexican independence from Spain, José María Luis Mora Lamadrid, publisher of the influential liberal newspaper *Semanario Político, Económico y Literario,* printed a translation of the Declaration of Independence. A Mexican Empire had been declared upon separation from Spain, but republicans were battling monarchists in the Mexican Congress to determine the future of the new nation. The twenty-seven-year-old Mora wanted to bolster the liberal cause by printing key documents "relating to the first revolution on the continent," as he put it. Following the Declaration, Mora printed translations of several U.S. State constitutions, all of which were referred to in debates in the Mexican Congress.[21]

In the wake of these revolutions, some Latin American countries, like Mexico, succeeded in forming republics, while others floundered. The relations of these new nations with the United States would be sometimes confrontational, even violent, but the fact that America had survived two wars of Independence validated its example of revolution. Appealing to a larger cause was fast becoming a global norm.[22]

Admired abroad, the Declaration faced new challenges at home. In the first weeks after the British withdrew from the Chesapeake Bay, it seemed possible that the scroll would once again find itself on the road. Many wanted to give up on Washington altogether. The fire-gutted walls of the President's House and Capitol Building were a smoldering symbol of the brief but searing national humiliation. President Madison and Congress returned to Washington within days, but normalcy was a long time in coming.

The U.S. Capitol was by necessity the focus of reconstruction. Both Congress and the Nation were encouraged when Charles Bulfinch, a Bostonian and the first professional architect in America, took over the Capitol project in 1818, ensuring not just a reconstruction, but an enhancement of the original plans. Bulfinch's domed central structure reopened in 1819, while still under construction, and was finished by the semicentennial of the Declaration, in 1826.[23]

Next to the Capitol, the most important structure in need of urgent attention was the President's House and the square around it. James Hoban, the original architect, returned to oversee the reconstruction. Over three years, the house was restored, reclaiming its position anchoring the west end of Pennsylvania Avenue. This time around, the mansion's sandstone walls were whitewashed, eventually giving a new name to the house.

Hoban was also tasked with rebuilding the other government buildings torched by the British. The most important of these was the one to house the State and War Departments. On April 1, 1816, a new building opened atop the ashes of its former home. It had no formal name but was ungainly referred to as the "Rebuilt Public Building West of the White House." Secretary of State James Monroe and his small staff brought the state papers from the cramped house on G Street and moved into their offices on the second floor. The Declaration was likely stored once again in the attic.[24]

By the time Hoban completed the White House, Monroe had been elected president. John Quincy Adams, son of the second president, succeeded him at the State Department, inheriting the priceless parchment. Did Secretary Adams ever feel pulled to go up into the attic and unroll the Declaration to gaze on its inspiring phrases? By now few Americans had seen the engrossed parchment that the nation more fervently celebrated. Within a few years, the Declaration—or at least its image—would become visible to ordinary citizens, beginning a fundamental transformation of the relationship between the American people and their founding document.

Chapter 7
Seeing the Declaration at Last

Declaration of Independence—We have no authentic copy of this most important state paper, the very basis that supports the proud column of American Liberty—*Why have we not?*"[1] Thus opened an advertisement in the March 26, 1816, edition of *Democratic Press*, a Philadelphia journal. The ad was written by John Binns, the journal's publisher, an avowed Jeffersonian Democratic-Republican who had started the journal back in 1807 "to advocate and defend the sacred principles of the American Revolution as they are laid down in the Declaration of American Independence."[2]

Binns proposed to take advantage of the upsurge in patriotism following the War of 1812 and create the first reproduction of the Declaration. Thanks to Binns and other creative entrepreneurs who followed him, the document suddenly became tangible after decades of invisibility. A new life had begun, making the Declaration both an object and a commodity, one Americans could see, buy, and connect with on a personal level.

In the decades leading up to John Binns's ad in the *Democratic Press*, Americans had seen dozens of reprints of the Declaration. As early as 1780, its text was included in a collection of original documents authorized by

Congress and sold in Philadelphia.[3] While annual printings were rare, the recent burst of national pride had led the *Essex Register* of Salem, Massachusetts, to note in its July 19, 1815, issue that "in our great cities the Declaration of Independence has been reprinted," urging that "copies of it should be multiplied, and circulated on all the annual celebrations of our independence."[4]

But all these were printed in newspapers or on single sheets. What John Binns proposed was radically new. As is so often the case, however, the original concept was not his. Back in 1810, a government clerk named William P. Gardner came up with the idea of creating and selling a decorative copy of the Declaration. Gardner brought some drawings to an engraver around 1813, and when he failed to follow up, the engraver took the plans to Binns, who immediately understood the commercial potential. A facsimile would reproduce—or claim to reproduce—the engrossed Declaration itself, something almost no Americans had seen and that many did not even know existed.[5]

Binns added to the parchment's mystique when he wrote in a follow-on advertisement in June 1816, that "The ORIGINAL Declaration of Independence, as deposited in the Secretary of State's office, was happily preserved when so many valuable papers were destroyed by the enemy."[6] With the Declaration's dramatic rescue from destruction at the hands of the British now common knowledge, Binns understood that the parchment's miraculous survival gave it a new importance, one he hoped to capitalize on.

Binns also knew there was a growing nostalgia for the Revolutionary generation, which was rapidly passing from the scene. He proposed to give Americans a chance to see how Jefferson's stirring phrases had first appeared, and to include all the signatures of the immortal leaders who had created the new country. In his June 1816 announcement he grandly promised that his reproduction would serve a noble purpose: "Such an embellished edition as will render an ornament to an apartment, will have a tendency to spread the knowledge of its contents, among those who would otherwise have turned their thoughts but lightly toward the subject . . . and familiarize those principles which form, the very bond and cement of political society."[7] Binns had a vision that the Declaration would become a daily visual reminder of America's origins, one that would bind the nation together across political differences.

But John Binns was too clever by half. He was convinced that what would appeal to buyers was the early-nineteenth-century equivalent of "bells and whistles." His reproduction would have elegant calligraphy and would be adorned with portraits of Washington, Hancock, and Jefferson. Other insets would include the arms of the United States, seals of the States, wreaths, depictions of key agricultural products, and the like. The signatures would be expertly redrawn, as he had secured access to the engrossed Declaration from Secretary of State Richard Rush. His plan

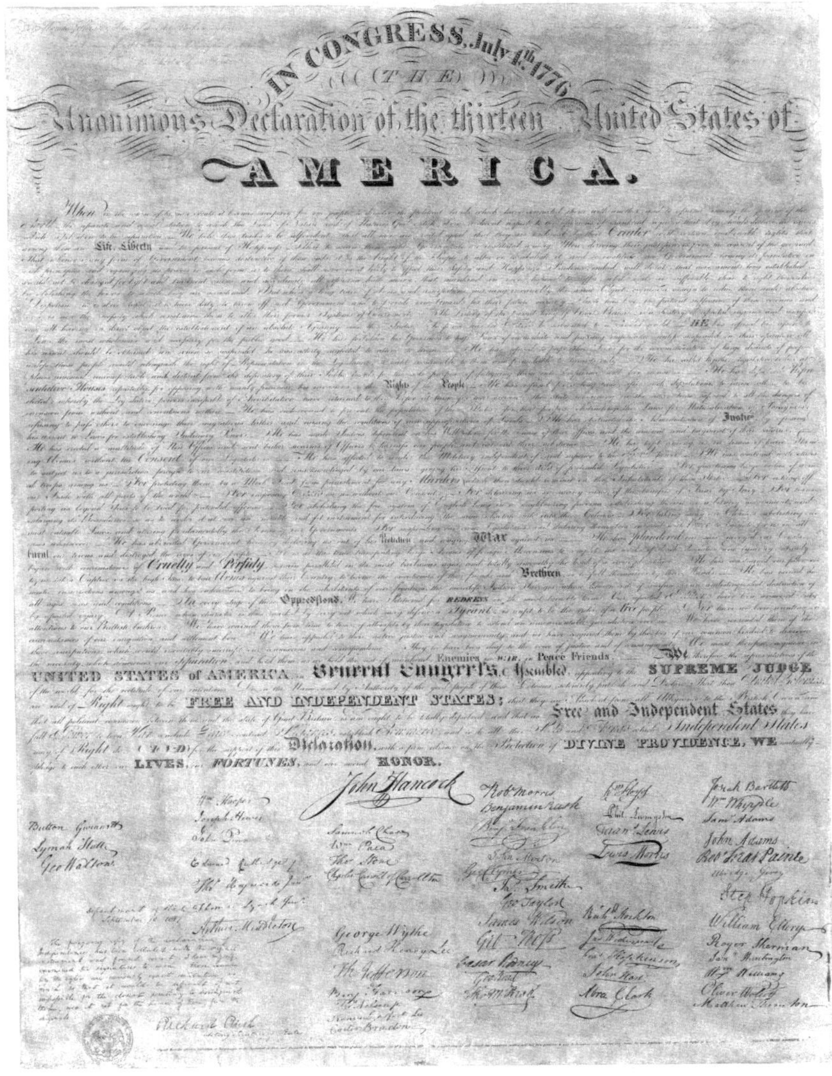

IN CONGRESS, July 4th 1776.
(THE)
Unanimous Declaration of the thirteen United States of
AMERICA.

The signatures on Benjamin Owen Tyler's 1818 engraving were considered so exact that "only the hand of time" could distinguish them from the originals.

required at least four artists to design, etch, and engrave this grand production. The whole would be even larger than the engrossed parchment, measuring 36 by 25½ inches. It took him three years to get this demanding and complicated product to market. By that time, he had been beaten to the punch by Benjamin Owen Tyler.

Tyler was a professional calligrapher based in Washington, D.C. He, too, had asked permission of Secretary Rush to copy the Declaration. Less grandiose than Binns, Tyler advertised in the *Vermont Republican*, in April 1818, that his aim was "to present to the American people a correct and elegant copy of that instrument, which secured to their fathers a deathless name, and to them extends liberty and happiness."[8] Tyler avoided overcomplicating his version, eschewing inset portraits or seals, which allowed him to produce his engraving far quicker than Binns. Yet he did not sacrifice accuracy for speed. The calligrapher copied the signatures so precisely that Secretary of State Rush certified on the prints that they were a "curiously exact imitation; so much so that it would be difficult if not impossible for the closest scrutiny to distinguish them, were it not for the hand of time, from the originals." Like Binns's planned reproduction, this was larger than the Declaration itself, at 32½ by 27 inches, prominently adorning any wall it was hung upon. Tyler was selling his reproduction of the Declaration by the spring of 1818, nearly a full year before John Binns's version came off the press in April 1819.[9] When Binns finally marketed his copy, he put "Declaration of Independence" boldly across the top, popularizing the unofficial title of the document.

Both men soon discovered that merchandising the Declaration was more difficult than they expected. They printed most of their copies on paper, but they also sold fabric and silk versions, a common practice at the time. They advertised widely in newspapers around the country and collected subscriptions. Sales apparently were brisk, and Tyler's leather-bound subscription book contained over a thousand signatures, including those of Thomas Jefferson and James Madison.[10] Self-publishing was a risky business, however, and both lost money from subscribers who failed to pay, from bootleg copies, and from unscrupulous agents. Binns also ran afoul of John Adams, who returned a complimentary copy in a huff, offended that his portrait was left off the reproduction. Despite the difficulties, Tyler never lost faith in his claim that "every American who duly appreciates the value of *liberty* and *independence* can point his children to it and say, 'there hangs the pledge which secured your liberty' . . ." It was

Declaration of Independence

IN CONGRESS JULY 4th 1776

The unanimous Declaration of the thirteen United States of America

John Binns was the first to embark on a decorative engraving of the Declaration, but his elaborate plans delayed its appearance until 1819.

a marriage of civic education with commercial ambition, celebrating the Declaration and at the same time turning it into a commodity.[11]

Binns and Tyler were soon joined by one William Woodruff, who in 1819 brought out an engraving remarkably similar in design to, but far cruder than, the one Binns produced—in other words, a pirated copy. Commercially available for the first time, the Declaration fell afoul of cutthroat practices. By now, Binns had had enough. He sued Woodruff for copyright infringement and for good measure accused Tyler of stealing his idea. This led to a nasty public exchange in the press into which poor William Gardner, the clerk who had originally come up with the idea, was drawn. That the Declaration had no sooner become a public commodity than it was embroiled in a legal dispute revealed both the rough-and-tumble ethos of the young Republic and the power the document was coming to hold in the public imagination.

On October 8, 1818, John Trumbull waited in the Academy of Fine Arts, in New York City, for his masterpiece to be unveiled in public. Recently commissioned by Congress, Trumbull had been working on a massive portrait scene of America's birth. When the crowds were let in, Trumbull's work instantly cemented the cultural status of the Declaration of Independence and forever changed American historical painting.

Trumbull was America's most famous artist. He had studied painting in England after the Revolutionary War with the brilliant American expatriate artist Benjamin West. The son of Connecticut's governor, Trumbull's social connections had made it possible for him to meet leading Americans abroad, like John Adams, minister to Great Britain in the mid-1780s. It was at Adams's residence that Trumbull first encountered Thomas Jefferson, who was then minister to France and visiting on diplomatic business. The two immediately formed a bond, sharing a belief that public art could strengthen patriotic feeling and instill the republican virtue so important to Jefferson.[12]

Trumbull had been planning an extended series of paintings celebrating the Revolutionary War, a genre for which he had gained renown. During a stay at Jefferson's residence in Paris in 1786, the two discussed commemorating the Declaration, which had begun to disappear from public consciousness. Jefferson encouraged the young Trumbull to pursue the idea and even made a sketch of the Assembly Room in Independence

Hall. They continued to discuss the idea when Trumbull returned a year later. Perhaps at Jefferson's urging, the young artist chose not to commemorate the act of adoption, but rather the moment when the Committee of Five presented the draft to the Continental Congress, on June 28, 1776. This, of course, would put Jefferson at the center of the composition.

For the next three decades, Trumbull worked on two versions of the painting, starting with a small one of 20 by 30 inches, which he eventually gifted to the Fine Arts museum at Yale in 1832. In 1817, Congress and President James Madison commissioned Trumbull to produce four paintings of the most important events of the Revolution, all to be placed in the rebuilt Capitol. Of these, the one entitled *The Declaration of Independence* was to be the centerpiece.[13]

Trumbull now started working on a 12-by-18-foot version of his painting. By October 1818, not long after Benjamin Owen Tyler's reproduction of the Declaration went on sale, Trumbull's massive canvas was displayed at the American Academy of Fine Arts. The timing was exquisite, for his painting entered a rapidly expanding art world, one that was becoming ever more commercialized. As Trumbull, now sixty-one, expected, *The Declaration of Independence* was lauded by the press. The painting is "magnificent," raved the *New-York Daily Advertiser*. "We doubt," continued the paper, "whether there is a work of the kind in the world . . . so well calculated to excite or to gratify public curiosity . . . in the most important and the most sublime political event in the history of our country—perhaps in the history of the world."[14]

With such glowing reviews in local papers, Trumbull sent the canvas to tour the East Coast. It was displayed in Boston, Philadelphia, and Baltimore, viewed by thousands and earning Trumbull over $4,000. The painting finally arrived in the new Capitol Building in early 1819, just as John Binns was preparing to put his facsimile engraving of the Declaration on the market. For the next seven years, Trumbull's canvas was hung or stored in various rooms in the Capitol until it was finally installed in December 1826 in the Rotunda, where it has hung ever since.

All told, Trumbull included forty-eight Signers in his tableau, painting thirty-six of them from life, including Thomas Jefferson and John Adams, whose likenesses he had first captured on sketches while they were together in Europe. At the center he grouped the Committee of Five with Jefferson, Adams, and Franklin the most prominent. Once the canvas was installed in the Rotunda, Americans by the thousands viewed a majestic scene of Jefferson handing over his draft to a regally enthroned John Hancock, attentively watched by the members of the Congress (see insert).

Only a handful of viewers knew that this magnificent portrayal was almost entirely an imaginative re-creation. It was also riddled with architectural errors, thanks to Jefferson's faulty memory. In reality, only Jefferson had handed his draft to Hancock, not the entire committee. And when he did so, Congress was still in its June recess and certainly not assembled in ranks to witness the moment. Compounding the confusion, most viewers of the painting naturally but erroneously believed it portrayed July 4, when the Declaration was adopted.

The work was criticized by some knowledgeable contemporaries. As luck would have it, when the painting giving Jefferson the starring role at the Nation's founding was unveiled, the Secretary of State was John Quincy Adams, the son of Jefferson's now archrival. Adams, who had inherited his father's famous prickliness and acerbic nature, described Trumbull's masterpiece as "immeasurably below the dignity of the subject." Adams was perhaps exercised by the relatively unflattering portrait of his squat father next to the leonine and commanding Jefferson.[15] An equally acerbic critic wrote in a New York newspaper that Trumbull's historical inaccuracies, due in no small part to Jefferson's faulty memories, had resulted in a "mongrel" picture.[16]

The public, however, embraced Trumbull's tableau as a faithful representation of the moment America gained its freedom. In 1823, taking advantage of the new public market for art, Trumbull decided to partner with Asher B. Durand, a young and eager engraver, to produce engraved reproductions of the painting. These would be sold through a subscription campaign for twenty dollars, a substantial sum for the time. There was a larger if less lucrative market to aim for, however, and within a few years, versions of the painting were available for as little as fifty cents.[17]

Trumbull's *Declaration of Independence* quickly became, and remains, the most famous portrayal of America's birth. It entranced viewers from its debut in New York and helped spark greater public interest in the dramatic events of July 1776. Just as importantly, it brought the Signers out of the shadows. Along with Emanuel Leutze's 1851 painting of George Washington crossing the Delaware, Trumbull's *Declaration* was one of the most famous American paintings of the nineteenth century.

The Signers began to reclaim their place in history, thanks in no small part to Trumbull's skill and to the re-creation of their autographs by John Binns and Benjamin Owen Tyler. The next decades saw a growing interest in the lives of the men who adopted the Declaration. By now, only a handful were left, among them Thomas Jefferson, John Adams, and Charles Carroll of Carrollton.

In August 1820, just two years after Trumbull's canvas was first displayed, a Philadelphia teacher named John Sanderson wrote to Thomas Jefferson, asking the aged statesman for any recollections he might have of John Hancock. Sanderson noted "the importance and sacredness of the task" upon which he was engaged, obliquely informing Jefferson that his interests went far beyond Hancock.[18] The wary Jefferson wrote a "strictly confidential" letter to the president of the American Philosophical Society, asking for background on the young teacher, then in his midthirties. "[W]hat is his character moral and political," Jefferson inquired, "does he write for money or fame, Etc?"[19] Despite Jefferson's qualms about this latest attempt to commodify the Declaration, Sanderson published the first volume of his *Biography of the Signers to the Declaration of Independence* that year. The volume was a roaring success and inaugurated an enduring and profitable cottage industry of books on the history of the Declaration.

Sanderson eventually became more of a general editor than author, given the immense task he had set himself. He soon employed ghostwriters to tackle the fifty-six biographies required to complete the project, selling the volumes initially for $2.50 each. Under subsequent editors, the series eventually reached nine volumes and created an entirely new genre. Sanderson's was the first of many histories of the men who had pledged their lives, fortunes, and sacred honor to the cause of freedom in 1776. There seemed to be an inexhaustible audience, young and old, ready for new retellings of the lives of the delegates and their fates. Before Sanderson's series was complete, the Reverend Charles Goodrich issued a popular one-volume *Lives of the Signers of the Declaration of Independence*, in 1829, and the following year Nathaniel Dwight published *Sketches of the Lives* . . . for use in schools. The following decade, the irrepressible Benson J. Lossing came out with his *Biographical Sketches of the Signers* . . . in 1848, followed by other similarly titled collections.[20] Well into the twentieth century, new group biographies of the Signers were churned out by various authors, some series reaching twenty volumes.[21]

Trumbull's inaccurate masterpiece, Sanderson's serial biographies, and Binns's and Tyler's reproductions all helped create a new, shared historical mythology of America's founding moment and a vibrant market for Declaration memorabilia.

On the morning of July 4, 1821, the *Daily National Intelligencer*, Washington's leading newspaper, ran a notice that "*To prevent the confusion which might be apprehended from so large a concourse of persons as are expected to attend, the following regulations are proposed . . .* " The short announcement was directed at the thousands of people expected to descend on the U.S. Capitol that day. Streaming in from early morning, they were there to participate in a ceremony unlike any other in American history.[22]

At precisely eleven o'clock, President James Monroe and Secretary of State John Quincy Adams entered the packed chamber of the House of Representatives. The crowd must have strained to see the chief clerk of the State Department following them, for he carried with him the original engrossed Declaration, though whether it was rolled up or placed in a special frame for the occasion is not known. Then, in the only recorded public display since its signing in 1776, the venerable scroll was read aloud by Secretary Adams in honor of its forty-fifth anniversary.

After his reading, Adams gave one of the most famous orations in American history. In it, he warned his countrymen against following an imperial path, memorably declaiming that America "goes not abroad, in search of monsters to destroy. She is the well-wisher to the freedom and independence of all. She is the champion and vindicator only of her own." Just as notably, Adams put the Declaration at the center of the American historical experience. It was not simply a pronouncement of sovereignty, Adams suggested; its philosophy was the inspiration for the formation of State governments and the federal Constitution itself. It was, he insisted, a living document. "The interest, which in this paper has survived the occasion upon which it was issued; . . . the interest which quickens with the lapse of years, . . . is in the principles which it proclaims," he said, making clear that Jefferson's soaring invocation of natural rights was the true and enduring legacy of the Declaration.[23]

Meanwhile, in Philadelphia that day, a frail eighty-nine-year-old man rose to recite the Declaration at the city's public celebration. It is possible that the soon-to-be nonagenarian did not even need to read the words of the document, for he was the one who, four and a half decades previously and in that very city, had so beautifully inscribed the calfskin vellum that John Quincy Adams was simultaneously reading at the U.S. Capitol.

Yet no one in the Philadelphia crowd, or throughout the nation, knew that Timothy Matlack was the scribe whose elegantly slanted script was now being read in Washington. The few remaining signers, John Adams, Thomas Jefferson, and Charles Carroll, may have remembered, but none of the brief news items reporting Matlack's recitation commented on his most important service to the United States. All that was mentioned was that he had written George Washington's commission as commander of the Continental Army and "was an early and persevering asserter of the principles of liberty." Matlack would outlive all the Founding Fathers, except for Charles Carroll, dying in 1829 a respected member of the Revolutionary generation who never advertised himself as the penman of America's founding document.[24]

Were one somehow to have seen both the engrossed Declaration and its scribe that day, one might uncharitably have been tempted to comment that both were the worse for wear. Indeed, the aged Matlack's labors were literally disappearing, for the engrossed Declaration was beginning to fade. Though no one knew how to stop the physical damage, by the time John Quincy Adams read the scroll at the Capitol in 1821, he had put in motion a plan to foil the ravages of time.

Adams was not the first official to have worried about the scroll. When former Secretary of State Richard Rush had certified the accuracy of Benjamin Owen Tyler's facsimile signatures in 1818, he had noted evidence of the "hand of time." Only forty-two years after its creation, the aging of the parchment was visible to the naked eye. It was a bitter irony that after decades of being ignored, just as the Declaration was coming to light as a symbol uniting the nation, it was physically fading away.

The parchment spent most of its time rolled up and stored in the library of the Department of State. But as it gained in public interest, it was increasingly taken out, unrolled, and shown to dignitaries and even ordinary citizens. When defending himself against John Binns's charges that he had stolen the idea for a facsimile, Tyler related that in July 1817, he had been shown the original Declaration in Washington by its custodian, Josias King, who had helped Stephen Pleasonton save the Declaration when the British were closing in on the capital back in August 1814.[25]

Those in charge of the parchment began to fear that it might soon be lost. No known science could preserve the document from deterioration, and little could be done to protect the scroll when it was repeatedly rolled and unrolled. There was a different problem, too, one more aesthetic than archival. From a historical perspective, neither Binns's nor Tyler's engravings presented the Declaration as it actually looked. A true image of the document had yet to be created.

This was the challenge, one among many, that John Quincy Adams set for himself. A polymath, deeply learned in science, Adams was one of the most far seeing of American statesmen. Considering the problem in his methodical way, he determined that the most logical option was to make an official, exact copy of the Declaration to preserve it for posterity. The question was how to do so.[26]

In 1820, the year before the Declaration was carried to the Capitol, Adams had approached William J. Stone, an English engraver living in Washington, D.C. The commission he offered to Stone was monumental: make a faithful facsimile of the engrossed parchment, as close to an exact duplicate as possible. Though Adams was eager to employ the most scientifically advanced process, the effort exacerbated the problem it was meant to solve.[27]

Stone was given full access to the engrossed Declaration in the State Department offices. It is possible that he traced the parchment by hand, but the most popular process of copying at the time was by making a "wet transfer." This entailed moistening absorbent paper and pressing it against an original document to capture some of the ink. This copy was in turn pressed onto a copper plate and engraved. It is possible that Tyler and Binns had used the wet transfer process to copy the signatures on the Declaration, and probable that Stone did the same for the entire document. The problem with the wet transfer process is that it lifts some of the ink off the original. No one knows for sure if Stone used this process or tracery, but for decades afterward it was charged that he had accelerated the fading of the Declaration by removing some of its iron gall ink.

Regardless of the method he used, Stone created the most exact replication of the Declaration ever achieved. It took three years, but his copperplate engraving was completed in May 1823, at almost life size. The press spread the word, with Washington, D.C.'s *National Intelligencer* celebrating that the "immortal and imperishable" document could now avoid unnecessary further exposure while being seen in faithful copy by far more people.

Once Stone's copperplate was ready, Adams called for two hundred official copies to be struck on parchment. At the top of the copies, on either side of the heading, was a line in tiny print reading "Engraved by W.I. STONE for the Dept. of State by order/ of J.Q. ADAMS Secy of State July 4th 1823." Stone oddly misspelled his own middle initial and failed to correct the copperplate (see insert).

Adams first sent two copies each to the Declaration's surviving Signers. To his father, he wrote formally but proudly:

> Of this Document, unparalleled in the Annals of Mankind, the original deposited in this Department exhibits your name as one of the Subscribers. The rolls herewith transmitted are copies as exact as the art of engraving can present of the Instrument itself, as well as of the signatures to it—While performing the duty thus assigned to me, permit me to felicitate you and the Country which is reaping the reward of your labours, as well that your hand was affixed to this record of glory, as that after the lapse of near half a century, you survive to receive this tribute of reverence and gratitude from your children, the present fathers of the Land.
>
> With every Sentiment of Veneration, I have the honour of subscribing myself, your Fellow-Citizen.

Adams sent copies to President Monroe and former President Madison, to the Marquis de Lafayette (who hung it in his bedroom), the Supreme Court, each governor in the United States, and heads of different government departments. He also sent twenty impressions to Congress. Realizing that the engravings had potential political value, he gifted several to influential Marylanders, at least one of whom was in the Electoral College, likely anticipating his upcoming run for the presidency.[28]

Adams was not the only one to understand the appeal of the print. After running the two hundred official impressions, William Stone struck off two hundred or so of his own copies on vellum for sale. For this run, he burnished out of the copperplate the line noting John Quincy Adams's order and instead at the bottom engraved "*W. J. STONE SC WASHn,*" correcting his middle initial. Stone also signed a contract with a young printer named Peter Force, to pull several thousand paper copies to be inserted into a monumental compilation of American documents called *American Archives*. Though copies of the Stone engraving would not become widely distributed until the very end of the nineteenth century, for the first time Americans could see an almost exact reproduction of the Declaration.[29]

By 1823, the Declaration had emerged from obscurity and become familiar to Americans. There were only three Signers alive, and awareness of the final passing of the great era of the Revolution was palpable. Independence Day celebrations were becoming less partisan, and the Declaration was increasingly honored. As the Declaration neared its half-century mark, it was taking its place as the crown jewel in America's treasures of state. This newfound prominence would soon embroil it in new feuds, raise it to even loftier heights, and inspire a new generation to appropriate it for its own purposes.

Chapter 8

Semicentennial

Thomas Jefferson survives."

Those were the last words of John Adams. As the ninety-year-old second President of the United States sat in his study in Quincy, his life ebbing away, his final thoughts were of his friend, rival, and colleague during one of the greatest eras in human history. But Adams was wrong. Thomas Jefferson had died earlier that day in his beloved mountaintop home of Monticello, at the age of eighty-three. A few hours after Jefferson's passing, Adams slipped away.

The date was July 4, 1826. Inconceivably, the author of the Declaration of Independence and the man who had pushed it through Congress died not only on the same day, but on the fiftieth anniversary of its adoption. Americans had been celebrating the great milestone with speeches, parades, fireworks, and bands. When the news made its way through the country a few days later, the shock was deeply felt. Many undoubtedly shared the feelings of the President, John Quincy Adams, for whom this was a personal as well as public loss.[1] The *Newburyport Herald* in Massachusetts lamented the "mournful yet glorious occasion of the deaths of the immortal signers of the Declaration of Independence."[2]

A few weeks later, in Boston, Representative Daniel Webster gave one of the most eloquent eulogies in American history, which is worth quoting at some length. "Adams and Jefferson are no more," he intoned:

> It cannot but seem striking and extraordinary, that these two should live to see the fiftieth year from the date of that act, that they should complete that year, and that then, on the day which had fast linked for ever their own fame with their country's glory, the heavens should open to receive them both at once.
>
> No two men now live, fellow-citizen, perhaps it may be doubted whether any two men have ever lived in one age, who, more than those we now commemorate, have impressed on mankind their own opinions more deeply into the opinions of others, or given a more lasting direction to the current of human thought.
>
> No age will come in which it shall cease to be seen and felt, on either continent, that a mighty step, a great advance, not only in American affairs, but in human affairs, was made on the 4th of July, 1776.[3]

News of the passing of these two great men added a somber significance to the jubilee. Fifty years after American Independence, the United States stretched from Maine to the Oregon Territory on the Pacific Ocean. Twenty-four States now composed the Union, whose population was nearing 12 million people. Growth westward was unstoppable, and from 1812 to 1826 a new State was added almost every year to the Union. Louisiana joined in 1812, followed by Indiana in 1816, Mississippi in 1817, Illinois in 1818, Alabama in 1819, Maine in 1820, and the fateful admission of Missouri, in 1821.

New York City, with some 25,000 residents at the outbreak of the Revolution, now had close to 200,000 people and Baltimore 80,000. Fewer than ten years later, a little village of 350 people on the shores of Lake Michigan would incorporate as Chicago, becoming within decades the Nation's second-largest city. New roads linked once isolated towns, bringing them into a national market economy. The opening of the Erie Canal in 1825 would ensure New York City's economic dominance, tying the Great Lakes to the Atlantic seaboard through the Hudson River and port of New York. The Baltimore and Ohio Railroad was begun in 1828, igniting a railway boom that would permanently alter life and the national economy. Just seven years later, there were already nearly one thousand miles of track laid along the East Coast.[4]

The pell-mell growth often seemed to ignore the country's history at the expense of its future, but on July 4, 1828, when Charles Carroll laid the first stone to commence construction on the Baltimore and Ohio, he linked the great events of the past to the promises of what was to come. "I consider what I have just now done," said the ninety-one-year-old, "to be among the most important acts of my life, second only to my signing the Declaration of Independence, if indeed, it be even second to that."[5] The link was made material for the thronging crowd by one of the floats in that day's parade, which carried a full printing press that ran off text copies of the Declaration on the spot for the eager spectators.[6]

Not all went smoothly in these years. Overexpansion and land speculation, combined with the issuance of too much paper money, had ignited inflation, caused bankruptcies, and led to the country's first financial panic, lasting from 1819 to 1821. Despite such disruptions, growth seemed largely unstoppable. These were decades of a surging national optimism, an embrace of what Herbert Hoover later called "rugged individualism," undimmed by the faint sign on the horizon of political storms brewing over slavery. If there was a manifesto for these years, it was Ralph Waldo Emerson's 1841 address "Self-Reliance," with its clarion call to "Trust thyself."[7]

The Declaration was not just a presence in America's founding cities, it followed the receding frontier. In his travels along the Atlantic Coast and out to Ohio in the mid-1830s, the Hungarian reformer Alexander Bölöni Farkas saw copies of the Declaration carefully framed and hung in pride of place in country inns. It was the "indispensable furnishing and handbook in the home of every citizen," he told his countrymen.[8] On the Western frontier, with its rough living and brash optimism, the Declaration remained a living gospel for the hardy pioneers, tying them to the far-off cities in the East. "The Declaration of Independence embodies, not only our rights but our duties, as men and citizens," Morris Birkbeck reminded his fellow townsmen in Edwardsville, Illinois, just four years after their village was founded in 1818 across the Mississippi River from St. Louis.[9]

Insisting on their equal status with older settlements, towns throughout the new States and territories vigorously celebrated the Declaration on July Fourth. Frontier newspapers proudly printed the document on their front page, as the *Edwardsville Spectator* did the week before Independence Day in 1821.[10] That same year, the few hundred residents of

Alton, on the Mississippi River in remote southwestern Illinois, turned out for an Independence Day celebration. While a crowd of notables in far-off Washington saw John Quincy Adams read from the original scroll, the townsfolk of Alton marched in a procession, then gathered to hear the Declaration read, followed by an oration given by a local notable and an evening of toasts and revelry.[11] Their recent addition to the Union and daily struggle to carve a society out of the woods and plains made the settlers of these territories at least as fervent as their Eastern counterparts in their embrace of the Declaration's promise of liberty and the pursuit of happiness. The cost of such expansion to the Great Plains Indians—driven off their ancestral lands, felled by disease, killed in skirmishes and raids that also left scores of settlers dead—was dismissed, celebrated, or grimly accepted as inevitable.

A number of years later, another Illinoisan, a twenty-eight-year-old lawyer, would invoke the Declaration in a plea to his fellow citizens to defend a spirit of liberty that he warned was slipping away in an era focused on expansion. "I do not mean to say, that the scenes of the revolution *are now* or *ever will be* entirely forgotten," Abraham Lincoln told the Young Men's Lyceum, a debating society in Springfield, "but that like every thing else, they must fade upon the memory of the world, and grow more and more dim by the lapse of time." "As the patriots of seventy-six did to the support of the Declaration and Laws," he beseeched, "let every American pledge his life, his property, and his sacred honor" to uphold the "proud fabric of freedom."[12]

Amid the sound of hammers raising houses and the laying of iron rails, however, disputes over the past found a way into the fabric of the young nation. A few years before the semicentennial, one of the most notable of public spats entangled Thomas Jefferson and John Adams, now in the twilight of their lives. The object of their dispute was the Declaration of Independence.

Decades of intense political partisanship and the bitter Election of 1800 had divided Adams's Federalists and Jefferson's Democratic-Republicans, and the two men themselves, leading to decades of silence. Only later in life, through the mediation of Dr. Benjamin Rush, did they begin a celebrated exchange of letters that rekindled their competitive friendship. The reverence accorded to the Declaration after the War of 1812 swept them into a surprising dispute over its authorship.[13]

The argument over who wrote the Declaration was another indication of the growing importance of the document. Since the early 1800s the copious praise heaped on Jefferson as father of the Declaration had nettled old Federalists like Timothy Pickering, who served as Secretary of State for Adams and was a longtime adversary of the Sage of Monticello. In 1822, in his late seventies, Pickering engaged Adams in an exchange on the origins of the Declaration, seeking to downplay Jefferson's role. Adams, perhaps unwisely, took the bait. In his reply, the always-prickly Adams took credit for appointing Jefferson to write the draft, before noting that "there is not an idea in it, but what had been hackney'd in Congress for two years before."[14] To drive the point home, Adams enumerated a number of the earlier resolutions on liberty that he assumed had influenced Jefferson. Hoping to spite Jefferson, Pickering publicly revealed Adams's comments during an Independence Day speech in 1823.

Once Adams's private thoughts were printed, Jefferson felt compelled to respond. He did so in a private letter to his old friend and successor James Madison. Jefferson charged Adams with having a faulty memory, but he reserved his firepower for Pickering, tarring him as an Anglophile, one of those lovers of monarchy with whom he had tangled decades before. Jefferson did not flatly reject Adams's assertions, acknowledging that a decade of colonial debate over natural law and the numerous local declarations floating around during those years may well have influenced him back in 1776. "I did not consider it part of my charge to invent new ideas altogether," he noted. The dispute was petty, to Jefferson (and probably to Adams, as well), but the meaning of the Declaration was not. Jefferson concluded his letter to Madison by stressing the public's new appreciation of the Declaration. The document was no longer seen by Americans as a narrow, legalistic defense of the long-ago vote for Independence, but rather as a living philosophy for all time: "[I]t is a heavenly comfort to see that these principles are yet so strongly felt," Jefferson wrote, "I pray God that these principles may be eternal."[15]

On July 4, 1826, as villages, towns, and cities across the land reflected on the great deeds of a half century before, Jefferson was in his final hours. Ten days earlier, in almost the last of his thousands of letters, he had declined an invitation from the mayor of Washington, Roger C.

Weightman, to join the festivities in the capital. He took the opportunity to express one last time his belief that the Declaration continued to inspire dreams of liberty. "May it be to the world," he wrote with his signature cadence, "the signal of arousing men to burst the chains under which monkish ignorance and superstition had persuaded them to bind themselves, and to assume the blessings and security of self-government." And to his fellow Americans, Jefferson enjoined the anniversary as an eternal obligation. "For ourselves, let the annual return of this day forever refresh our recollections of these rights, and an undiminished devotion to them." Jefferson closed on a personal note, apologizing that it was only the "sufferings of sickness" that prevented him from participating in this most notable of anniversaries.[16] If he could not participate in person in celebration of his most notable achievement, one he had asked to be chiseled into his gravestone, Jefferson undoubtedly took pleasure at the thought of the commemorations occurring throughout the country.

Amid the cannon salutes, fireworks, parades, and feasts, we may take one speech as representative of the mixture of national and local pride expressed in cities and towns across America. In Boston, Mayor Josiah Quincy (a distant relative of John Adams) stayed true to his roots in a long oration on American history in which he gave Massachusetts pride of place. Quincy started his address with a more national outlook, praising the "Generous men! Exalted patriots! Immortal Statesmen!" of the Continental Congress.[17] Neither Quincy nor anyone in the crowd knew that as he spoke, two of these "immortal statesmen" lay dying. By the end of the day, Charles Carroll was the only living Signer.

Not every American on that fiftieth anniversary engaged in the traditional festivities as a simple expression of patriotism. As Jefferson had written, he hoped the Declaration's eternal principles would arouse men to burst the chains binding them. If this was radicalism, it remained radicalism of a relatively sober kind, for the Enlightenment rationalist identified "monkish ignorance and superstition" as the justification for rebellion against established norms and structures. Yet in an America more than a generation removed from the Revolution, some just as passionate and less restrained were to enlist the Declaration's spirit in various attempts to reform the evils they saw in American society.

For decades, contending political parties had claimed to be the true inheritor of the Declaration's principles. Out in New Harmony, Indiana, however, a wealthy utopian socialist was preparing to celebrate the document in a very different way. Robert Owen was about to invoke the Declaration for purposes far different from those of vote-seeking politicians.

Owen was a successful Welsh textile manufacturer who, driven by visions of global equality, had set up a collective on a farm he had bought with the proceeds from his industrial concerns. On that Independence Day, he gathered several hundred disciples and read to them a "Declaration of Mental Independence." He began by acknowledging the importance of July Fourth. It was, he noted, "the period, when the inhabitants of this new world attained the power to withdraw from the control of the old world, and to form a government for themselves." What started as a traditional reflection quickly turned into a passionate—even hysterical—condemnation of the entire American system. Owen excoriated "PRIVATE, OR INDIVIDUAL PROPERTY — ABSURD AND IRRATIONAL SYSTEMS OF RELIGION — AND MARRIAGE, FOUNDED ON INDIVIDUAL PROPERTY COMBINED WITH SOME ONE OF THESE IRRATIONAL SYSTEMS OF RELIGION." He did not call on his followers to assault the citadels of democracy, so much as to turn inward to destroy "this HYDRA OF EVILS" and usher in an egalitarian utopia. Owen linked his cause directly to the founding document of the country, celebrating the fact that "the Declaration of Political Independence, in 1776, has produced its counterpart, the Declaration of Mental Independence in 1826."[18]

Despite his fervent socialist beliefs, Owen's utopian experiment collapsed the following year, doomed by internal disagreements, poor town planning, and an inability to become self-supporting. Owen soon returned to England, his call for a mental and social revolution falling on deaf ears. But he was a harbinger of things to come. Owen had shown how the Declaration could be a living force for reformers and dreamers. Over the coming decades, as the economy grew, labor groups and socialists would take up his call, attacking capitalism and criticizing workplace conditions and wage rates by imitating the Declaration. At least six such declarations appeared by 1845, including by the New York Working Man's Party in December 1829, the Boston Trades' Union in June 1834, and the Equal Rights Advocates and Anti-Monopolists of New York in September 1836.[19]

One of the most radical, and bellicose, of labor platforms appeared in the New York *Working Man's Advocate*, in September 1844, as the "Declaration of Independence of the Producing from the Non-Producing

Class." Written by Lewis Masquerier, who believed land reform was vital to achieving the republican equality promised in Jefferson's document, it began

> When in the course of human events, the producers of property have been reduced to the lowest state of degradation and misery by the almost universal usurpation of all property and power by a non-producing, tyrannical, and aristocratic class, a decent respect for the opinions of mankind requires that they should declare the causes which impel them to cease ultimately being tenants to land usurping and non-producing lords . . . We hold these truths to be self-evident: That as the natural wants and powers of production of all men are nearly equal, all should be producers as well as consumers.[20]

Little of such dreams would be realized. Though labor unions and the socialist movement would grow throughout the nineteenth century—sometimes cooperating, sometimes at odds—ever more workers were drawn from rural areas and overseas to feed the insatiable manpower needs of manufacturing centers. Even with these difficult working conditions, the new economy generally offered a better life than in the Old World. If labor agitators' hopes were frustrated, others would soon seek to appropriate the Declaration for more disruptive causes.

Life on the country's successive frontiers engendered a rough, if free, culture that was unforgiving of weakness and timidity. American folklore celebrated men like Mike Fink and Davy Crockett, who could brawl, shoot and wrassle alligators and bear, all while being "ramsquaddled with whiskey."[21] It may have seemed inconceivable to end the brawling, but drinking soon became a target of reformers, who brought to their mission the religious fervor of the Great Awakenings that had swept through America in the eighteenth century and was about to do so again.

In both America and Europe, the mid-nineteenth century had seen a flourishing temperance movement, inspired by the religious revivals of Evangelical Protestants. Attracting women in particular, the temperance crusade became one of the largest social reform movements in American history.[22] Advocates attracted attention by publicly linking their cause with the country's founding document. On July 4, 1833, the Connecticut

State Temperance Society released a sermon entitled, "A Second Declaration of Independence, A Temperance Address," calling for a widespread abstention from liquor and other intoxicants.

This 1833 temperance manifesto was followed on Independence Day in 1841 by another edition of the "Second Declaration of Independence," now published as a national effort by "all the Washington Total Abstinence Societies of the United States of America." Delivered initially as an address in Worcester, Massachusetts, this pamphlet consciously mimicked the Declaration, amateurishly if earnestly playing off Jefferson's eternal phrases:

> We hold these truths to be self-evident; that all men are created *temperate*; that they are endowed by their Creator with certain natural and innocent desires; that among these are the appetite for COLD WATER and the pursuit of happiness!

Then followed a long list of charges against an anthropomorphized Alcohol. The conclusion clumsily mimicked the Declaration's stirring vow: " . . . we mutually pledge to each other our adhesion to PURE WATER, TOTAL ABSTINENCE, and the CAUSE OF HUMANITY."[23]

The temperance movement became a national force, though it never managed to eradicate drinking as a defining feature of American society. It was notable, however, not only for daring to tackle man's oldest intoxicant, but because it was the first major political movement led by women. As the struggle for sobriety continued, American women would invoke the Declaration on behalf of an even more personal cause. On July 19, 1848, thirty-three-year-old Elizabeth Cady Stanton opened the first American Women's Rights Convention in Seneca Falls, New York.

Stanton and her husband, Henry, were ardent abolitionists, committed to the eradication of slavery. On their honeymoon trip to London in 1840, they had attended the World Anti-Slavery Conference, where women delegates were forbidden from the main floor. While in London, Stanton met the Quaker women's rights advocate Lucretia Mott. In the summer of 1848, Stanton, Mott, and several other women organized a meeting in Stanton's new hometown of Seneca Falls to advocate for women's rights. Among the forty or so men in attendance was the Black abolitionist and intellectual Frederick Douglass.[24]

The centerpiece of the convention was the adoption of the "Declaration of Sentiments." Drafted by Stanton, it consciously and solemnly rephrased the Declaration of Independence, expanding Jefferson's philosophy to embrace equality between the sexes:

> We hold these truths to be self-evident: that all men and women are created equal; that they are endowed by their Creator with certain inalienable rights; that among these are life, liberty, and the pursuit of happiness; . . .
>
> But when a long train of abuses and usurpations, pursuing invariably the same object, evinces a design to reduce them under absolute despotism, it is their duty to throw off such government, and to provide new guards for their future security. Such has been the patient sufferance of the women under this government, and such is now the necessity which constrains them to demand the equal station to which they are entitled . . .
>
> The history of mankind is a history of repeated injuries and usurpations on the part of man toward woman, having in direct object the establishment of an absolute tyranny over her. To prove this, let facts be submitted to a candid world . . .

Stanton's Declaration concluded with a set of twelve resolutions, summoning Jefferson's language of natural rights. The most radical of these was the demand for women's "sacred right to the elective franchise."[25] In mid-nineteenth-century America, this was a revolutionary manifesto.

Stanton's Declaration did not change centuries of legal codes overnight. It would take women another seven decades to win the right to vote, but she had forever changed the national debate over civil rights. By founding her movement on an appeal to the Declaration, Stanton acknowledged that the scroll was now the most unassailable symbol of America's promise of equality. It was a logical and inevitable expansion of the philosophy expressed by Thomas Jefferson, and a belated response to Abigail Adams's admonition to her husband, John, to "Remember the Ladies."

Even as Americans enlisted the Declaration in new causes, it retained its power as an independence manifesto. In the American southwest, it was the inspiration to add a huge new territory to the Union. Texas had been a part of Mexico since Mexico had invoked the Declaration to declare its separation from Spain in 1821. In the succeeding fifteen years, Texas filled with American settlers who soon sought their own political freedom. On March 2, 1836, fifty-nine men gathered in the small, wooden Independence Hall at Washington-on-the-Brazos to sign a "Unanimous Declaration of Independence," declaring the Republic of Texas independent from Mexico. Drafted by George C. Childress, the Texians' Declaration

UNANIMOUS

DECLARATION OF INDEPENDENCE,

BY THE

DELEGATES OF THE PEOPLE OF TEXAS,

IN GENERAL CONVENTION,

AT THE TOWN OF WASHINGTON,

ON THE SECOND DAY OF MARCH 1836.

The Texas Declaration of Independence of 1836.

of Independence consciously reflected Thomas Jefferson's language and pronounced similar universal claims:

> When a government has ceased to protect the lives, liberty and property of the people, from whom its legitimate powers are derived . . . A statement of a part of our grievances is therefore submitted to an impartial world, in justification of the hazardous but unavoidable step now taken, of severing our political connection with the Mexican people, and assuming an independent attitude among the nations of the earth.[26]

By the time of their Declaration, the Texians, most of them American emigrants, had been fighting Mexico for a year, led by Sam Houston. While they were proclaiming their Republic, two hundred and fifty Texians were desperately fighting for their lives at a small mission called the Alamo, in San Antonio. After a two-week siege, Mexican general Santa Anna's troops massacred the entire garrison, including frontiersmen Jim Bowie and Davy Crockett. "Remember the Alamo!" soon held for the Texians the power that "Give me Liberty, or give me Death!" had for the colonists. Within a decade, the government of U.S. President James K. Polk would annex Texas, and then go to war with Mexico in 1846 to draw Texas into the Union.[27]

Whether utopians like Robert Owen, activists like Elizabeth Cady Stanton, or Texian revolutionaries, those seeking to create a more perfect Union had found their lodestar in the Declaration. No longer was it simply a static part of the political firmament. In an expanding and modernizing America, the Declaration had become a living document, dragged into supporting new causes not imagined back in 1776. Within another generation, it would face its severest test in the struggle to end America's greatest evil. Before that, however, the now venerable parchment would be brought into the light for all Americans to see.

Chapter 9
Into the Light

On November 14, 1832, Charles Carroll, the last living Signer of the Declaration, died at the astounding age of ninety-five. The *Alexandria Gazette* lamented,

> Charles Carroll of Carrollton *is no more!* . . . The only remaining link which connected this generation with the past, with that illustrious race of statesmen, philanthropists and patriots, the founders of American Independence, and the benefactors of the world, now and for all time hereafter—is broken . . . Henceforth the DECLARATION OF INDEPENDENCE is sacred to History—part of the mighty Past. THE LAST OF THE SIGNERS IS DEAD![1]

With the passing of Carroll, the "American Cicero," the Declaration of Independence had outlived the Founders.[2] But it was now connected to the American people more deeply than at any time since the Revolution, celebrated with pride in villages and towns across the nation, lauded as a harbinger of freedom throughout the world, and visibly present in daily life, thanks to the efforts of John Binns and John Trumbull.

Yet despite this growing reverence, the physical scroll remained all but hidden. After its rescue in 1814, the engrossed Declaration had lain quietly in the State Department's Bureau of Archives and Laws, located since 1819 on the second floor of the new Northeast Executive Building next to the President's House. Within a few years however, the venerable parchment would make its most important move since 1776.

Outside the walls of the new State Department, interest in the founding generation continued to grow. Trumbull's prints were perennial bestsellers while John Sanderson's and Charles Goodrich's biographies of the Signers poured off the press. The following year, the *Charleston Courier* advertised a new edition of the *Works of Thomas Jefferson*. One of the main selling points of the new edition was the inclusion of an accurate facsimile of the "rough draught" of the Declaration in Jefferson's own hand, possibly having been copied from one of the six handwritten versions that Jefferson had sent to friends.[3]

Attention was being paid to the Declaration for more concerning reasons, as well. Tensions over the extent of federal power had grown over the previous decade, forming fissures beneath the surface of what seemed a united nation. Missouri had been the first great crisis, over whether to admit the territory as a slave or free State. Guided by the legislative finesse of Speaker of the House Henry Clay, a political bargain was struck to maintain a balance between Free States and Slave States. Human bondage would be prohibited in new States created north of a line drawn at 36°30', except Missouri, which was allowed to be a Slave State. For a generation, the Missouri Compromise settled the slavery question, but the underlying problem festered.

Slavery was not the only national divide. In response to Northern manufacturers' pleas for protection from British goods, Congress in 1828 passed what became known as the Tariff of Abominations, totaling nearly 49 percent. The tariff threatened to impoverish the Southern States, which imported most of their manufactured goods. South Carolina's John C. Calhoun, who became Vice President the following year, sought to cancel the tariffs by putting forth the concept of State nullification of federal laws. Seeing nullification as a direct threat to the integrity of the nation, Senator Daniel Webster gave a passionate refutation to a speech by pro-nullification Senator Robert Hayne over two days in January 1830. His immortal conclusion pleaded for unity:

> When my eyes shall be turned to behold for the last time the sun in heaven, may I not see him shining on the broken and dishonored fragments of a once glorious Union; on states dissevered, discordant, belligerent; on a land rent with civil feuds, or drenched, it may be, in fraternal blood! . . . *Liberty and Union, now and forever, one and inseparable!*[4]

Divisions grew after another punitive tariff passed in 1832. Then, on November 14, South Carolina declared the Tariffs of 1828 and 1832 null and void. The *Charleston Courier* defended the move, writing that "the only foundation upon which we can safely erect the right of a State to protect its citizens, that South Carolina, by the Declaration of Independence, became and has since continued a Free, Sovereign and Independent State."[5] This assertion resurrected questions that went back to the debates over the Articles of Confederation and Constitution.

President Andrew Jackson challenged Calhoun in what became known as the Nullification Crisis. Though he was himself a Southerner, Jackson threatened to use federal troops to enforce the tariffs, and Congress passed the Force Bill in March 1833 to authorize such action. At the same time, the legislators passed a more lenient tariff, ending the standoff. This resolution did not assuage the deeper fears of Southern States, who increasingly felt themselves a minority in the face of the growing industrial and mercantile power of the North. The threat of sectional division emerged again, as it had during the Missouri Compromise.

In 1830, at the same time as the Nullification Crisis, Jackson signed the narrowly passed Indian Removal Act, allowing him to break longstanding treaties and exchange lands in the west for Indian territory stretching from Wisconsin to Florida. These negotiations were backed by threats of force, leaving the tribes, some of whom like the Cherokee held thousands of Black slaves, little choice but to accede. Six years earlier, a Cherokee delegation headed by Principal Chief John Ross had presented a letter to Congress requesting assistance in protecting "the rights, liberty, and lives of the Cherokee people" from Georgia's attempts to remove them from their lands. The memorial included an appeal to that "*memorable* declaration, 'that all men are created equal; that they are endowed by their Creator with certain unalienable rights; that among these are life, liberty, and the pursuit of happiness.'"[6]

In 1831, the Cherokee sued in the Supreme Court to retain their lands

A cartoon by Joseph Arnold from 1839 linking Independence with the preservation of the union after tensions over slavery threatened sectional division.

in Georgia, claiming the status of a foreign nation, but the State successfully opposed the suit. The next year the Court reversed course and ruled that the Cherokee had the protection of federal law against Georgia State law. Jackson infamously said that Chief Justice John Marshall had made his decision and dared him to enforce it. Jackson was happy to assert federal authority inside the States, but he had no intention of granting the Cherokee federal protections. By the time he stepped down, after two terms, paving the way for his Vice President, Martin Van Buren, government policy toward the Indians was set. In 1838, Van Buren ordered the Cherokee forcibly moved off their lands. Over four thousand Cherokee died on the "Trail of Tears" that would soon see tens of thousands of Seminoles, Chickasaw, Muskogee, and Choctaws removed from the Southeast and forced into government reservations in Oklahoma.[7]

Despite this tragic marriage of Federal and State convenience at the expense of the Indians, those who appealed to the Declaration's assertion of State sovereignty were beginning to build sophisticated constitutional arguments that would threaten the future of the Union. Yet even as greater attention was paid to the Declaration, the actual scroll never left the State Department. All that changed suddenly in the early summer of 1841.

On June 11, 1841, Secretary of State Daniel Webster, the fearsome orator and once-and-future Senator from Massachusetts, sent a letter to Henry Ellsworth, Commissioner of Patents. "Having learned that there is in the new building appropriated to the Patent Office suitable accommodations for the safe-keeping, as well as the exhibition of the various articles now deposited in this Department," wrote Webster, "I have directed them to be transmitted to you." These "various articles" included those "which, having been usually exhibited to visitors at this Department, may be interesting to those calling at the Patent Office." On the attached inventory was "Schedule C, 6. The Original Declaration of Independence."[8]

Like Richard Rush and John Quincy Adams before him, Webster discovered that he had custody of one of the capital's more popular artifacts. How much time he or his clerks spent unrolling and rolling the scroll is not known, but that it was "usually exhibited" gives some indication that the available reproductions were not sating public interest. Nor did the popularity of the Declaration spill over to that other great document of American history, the Constitution. However important it may have been, the Constitution, written out over four large leaves, seemed not to call forth the same fascination or emotions. It lay relatively undisturbed in the Department of State's library, spared from the physical wear and tear that had so damaged the Declaration.

The building to which Webster sent the Declaration was one of the newest jewels of Washington, D.C., a symbol of America's growing power. Once the capital city had recovered from the destruction wrought by rampaging British troops, it had grown and prospered, its population increasing from roughly 25,000 in 1814 to over 43,000 by 1840. When Andrew

Jackson soundly defeated John Quincy Adams in 1828, he became the first president from outside Massachusetts or Virginia, ushering in an era of populist democracy. The unruly mobs that crowded into the Capitol and White House for his inauguration on March 4, 1829, held new expectations for civic participation.[9]

Both Adams and Jackson presided over a burst in scientific investment by the federal government, and welcomed the establishment of a new national institution devoted to science, funded by a bequest from an unknown Englishman named James Smithson. Since colonial days America had been a land of inventors and tinkerers, what Benjamin Franklin called "mechanics," and as the nineteenth century reached its midpoint, America's twenty-three million citizens were inventing and patenting more than ever, issuing more than double the number of patents in either England or France, despite being a third smaller in population than France and only slightly larger than Great Britain.[10]

Americans were also taking their place as great explorers. The epochal expedition led by Meriwether Lewis and William Clark from 1804 to 1806 explored the Louisiana Purchase and looked for a passage to the Pacific Northwest. Three decades later, the United States Exploring Expedition commanded by Lieutenant Charles Wilkes covered the Pacific Ocean and circumnavigated the globe. The tens of thousands of American inventions and equal number of artifacts collected in North America and around the world fascinated a public more interested than ever in different cultures of the world around them.[11]

The need for a new building, and a better patent system, was recognized by President Jackson. He approved the construction of a new Patent Office, which was begun in 1836, opened in 1841, and finished three decades later, in 1868, after the convulsions of the Civil War. Construction was supervised by the architect Robert Mills, a Charleston native. Taking up a full city block on F Street, between Seventh and Ninth Streets, the Patent Office's main portico was modeled on the ancient Greek Parthenon, making it one of the "noblest of Washington buildings," as Walt Whitman was soon to proclaim.[12]

In this new era of populist democracy, the building was designed for more than office space. Over half of it was set aside for public exhibitions of the models held by the Patent Office and for the various collections and specimens held by the U.S. Government. Its massive top floor was 266 feet long, 63 feet wide, and 30 feet high, the ceiling a series of arches supported by two double rows of massive columns. One of the largest exhibition halls in the world, the space became known as the "National Gallery." The gallery grew out of the holdings of the National Institution for the Promotion of Science, Washington's first learned society, founded by Joel R. Poinsett, the Secretary of War, and Peter Force, a former Washington mayor and publisher of *American Archives*. The National Institution held the collections bequeathed by James Smithson and those sent to the government by American explorers, now displayed in the grand gallery. Also called the "Hall of Curiosities" or the "National Museum," the gallery quickly became one of the most popular venues in Washington. It was here that Webster sent the engrossed Declaration of Independence.

Webster left no explanation as to why he would take the nation's most precious document from secure storage in the State Department and send it to a public exhibition hall. Were its popularity and the desire to spare it further physical handling justification enough for such an unprecedented move? His reasoning may have been more practical: the danger of fire. In 1833, fire consumed the old Treasury Building, destroying thousands of irreplaceable records, just yards from where the Declaration lay in the Northeast Executive Building. And in 1836, over ten thousand patent documents and seven thousand patent models were lost when the old Patent Office had burned down. The danger of fire was ever present.

The new Patent Office Building seemed the answer. Built from thick sandstone and deliberately designed to be fireproof, it could protect records, models, and specimens from accidental conflagration. That exhibiting the Declaration in the National Gallery might obviate the need for unnecessary handling could only be a plus. To cap it off, displaying the country's founding document fit the tenor of the times, as a curious, exuberant, and increasingly wealthy America entered the age of museum building and collecting.

If Webster felt the safety of the document would be assured after sixty-five years of being rolled, folded, and stashed away, his decision led to new challenges and unanticipated problems. The scroll had not been created for exhibition, and its custodians suddenly found themselves having to consider the parchment's physical properties. Since this was the first government document to be put on permanent display, there was no precedent for the best way to exhibit it. Responsibility for deciding how to exhibit the Declaration fell to Dr. Henry King, the first curator of the National Institution. King was a medical doctor, geologist, and mining expert most recently employed by the War Department. He was among the first in the country to write manuals on how to make natural history collections.[13]

The questions, both artistic and scientific, surrounding the display were unique. If discussions took place over whether the scroll should be in a particular location, dedicated case, or even its own hall, no record exists of such deliberations. Most likely, King and his staff simply treated it as one of thousands of items in the National Gallery and decided to display it like other items in the collection, namely hung up in one of the many cases. Institutional records show no mention of concern about the scroll's physical safety in such an unguarded public spot. Such assumptions may have been strained just a few months later, when foreign gifts to the president worth as much as $15,000 were stolen from the Patent Office collection (and later recovered). But no changes appear to have been made to the exhibit.[14]

With no serious science of conservation, little was understood about how best to maintain such a fragile artifact. There were no climate-controlled cases in 1841 and no understanding of how exposure to the air might affect parchment through changes in humidity, temperature, and light. Written as it was on animal skin, the Declaration expanded, contracted, and curled depending on the moisture levels and heat. Few at the time realized that this, too, would cause physical deterioration.

To be displayed, the Declaration would have to be unrolled and kept flat. King and his staff decided to secure the Declaration to a wooden frame using string mounts. This required making Y-shaped punctures along the edges of the parchment, a few of which remain visible today. The tighter the Declaration was secured, the more stress the scroll would undergo as it contracted and expanded. Yet this, too, was not understood, so the fragile skin was duly affixed to the backing of the frame, covered with a simple pane of glass, and hung in the majestic National Gallery.

The Declaration was in good company in its new home. Among the Gallery's sixty-three glass-fronted cases were those holding Benjamin Franklin's cane and printing press, a piece of Plymouth Rock, Andrew Jackson's uniform at the Battle of New Orleans, and Davy Crockett's tomahawk. Around them were displayed Egyptian mummies, pieces of lava and coral, plants familiar and strange, minerals and shells, hundreds of stuffed animal specimens, and five thousand exotic curiosities from the Wilkes Exploring Expedition.

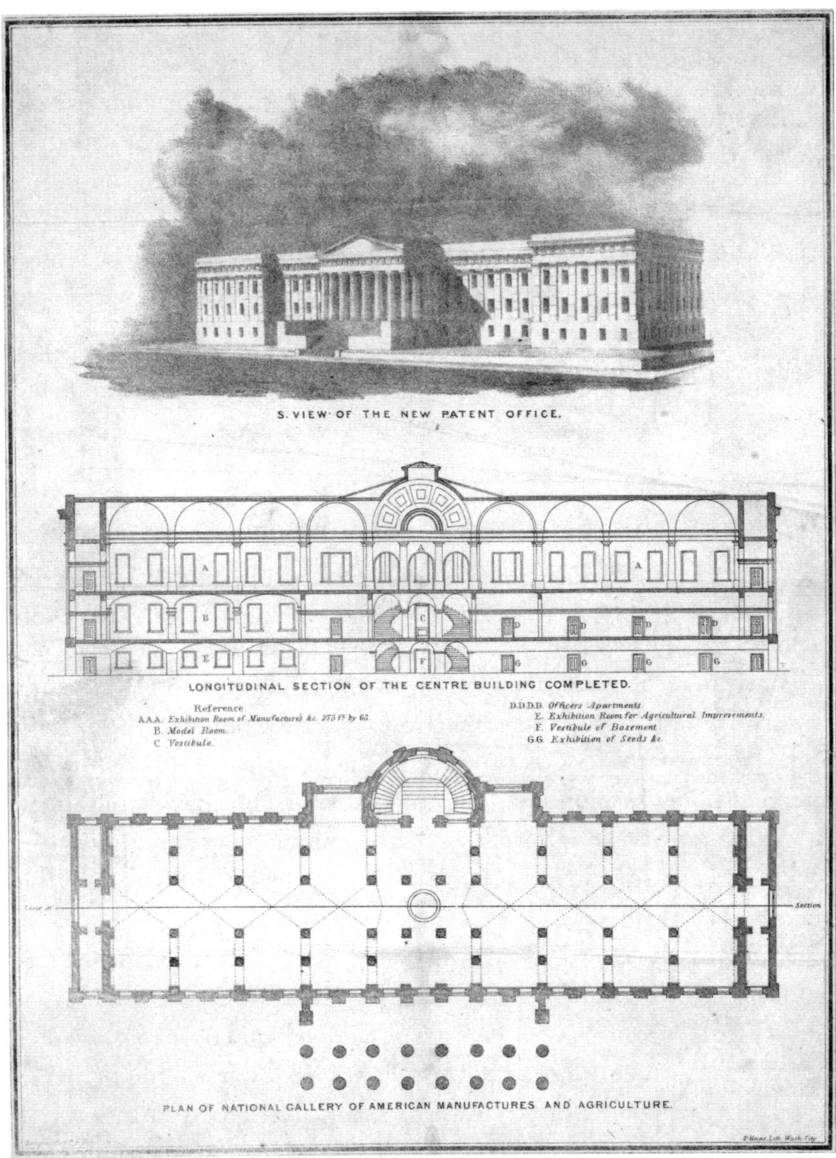

The new Patent Office circa 1845, showing the plan of the National Gallery, where the Declaration was first put on public display.

The Declaration was placed in case number 24, on the outer wall, where it immediately attracted attention. Soon after its installation, a newspaper account informed readers of the scroll's display, "suspended above your reach" near a formal statue of George Washington.[15] The case also held George Washington's commission as commander of the Continental

Army, and Washington's camp chest, coat, and sword. Almost immediately, the public could see for themselves why Daniel Webster had worried about the physical condition of the scroll. "The Declaration appears much thumbed and soiled," noted the same article. Though it was encased and seemingly protected for the first time, it would be damaged beyond the stress of being hung vertically. King had chosen a central location in the hall, but unfortunately it was subject to both direct and indirect sunlight and reflected glare from the gallery's tall windows. While there was no way to accurately measure the fading to the document, observers repeatedly noted over the next three decades that the ink was growing more and more faint.[16]

The Declaration was put on display just as Washington was becoming a major tourist destination. The Baltimore and Ohio Railroad, the nation's first rail system, opened a station in 1835 at Pennsylvania Avenue and Second Street, just west of the Capitol, serving over seventy-five thousand passengers in its first year of operation. Branches soon ran up to New York City, and within two decades the B&O offered service to the Nation's capital from as far west as St. Louis.[17] In the city, eighteenth-century inns were giving way to more modern hotels. Dozens of new establishments crowded the streets along with boardinghouses servicing both tourists and Congressmen during their legislative sessions, from Willard's by the White House to Tunnicliff's near the Capitol.

Watching the crowds from his post in the old Patent Office, an enterprising clerk named William Elliot saw an opportunity. In 1837, he published the *Washington Guide*, one of the first handbooks to the capital. Four years later, Elliot moved to the Patent Office's new building, which hosted the National Institute (renamed from National Institution) and its museum collection. Guidebooks soon vied to extol the treasures of the capital. After a detailed description of the National Gallery in his *Picture of Washington and Its Vicinity* (1845), William Q. Force noted it was a "place of great resort for both citizens and strangers."[18]

By the mid-1840s, amid the sights of Washington the Declaration was inescapable. Guidebooks made it a highlight of any visit. Handbooks like *Morrison's Stranger's Guide to the City of Washington* directed visitors to Trumbull's massive panorama in the Rotunda and to the bronze statue of Thomas Jefferson, sculpted in France by Pierre-Jean David d'Angers, which went up in the Capitol in 1834.[19] The statue had been commissioned and donated by Uriah P. Levy, a Jewish veteran of the U.S. Navy and admirer of Jefferson who two years later would purchase the decaying Monticello, saving it from destruction.[20]

D'Angers's imposing statue depicted Jefferson holding a quill pen in one hand while the other clutched an enlarged scroll on which the entire Declaration had been pressed into the sculptor's clay and then cast in bronze. By the mid-1840s, it had been moved to the front lawn of the White House, where thousands of passersby would see it over the next quarter century. Force, in his *Picture of Washington*, rhapsodically wrote it seemed as if Jefferson "had just finished that immortal instrument, and was anticipating the glorious results of its influence—the terror it would strike among the foes of freedom—the strength with which it would nerve the patriot's heart—the bitter opposition with which it would meet from some—the joy with which it would be hailed by more—and, if adopted, the high destinies which awaited young America." Now back in the Rotunda, the statue has lost none of its power.[21]

Wherever visitors went in Washington, they were likely to run into the Declaration in some form. In a way, as one followed the guidebooks through the stations around the city, a living tapestry of this moment of national creation played out, from the statue of Jefferson to Trumbull's panorama of the presentation to Congress, culminating in the venerable scroll itself in the Patent Office, encased for all to see. These objects provided a patriotic education outside the classroom, celebrating an increasingly mythic view of the nation's founding.

But not all those who gazed upon the Declaration were equally enraptured. One luminary who cast a jaundiced eye was the famed English novelist Charles Dickens, who visited the Patent Office in 1841. In *American Notes*, an account of his visit to the United States published the following year, Dickens recounted how he had been to Washington just a few months after former President John Quincy Adams had argued before the Supreme Court in the *Amistad* case, defending a group of African Mende abducted by Portuguese slavers who hoped to sell them in Cuba. The Mende, led by Joseph Cinque, had taken over the ship by force and then been captured by the U.S. Navy off Long Island.[22]

Though Adams had successfully restored their freedom to the captured Mende, he had been pilloried by pro-slavery sympathizers and threatened with censure by the House of Representatives. This treatment incensed Dickens, whose country had outlawed the slave trade in 1807 and abolished slavery throughout the empire in 1833. Far from withering, as Thomas Jefferson had half hoped, half expected, slavery had been institutionalized and codified and was now completely enmeshed in the plantation system. Though the slave trade was banned starting in 1807, and Northern states began passing gradual emancipation laws as early as 1780, freeing the children of existing slaves when they reached the age of maturity, the number of people held in chattel slavery—considered as property of "owners"—reached over 2.4 million, tripling from less than a century earlier.[23]

Dickens was a passionate antislavery advocate. Instead of being inspired by Jefferson's elegant phrases and promises, he was disgusted. All he saw was hypocrisy. To his mind, the Declaration's great claims were negated by the "infamy" of slavery. When he viewed the venerable document, newly installed in the Patent Office, he could hardly contain his contempt:

> gilded, framed and glazed; hung up for general admiration; shown to strangers not with shame, but pride; its face not turned towards the wall, itself not taken down and burned; is the Unanimous Declaration of the Thirteen United States of America, which solemnly declares that All Men are created Equal; and are endowed by their Creator with the Inalienable Rights of Life, Liberty and the Pursuit of Happiness![24]

Two decades before the Civil War, Dickens had touched the rawest nerve in the American body politic. Westward expansion had raised the unavoidable question of whether slavery should be allowed in new States, though this divisive issue had been papered over by the contentious Missouri Compromise of 1820. In 1841, few thought that the question of slavery would tear the nation apart. Despite Dickens's scorn, the Declaration continued to draw fascinated visitors.

On July 4, 1848, *Brother Jonathan*, America's first illustrated newspaper, reprinted a facsimile of Thomas Jefferson's handwritten rough draft of the Declaration. The full-page reproduction included the Signers' autographs and a capsule history of the document, adapted from the prolific historian Benson J. Lossing's *Biographical Sketches of the Signers of the Declaration of American Independence.*[25] Prints of the rough draft itself would become perennial sellers. Reprintings in periodicals like *Harper's Weekly* helped ensure that Jefferson's reputation never dimmed.

In a culture increasingly oriented toward mass communication, the Declaration gained in popularity from this constant exposure. The country's relentless growth, endless immigration, and the transformation of the landscape led to a sense of upheaval but also of patriotic optimism.[26] In the two decades between 1840 and 1860, the population of the United States nearly doubled, rising from 17 million to 31.4 million. The Irish Potato Famine, which broke out in 1845, was followed on the Continent by the 1848 Revolutions. Both brought waves of Northern European immigrants to America, joined by those seeking to escape the rapid industrialization of Europe and settle on their own land. The number of Irish doubled, to 1.6 million, while Germans tripled by 1860 to 1.3 million, settling heavily in Illinois, Minnesota, and especially Wisconsin. Rapidly growing Western towns absorbed many of the immigrants, as in St. Louis, where more than 43 percent of its population in 1850 was born in either Ireland or Germany.[27]

Meanwhile, the discovery of gold at Sutter's Mill in 1848 in the territory of California lured hundreds of thousands west to seek their fortunes. Immigrants arrived from around the world over the next seven years, driving California's non-native population from roughly 1,000 to 380,000 by 1860. The massive amount of land conquered in the 1846–1848 Mexican War drew thousands of new settlers into the Southwest, and California was officially admitted as a State in 1850.[28] While many made their way to San Francisco and the gold mines by ship around the tip of South America, thousands traveled overland in caravans of covered wagons, continuing a process of movement toward the Pacific Coast that had begun in the early 1840s with the settlement of the Oregon Territory. Untold numbers stopped along the way, or "having seen the elephant," returned disappointed from California, settling new territory and founding new towns.[29]

The Declaration moved west into the new territories, as arrivals from the East Coast and Old Northwest around the Great Lakes brought with them long-established traditions. As early as 1850, the *Daily Alta California*, in San Francisco, reported on a "Soiree to be given in honor of the Anniversary of American Independence" at the St. Francis Hotel. Hoping to ensure that the celebration would not turn into a drunken melee of gold prospectors, the organizers informed the newspaper that "upwards of forty ladies have signified their intention of gracing the *fete* with their presence."[30] Later that year, at a dinner given to pay off the debts of the First Methodist Church of Sacramento City for the Colored People, a resolution was adopted to "cherish with gratitude the names and memories of the men who framed and signed the Declaration of Independence of these United States of America, for the clause in that instrument, which declares all men to be born 'free and equal.'"[31] Three years later, Salt Lake City enjoyed a day of July Fourth festivities beginning with a dawn artillery salute, a rendition of the "Star-Spangled Banner" as the flag was raised, and bands and parades. At a grand feast later that evening, the Declaration was toasted as "stereotyped in the hearts of the American people."[32]

Whether East Coast émigrés or foreign immigrants, tales of '76 and the history of the Declaration reached those in the new settlements through civic celebration and individual interest. Booksellers in heavily German and Irish St. Louis, for example, advertised copies of Nathaniel Dwight's *Lives of the Signers* in 1851, while books aimed at younger readers, many of them children of immigrants going to public schools for the first time, frequently appeared.[33]

In these years the Declaration became encrusted with apocryphal stories, which only served to deepen its appeal, particularly among the young. One that lodged in American folklore was the legend of the ringing of the Liberty Bell with the signing of the scroll on July 4, 1776. A version of the tale was dramatically related by Benson Lossing, in his 1848 work, *Biographical Sketches of the Signers*:

> On the morning of the day of its adoption, the venerable bell-man ascended to the steeple, and a little boy was placed at the door of the Hall to give him notice when the vote should be concluded. . . . Suddenly a loud shout came up from below, and there stood the blue-eyed boy, clapping his hands and shouting 'Ring! ring!' Grasping the iron tongue of the old bell . . . backward and forward he hurled it a hundred times, its loud voice proclaiming 'Liberty throughout all the land, unto all the inhabitants thereof.'[34]

Generations of schoolchildren would be taught that the fatefully cracked Liberty Bell had pealed when the Declaration was signed on July Fourth, yet few likely learned that no bell was rung and no parchment signed on that historic day. A few decades later, Lossing would pen another patriotic myth that stirred the hearts of boys and girls alike, weaving a dramatic tale of the rescue of the Declaration by Dolley Madison from the approaching British in 1814.

These stories may have imaginatively re-created elements of famous events, but they served to put the Declaration at the center of a shared American past, one that embraced newcomers as well as descendants of colonial rebels. It was a period of intense interest in American history, driven by social changes and national expansion.[35] As New Englanders left their stony soil and moved west, they encountered recently arrived immigrants, creating new social alloys in the growing towns beyond the Alleghenies. The small fictions offered by writers such as Lossing served a larger purpose by inculcating an enduring patriotism, one that encouraged new citizens to adopt the beliefs and norms of the existing population. The Declaration was perhaps the most easily identifiable object to which such stories and lessons could be attached.

From hidden artifact to commodified object and tourist attraction, the Declaration of Independence by the mid-nineteenth century was firmly woven into American myth and culture. By 1860, some sixty-five different reproductions of the Declaration were available in the thirty-three States that then made up the country. They ranged from broadsides to facsimiles and were printed on paper, cloth, and silk. Some were fanciful artistic reinterpretations, while others were more accurate copies. Many incorporated John Trumbull's iconic painting or included a portrait of George Washington, who never signed the document. They ranged in price, but almost all were affordable to the masses, framed on living room walls or pressed between pages of the family Bible across the Nation.[36] Thousands of visitors saw the engrossed parchment in the Patent Office in Washington every year and then read biographies of the Signers once they were back home. The Declaration had become a regular presence in American life.

At this moment of its greatest visibility, the Declaration would be dragged into America's greatest crisis, leading to a war that would tear apart the Nation it had called into being.

Chapter 10

The "Apple of Gold" and the Coming of the Civil War

An eagle-eyed reader of *Brother Jonathan*'s 1848 reproduction of Thomas Jefferson's handwritten rough draft of the Declaration of Independence would have made out, among the small print, a paragraph condemning King George III's "cruel war against human nature itself, violating it's most sacred rights of life & liberty in the persons of a distant people who never offended him, captivating & carrying them into slavery in another hemisphere . . ." Those who knew their Declaration might have wondered about these sentences, for they were nowhere evident in the venerable document.[1]

When, in July 1776, the Continental Congress struck out Jefferson's denunciation of the British slave trade in his draft, it foreshadowed a fracture at the heart of the American experience. Jefferson had referred to Africans as a "distant people" in his draft, and thus not part of the "one people" of the colonies, but he had also made clear that the trade violated their most sacred rights and liberties, attributing to them a common humanity.[2] At the time, both Northern shipping interests and Southern plantation interests (primarily in Georgia and South Carolina) had a vested stake in the continuation of what became known as the "peculiar institution" and the entire paragraph had been removed. The vast majority of Americans never held slaves, but the issue was, as a later historian wrote, a "sleeping serpent," waiting to rouse and strike.[3]

Southern statesmen, including Jefferson and Washington, hoped or even assumed that slavery would die out on its own accord. Yet slavery steadily became more economically efficient, as "King Cotton" supplanted lands exhausted from tobacco farming, eventually cementing it as the mainstay of the South's economy. The cotton trade tied the South into a global market, especially the British textile industry, and made the practice ever more profitable, accounting for over half of American export earnings. The region's wealth rested on the commercial commodities slavery produced, which covered an area of up to thirty million acres, more than Britain's entire arable and pasture land.[4] With a steady supply of cotton flowing to the new industrial mills in New England and across the Atlantic, mercantile and financial interests in the North found themselves nearly as invested as Southern plantation farmers in the perpetuation of slavery.[5] The Southern States translated their economic clout into political programs that promoted and protected the practice.

In the decades of debate over slavery, the Declaration initially played little role, though its equality claim was regularly quoted by the earliest abolitionists in the 1780s and 1790s. Moves to abolish slavery began in the North soon after Independence, beginning with Vermont in 1777 before it even achieved statehood, while Pennsylvania passed a law for gradual emancipation in 1780. In Massachusetts a series of legal cases led to the banning of the practice by appealing to the assertion in the State's 1780 constitution (largely written by John Adams) that all people were born free. In the mid-1780s, Alexander Hamilton and John Jay were members of the New York Society for the Manumission of Slaves, while down in Philadelphia, Ben Franklin became president of the Pennsylvania Abolition Society. In the South, a bill banning the importation of slaves into Virginia, likely authored by Thomas Jefferson, was passed in 1778, though emancipation of those currently enslaved was not proposed.[6]

Jefferson had failed to protect his condemnation of the national slave trade in the Declaration, but a decade later the question of the trade reemerged during the Constitutional Convention. With no prospect of abolishing slavery nationwide, the Convention focused on cutting the source, the transatlantic network that procured human beings from local slavers on the African Coast and forcibly transported them to America. Yet given the confluence of mercantile and agrarian interests, the best the

Convention could do was another compromise, agreeing to prevent Congress from banning the trade for twenty years. Congress did indeed prohibit the trade starting in 1808, but that did little to dent the practice. In lieu of the transatlantic voyage, a massive domestic slave market emerged, using both maritime and overland routes between the States, and making Virginia one of the largest suppliers to the growing Southern economy.[7]

It was the expansion of the United States across the continent that brought the issue of slavery to the fore and ultimately dragged the Declaration into the dispute. While Northern abolitionists had fought against the practice based on moral reasons, the reality of electoral politics hardened positions across the country. The Northwest Ordinance of 1787 banned slavery in the territories north of the Ohio River, but when Missouri applied for admission to the Union as a Slave State, fear for the balance between Northern and Southern representation in Congress erupted.[8]

The issue turned on a proposal to admit Missouri as a Slave State and Maine as a Free State, while prohibiting the expansion of slavery north of a line drawn at 36°30' latitude. During the debate in Congress, Representative Timothy Fuller, of Massachusetts, explicitly invoked the Declaration of Independence, arguing that no reading of the document "can endanger the rights, or merit the disapprobation, of any portion of the Union." Yet Southern slavery interests felt threatened by just such a reading, with its assertions of equality. The fault lines exposed by the Declaration were but temporarily paved over by the Missouri Compromise of 1820, putting off the reckoning for a generation.[9]

Over the next thirty years, the United States grew exponentially as the Indian Treaties and Andrew Jackson's Removal Act pushed American Indians off their ancestral lands and as settlers jockeyed with Britain and Russia for full control of the Oregon Territory, which stretched from the Rocky Mountains to the Pacific Coast. Agreement with Britain over Oregon and victory in the Mexican War in 1848 would add almost all the rest of the continent south of Canada to the United States, tacking on fully one-third of the total area the country ultimately came to include. As new States were formed or planned in the vast territory, slavery now became the country's overriding political issue, sparking a foreign policy struggle in the Caribbean and raising constitutional questions. Slaveholding interests continued to push for the expansion of the practice into new lands to the west. Were new States to be slave or free? The answer would determine the balance of political power in Washington, representation in Congress, and electoral votes for the presidency.[10]

The Declaration was intimately tied to the abolitionist movement, which had begun with the birth of the country and included Black as well as White voices. The French-born Quaker Anthony Benezet, who in 1775 founded the Society for the Relief of Free Negroes Unlawfully Held in Bondage, repeated the Declaration's equality claim in his influential writings after 1776. Maryland's Benjamin Banneker, a free Black polymath, boldly wrote Thomas Jefferson himself in the summer of 1791, quoting back to the then–Secretary of State his own lines from the Declaration in a plea for equal treatment. In 1813, James Forten, publishing anonymously his *Letters from a Man of Colour*, began his criticism of a Pennsylvania bill to limit the rights of free Blacks by asserting that "We hold this truth to be self-evident, that GOD created all men equal, and is one of the most prominent features in the Declaration of Independence."[11]

As the specter of slavery expanding across the continent grew, opposition mounted in the North, coalescing into an organized abolition movement. Black writers such as David Walker appealed to the Declaration and to Christianity in condemning the evil. Walker, born free in North Carolina and living in Boston, penned *An Appeal to the Colored Citizens of the World*, a fiery tract circulated in 1829 that helped inspire a more formal movement. "Compare your own language from your Declaration of Independence," Walker insisted, after quoting Jefferson's famous words on equality, "with your cruelties and murders inflicted by your cruel and unmerciful fathers and yourselves on our fathers and on us . . ."[12]

Walker's call for direct resistance, even insurrection, was too strong for many opposed to slavery and to the use of violence. One such was William Lloyd Garrison, who starting in 1831 published the abolitionist newspaper *The Liberator* in Boston. In December 1833, under Garrison's lead, abolitionists gathered in Philadelphia to establish the American Anti-Slavery Society. Seeking reform through moral suasion, Garrison's movement tackled political questions that were constitutional in nature by firmly attaching the Declaration to their cause.[13]

The twenty-eight-year-old Garrison composed the Society's 1833 platform, "A Declaration of Sentiments," whose title would be taken fifteen years later by Elizabeth Cady Stanton in her campaign for women's rights. Garrison lightly rephrased parts of Jefferson's document, writing of the Founders that "the corner-stone upon which they founded the Temple of Freedom was broadly this – 'that all men are created equal; that they are endowed by their Creator with certain inalienable rights; that among these are life, LIBERTY, and the pursuit of happiness.'" In his summation, Garrison vowed of the delegates that "we plant ourselves upon the Declaration of our Independence and the truths of Divine Revelation" before concluding with a Jeffersonian flourish and appeal to natural rights: "Submitting this Declaration to the candid examination of the people of this country, and of the friends of liberty throughout the world, we hereby affix our signatures to it; pledging ourselves that, under the guidance and by the help of Almighty God, we will do all that in us lies, consistently with this Declaration of our principles, to overthrow the most execrable system of slavery that has ever been witnessed upon earth."[14]

If Garrison and other abolitionists drew on the Declaration as the moral spirit of their quest, Southerners sought to justify their continued adherence to slavery by denying the document's central claim. Speaking on the Oregon Bill of 1848, which would have prohibited slavery in the territory encompassing the future States of Oregon, Washington, and Idaho, the powerful Senator John C. Calhoun of South Carolina thundered that the assertion that "all men are created equal" was "the most false and dangerous of all political errors." Six years after that, when the Missouri Compromise was undone by the 1854 Kansas-Nebraska Act, allowing new States to vote on whether to allow slavery, Senator John Pettit of Indiana echoed Calhoun's words, insisting that the Declaration's claim of equality was a "self-evident lie."[15]

Such attempts to denigrate the Declaration were widespread as America became ever more divided. But while the battle over slavery was fought largely on constitutional grounds, slavery's defenders often inverted the language and spirit of the Declaration. In 1857, a Southern clergyman named Frederick A. Ross wrote a book entitled *Slavery As Ordained of God*, denying Jefferson's natural rights theory: "God gives no sanction to the affirmation that he has *created all men equal*; that this is *self-evident*, and that he has given them *unalienable rights*," charged Ross. "All this—every word of it, every jot and tittle—is the liberty and equality claimed by infidelity . . . Sir, that paragraph is an *excrescence* on the tree of our liberty. I pray you take it away." Here was the Southern understanding of the "liberty" promised by the Declaration: the freedom to shape their society as they saw fit, including through the bondage of those deemed unequal.[16]

While Southerners sought to impose their own conception of liberty, which meant denying that the Declaration contained a message of universal equality, those opposed to slavery criticized the country's failure to live up to the document's promises. Among the most eloquent and influential of these critics was Frederick Douglass. Born enslaved in 1818 in Maryland, Douglass escaped from Baltimore in 1838, making his way to New York, where he came to know William Lloyd Garrison. Douglass wrote a bestselling *Narrative* of his life in 1845 and became the leading Black voice for the abolition of slavery.[17]

On July 5, 1852, Douglass gave an oration in front of six hundred people in Rochester, New York, in which he condemned the hypocrisy of those celebrating Independence Day while ignoring its core claims. "What, to the American slave, is your Fourth of July?" he famously asked. "I answer: a day that reveals to him, more than all other days in the year, the gross injustice and cruelty to which he is the constant victim." "Your prayers and hymns," Douglass continued, "your sermons and thanksgivings, with all your religious parade, and solemnity, are, to him, mere bombast, fraud, deception, impiety, and hypocrisy." He could not celebrate, for "This Fourth of July is yours, not mine. You may rejoice, I must mourn." And yet, believing in the promise of the Declaration, Douglass concluded with a hope that few felt at the time: "I do not despair of this country. There are forces in operation, which must inevitably work the downfall of slavery . . . While drawing encouragement from the Declaration of Independence, the great principles it contains, and the genius of American institutions, my spirit is also cheered by the obvious tendencies of the age."[18] Douglass's hope in the founding document powerfully contrasted with William Lloyd Garrison's more radical turn, marked by a public burning of the Constitution in 1854, a document Garrison called a "covenant with death."[19]

A portrait of Frederick Douglass in 1856, four years after his famous "What to the Slave Is the Fourth of July?" speech.

For the first time since 1776, the Declaration was embroiled directly in a political crisis, attacked by proponents of slavery for offering false promises and by opponents of slavery for failing to make true on its word. No longer did it float serenely above the political sphere, innocuously claimed by contending parties as it was in the old fights between Federalists and Jeffersonian Democratic-Republicans. The Declaration's very legitimacy was now questioned in a way that cut to the core of the American experiment.

But if the Declaration was now vulnerable to attacks, it also found defenders. Among them was a tall, lanky, and relatively unknown Illinois lawyer. After serving one term in the U.S. Congress, with his political career seemingly over, Abraham Lincoln had returned to practice law in Springfield, the state capital. It was the Kansas-Nebraska Act of 1854 that reignited his political passions.[20]

The brainchild of Senator Stephen Douglas, a fellow Illinoisan, the Act overturned the ban on slavery north of 36°30' agreed to in the 1820 Missouri Compromise. Instead, each territory would be allowed to vote on whether to be slave or free. This, claimed Douglas, was the exercise of "popular sovereignty," the consent of the governed promised in the Declaration. To Lincoln, it was an abomination that repudiated the founding principles of the United States. Those principles were expressed with crystal clarity in the Declaration of Independence, and it was on the Declaration that Lincoln now focused his incomparable moral compass and lyrical abilities.

Through his election as President in 1860, defense of the Declaration—as he understood it—was the animating force in Lincoln's public career. In speeches inveighing against the Kansas-Nebraska Act, the Supreme Court's *Dred Scott* decision, and in the debates he held with Douglas during their campaign for the U.S. Senate in 1858, Lincoln placed the Declaration at the center of his governing philosophy. Never before had Jefferson's document animated the core of a coherent and militant political program, helping make Lincoln the "redeemer president," in the words of a later historian.[21]

On October 16, 1854, in Peoria, Illinois, Lincoln gave his main reply to the passage of the Kansas-Nebraska Act, warning his listeners, "Let no one be deceived. The spirit of seventy-six and the spirit of Nebraska, are utter antagonisms." Lincoln ridiculed those justifying human bondage, denying any legitimacy to the claims "that for SOME MEN to enslave OTHERS is a 'sacred right of self-government.'" Support for slavery threatened the legitimacy of democratic equality, "because it forces so many really good men amongst ourselves into an open war with the very fundamental principles of civil liberty—criticizing the Declaration of Independence, and insisting that there is no right principle of action but *self-interest*." Lincoln ended his attack on Douglas's Act by urging "Let us re-adopt the Declaration of Independence, and with it, the practices, and policy, which harmonize with it." It was a position he held fast to as the crisis deepened.[22]

Three years later, Lincoln was even more exercised by the Supreme Court's *Dred Scott* ruling. Held in bondage in Missouri, Scott had sued for his freedom based on brief residence in Free States, including Illinois. In a 7–2 decision, the Court decided that Scott and his family were to remain enslaved. However, driven by the pro-slavery convictions of Chief Justice Roger Taney of Maryland, the Court went farther than the case before it, ruling that the Declaration of Independence did not, and had never intended to, include Blacks in its claim of equality. Instead, the Court decreed, they could not be citizens but only be considered as property. For Lincoln, this was a defilement of the Declaration's clear intent.[23]

At a speech given in Springfield, Illinois, on June 26, 1857, he fought to redeem the Declaration from its mutilation at the hands of the Court. "In those days," he charged, harking back to the Founding, "the Declaration of Independence was held sacred by all, and thought to include all; but now, to aid in making the bondage of the negro universal and eternal, it is assailed, and sneered at, and construed, and hawked at, and torn, till, if its framers could rise from their graves, they could not at all recognize it." Lincoln linked the damage done by Taney's *Dred Scott* case to Douglas's equally illegitimate Kansas-Nebraska Act, indicting "both the Chief Justice and the Senator, for doing this obvious violence to the plain unmistakable language of the Declaration."

So far, Lincoln had defended the Declaration on conventional grounds, if passionately. Now, however, he introduced into the mainstream political debate a position that previously had been made by abolitionists, including Black abolitionists like David Walker. This began a fundamental transformation of the meaning of the Declaration, one that would reshape the ideals of the document in the minds of Americans, and indeed the world. The Declaration, Lincoln explained, may have been written primarily to justify revolution, but its philosophy went far beyond the exigencies of 1776. "The assertion that 'all men are created equal' was of no practical use in effecting our separation from Great Britain," claimed

Lincoln. In reality, he continued, that assertion "was placed in the Declaration, not for that, but for future use [as] a stumbling block to those who in after times might seek to turn a free people back into the hateful paths of despotism." Slavery was despotism and the Declaration was a clarion call for liberty and equality, in Lincoln's formulation. It held universally, for all races.[24]

Fired with indignation at the harm being done to the American ethos, Lincoln decided to challenge Douglas for the U.S. Senate seat from Illinois. Their debates over the summer of 1858 would go down as one of the great philosophical battles in American political history. During the campaign, Lincoln was forced to deflect questions on whether, in arguing that Blacks had equal human rights to Whites, he agitated for full civil equality and the mixing of the races, and thus whether he truly believed in the standard set by the Declaration.[25] Yet throughout, he held to his fundamental belief in the promises of 1776.

In a July speech in Chicago the month before his first debate with Douglas, Lincoln celebrated the "electric cord in that Declaration that links the hearts of patriotic and liberty-loving men together, that will link those patriotic hearts as long as the love of freedom exists in the minds of men throughout the world." In this same speech Lincoln also asserted that new immigrants have as much claim on the moral principle of equality as the first settlers, noting they were "blood of the blood, and flesh of the flesh of the men who wrote that Declaration."[26] Lincoln lost the senatorial election to Douglas that fall, but through his unrelenting defense of the Declaration, he had become a leading voice on the slavery issue.

In February 1860, Lincoln gave a speech at New York's Cooper Union that cemented his position as a national figure. The main issue he addressed was the question of the expansion of slavery into Free States and Federal territory. In front of nearly fifteen hundred listeners, Lincoln asserted that his position was no different from George Washington's, reminding his listeners that Washington had approved the ban on slavery in the Northwest Territory and noting the first President's "hope that we should at some time have a confederacy of free States." At the same time, Lincoln took pains to deny that his Republican Party sought to eradicate slavery in the South or provoke insurrection among slaves. Coming on the heels of John Brown's bloody failed attempt in October 1859 to take over the Harper's Ferry arsenal and spark a slave rebellion, Lincoln's logical refutation of the argument that the Constitution included "the right of property in a slave" only helped convince Southerners that he was in reality a radical abolitionist.[27]

Heading into the 1860 presidential election, Lincoln had stage-managed an unprecedented political resurgence, just two years after first contending for major office. Skillful maneuvering at the Republican National Convention in Chicago vaulted him above the heavily favored William Seward to become the party's presidential nominee. That November, he bested Stephen Douglas and two others in the presidential election, bringing the young Republican Party its first national victory.[28] Yet due in no small part to his passionate stance on slavery, Lincoln's election hastened the division of the nation. Southern States had tarred him as a "Black Republican" during the campaign, though he had done his best to assure them that he sought not to abolish slavery, but only to prevent its further spread. All was in vain. Lincoln's victory in November 1860 was the signal for the secession of South Carolina the following month.[29]

This was the great nightmare of American statesmen since 1776, one they had striven to avoid by any means. The need for unanimity had driven John Adams during the Continental Congress, secured the controversial three-fifths clause in the Constitution, and forced James Madison to tamp down New England separatism in the lead-up to the War of 1812. The compromises of 1820 and 1854, wise and foolish in turn, had been taken in an effort to keep the Union together in the face of irreconcilable differences over slavery.

Now the moment of division had come. Yet even as it sought to sever ties with the rest of the United States, South Carolina defended its decision by invoking the language and promise of the Declaration. On December 24, the state's legislature published a "Declaration of the Immediate Causes Which Induce and Justify the Secession," which directly relied on Jefferson's political argument. "Having resumed her separate and equal place among nations," South Carolina reminded Americans and the world that the Founders "solemnly declared that whenever any 'form of government becomes destructive of the ends for which it was established, it is the right of the people to alter or abolish it, and to institute a new government' . . . In pursuance of this Declaration of Independence, each of the thirteen States proceeded to exercise its separate sovereignty . . ." Now reclaiming that sovereignty, the Palmetto State would act "with full power to levy war, conclude peace, contract alliances, establish commerce, and to do all other acts and things which independent States may of right do."[30]

South Carolina's proclamation stripped Jefferson's phrases down to what Lincoln called the "merely revolutionary" reading of the Declaration: State sovereignty as the fundamental axiom of American politics. On this narrow, reductionist view, the core of the Declaration was its assertion that government

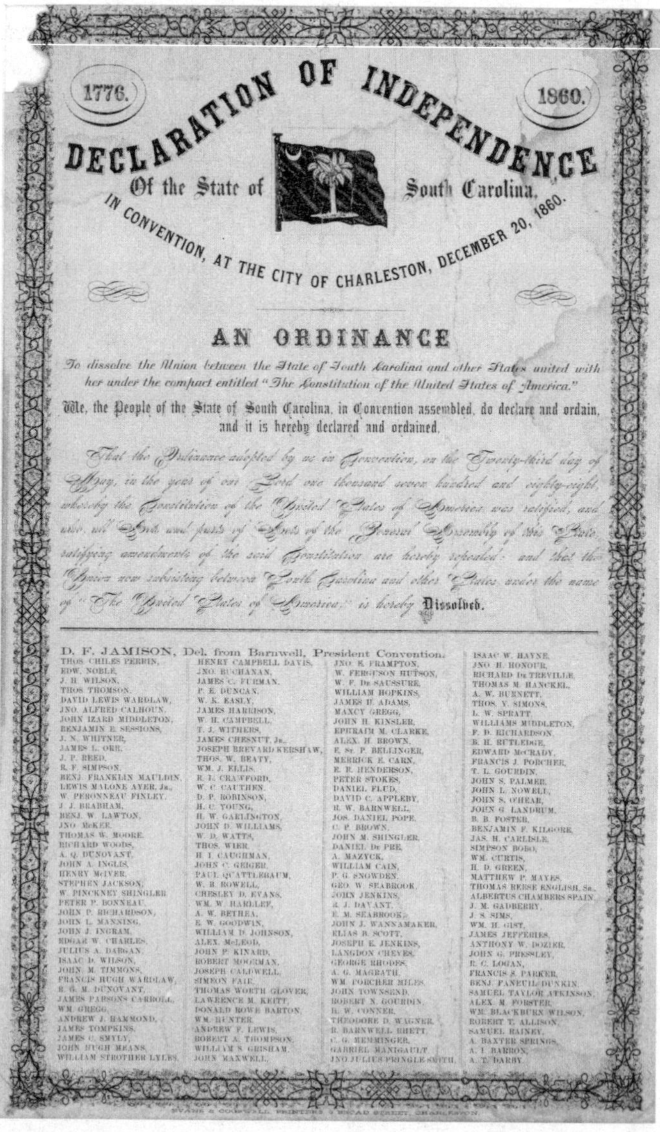

1776. 1860.

DECLARATION OF INDEPENDENCE

Of the State of South Carolina,

IN CONVENTION, AT THE CITY OF CHARLESTON, DECEMBER 20, 1860.

AN ORDINANCE

To dissolve the Union between the State of South Carolina and other States united with her under the compact entitled "The Constitution of the United States of America."

We, the People of the State of South Carolina, in Convention assembled, do declare and ordain, and it is hereby declared and ordained,

That the Ordinance adopted by us in Convention, on the Twenty-third day of May, in the year of our Lord one thousand seven hundred and eighty-eight, whereby the Constitution of the United States of America was ratified, and also, all Acts and parts of Acts of the General Assembly of this State ratifying amendments of the said Constitution, are hereby repealed; and that the Union now subsisting between South Carolina and other States, under the name of "The United States of America," is hereby Dissolved.

D. F. JAMISON, Del. from Barnwell, President Convention.

THOS. CHILES PERRIN, EDW. NOBLE, J. H. WILSON, THOS. THOMSON, DAVID LEWIS WARDLAW, JNO. ALFRED CALHOUN, JOHN IZARD MIDDLETON, BENJAMIN E. SESSIONS, J. N. WHITNER, JAMES L. ORR, J. P. REED, R. F. SIMPSON, BENJ. FRANKLIN MAULDIN, LEWIS MALONE AYER, Jr., W. PERONNEAU FINLEY, J. J. BRABHAM, BENJ. W. LAWTON, JNO. McKEE, THOMAS W. MOORE, RICHARD WOODS, A. Q. DUNOVANT, JOHN A. INGLIS, HENRY McIVER, STEPHEN JACKSON, W. PINCKNEY SHINGLER, PETER P. BONNEAU, JOHN P. RICHARDSON, JOHN L. MANNING, JOHN J. INGRAM, EDGAR W. CHARLES, JULIUS A. DARGAN, ISAAC D. WILSON, JOHN M. TIMMONS, FRANCIS HUGH WARDLAW, R. G. M. DUNOVANT, JAMES PARSONS CARROLL, WM. GREGG, ANDREW J. HAMMOND, JAMES TOMPKINS, JAMES C. SMYLY, JOHN HUGH MEANS, WILLIAM STROTHER LYLES,

HENRY CAMPBELL DAVIS, JNO. BUCHANAN, JAMES C. FURMAN, P. E. DUNCAN, W. K. EASLY, JAMES HARRISON, W. H. CAMPBELL, T. J. WITHERS, JAMES CHESNUT, Jr., JOSEPH BREVARD KERSHAW, THOS. W. BEATY, WM. J. ELLIS, R. L. CRAWFORD, W. C. CAUTHEN, D. P. ROBINSON, H. C. YOUNG, H. W. GARLINGTON, JOHN D. WILLIAMS, W. D. WATTS, THOS. WIER, H. I. CAUGHMAN, JOHN C. GEIGER, PAUL QUATTLEBAUM, W. B. ROWELL, CHESLEY D. EVANS, WM. W. HARLLEE, A. W. BETHEA, E. W. GOODWIN, WILLIAM D. JOHNSON, ALEX. McLEOD, JOHN P. KINARD, ROBERT MOORMAN, JOSEPH CALDWELL, SIMEON FAIR, THOMAS WORTH GLOVER, LAWRENCE M. KEITT, DONALD ROWE BARTON, WM. HUNTER, ANDREW F. LEWIS, ROBERT A. THOMPSON, WILLIAM S. GRISHAM, JOHN MAXWELL,

JNO. E. FRAMPTON, W. FERGUSON HUTSON, W. F. De SAUSSURE, WILLIAM HOPKINS, JAMES H. ADAMS, MAXCY GREGG, JOHN H. KINSLER, EPHRAIM M. CLARKE, ALEX. H. BROWN, E. St. P. BELLINGER, MERRICK E. CARN, E. R. HENDERSON, PETER STOKES, DANIEL FLUD, DAVID C. APPLEBY, R. W. BARNWELL, JOS. DANIEL POPE, C. P. BROWN, JOHN M. SHINGLER, DANIEL De PRE, A. MAZYCK, WILLIAM CAIN, P. G. SNOWDEN, GEO. W. SEABROOK, JOHN JENKINS, R. J. DAVANT, E. M. SEABROOK, JOHN J. WANNAMAKER, ELIAS B. SCOTT, JOSEPH E. JENKINS, LANGDON CHEVES, GEORGE RHODES, A. G. MAGRATH, WM. PORCHER MILES, JOHN TOWNSEND, ROBERT N. GOURDIN, H. W. CONNER, THEODORE D. WAGNER, R. BARNWELL RHETT, C. G. MEMMINGER, GABRIEL MANIGAULT, JNO. JULIUS PRINGLE SMITH,

ISAAC W. HAYNE, JNO. H. HONOUR, RICHARD De TREVILLE, THOMAS M. HANCKEL, A. W. BURNETT, THOS. Y. SIMONS, L. W. SPRATT, WILLIAMS MIDDLETON, F. D. RICHARDSON, B. H. RUTLEDGE, EDWARD McCRADY, FRANCIS J. PORCHER, T. L. GOURDIN, JOHN S. PALMER, JOHN L. NOWELL, JOHN S. O'HEAR, JOHN G. LANDRUM, B. B. FOSTER, BENJAMIN F. KILGORE, JAS. H. CARLISLE, SIMPSON BOBO, WM. CURTIS, H. D. GREEN, MATTHEW P. MAYES, THOMAS REESE ENGLISH, Sr., ALBERTUS CHAMBERS SPAIN, J. M. GADBERRY, J. S. SIMS, WM. H. GIST, JAMES JEFFERIES, ANTHONY W. DOZIER, JOHN G. PRESSLEY, R. C. LOGAN, FRANCIS S. PARKER, BENJ. FANEUIL DUNKIN, SAMUEL TAYLOR ATKINSON, ALEX. M. FORSTER, WM. BLACKBURN WILSON, ROBERT T. ALLISON, SAMUEL RAINEY, A. BAXTER SPRINGS, A. I. BARRON, A. T. DARBY.

EVANS & COGSWELL, PRINTERS, 3 BROAD STREET, CHARLESTON.

A convention of South Carolina delegates declared independence from the Union in December 1860, basing their claims on Jefferson's document and its appeal to the consent of the governed. Ten other Southern states joined South Carolina and formed the Confederate States of America the following year.

derived its just powers from the consent of the governed. Thus, if the people of South Carolina withdrew their consent, did not the Declaration defend their right to do so? Even some Northern voices acknowledged the Southern position. On November 21, 1860, just weeks after Lincoln's election, the *Cincinnati Daily Press* had written, "We believe that the right of any member of this Confederacy [the United States] to dissolve its political relations with the others and assume an independent position is absolute . . . This we suppose to be the doctrine of the Declaration of Independence," though the paper justified instituting a new government only if done through peaceful means.[31]

While all within the Southern camp agreed on the question of consent of the governed as a justification for secession, they were not united over how to interpret the Declaration's statement of equality. One position was expressed by Jefferson Davis, U.S. Senator from Mississippi and the acknowledged leader of Southern interests in Congress. On January 21, 1861, two weeks after Mississippi joined South Carolina and seceded from the Union, Davis gave his Farewell Address to the Senate. In it, he repeated Chief Justice Taney's *Dred Scott* argument that the Declaration did not include Black men in its assertion that all were created equal.

Acknowledging that "the sacred Declaration of Independence has been invoked to maintain the position of the equality of the races," Davis argued that such was an incorrect reading of the document. "That Declaration of Independence is to be construed by the circumstances and purposes for which it was made," which he asserted were far more limited. "The communities were declaring their independence; the people of those communities were asserting that no man was born—to use the language of Mr. Jefferson—booted and spurred to ride over the rest of mankind; that men were created equal—meaning the men of the political community; . . . these were the purposes for which they made their declaration; . . . They have no reference to the slave." Davis was about to be elected as President of the Confederacy, and his view reflected the majority opinion in the South.[32]

A different Southern position was taken by the man who became Davis's Vice President, Alexander Stephens. A former Representative from Georgia, Stephens ardently defended slavery but counseled against secession. On March 21, 1861, just weeks before hostilities broke out, he offered a different reading of the Declaration from Jefferson Davis's. Stephens would agree with Abraham Lincoln's interpretation, but he drew from it very different conclusions.

In the address, which came to be known as the "Cornerstone Speech,"

Stephens acknowledged that the Declaration indeed saw all races as equal. "The prevailing ideas entertained by [Jefferson] and most of the leading statesmen at the time of the formation of the old constitution," Stephens admitted, "were that the enslavement of the African was in violation of the laws of nature; that it was wrong in principle, socially, morally, and politically. It was an evil they knew not well how to deal with, but the general opinion of the men of that day was that, somehow or other in the order of Providence, the institution would be evanescent and pass away." Stephens now shifted tack, arguing that "Those ideas, however, were fundamentally wrong. They rested upon the assumption of the equality of races. This was an error." The Declaration and Lincoln thus were in agreement, according to Stephens, but were incorrect. The Declaration was, on this view, illegitimate, and therefore could not command loyalty.[33]

There could be no answer to this fundamental disagreement by the time Lincoln arrived in Washington to take office in March. Yet South Carolina and Mississippi no longer stood alone: they had been joined in secession by Florida, Alabama, Georgia, Louisiana, and Texas. On February 8, 1861, they formally declared themselves the Confederate States of America, with a new capital, in Montgomery, Alabama.[34]

A few months later, the Confederates gained an unlikely ally. The Cherokee Nation, who held thousands of Black slaves, declared themselves "a free people, independent of the Northern States of America, and at war with them by their own act." Beginning their declaration with a paraphrase of Jefferson's opening lines, they observed that the Confederacy "claimed only the privilege asserted by the American Declaration of Independence . . . of altering their form of government when it became no longer tolerable," while in the North, the Cherokee "saw with alarm a violated Constitution, all civil liberty put in peril." Thus believing that "their interests and their destiny are inseparably connected with those of the South," the Cherokee condemned the "war of Northern cupidity and fanaticism against the institutions of African servitude; against the commercial freedom of the South, and against the political freedom of the States . . ."[35]

Two weeks after the formation of the Confederacy in February, Abraham Lincoln stopped in Philadelphia, on his long rail journey from Illinois to Washington, D.C., for his inauguration. In the face of a country coming apart, he proceeded to Independence Hall, the old Pennsylvania State House. Coming to the spot where the Declaration had been signed nearly eighty-five years previously filled him with "deep emotion," he told the crowd. Though he was

HARPER'S WEEKLY.

A JOURNAL OF CIVILIZATION.

Vol. V.—No. 219.] NEW YORK, SATURDAY, MARCH 9, 1861. [Price Five Cents.

Entered according to Act of Congress, in the Year 1861, by Harper & Brothers, in the Clerk's Office of the District Court for the Southern District of New York.

PRESIDENT LINCOLN HOISTING THE AMERICAN FLAG WITH THIRTY-FOUR STARS UPON INDEPENDENCE HALL, PHILADELPHIA, FEBRUARY 22, 1861.

From Photographs by F. D. Richards, Philadelphia.—[See next Page.]

President-elect Abraham Lincoln raising the American flag at Independence Hall on February 22, 1861. During his speech, Lincoln indicated he would rather be assassinated than surrender the principles of the Declaration. (*Harper's Weekly*) just days away from taking an oath to uphold the Constitution, he confided to the cheering spectators, "I have never had a feeling politically that did not spring from the sentiments embodied in the Declaration of Independence."[36]

To his Philadelphia audience Lincoln once again invested the document with the broader meaning that he had attached to it after the *Dred Scott* case. The scroll's importance "was not the mere matter of the separation of the colonies from the mother land; but something in that Declaration giving liberty, not alone to the people of this country, but hope to the world for all future time . . . that *all* should have an equal chance." But that hope had never been more threatened, Lincoln acknowledged, asking, "Now, my friends, can this country be saved upon that basis?"

Lincoln's next words were spoken in full knowledge that he was about to pass into Maryland, a Southern State where rumors of plots against his life had been reaching his ears for months: "But if this country cannot be saved without giving up that principle—I was about to say I would rather be assassinated on this spot than to surrender it." In no starker way could Lincoln have tied his very life to the survival of the ideals of the Declaration of Independence as he understood them. The words would come to haunt those who remembered them a few terrible years hence.

Sometime in between his election and inauguration, Lincoln composed a fragment of a speech in which he lyrically and metaphorically expressed his deepest feeling about the Declaration. Employing an image from Proverbs 25, he wrote that the Constitution, and even the Union:

> are not the primary cause of our great prosperity. There is something back of these, entwining itself more closely about the human heart. That something is the principle of "liberty to all"—the principle that clears the path for all— . . . The expression of that principle, in our Declaration of Independence, was most happy and fortunate . . . The assertion of that principle . . . has proved an "apple of gold" to us. The Union and the Constitution are the picture of silver, subsequently framed around it. The picture was made not to conceal or destroy the apple but to adorn, and preserve it. The picture was made for the apple—not the apple for the picture . . . So let us act, that neither picture or apple shall ever be blurred or bruised or broken.[37]

Lincoln would spend the rest of his few years striving to protect that apple and to preserve the Union.

Chapter 11
The Last Civil War Mystery

On Saturday, April 13, 1861, students at the University of Virginia, in Charlottesville, held a parade and military display. Later that day, the Jefferson Literary and Debating Society, founded in 1825, hosted an oration and then a crowd assembled for the highlight of the day, a reading of the Declaration of Independence. It was the 118th anniversary of Thomas Jefferson's birth, and the festivities were an annual occurrence on the campus, which had been created by Jefferson in 1819.

As a Mr. Chauncey recited the Declaration in Charlottesville, U.S. soldiers were huddling under a hailstorm of cannon shot in Fort Sumter, 375 miles to the south in South Carolina. Nearly thirty-six hours earlier, the forces of P. G. T. Beauregard, commanding general of the military of the Confederate States of America, had unleashed the bombardment against the tiny island in the mouth of Charleston Harbor, ultimately firing three thousand shells at the Union fortification.

At two thirty in the afternoon, Major Robert Anderson of the U.S. Army formally surrendered, though he only would admit to "evacuating" his eighty-five men, none of whom, miraculously, had been killed. While the students at the University of Virginia celebrated Thomas Jefferson's birth, the country he had helped call into existence descended into civil war.[1]

A few days later, Washington, D.C., prepared for attack. Though Virginia still wavered between loyalty and secession, Washington already felt like a frontline city. President Lincoln, in office barely a month, called for seventy-five thousand Union troops to protect the capital and suppress the Southern rebellion. Later he would describe Washington as having been "put into the condition of a siege." A Confederate attack was expected at any time.[2]

While the President began planning a response to Fort Sumter, Washingtonians nervously awaited news of a Confederate move on the capital. Washington was a Southern city, sandwiched between two Slave States and filled with thousands of Confederate sympathizers, who were likely a majority of the roughly seventy thousand residents. There was no defense strategy in place for the capital and in these first days of war, little to no coordination of any effort to prepare for an assault. No Union troops had reached the city. Only those soldiers already there, numbering perhaps fifteen hundred, could be called on to defend the White House, the still-unfinished Capitol, and other important public buildings.

Seven blocks east of the White House stretched the massive bulk of the Patent Office. Since the Declaration had arrived there in 1841, two large wings had been added and an even larger fourth wing was under construction. Inside its thick walls were tens of thousands of patent models, hundreds of thousands of pages of records, and what remained of the collection of the National Institute. In 1857, most of the natural history collection had been transferred to the Smithsonian Institution's just-completed redbrick "castle" across the National Mall. Yet the Patent Office refused to surrender the objects connected with American history. These remained in the second-floor gallery, still in their old cases, ogled by visitors to the building, but now with no one responsible for their safety.[3]

Foremost among these relics was the Declaration of Independence. It had hung quietly in the vast exhibition hall, exposed to sunlight, for two decades, gazed at by thousands of visitors. If there was a treasure house in Washington, the Patent Office was it. It would have been a prime target for any invading force, as burning the records there could throw the Union economy into chaos. Even more symbolically, capturing or destroying the Declaration would have been a blow to Northern morale and a coup for the Confederacy.

There were few troops and fewer weapons to guard the Patent Office, but in those early, fraught days of civil war, a makeshift defense force suddenly emerged. Colonel Ambrose Burnside, a burly, thirty-six-year-old Rhode Islander distinguished by his prominent whiskers, had some soldiers at his disposal. He organized these troops, along with the roughly five hundred employees of the Patent Office, into an "Interior Guard." Night after night, Burnside's makeshift defenders patrolled the long halls, passing by the Declaration in its fragile frame.[4]

Though no Confederate invasion materialized in April 1861, the priceless scroll would remain at risk throughout the four years of war. What happened to the Declaration during the bloodiest conflict on American soil remains one of the last great mysteries of the Civil War.

When Ambrose Burnside organized his Interior Guard to patrol the Patent Office, he was improvising a defense strategy in a largely defenseless capital. Washington at the beginning of the war was a sleepy Southern town. Except for Pennsylvania Avenue, its streets were dirt roads. Impressive buildings like the Patent Office and Capitol were surrounded by ramshackle structures, outbuildings, row houses, and hovels. The capital's population of 70,000 or so included over 11,000 free Blacks and more than 3,000 slaves. A small upper-class slice of society frequented balls, soirees, and promenades, while the majority of residents worked at professional or menial jobs in and around the federal government.

After the attack on Fort Sumter, Washington became the nerve center of the Union war machine. Within days of the outbreak of war *The New York Herald* reported that Washington was "rapidly assuming the aspect of a vast military camp. The streets are crowded with regulars and volunteers, and warlike din resounds in every direction."[5] An initial panic broke out when mobs in Baltimore, abetted by Maryland authorities, had tried to prevent the first militia companies sent by Massachusetts and New York from reaching the capital. Soon, however, troops poured in. Even as the government welcomed the relief, Washington remained a city unprepared either to host Union forces or repel Confederate ones.

At the end of April, the Virginia Secession Convention had voted to join its Southern neighbors and leave the Union. On May 24, 1861, the people of Virginia ratified the decision to secede, and on June 1, Colonel Robert E. Lee took command of the Army of Northern Virginia, having rebuffed President Lincoln's offer to head up all Union forces and resigned his commission in the U.S. Army. Instantly, the capital became a frontline city, facing the enemy just across the Potomac River. Worse, it was in a terrible defensive position.

The Potomac could be forded from the Virginia side a few dozen miles upriver, past the Great Falls, while three bridges gave access to the heart of the city across the river's wide, flat tidal sweep. To the north, the gently rising Piedmont Plateau in Maryland left the city equally vulnerable to attack. The only permanent defensive post near the national capital was Fort Washington, twenty miles south of the White House, high above the Potomac across from Mount Vernon. Built originally in 1809, Fort Washington had been strengthened in 1812 to prevent a British naval attack from the Chesapeake Bay.

As soon as Virginia seceded, seventy-four-year-old Lieutenant General Winfield Scott, hero of the Mexican War and commander of the U.S. Army, went to President Lincoln and recommended that he occupy Arlington Heights, directly across the Potomac from Washington. Lincoln approved, and Union troops moved across the river, where army engineers directed them in building the first defenses and fortifications. Within six months, under the leadership of Major John Gross Barnard, a comprehensive system of interlocking defenses was constructed. Eventually, Washington would be ringed by 68 forts and 93 batteries, along with 20 miles of infantry trenches and 32 miles of military roads, among the most extensive fortifications ever built for a national capital. Nine hundred cannon and mortars were mounted to defend the approaches to the city.[6]

During these frenetic months, the Declaration of Independence hung quietly in the Patent Office. Yet the war and the activity consuming Washington swirled around it in ways not immediately appreciated by those rushing to defend the capital. As the crisis deepened, it should have been obvious that the nation's founding charter, a source of inspiration and legitimacy for both sides, was in a dangerously vulnerable location.

An unexpected threat came from the very forces supposedly protecting Washington. There were no barracks available nor were camps laid out for the thousands of troops flooding the city. Hastily mustered men from New York, Pennsylvania, Massachusetts, and Rhode Island in ill-fitting blue uniforms pitched tents and laid out fields for military drilling on the National Mall and in open spaces throughout the city. Others threw down mattresses in the Capitol and took over the campus buildings of Georgetown College, among other places. Within weeks of the outbreak of war the First Rhode Island Regiment, placed under the command of Ambrose Burnside, set up their barracks in the Patent Office.

While the Union troops should have given a sense of safety to the capital, many wondered if they were not more of a menace than the Confederates would have been. Arguing that "great armies are great evils," the *New-York Tribune* reported from the capital early in the war that "the streets of this city, from day to day and night after night, are filled with drunken, riotous, quarrelsome soldiers, who are permitted to crowd saloons and hotels, and to engage in brawls . . . Fights are frequent and bloody."[7]

Such behavior was brought into the makeshift camps and barracks at night, including in the Patent Office, where Burnside's Rhode Island Volunteers remained housed through July. When they finally were mustered out, the building was "ruined with their filth," according to a story in *The Philadelphia Inquirer* that graphically quoted Confederate Vice President Alexander Stephens, whose claims might have been dismissed as propaganda had others not reported the same.[8] As early as May, *Scientific American* magazine noted that the Rhode Islanders had broken the glass panes of four hundred cases and stolen an unknown number of patent models.[9] With no National Institute staff left to guard the treasures in the upstairs gallery, they were the most vulnerable of the items stored in the building.

Union casualties mounted throughout the summer, straining the capital's medical resources. As one of Washington's largest buildings, the Patent Office had space that was vitally needed. In September it became a military hospital, crammed with three thousand beds. The poet Walt Whitman, who volunteered in the hospital during the war, left a vivid description of the scene: " . . . that noblest of Washington buildings was crowded close with rows of sick, badly wounded and dying soldiers . . . The glass cases, the beds, the forms lying there, the gallery above, the marble pave-ment under foot—the suffering, and the fortitude to bear it . . ."[10] Patients, medical staff, visitors, and soldiers roamed freely through the halls.

A second danger lurked in the shadows. Despite being the federal capital, Washington was filled with sympathizers. Rumors swirled that Confederate agents moved freely through its streets, hatching plots to kidnap or murder the President and his Cabinet, take over the Capitol and Treasury, and dismember the government. General Scott warned that " . . . machinations against the Government & this Capital, are secretly going on, all around us—" while Lincoln's personal secretary, John G. Nicolay, wrote his wife that "We were not only surrounded by the enemy, but in the midst of traitors."[11] Just as Robert E. Lee was forced to choose between his country and his state, Washingtonians were dividing into loyalists and secessionists.

It was difficult to know who could be relied on. The city's own District Attorney was a secessionist and Rose O'Neale Greenhow, a Washington socialite, passed to the Confederates military intelligence picked up at the parties she hosted. Not even the officers and men of the District of Columbia militia could be trusted.[12] Spies were roaming throughout the city and one of the leading targets in Washington for any covert action was the Patent Office. An arsonist determined to sow chaos by destroying patent models and records would likely have caught up everything inside the building in his path. Saboteurs eager to demoralize Lincoln and his supporters could easily have targeted the Declaration for theft or mutilation.

Such was not idle speculation, for in June soldiers from the Rhode Island First Regiment captured a spy skulking around the Patent Office. A few days later, they observed the same spy among the ranks of a Pennsylvania regiment and arrested him again.[13] With all the comings and goings at the Patent Office, agents could easily have made their way to the second-floor gallery and targeted the Declaration. A late-night operation could have reduced it to shreds or seen it spirited out of Washington, only to reappear in Richmond, the Confederate capital, as the most prized booty of the war.

The most obvious danger to the scroll was the threat of a Confederate attack on the capital. Washingtonians who had been in the city in August 1814 could well remember the damage wrought by the British. The Confederates could invade with far more men, bringing even greater devastation. Though no attack had materialized in April, by July fears again were on the rise, as shown in an article from the *Memphis Appeal* reprinted in the capital's *Daily National Intelligencer*. "The Confederates can take Washington when they [like]," the writer noted with seeming glee, "which would inevitably have to be followed by the destruction of all the public property within its limits."[14]

These fears took on epic proportions after the rout of Union forces at Manassas on July 21, 1861, in the Battle of Bull Run, the first major clash of the war. Washingtonians flocked "in stylish carriages, others in city hacks, and still others in buggies, on horseback and even on foot," many packing picnic baskets, to watch what they assumed would be a thrashing of the Confederates that would bring the conflict to a speedy close.[15]

Instead of a resounding victory, the poorly trained Union soldiers were outmaneuvered by an equally ill-prepared Confederate force and driven from the field, at a cost of forty-seven hundred dead and wounded on both sides.

As Federal troops fled back to the capital in disarray, panic seized Washington. Over the next weeks, nearly everyone thought the city was in for a Confederate attack. "Many soldiers had deserted and the streets of Washington were crowded with straggling officers and men, absent from their stations without authority," wrote General George B. McClellan, who was given command of Union forces after the defeat.[16] Most believed that Southern sympathizers in the capital and Maryland were prepared to join General Robert E. Lee's forces when they made their inevitable move on the city. "Is Washington Safe?" worried *The Boston Post*, while *The New York Herald* confidently informed its readers that Lee "intends to direct his force upon the upper Potomac, . . . Once there, he will be joined by the secessionists, who are secretly organizing all over Maryland, and will then attack Washington on its unfortified and defenceless side . . ." Lee would then capture the city, "archives . . . and all."[17]

Not since the British approached Washington in 1814 was the Declaration in as much danger.

Here we must pause our narrative. Every history of the Declaration of Independence without exception states definitively that the engrossed parchment was kept in the Patent Office, hung on public display from 1841 through 1876. From William H. Michael's 1904 government-sponsored volume to Dumas Malone's 1954 history and official publications of the National Archives, it has never been suggested that the Declaration was stored anywhere but the Patent Office from the day Daniel Webster sent it over to the moment that it left Washington for the Philadelphia Centennial Exposition thirty-five years later.[18]

But is it true that the Declaration remained hanging on the walls of the Patent Office throughout the four years of the Civil War? Our account of the dangers in wartime Washington should at least raise doubts. Is there a missing chapter in the history of the Declaration?

In the manner of a prosecutor making a case, let the following questions be put before a jury of readers:

- Would Abraham Lincoln, who made the Declaration the centerpiece of his entire political philosophy, leave it unprotected during the most dangerous period in American history?
- With public knowledge of the damage inflicted on the Patent Office building and its collections by barracked troops, and with thousands of wounded soldiers, medical staff, and visitors wandering the halls freely, would the State Department have risked leaving the Declaration exposed for four years?
- With the certain knowledge that Confederate sympathizers, spies, and saboteurs were actively plotting in Washington, and with no staff to watch over the collection, is it likely that Lincoln's government would have allowed the country's most precious document to remain so unprotected?
- Finally, in the dark days of July 1861, after the crushing defeat of Union forces at Bull Run, when fears of a Southern invasion of the capital ran rampant, resurrecting memories of the British burning of Washington in 1814, is it credible that Lincoln and his officials would have done nothing to protect the document encapsulating the ideal for which they were fighting?

These questions having been submitted to a candid world, some may dismiss them as merely of antiquarian interest. Yet in the long life of the Declaration, this missing piece of the story is more than just a diversion. To Abraham Lincoln, the war to save the Union was a war to defend the American principle of freedom. And that principle, for Lincoln, was embodied in the Declaration of Independence. Never before had the symbolic importance of the Declaration risen so high. If it was important enough for James Monroe to urge that it be saved in 1814, how much more critical would it have been to Lincoln in 1861?

No contemporary account records that the Declaration was moved from the Patent Office. But it seems hard to believe that the fragile scroll was left hanging undefended on a wall in a building that had become a hospital ward seven long blocks from the White House. Those in Washington during the early days of war would not have been surprised to learn the Declaration had been secreted away. In fact, even before the defeat at Bull Run, rumors briefly flew around the capital that the Declaration and other vital documents were evacuated from the city. On July 12, the

Daily National Intelligencer repeated a Southern report that "the Lincoln Government is already clandestinely removing the national archives to Philadelphia" in sealed rail cars. While this rumor was quickly dispelled, such a move would have made eminent sense.[19]

As the idea for an adventure story, Lincoln secretly moving the Declaration out of wartime Washington has great appeal, but there is little evidence to support it. Nevertheless, for the first time, we can offer a fact-based alternative explanation for what might have happened to the Declaration during the Civil War. Thanks to the digitization of long-forgotten newspapers and guidebooks, we can now search more widely than before and dig through scattered reports, letters, and descriptions. Such a search reveals tantalizing evidence, both direct and indirect, that the Declaration was removed from the Patent Office and protected from the risk of capture or destruction.

Marshalling the evidence, our revisionist history goes something like this:

For three months after the outbreak of war, the Declaration remained on the wall in the National Gallery of the Patent Office. It stayed there until just days after the defeat at Bull Run. We know it was there until the battle, based on a recollection of the Reverend J. B. Wakeley, who saw it in the Patent Office the weekend before the Army of the Potomac marched off to Bull Run. In an 1873 article, Wakeley recounted that on the last Sabbath that the Army spent in Washington, he visited the Patent Office, where he "stumbled upon the original Declaration of Independence . . . it was very much faded." It made such an impression on the good reverend during this trying time of war that he wept tears of joy at the sight.[20]

Yet just a few weeks later, the Declaration was conspicuously missing from the treasures of Washington recounted in a "Soldier's Letter," printed on August 9, 1861, in the *Jamestown Journal*. In his letter, the young soldier expressed his awe at the sights, from the Capitol and White House to the Washington Monument. Of particular note was the Patent Office, where he explained "you can see a model of every patent yet issued—from a buckle to a steam engine . . . But I will not attempt to enumerate the many things to be seen, for it is impossible." One might well have expected this perceptive visitor to have singled out the Declaration, as did Reverend Wakeley and almost every other correspondent who had viewed the Patent Office's collections over the previous two decades.[21]

Nor did the ever-observant Walt Whitman mention the scroll in his description that September of the chaos in the hospital set up in the Patent Office, though one could easily see him lyrically linking the suffering and sacrifices of the wounded soldiers on the first floor with the moral imperative of the venerable parchment up on the second—had it been there.

Did the young soldier writing back home to Jamestown, New York, or America's greatest poet simply miss the Declaration hanging in the museum? Perhaps, but long-forgotten evidence exists to suggest that by the beginning of August, the Declaration no longer hung in the Patent Office. Instead, just after the Union defeat at Bull Run, the scroll was quietly moved to a far safer location: back to the State Department, next to the White House.

During the first week of August, Washington hosted Prince Napoleon Joseph Charles Paul Bonaparte, the nephew of Napoleon and cousin of reigning French Emperor Napoleon III. "Plon Plon," as the prince was known, met President Lincoln at the White House and was given a

The White House in 1861, with a statue of Thomas Jefferson holding the Declaration of Independence (now in the U.S. Capitol).

private tour of Mount Vernon. He was accompanied around the capital city by Secretary of State William Seward, the most powerful member of Lincoln's Cabinet.

Prince Napoleon arrived from New York on August 2. That day, Seward brought him to the State Department, still located in the Northeast Executive Building, next to the White House. According to contemporary news accounts, Seward took Napoleon to see the "documents and letters which are piled up on the shelves of the library, covered with the thick dust of some fifty years and upwards." And there, the *Daily Evening Bulletin* reported, the Prince saw "such articles of antique workmanship as the Declaration of Independence." This report is buttressed by a second news item, from the *Newport Mercury*, which relayed similar information, reporting that Napoleon "looked over the musty Declaration of Independence" at the State Department.[22]

Should these reports be believed? There is no contemporary mention by those who would know best, such as Seward. It is certainly possible the newspapers might have been misinformed or that they could have misreported events. However, given the widespread national coverage of Napoleon's visit and his well-publicized activities with senior officials while in Washington, it seems more likely that the stories that he was shown the original Declaration in the State Department as part of his red-carpet treatment are accurate.

Three years later, in 1864, William F. Richstein, in his *Strangers' Guide-Book to Washington City*, added more evidence. Tourism was not a priority during the war, unsurprisingly, but there were thousands of new government workers, contractors, suppliers, and troops who now called the city home, and Richstein offered them a guide to the sights of the bustling capital. Deep inside his wartime *Guide-Book,* he informed his readers that the "original" Declaration could be seen in the library of the State Department.[23] Once again, the comment may have been inaccurate. Yet given that numerous letters, accounts, newspapers articles, and every guidebook for two decades had noted the Declaration's location in the Patent Office, it is hard to believe that Richstein would not have known that, and thus his assertion that the Declaration was in the State Department reflected new information.

Have we solved the mystery of where the Declaration of Independence was kept during the Civil War? At one level, the idea that it would have been brought back to the State Department makes perfect sense. In the shadow of a looming invasion, with the unguarded Patent Office a scene of crowding and chaos, it must have seemed simple prudence for someone to have quietly removed the Declaration sometime between July 21 and August 2, 1861, and taken the priceless parchment back to the State Department.

That venerable building, constructed in 1819 and already slated for demolition to accommodate the expansion of the Treasury Department, had been described in a newspaper article earlier that year as "a fitting repository for the state papers, so jealously guarded."[24] The State Department was part of the "Executive Square" that included the White House; the War, Navy, and Treasury Departments; and Army Headquarters. True, there was little overt security around the square in the early days of the war. Visitors could all but walk freely into the White House, but the area was constantly filled with officials, clerks, and the new Provost Guard passing by. Eventually, troops would be detailed to guard the area.[25]

If the Declaration was to remain in Washington, it could not be better protected than in its old home. Inside the State Department, it would have been kept in the library, located deep inside the building. From the White House next door, President Lincoln could all but keep in sight the "apple of gold" for which the Union was fighting such a desperate battle. It would have been safe there in July 1864, when Confederate General Jubal Early attacked Fort Stevens, just four miles away, sparking a battle that President Lincoln went in person to observe and where Confederate sharpshooters famously targeted his tall stovepipe hat. The engrossed Declaration would have remained at the State Department until the War Between the States came to its bloody conclusion in April 1865.

This speculative reconstruction is based on newly discovered evidence as well as common sense. There are no smoking guns—no transfer order from the Patent Office to the State Department, no mention of a move in contemporary diaries or letters. But as not all orders were recorded by the Bureau of Rolls and Library back in those days, this absence of documentation is explainable. Besides, given the chaos of the war, a spur-of-the-moment transfer order may well have been verbal.

As to the case presented here, the reader will have to serve as judge and jury.

Whatever may have happened to the Declaration during the Civil War, it remained the ultimate symbol of American aspirations to equality in the North and of the right of rebellion in the South. All through the terrible struggle, its anniversary was celebrated and the document solemnly recited across the land, invoked by each side for its own purposes.

On April 12, 1861, John Wilson, a Baltimore composer, deposited in the Library of Congress the sheet music for his arrangement of the Declaration of Independence in four-part harmony for "vocal and instrumental music." As he dropped off his "Great National Chant," whose final page reproduced facsimiles of the document's famous signatures, Confederate guns opened upon Fort Sumter.[26] During the early, dark months of war, Massachusetts set aside money to construct a monument to commemorate the Declaration in Boston. That same month, in New York's Institute of Fine Arts, Peter Frederick Rothermel, Philadelphia's most famous artist, exhibited for the first time his panoramic painting entitled *Reading of the Declaration of Independence*. This vibrant composition imagined the scene outside Independence Hall on July 8, 1776, portraying Colonel John Nixon orating from the packed astronomical stand to the dozens of citizens crowded below while members of the Continental Congress huddled among the crowd in conversation (see insert). Like Trumbull's masterpiece, Rothermel's painting wove another strand of myth in the collective memory surrounding the Declaration.[27]

In his immortal Gettysburg Address, on November 19, 1863, Abraham Lincoln offered his deepest reflection on the founding document. The brief speech recast American history on the rock of a Declaration whose invocation of equality spoke for all people and all time. Lincoln dedicated himself to saving a "nation, conceived in Liberty, and dedicated to the proposition that all men are created equal," so that such inspiring and eternal principles "shall not perish from the earth." Forever more would that interpretation of the Declaration influence American minds.[28]

Gettysburg marked the high tide of the Confederacy, but there would still be nearly two more terrible years of war. Fighting ranged over nearly half the continent, along the Mississippi River and down to the Gulf of Mexico. Lincoln's invocation of the equality principle of the Declaration accompanied Union troops wherever they marched, while his Emancipation Proclamation of January 1863, freeing slaves held in Confederate territory, appeared to show the spirit of the document in action. The year after Gettysburg, as Union troops steadily pushed back the Confederates, the poet Ralph Waldo Emerson could assert that "The sharp words of the Declaration of Independence, lampooned then and since as 'glittering generalities' have turned out blazing ubiquities that will burn forever and ever."[29] In rejecting Senator Rufus Choate's dismissal of the Declaration, Emerson foresaw a Union victory that would bring the founding document back to every corner of a reunited country.

Throughout the conflict, Confederates clung to the document's assertion that consent of the governed was the *sine qua non* of just government. Speaking in Richmond in January 1863, Jefferson Davis equated the Southern cause with the Revolution, calling the Confederacy "the last hope, as I believe, for the perpetuation of that system of government which our forefathers founded . . . the home of true representative liberty."[30] The virtues of courage and sacrifice that animated the Southerners, in Davis's view, provided a shining example to mankind, a counter to Northern presumptions that the Declaration's assertion of equality was universal.

The unstoppable Northern war machine ground down the Confederates, bringing ruin and defeat and with it the triumph of Lincoln's vision of the Declaration. As the war began to draw to a close, *The Jewish Messenger* of New York could write in February 1865, "When Americans next celebrate the anniversary of the 'Declaration of Independence,' they will be enabled to rejoice in the full realization of the hopes that animated the founders of the republic—'this is a land of liberty.'"[31] With victory in sight, Northerners, whether old Puritan stock or newcomers, knew what they had fought for.

For Southerners, their relationship to the Declaration would be far more complicated. By the time Robert E. Lee surrendered the Army of Northern Virginia to General Ulysses S. Grant at Appomattox Courthouse, on April 9, 1865, the Confederate interpretation of the Declaration had been thoroughly and bloodily refuted. Though a few weeks of desultory resistance were to continue, the Southern concept of liberty had been defeated by a powerful government whose war-fighting mobilization would indelibly transform the nation away from the Southern agrarian ideal and State sovereignty.

On April 11, 1865, President Lincoln addressed a jubilant crowd in front of the White House. Now, with victory at hand, an exhausted and prematurely aged Lincoln soberly addressed the fraught process of readmitting the former rebel States back into the Union. Having all but triumphed in an existential struggle for the future of the nation, Lincoln's speech revealed the limits even he imposed on the exercise of equality. In speaking of readmitting Louisiana to the Union and demands by radicals that the vote be given to freed males, he noted, "It is also unsatisfactory to some that the elective franchise is not given to the colored man. I would myself prefer that it were now conferred on the very intelligent, and on those who serve our cause as soldiers." But not, he did not have to say, on all newly freed Blacks, most of whom had no schooling and none of whom had any experience of democratic participation. Such limits reflected the political realism that tempered Lincoln's idealism, as well as deeper questions of just what equality meant even after the war.

Lincoln could have let such looming complexities of reconstruction politics blur his focus on the permanent things, but he held to his philosophical North Star. His speech ended with the firm assertion that "Important principles may, and must, be inflexible."[32] Those who knew what lay closest to Lincoln's heart, what had driven him to persevere during the terrible struggle, could have had no doubt as to what he was referring. As he contemplated a restored, even refounded, United States, he must have given great thanks for having been able to save for posterity both the body and the spirit of the Declaration.[33] Three days later, Abraham Lincoln was assassinated.

On April 22, his funeral train reached Philadelphia on its way back to Springfield, Illinois. Lincoln's casket was carried to Independence Hall, where in February 1861 he had said he would rather be assassinated than surrender the principles of the Declaration. For two days his body lay in state in the very room where the document he defended at the cost of his life had been signed.

Chapter 12
CENTENNIAL

July 4, 1876. Crammed around a formal stand in nearly one-hundred-degree heat, a packed crowd behind Philadelphia's Independence Hall craned to watch as Richard Henry Lee, grandson of the Founding Father who had first called for Independence, laid the engrossed Declaration on a makeshift lectern and began to read its sonorous phrases. Only the second public reading from the original scroll in its history, the recitation was the highlight of the Centennial Exposition, the national celebration marking the birth of America a century before.

Those gathering in Philadelphia were celebrating the anniversary of a country now forcibly reunited, in which the great question of slavery had at last been resolved. Ratified on December 6, 1865, the Thirteenth Amendment had irrevocably outlawed human bondage, while the Fifteenth, ratified on February 3, 1870, guaranteed the right to vote regardless of race or prior condition of servitude.[1] To Lee's listeners, the words of the Declaration may have conjured ties to America's long-ago founding, but Abraham Lincoln had fundamentally changed most of his countrymen's understanding of their founding document. Some of those who had made their way to Philadelphia were eager to test whether Lincoln's promise of equality for all would extend beyond slavery.

Seated in the audience at Independence Hall were Susan B. Anthony, a fifty-six-year-old schoolteacher from New York, and four of her colleagues in the National Woman Suffrage Association, which Anthony had founded in 1869 along with Elizabeth Cady Stanton. As Lee finished his recitation, Anthony rose from her seat and led her colleagues to the stage. There, she handed to a pale and silent Thomas W. Ferry, Acting Vice President of the United States, a document she had been denied permission to formally present during the ceremony. The Association's "Declaration of Rights of the Women of the United States" was a passionate rebuke to a quarter century of inaction since Stanton had promulgated her "Declaration of Sentiments" at the Seneca Falls Convention back in 1848.[2] Returning to their seats, Anthony and her comrades passed out copies of their declaration to the crowd.

Susan B. Anthony's bold disruption of the Centennial ceremonies may have struck a brief discordant note into the day's festivities, but the protest reflected the unsettled state of a country still recovering from the Civil War. While the Declaration of Independence returned to the city of its birth in celebration, the country around it was beginning a half-century transformation into a modern nation. The question of how the Declaration would fit into the new, postwar America dominated the next phase of the scroll's history.

The generation after the Civil War underwent a transformation that was not just material, but philosophical, changing the nation's ideals and self-identity. America in 1876 would have been almost unrecognizable to the Founding Fathers. The more farsighted of them, like George Washington and Thomas Jefferson, had long advocated the importance of the West and even the Pacific to the future of the United States.[3] But it is doubtful they could have foreseen just how inexorably their nation would spread across the thousands of miles of plains, valleys, deserts, and mountains.

During and after the Civil War, the remainder of the North American continent south of Canada was organized into vast new territories: Arizona, Colorado, Dakota, Idaho, Montana, and Wyoming among them. Soon, these territories would be carved into new States, adding a dozen in less than half a century. In the West, new agricultural kingdoms were emerging, from the Texas cattle drives that saw herds of hundreds of thousands brought up the Chisholm Trail to Abilene, Kansas, and beyond, to the ocean of wheat that now stretched from Illinois across the Great Plains, turning what was once dismissed as a great desert into the most productive farmland in the world. By 1890, just a quarter century after Appomattox, the Census Bureau would declare that the frontier had "closed," and the line of settlement that had defined American existence since Jamestown in 1607 was no more.

At the same time, a new economic structure and legal construct emerged that swept away the old local patterns of production. The corporation, forged by ambitious builders, transformed America's economy and drove technological innovation. The war had spurred the growth of industry in the North, but the postwar era saw even greater productivity. It was the era of telegraphy and "telephony," making the dissemination of news all but instantaneous. Massive new factories were built in the Middle West, pouring out uncountable miles of steel that was forged into rail tracks laid across the nation and indestructible girders that soon let architects raise skyscrapers to dizzying heights. Electric lighting banished the night, illuminating cities and homes. Before the century was out, the United States would become the world's leading industrial power.

Economic growth was fueled by a revolution in transportation that created a true national market. From modest beginnings, spurred by generous government land grants and tax incentives, the rail network spread across the continent, quickly outstripping all the track in Europe.[4] The Transcontinental Railroad, which Abraham Lincoln had approved during the war, was completed on May 10, 1869, when the Union Pacific and Central Pacific met at Promontory Point, Utah, effectively linking the Golden Gate with New York Harbor. Traditional concepts of space were obliterated, making it possible to travel in a matter of hours across a distance that only recently would have taken weeks. The need to coordinate rail schedules even led to the nationwide establishment of time zones, giving the clock dominance over daily life.

The growing pains that accompanied these changes were often traumatic. For the South, recovery from the war remained the imperative, especially once Reconstruction ended and political control reverted to the States of the former Confederacy. Manipulation of financial markets by speculators like Jay Cooke and Jay Gould led to widespread crashes in the postwar years, especially in 1873. Labor strikes were called as working conditions in the massive new factories became worse. Racial tension grew with immigration, while local communities became dependent on national industry for consumer goods. Political corruption of the type represented by the Tweed Ring in New York City became endemic.

For Southern Blacks, the end of Reconstruction in 1877 began the undoing of much of the gains of the past decade, while the American Indian faced a "greater disaster" as "his hunting ground is pierced by the iron rail," as Philadelphia's *The Press* admitted in 1868, bringing ever more waves of settlers.[5] The final reckoning between American Indians and those taking over their lands was about to unfold. Open warfare erupted and massacres of Indians became more common as the U.S. Government moved to push the remainder of the tribes farther west into new reservations and open the land to homesteaders or the railways.

Although such economic and social dislocations were permanent, and the human cost often high, growth and progress were also undeniable. Standards of living were increasing, innovation was boosting the economy, immigrants continued to pour in, and opportunity was abundant for the innovative and ambitious.[6] There was broad national optimism amid the uncertainties, summed up by *The Cincinnati Daily Enquirer*, which wrote on the opening day of the centennial year, "we have but commenced on our career of human progress. Like a rolling snow-ball we go on accelerating in magnitude."[7]

The evolution of the country from a rural, largely agricultural republic into an urban industrial empire swept away age-old patterns of life in a few decades, forever altering the relationship of the American citizen to his society and government in ways both superficial and profound. These changes may have seemed unconnected with the Declaration of Independence, but in 1868, the *Quincy Daily Whig*, in central Illinois, warned that the transformation of life was erasing the memory of 1776. "The ancient method of observing the anniversary of the nation's birthday appears to be entirely abandoned," the paper lamented, as citizens were more likely to "go off on railroad and steamboat excursions" than to celebrate their inheritance.[8]

Whether an eighteenth-century natural rights argument penned by an agrarian philosopher could represent modern America—or, as a later historian put it, "the supreme problem of whether a Jeffersonian democracy could survive in a Hamiltonian economy"—was the great question facing the Declaration as it entered its second century.[9] In his successful 1867 campaign for governor of Ohio, General Rutherford B. Hayes (who a decade later would be elected President) hinted at a new relationship between Americans and their founding charter. "The sentiment of nationality is the sentiment of the Declaration of Independence," asserted

Hayes, highlighting the document's communal role.[10] In his view, liberty and equality were not ends in themselves but necessary elements of a new postwar nationalism. Just two years after Lincoln's tragic assassination, Hayes looked to the Declaration as the glue fastening Americans to their rapidly changing country.

Some uncertainty attends the whereabouts of the physical Declaration in these early postwar years. For the first decade after the Civil War, the parchment moved between buildings in Washington, just as it had in its early years. It stayed in the State Department building next to the White House until November 1866, when the old structure was torn down to allow for the expansion of the Treasury Department. By some accounts, the Declaration was packed up and moved with the State Department half a mile away, to its temporary location in the old Washington City Orphan Asylum, on Fourteenth Street.

The return of peace and the resurgent power of the federal government once again turned Washington, D.C., into a tourist destination. The thousands of visitors streaming into the city helped return the Declaration to the public eye as they poured into the Capitol Rotunda and Patent Office. John F. Ellis's 1868 *Guide to Washington City and Vicinity* highlighted the treasures of the capital for visitors, including the relocated State Department. Ellis informed his readers that the library in the temporary building "contains a very fine collection of books . . . especially the original Declaration of Independence."[11] It is possible that such attention became a problem, for it appears that the Declaration was soon back in its old haunts in the Patent Office. An 1869 guidebook entitled *Sights and Secrets of the National Capital*, by a Dr. John B. Ellis—likely the same author, despite the different middle initial—directed visitors to the massive building, where they could again see the Declaration on public display.

This was the same year that Benson Lossing published his popular history of the War of 1812 with its mythical tale of Dolley Madison saving the Declaration from the invading British. Two years later, a new generation of schoolchildren was introduced to the fanciful tale that the Liberty Bell was rung as the Declaration was signed in a poem in George S. Hilliard's widely used *Franklin's Fifth Reader*. Entitled "Independence Bell, July 4, 1776," the poem stirringly described the scene:

Hushed the people's swelling murmur,
Whilst the boy cries joyously;
"Ring!" he's shouting, "ring, grandfather,
Ring! Oh, ring for Liberty!"[12]

What visitors to Washington did not know was that, despite the Declaration being a great tourist attraction, there were plans to take it away from the public. The State Department wanted the Declaration back and intended to transfer the scroll to its new building when construction was completed. Before that could happen, however, the parchment would make yet another journey.

On the morning of May 6, 1876, Alonzo Bell walked into the Baltimore and Ohio Railroad's Washington, D.C., station, just north of the Capitol at New Jersey and C Streets. The forty-year-old Bell was the chief clerk of the Department of the Interior, and he carried with him a large rectangular-shaped package. Bell boarded the 9:23 a.m. "limited express" to Philadelphia. Around one o'clock, he arrived at the West Philadelphia Depot, where he was met by a small party and escorted by carriage to Independence Hall. There, he unwrapped his package: the engrossed Declaration of Independence. With no security and apparently no concern for its safety, Bell had brought the irreplaceable parchment back to its birthplace.[13]

Bell's mission was the result of four months of hard bargaining between the leading citizens of Philadelphia and the administration of President Ulysses S. Grant, the former commander of the Union Army who had been elected president in 1868. The driving force behind returning the Declaration to Philadelphia, Colonel Frank M. Etting, was a Civil War veteran whose primary public service was as chairman of the Committee for the Restoration of Independence Hall. In Etting, whose Jewish ancestors had fought in the Revolutionary War, Philadelphia's claim to the Declaration found a dogged champion.

There was little by way of formal historic preservation in the United States when Etting took charge of the committee to restore Independence Hall. Only the work of committed individuals had kept a few historic sites from disappearing, such as Thomas Jefferson's mountaintop

Monticello. The famed house, which Jefferson had designed himself, had fallen into disrepair until it was restored by Commodore Uriah P. Levy, who bought it in 1834. Even George Washington's historic home was at risk of collapse before it was purchased in 1858 by the Mount Vernon Ladies' Association, the first national organization dedicated to preservation of an historic structure, founded by the South Carolinian Ann Pamela Cunningham.[14]

The Philadelphia State House—renamed Independence Hall in 1824—had fared somewhat better. After its historic role in 1776 it had been the site of the 1787 Constitutional Convention and continued to house the Pennsylvania legislature. When the state government moved out of Philadelphia in 1799, it was used as a court while the upstairs was rented to the artist Charles Willson Peale for his natural history museum, the first in the country. The hall was narrowly saved from destruction in 1816 and when the Marquis de Lafayette visited Philadelphia on his triumphant return to the United States in 1824, a new interest in the old building emerged. It had long since lost its steeple, and a new one, the familiar one we see today, was completed in 1828. Plans were established to restore the "Hall of Independence," the first-floor room where the Continental Congress assembled, but little came of them. Fondly praised and generally kept up, Independence Hall nonetheless had little connection to its most famous moment as the centenary approached.

All that changed starting in 1872, when Frank Etting's Committee for the Preservation of Independence Hall was organized. Its goal was not only to maintain the building but to re-create how it looked in 1776. Within four years, the committee had acquired furniture believed to have been in place when the Continental Congress sat, including John Hancock's oversize chair (which most likely was George Washington's used at the Constitutional Convention) and the table on which the engrossed Declaration was signed. Coats of paint were stripped away, revealing intricate carved ornamentation in the room. Portraits of the Founding Fathers were hung along the walls, along with Robert Pine and Edward Savage's early nineteenth-century group painting, *Congress Declaring Independence*. A new bell, to replace the long-cracked and silent Liberty Bell, was installed in the clock tower.[15]

Even the silver inkstand used by John Hancock and other members of Congress to sign the Declaration was reverentially returned. As the *American Stationer* reported, "After a short ceremony the Mayor placed [the inkstand] upon the original table in Independence Hall, and efforts will at once be made to secure its ancient companion, the original copy of the Declaration of Independence."[16] The *Stationer* thus revealed Etting's larger vision: to engage a new generation of Americans by instilling the feeling of being in the hall when Independence was declared. It would be a dramatic change from simply viewing the Declaration in a case hung on a wall.[17]

To better explain his vision and promote the restoration committee's work, Etting wrote a lavishly illustrated history of the State House, expressing his "hope that the general public would ultimately share in the interest which every brick of this old building possesses for me, and thus be inclined to lend each his individual aid toward its preservation, and to insure its proper custodianship for all time." In early 1876, he turned his energies to a new goal: getting the Declaration returned to Philadelphia for the Centennial.[18]

Aside from its dramatic rescue in 1814, the scroll had not left Washington since 1800. It would take months of wrangling, numerous rebuffs, and the employment of a spy for Etting to secure approval. In a letter of February 1, 1876, he informed Secretary of the Interior Zachariah Chandler that there was now installed in Independence Hall a "first class fire-proof safe . . . when the doors are opened the contents will be securely presented by a heavy plate glass inner door—the fire-proof doors to be opened by day & closed at night." He went on to promise that his committee was "ready & willing to adopt whatever more you may point out to ensure the perfect safety of this inestimable document." Then he enlisted George W. Childs, publisher of the Philadelphia *Public Ledger* and a close friend of Ulysses S. Grant, to sway the President.

As it turned out, Secretary Chandler had already proposed to display the Declaration in Philadelphia, in a building specially constructed for the Centennial Exposition. But Etting's restoration of Independence Hall offered a unique opportunity to reunite the parchment with its original surroundings. Just days before the opening of the Exposition, Alonzo Bell took the Declaration down from the Patent Office wall, wrapped it carefully, and boarded the train to Philadelphia.[19]

To some observers, it was not the most propitious time to hold a gala celebration. The country was in the grips of a depression, begun with a bank panic in 1873, that had shattered thousands of businesses and caused the collapse of dozens of railroads. As the *New-York Daily Tribune* lamented,

> It is doubly unfortunate, therefore, that those who come from other lands to inspect this nation on its centennial anniversary will see it at its worst . . . Our commerce and industry are suffering from a prostration extraordinarily prolonged and severe . . . perhaps the worst feature in our condition is that our business misfortunes are largely due to incompetence or corruption in Government.[20]

Others took a more optimistic view. At the beginning of the centennial year Chicago's *The Inter Ocean* had written that "the growth of the country in a hundred years, in population, territory, wealth, and influence among the nations of the earth, cannot fail to inspire feelings of the liveliest satisfaction in the breast of every citizen."[21] The Republican paper was more in tune with the national mood as Americans flocked to celebrate the great anniversary.

On May 10, President Grant formally opened the Centennial Exposition, which extended over three hundred acres in Philadelphia's Fairmount Park along the Schuylkill River. From agricultural products to massive steam engines, the fair showcased America's wealth and vitality and drew exhibits from around the world. Among the new technologies on display was a little-noticed invention by the Scottish-American engineer Alexander Graham Bell that allowed people to talk to each other over an electrical wire. In all, more than nine million people thronged the Exposition before it closed in November.[22]

The revelers descended on a city dramatically changed from the one Benjamin Franklin had called home. The narrow dirt streets of colonial times were now paved and development reached out into the countryside. When the Continental Congress had assembled in 1776, Philadelphia had 30,000 residents; now, it was home to 817,000 people. Centennial activities spilled out of Fairmount Park as the millions of visitors poured into the city. One Southern newspaper painted a vibrant picture for its readers: "the streets of the city were all ablaze with flags, and the patriotic decorations were numerous."[23]

Historic sites throughout Philadelphia became part of the pageant. One of these was a narrow four-story house on the corner of Market and Seventh Streets, one story taller than it had been a century earlier. During the day, passersby would likely have paid no attention to the building, which until a few years previously had featured in a local advertisement as

BIRTHPLACE OF LIBERTY
CLOTHING HOUSE
700 Market Street,
Philadelphia
The identical spot where Jefferson penned the
Declaration of Independence
MEN'S AND BOY'S CLOTHING,
which we offer at low prices.
Wm. Brown and Company[24]

Centennial strollers passing the house after dark could see through windows illuminated by candles the silhouette of a young man bent over a writing desk with quill in hand, one of many celebratory transparencies set up throughout the city center.[25]

We don't know if the sight of a clothing store and real estate agency occupying the spot where the Declaration of Independence had flowed from Jefferson's pen troubled the thoughts of visitors. To a philosophical mind, it may well have summed up the triumph of a Hamiltonian economy over Jefferson's agrarian republic. In 1801, as Jefferson became president, the house he had lived in while writing his draft was sold to the Gratz family, who eventually remodeled the second-floor suite of rooms, turning them into offices. In 1883, the historic house would be torn down, with only a few brass doorknobs, wooden lintels, and a lock and keys kept for posterity.[26]

It was Independence Hall that was the center of the celebrations. All day, long lines of spectators passed by the Declaration, now propped up inside its indestructible safe. Visitors also saw the re-created assembly room, carefully staged as though the Continental Congress was still in session. For Frank Etting, whose abrasive personality had led to his dismissal that year from the committee on restoring Independence Hall, it was a vindication of his vision of reuniting the Declaration with its place of birth.

On the night of July 3, a crowd estimated at three hundred thousand crammed Philadelphia's streets for a grand torchlight parade. At midnight, the replica of the Liberty Bell pealed thirteen times to ring in the centenary. Throughout the early morning hours, bands played nonstop, starting with the "Star-Spangled Banner," and cannon salutes started soon after dawn on the Fourth. A morning military review of the "Centennial

Richard Henry Lee reading the original Declaration of Independence in Philadelphia on July 4, 1876. From *The Illustrated London News*, July 29, 1876.

Legion," with ten thousand troops from the original thirteen colonies, paraded to Independence Hall. Then the formal ceremonies began. The hall was draped in the national colors, while flag-covered stands were reserved for four thousand invited guests. Over three hundred Members of Congress had traveled from Washington for the occasion, taking their place on the covered platform alongside the Emperor of Brazil and other foreign dignitaries.

Inside the hall, the heavy safe was unlocked and the Declaration was given to Mayor William S. Stokley, who carried it out to Independence Square. Acting Vice President Thomas Ferry made brief remarks, linking the country's upsurge in nationalism to the "majesty of the Declaration of 1776" and claiming that the "worth of American citizenship, its force, is fast supplementing the assumption of divine rights of kings by virtue of the supreme law of the Nation that the people alone hold sole power to rule."[27] When Ferry sat down, prayers were offered by the Episcopal Bishop of Pennsylvania, and hymns were sung.

Then, in the "intense" ninety-five-degree heat, Mayor Stokley handed the Declaration to Richard Henry Lee. For five minutes the crowd cheered, then Lee gingerly placed the document on the rostrum and read to the assembled throng in a "clear, ringing voice."[28] When he was done, "The faded and crumbling manuscript, held together by a simple frame was then exhibited to the crowd and was greeted with cheer after cheer."[29] For those in the square, old war wounds seemed mostly to have healed. Among the raucous crowd was a young boy from Plymouth Notch, Vermont, Calvin Coolidge, brought by his parents to celebrate his fourth birthday, who fifty years later would preside over the Nation's Sesquicentennial as President.[30]

As the crowd settled down, Susan B. Anthony approached the stage to deliver her counter declaration, a moment likely missed by many in the teeming throng. The protest was the high point of several years of effort to publicize women's suffrage, often using the language of Jefferson's Declaration. In January 1871, Victoria Woodhull, the wealthy publisher of a feminist newspaper, printed an appeal for "Constitutional Equality" in which she argued that "Women have the same inalienable right to life, liberty, and the pursuit of happiness that men have. Why have they not this right politically, as well as men?"[31]

Charged with voter fraud for illegally casting a ballot in the presidential election of 1872, Susan B. Anthony had challenged the authority of the court in her highly publicized trial. "Your denial of my citizen's right

Leading suffragists Elizabeth Cady Stanton and Susan B. Anthony in 1870.

DECLARATION AND PROTEST

OF THE

WOMEN OF THE UNITED STATES

BY THE

NATIONAL WOMAN SUFFRAGE ASSOCIATION,

JULY 4th, 1876.

WHILE the Nation is buoyant with patriotism, and all hearts are attuned to praise, it is with sorrow we come to strike the one discordant note, on this hundredth anniversary of our country's birth. When subjects of Kings, Emperors, and Czars, from the Old World, join in our National Jubilee, shall the women of the Republic refuse to lay their hands with benedictions on the nation's head? Surveying America's Exposition, surpassing in magnificence those of London, Paris, and Vienna, shall we not rejoice at the success of the youngest rival among the nations of the earth? May not our hearts, in unison with all, swell with pride at our great achievements as a people; our free speech, free press, free schools, free church, and the rapid progress we have made in material wealth, trade, commerce, and the inventive arts? And we do rejoice, in the success thus far, of our experiment of self-government. Our faith is firm and unwavering in the broad principles of human rights, proclaimed in 1776, not only as abstract truths, but as the corner stones of a republic. Yet, we cannot forget, even in this glad hour, that while all men of every race, and clime, and condition, have been invested with the full rights of citizenship, under our hospitable flag, all women still suffer the degradation of disfranchisement.

Our history, the past hundred years, has been a series of assumptions and usurpations of power over woman, in direct opposition to the principles of just government, acknowledged by the United States at its foundation, which are:

First. The natural rights of each individual to self-government.

Second. The exact equality of these rights.

Third. That these rights, when not delegated by the individual, are retained by the individual.

Fourth. That no person can exercise the rights of others without delegated authority.

Fifth. That the non-use of these rights does not destroy them.

And for the violation of these fundamental principles of our Government, we arraign our rulers on this 4th day of July, 1876,—and these are our

ARTICLES OF IMPEACHMENT.

BILLS OF ATTAINDER have been passed by the introduction of the word "male" into all the State constitutions, denying to woman the right of suffrage, and thereby making sex a crime—an exercise of power clearly forbidden in Article 1st, Sections 9th and 10th of the United States Constitution.

Susan B. Anthony disrupted the Centennial ceremonies to present this Declaration of the Rights of Women of the United States to Vice President Thomas Ferry.

to vote," she proclaimed in her closing statement, "is the denial of my right of consent as one of the governed, the denial of my right of representation as one of the taxed, the denial of my right to trial by a jury of my peers as an offender against law; therefore, the denial of my sacred right to life, liberty, property."[32]

Now, in front of Independence Hall, she publicly read the National Woman Suffrage Association's "Declaration of Rights of the Women of the United States." She and her fellow suffragists then moved to the

First Unitarian Church a few blocks away, where Elizabeth Cady Stanton chaired a meeting of "considerable enthusiasm." Stanton read their declaration again. "Our faith is firm and unwavering in the broad principles of human rights proclaimed in 1776," she told the crowded hall, "not only as abstract truths, but as the corner stones of a republic." A bill of particulars followed, arguing for the extension of all legal rights to women and for women to be counted as full members of society. It was in the interest of the United States to rectify this "absolute and cruel despotism," the declaration concluded, for it "was the boast of the founders of the republic, that the rights for which they contended were the rights of human nature."

Unlike socialists, the suffragists insisted that their goal was to strengthen the country. "If these rights are ignored in the case of one-half the people, the nation is surely preparing for its downfall."[33] It would take another forty-four years before the Nineteenth Amendment would extend the franchise to women. Yet, much like Frederick Douglass's 1852 mourning speech, the "faded and crumbling manuscript" gave reason for hope.[34]

While millions celebrated the country's progress and some called for change, the Centennial became the first great commercial anniversary in American history. Playing a large role in this chapter was General James D. McBride, a Civil War veteran from Ohio who had done well with historical prints, including one of the recent impeachment of President Andrew Johnson in 1868, and thought he might profit from the new appetite for mementos of American history. In 1874, with admirable foresight, McBride had released a "Centennial Memorial" engraving of the Declaration. He received permission from the Patent Office to use the official Stone engraving to make a facsimile with the signatures and got the Secretary of the Interior to certify the work with an official seal. Surmounted by an American eagle and U.S. flags, with a border of Roman *fasces*, McBride's reproduction went through at least ten variants, making it the most popular image of the Declaration in its time.

McBride's engraving was the most authentic replica of the engrossed parchment produced to date. Two years later he sold it at the Centennial Exposition, charging one dollar, double the price in New York, but he did not stop there. Up till now, facsimiles could be purchased directly from the engravers or booksellers, often by subscription. McBride came up with the idea of selling his reproduction in bulk to merchants and

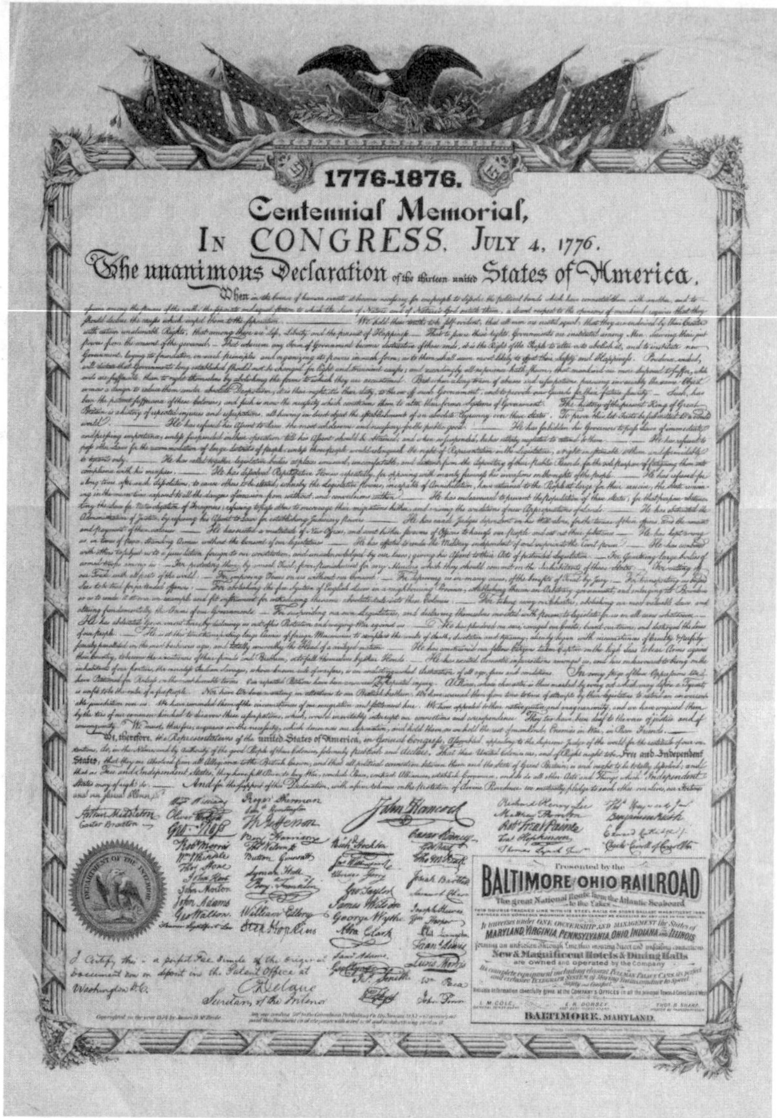

1776-1876.

Centennial Memorial,

In CONGRESS. July 4, 1776.

The unanimous Declaration of the thirteen united States of America.

Presented by the

BALTIMORE & OHIO RAILROAD

BALTIMORE, MARYLAND.

1776–1876 Centennial Memorial facsimile, by General James McBride, was the most popular reproduction of its time. This one was licensed to the Baltimore and Ohio Railroad as a promotional giveaway.

other companies. He sold his facsimile to national powerhouses such as the Baltimore and Ohio Railroad, as well as local businesses such as the S. Freedman Company of Detroit, Michigan, a purveyor of dry goods and carpets, or Baltimore's R. J. Baker and Company, which specialized in fertilizers. These companies then put an ad for their products or services in the lower right-hand corner of the print and handed them out to customers. Such mass-produced, lower-quality reproductions were now distributed around the nation as promotions, reaching many who would not have purchased a copy of the Declaration on their own.[35]

Images of the Declaration were by now so widespread that in the Centennial year alone over a dozen reproductions and imaginative facsimiles of the text were produced and distributed nationally by engravers and commercial businesses. Many of these were as ornate as John Binns's first facsimile, with decorative borders composed of Corinthian columns or Roman *fasces*, surmounted by eagles or personifications of Liberty. Images crowded the prints, often including John Trumbull's iconic portrayal of Jefferson presenting the Declaration to Congress. Also popular were cartouches of individual Signers, Presidents, or State seals. One particularly imaginative

Some prints artistically varied the size of the Declaration's text to create an image. This one, by the artist Augustus Hageboeck, forms a portrait of George Washington.

version varied the size and boldness of the Declaration's text to turn it into a portrait of George Washington. Other reproductions included key dates in American history or basic statistical information about the various States such as size and population. Many were printed on fragile paper, while some were impressed on heavy-duty stock suitable for framing.[36]

The Centennial spurred the release of a seemingly inexhaustible supply of patriotic scenes that fixed the Declaration in the American mind. Trumbull's painting remained the most famous, but it was joined in 1876 by a series of prints produced by the famous house of Currier and Ives. One portrayed Jefferson and his colleagues on the Committee of Five seated around a table, earnestly debating their draft of the Declaration, while another, entitled "John Hancock's Defiance," showed the president of the Continental Congress boldly signing the parchment. Following McBride's innovation, businesses sent out such scenes as promotions. One such was a calendar distributed by the Home Insurance Company, whose centerpiece showcased the first reading of the Declaration in front of Independence Hall, on July 8, 1776.[37]

Beyond prints and facsimiles, entrepreneurial spirit produced a variety of Declaration-related items for sale. Particularly popular were cotton and silk handkerchiefs imprinted with the text of the Declaration, the autographs of the Signers, and the Liberty Bell. One offered the Declaration printed on it in English, French, and German, so a "man can blow his nose in three different languages" into the text of the country's founding document.[38]

More durable collectibles emerged, as well. The U.S. Medallion Company, located at 212 Broadway, in New York, advertised a Centennial gilt medallion stamped with Trumbull's iconic representation, "equal in appearance, wear and color to SOLID SILVER OR GOLD," for $3.50.[39] Those in Albany, New York, who were interested in subscribing for the medallion were invited to view it at Marshall and Wendell's downtown music store. The *Albany Evening Journal* printed an enticing description of the "patriotic keepsake," which "embraces the text of the Declaration surrounding a sunken circle in which is a view of the interior of Independence Hall and the members of the Continental Congress signing the immortal document. Underneath are facsimiles of the signatures, which, though reduced in size from the original, are cut with great accuracy and beauty."[40]

The Declaration was not just an object for sale in its own right, it was enlisted to help sell other goods and services. In bustling Chicago, the Rand McNally Company produced a "Guaranteed Correct Copy" of the Declaration in 1876, assuring those journeying to the Centennial Exposition that had the Signers been able to see into the future, they would have included "a unanimous recommendation . . . to travel via the Chicago, Milwaukee and St. Paul Railway" or the Chicago and North Western Railway. In New York, meanwhile, G. Nicholson, located at 111 Broadway, took out a striking ad that read, "**IMPORTANT!** Every Purchaser of COAL Presented with a copy of the 'Declaration of Independence.'"[41]

Back in the 1820s, Benjamin Owen Tyler had hoped to see a copy of his engraving of the Declaration on every wall to promote patriotism; now, every time a New York family fired up their kitchen stove, they might remember the soot-begrimed Declaration presented by coal merchant G. Nicholson. Ubiquitous in popular media and advertising, thanks in no small part to the Centennial, the Declaration of Independence had in a sense been domesticated. As it reached its one-hundredth anniversary, it was no longer a majestic, if remote and sometimes abstract symbol of America's origins. Though at times commercially crass, selling the Declaration and using it in advertising served to create a constant, even personal, relationship between Americans and their founding document.

Chapter 13
The Gilded Age

The Centennial Exposition closed on November 10, 1876, the longest and greatest birthday party in the history of the United States. The crowds were gone, most of the makeshift buildings erected for the festivities had been taken down, and Philadelphia's Fairmount Park had settled back into its daily rhythm. Yet the Declaration of Independence still lay inside its steel safe in Independence Hall.

Despite Susan B. Anthony's protest that half the country had yet to receive full political or legal equality and the fact that legal equality for Black Americans in no way meant economic or social equality, millions had patriotically celebrated the Declaration as the guiding spirit of a free, powerful, and growing Nation. From Nantucket to Napa, Americans gathered to hear it read on July Fourth, and many undoubtedly remembered Abraham Lincoln's passionate insistence that it was the soul of America. The hundreds of thousands, if not millions, who had journeyed to see the ancient parchment at Independence Hall testified to its magnetic attraction. Perhaps it is not surprising that at this moment of its greatest popularity, the first of several battles over who should own this national treasure would erupt.

Philadelphia's civic leaders knew they had a priceless artifact on their hands. Despite having promised that the Declaration would be sent back to Washington, they weren't about to let it go without a fight. Basking in the glow of the Exposition and hoping to capitalize on the boost of tourism at Independence Hall, they were eager to keep it permanently.

Throughout the winter, the Declaration stayed quietly in its safe. It was only in February 1877 that the battle lines were drawn. One of the first public intimations of Philadelphia's plan was revealed on Valentine's Day 1877, in the city's *North American* newspaper. The paper opined (unsurprisingly) that its hometown was the best place to keep the Declaration in the public eye, arguing that "where ten thousand will do it reverence here not one will see it in the chamber of the Department of State at Washington, where it is to be buried with the other official archives of the government." Word of the plan to move the Declaration from the Patent Office had obviously leaked, and it must have seemed the time to make a play for the document.[1]

The next day, the Common and Select Councils of Philadelphia passed a formal resolution that, as the restored Independence Hall was dedicated by Philadelphians to all Americans as a "perpetual monument to the founders of American Independence," the engrossed Declaration "should be permitted to remain permanently in the building where it was signed." The city councils thus requested the federal government "to take the necessary action, legislative or otherwise, by which the said Chart may be suffered to remain deposited hereafter on exhibition in Independence Hall."[2]

It was a bold gamble, and it even made a certain sense. But the Declaration had overstayed its loan by three months, and the State Department was not pleased. In early February, Secretary of State Hamilton Fish had written a terse letter to Interior Secretary Zachariah Chandler, noting that "the articles transferred to the Patent Office . . . were not returned to this Department." Two years earlier, the diplomats had moved into the new State, War, and Navy Building, on the west side of the White House, and Fish went on to inform Chandler that "This Department now occupies the new, fire-proof and spacious edifice . . . it is considered that it would be preferable for such of the articles which were sent to the Patent Office . . . should be returned here for future custody . . . I would consequently request the return of the original Declaration of Independence."[3] Fish's letter revealed that there was more than one custody battle going on. Philadelphia may have been trying to wrestle the Declaration from the federal government, but inside the capital, the State Department was flexing its muscles against Interior.

Philadelphia's appeal, and Fish's demand, raised the strange question of who, if anyone, actually owned the Declaration of Independence. After 1789, the scroll had resided in the State Department, and when Daniel Webster had transferred it to the Patent Office in 1841, that bureau was still under the control of State. Just eight years later, however, the Patent Office was moved to the Interior Department, and along with it, the parchment. For a quarter century now, Interior had considered itself the owner of the Declaration.

When Frank Etting and George Childs had proposed sending the scroll to Philadelphia for the Exposition, Secretary Chandler initially based his firm opposition on the grounds that he was not at liberty to let the Declaration pass from his physical custody without Congressional authorization, which had first sent it to the State Department. The need for such an order had not troubled Daniel Webster when he had sent the scroll to the Patent Office back in 1841, but views had changed. Chandler's Commissioner of Patents, Robert Holland Duell, reinforced this position in mid-April, writing a formal judgment that "the Declaration of Independence, and the Commission of General Washington, associated with it in the same frame, belong to your Department as heirlooms, the right being prescriptive," given Interior's long possession.[4] In the end, Chandler had agreed to loan the scroll to Independence Hall, but who had ultimate authority over the Declaration?

It was an unprecedented question, but in some ways a nonsensical one, for most Americans undoubtedly believed that they "owned" the Declaration and that whoever managed it had no permanent claim on it of any kind. Though legally and even philosophically interesting, the issue was of no interest to the bluff ex-soldier who was now President. On February 8, 1877, just three days after receiving Fish's letter, Chandler wrote back to say that, on order of President Grant, "measures will immediately be taken by this Department to return the papers referred to, to the custody of the Department of State." Grant, ever blunt, had rejected the Philadelphians' proposal and clarified where the Declaration would be kept on its return. But as Chandler had to inform Fish in the same letter, the Declaration "has not yet been returned to this Department."[5] The next week, the Philadelphia city council published its resolution, arguing that it was "peculiarly appropriate that the Original Chart of the Declaration should be permitted to remain permanently in the building where it was signed and originally promulgated, as an enduring object of interest to the ceaseless throng of visitors to that Historic spot."[6]

1

Thomas Jefferson's original Rough Draft of the Declaration, composed in June 1776, was called "the most extraordinarily interesting document in American history." Jefferson deplored the "mutilations" of his draft by the Continental Congress, which cut around a quarter of the text, including a passionate denunciation of the slave trade.

2

Portrait of Thomas Jefferson by Mather Brown, 1786.

Thomas Jefferson and John Adams allied their talents in the push for Independence, but fell out over political differences exacerbated by the bitter presidential campaign of 1800. Later in life they reconciled, though they still sparred over how much credit Jefferson deserved for writing the Declaration. They both died on July 4, 1826, the fiftieth anniversary of the adoption of the Declaration.

3

Portrait of John Adams, known as "the Atlas of Independence," by John Trumbull, 1793.

IN CONGRESS, JULY 4, 1776.

A DECLARATION

BY THE REPRESENTATIVES OF THE

UNITED STATES OF AMERICA,

IN GENERAL CONGRESS ASSEMBLED.

WHEN in the Course of human Events, it becomes necessary for one People to dissolve the Political Bands which have connected them with another, and to assume among the Powers of the Earth, the separate and equal Station to which the Laws of Nature and of Nature's God entitle them, a decent Respect to the Opinions of Mankind requires that they should declare the causes which impel them to the Separation.

We hold these Truths to be self-evident, that all Men are created equal, that they are endowed by their Creator with certain unalienable Rights, that among these are Life, Liberty, and the Pursuit of Happiness—That to secure these Rights, Governments are instituted among Men, deriving their just Powers from the Consent of the Governed, that whenever any Form of Government becomes destructive of these Ends, it is the Right of the People to alter or to abolish it, and to institute new Government, laying its Foundation on such Principles, and organizing its Powers in such Form, as to them shall seem most likely to effect their Safety and Happiness. Prudence, indeed, will dictate that Governments long established should not be changed for light and transient Causes; and accordingly all Experience hath shewn, that Mankind are more disposed to suffer, while Evils are sufferable, than to right themselves by abolishing the Forms to which they are accustomed. But when a long Train of Abuses and Usurpations, pursuing invariably the same Object, evinces a Design to reduce them under absolute Despotism, it is their Right, it is their Duty, to throw off such Government, and to provide new Guards for their future Security. Such has been the patient Sufferance of these Colonies; and such is now the Necessity which constrains them to alter their former Systems of Government. The History of the present King of Great-Britain is a History of repeated Injuries and Usurpations, all having in direct Object the Establishment of an absolute Tyranny over these States. To prove this, let Facts be submitted to a candid World.

HE has refused his Assent to Laws, the most wholesome and necessary for the public Good.

HE has forbidden his Governors to pass Laws of immediate and pressing Importance, unless suspended in their Operation till his Assent should be obtained; and when so suspended, he has utterly neglected to attend to them.

HE has refused to pass other Laws for the Accommodation of large Districts of People, unless those People would relinquish the Right of Representation in the Legislature, a Right inestimable to them, and formidable to Tyrants only.

HE has called together Legislative Bodies at Places unusual, uncomfortable, and distant from the Depository of their public Records, for the sole Purpose of fatiguing them into Compliance with his Measures.

HE has dissolved Representative Houses repeatedly, for opposing with manly Firmness his Invasions on the Rights of the People.

HE has refused for a long Time, after such Dissolutions, to cause others to be elected; whereby the Legislative Powers, incapable of Annihilation, have returned to the People at large for their exercise; the State remaining in the mean time exposed to all the Dangers of Invasion from without, and Convulsions within.

HE has endeavoured to prevent the Population of these States; for that Purpose obstructing the Laws for Naturalization of Foreigners; refusing to pass others to encourage their Migrations hither, and raising the Conditions of new Appropriations of Lands.

HE has obstructed the Administration of Justice, by refusing his Assent to Laws for establishing Judiciary Powers.

HE has made Judges dependent on his Will alone, for the Tenure of their Offices, and the Amount and Payment of their Salaries.

HE has erected a Multitude of new Offices, and sent hither Swarms of Officers to harrass our People, and eat out their Substance.

HE has kept among us, in Times of Peace, Standing Armies, without the consent of our Legislatures.

HE has affected to render the Military independent of and superior to the Civil Power.

HE has combined with others to subject us to a Jurisdiction foreign to our Constitution, and unacknowledged by our Laws; giving his Assent to their Acts of pretended Legislation:

FOR quartering large Bodies of Armed Troops among us:

FOR protecting them, by a mock Trial, from Punishment for any Murders which they should commit on the Inhabitants of these States:

FOR cutting off our Trade with all Parts of the World:

FOR imposing Taxes on us without our Consent:

FOR depriving us, in many Cases, of the Benefits of Trial by Jury:

FOR transporting us beyond Seas to be tried for pretended Offences:

FOR abolishing the free System of English Laws in a neighbouring Province, establishing therein an arbitrary Government, and enlarging its Boundaries, so as to render it at once an Example and fit Instrument for introducing the same absolute Rule into these Colonies:

FOR taking away our Charters, abolishing our most valuable Laws, and altering fundamentally the Forms of our Governments:

FOR suspending our own Legislatures, and declaring themselves invested with Power to legislate for us in all Cases whatsoever.

HE has abdicated Government here, by declaring us out of his Protection and waging War against us.

HE has plundered our Seas, ravaged our Coasts, burnt our Towns, and destroyed the Lives of our People.

HE is, at this Time, transporting large Armies of foreign Mercenaries to compleat the Works of Death, Desolation, and Tyranny, already begun with circumstances of Cruelty and Perfidy, scarcely paralleled in the most barbarous Ages, and totally unworthy the Head of a civilized Nation.

HE has constrained our fellow Citizens taken Captive on the high Seas to bear Arms against their Country, to become the Executioners of their Friends and Brethren, or to fall themselves by their Hands.

HE has excited domestic Insurrections amongst us, and has endeavoured to bring on the Inhabitants of our Frontiers, the merciless Indian Savages, whose known Rule of Warfare, is an undistinguished Destruction, of all Ages, Sexes and Conditions.

IN every stage of these Oppressions we have Petitioned for Redress in the most humble Terms: Our repeated Petitions have been answered only by repeated Injury. A Prince, whose Character is thus marked by every act which may define a Tyrant, is unfit to be the Ruler of a free People.

NOR have we been wanting in Attentions to our British Brethren. We have warned them from Time to Time of Attempts by their Legislature to extend an unwarrantable Jurisdiction over us. We have reminded them of the Circumstances of our Emigration and Settlement here. We have appealed to their native Justice and Magnanimity, and we have conjured them by the Ties of our common Kindred to disavow these Usurpations, which, would inevitably interrupt our Connections and Correspondence. They too have been deaf to the Voice of Justice and of Consanguinity. We must, therefore, acquiesce in the Necessity, which denounces our Separation, and hold them, as we hold the rest of Mankind, Enemies in War, in Peace, Friends.

WE, therefore, the Representatives of the UNITED STATES OF AMERICA, in GENERAL CONGRESS, Assembled, appealing to the Supreme Judge of the World for the Rectitude of our Intentions, do, in the Name, and by Authority of the good People of these Colonies, solemnly Publish and Declare, That these United Colonies are, and of Right ought to be, FREE AND INDEPENDENT STATES; that they are absolved from all Allegiance to the British Crown, and that all political Connection between them and the State of Great-Britain, is and ought to be totally dissolved; and that as FREE AND INDEPENDENT STATES, they have full Power to levy War, conclude Peace, contract Alliances, establish Commerce, and to do all other Acts and Things which INDEPENDENT STATES may of right do. And for the support of this Declaration, with a firm Reliance on the Protection of divine Providence, we mutually pledge to each other our Lives, our Fortunes, and our sacred Honor.

Signed by ORDER *and in* BEHALF *of the* CONGRESS.

JOHN HANCOCK, PRESIDENT.

ATTEST.
CHARLES THOMSON, SECRETARY.

PHILADELPHIA: PRINTED BY JOHN DUNLAP.

John Dunlap worked through the night of July 4 to print broadsides announcing Independence. Copies were sent to George Washington in New York and throughout the colonies. Only twenty-six Dunlap broadsides are known to exist today. This copy was inserted into the Continental Congress's *Rough Journal* by Charles Thomson, secretary of Congress.

5

IN CONGRESS. JULY 4. 1776.

The unanimous Declaration of the thirteen united States of America.

Timothy Matlack engrossed the Declaration of Independence onto parchment starting on July 19, 1776. It was not signed on July 4 as is commonly believed. Members added their signatures over months beginning on August 2. The parchment was kept secret and displayed to the public only starting in 1841.

6

John Trumbull's masterpiece *The Declaration of Independence* imaginatively portrays Jefferson and the Committee of Five presenting their draft to Congress. This painting, which went on display in 1818, would become the best-known image of this iconic moment, spawning countless reproductions.

7

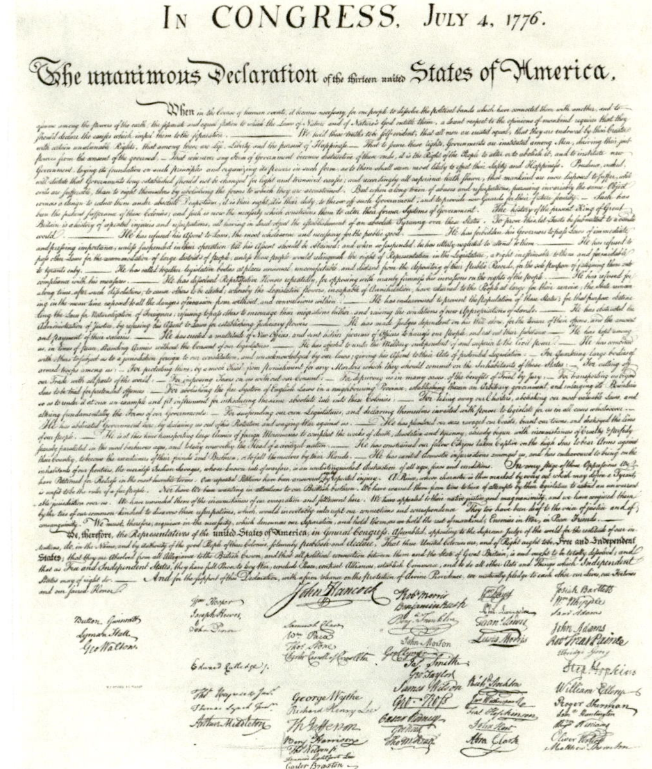

IN CONGRESS, JULY 4, 1776.

The unanimous Declaration of the thirteen united States of America.

Commissioned by Secretary of State John Quincy Adams in 1820, William J. Stone's official engraving took three years to complete. The most accurate representation ever made, it became the iconic image of the Declaration.

 8

First Reading of the Declaration of Independence by Philadelphia artist Peter Frederick Rothermel. Appearing in 1861, soon after the outbreak of the Civil War, the painting mythologizes the scene in front of Independence Hall on July 8, 1776. The unity it portrays reflected Abraham Lincoln's wartime appeal to the Declaration as a set of noble principles that bound all Americans. At the same time, Jefferson Davis wrapped his argument for secession in the language and precedent of the Declaration.

9

The writing of the Declaration was a popular theme for artists during the nineteenth and twentieth centuries. J. L. G. Ferris produced a heroic and mythical scene of Thomas Jefferson, John Adams, and Benjamin Franklin struggling over the draft. This was reproduced as a popular postcard around 1932.

10

During World War II, the Declaration was hidden in Fort Knox, with the Constitution, Bill of Rights, and Magna Carta. Here U.S. Marines struggle to carry the engrossed Declaration in its steel case into the Jefferson Memorial for its dedication on April 13, 1943, after which it was hastily returned to Fort Knox.

11

Visitors to the National Archives in the 1950s admiring the Declaration in its commanding shrine. (The Constitution is in the case below.) This is how Americans and visitors from around the world saw and experienced the Declaration for half a century.

12

Leaders of the March on Washington inside the Lincoln Memorial on August 28, 1963. In the back row are leaders of Catholic and Jewish civil rights organizations, including John Lewis, Eugene Carson Blake, and labor leader Walter Reuther. Seated left to right are Whitney Young, Cleveland Robinson, A. Philip Randolph, Martin Luther King, Jr., and Roy Wilkins. King's famous speech on that day spoke of the Declaration's "promissory note" of racial equality and urged all Americans to live up to Lincoln's calls for equality. The Civil Rights Act was signed the following year.

13

The Rotunda at the National Archives after its renovation in 2003. The case holding the Declaration is on the left, the Constitution is in the middle, and the Bill of Rights to the right.

Despite the appeal, Grant's decision was final. Two weeks later, on March 2, 1877, State Department clerk Alonzo Bell returned to Philadelphia. This time, his trip was reported in the local press. After presenting his credentials to Mayor William Stokley, Bell went to Independence Hall, where the safe was opened and the Declaration handed over. Bell wrapped up the framed parchment and returned with his precious cargo to Washington. The next day, Interior Secretary Chandler hurriedly wrote Hamilton Fish at the State Department, "I have the honor . . . to forward, herewith, the original Declaration of Independence." Chandler added that "Compliance with your request . . . was delayed by an effort on the part of prominent citizens of Philadelphia to have [it] retained permanently in Independence Hall," possibly an attempt to deflect any lingering blame.[7] The scroll was handed back to the State Department, and with no other ceremony, it was all but removed from the public eye.

The Declaration's return to the State Department was providential. In the late morning of September 24, 1877, smoke began pouring out of the Patent Office. A fire set in one of the building's fireplaces had ignited the roof. For several hours, flames consumed large parts of the north and west wings of the building. Staff and volunteers raced through the structure, carrying out as many patent models and records as they could. By the time the conflagration was brought under control, 100,000 models had been destroyed, while another 27,000 were damaged, along with 300 patent drawings. Though the blaze did not reach the old National Gallery in the original south wing, it easily could have. Had the Declaration been returned to this supposedly fireproof structure, it could for the third time in its history have gone up in flames.[8]

Instead, as the Patent Office burned on that September morning, the Declaration was stored in its new home half a mile away. The new State, War, and Navy Building was one of the architectural wonders of Washington, D.C. Standing on the site of the old War Department, directly west of the White House, across what became known as West Executive Drive, the new building encompassed an entire city block. It cost over $10 million to build the whole complex, an enormous sum at the time, and took a total of seventeen years from the first groundbreaking in 1871.

The new building towered over the White House, its florid French Second Empire style clashing with the neoclassical and Federal architecture of the rest of the capital. Clad in gray granite, with a distinctive dark gray sloping mansard roof, it was hated by architectural critics, denounced as a perfect reflection of the frenetic excess of Gilded Age America. It seemed proof that Thomas Jefferson's ideal of a decentralized agrarian republic had been swept away by a powerful central government in thrall to financial and industrial interests. The new building's offices were filled with appointees to the growing civil service, another sign of the bureaucratization of American society.

The State Department was the first department to move into the new building, in June 1875, occupying the south wing even before it was completed. Among the records brought over was the engrossed Declaration. The Washington *Evening Star* reported on June 29 that "The work of removing the archives of the Department of State from the hospital building on Fourteenth street to the new building on the southwest corner of Executive Square has already been commenced." On July 20, Hamilton Fish wrote, "We have just moved into our new State Dept Building. I experience a freedom from the anxiety which the Combustible nature of the old building kept ever present in my mind," a prescient comment.[9]

When the final wings opened in January 1888 it was reputed to be the largest office building in the world. It rose over six stories and covered five acres, easily the largest government building yet built. Just as importantly, it was said to be "as nearly fire-proof as buildings can well be that are filled with records."[10] This was, as Hamilton Fish had told Zachariah Chandler, the main reason for transferring the Declaration from the Patent Office.

In one of his last acts as secretary, Fish chose not to consign the Declaration to storage. He decided to place it on display in the State Department's new library, located on the upper floors of the south wing. An open four-story atrium let light pour down on the central hall. Ornate wrought-iron railings ran the circuit of the open galleries, which held eighty thousand volumes on international law, history, and diplomacy, along with rare maps.[11] Cases on the main floor were filled with some of the exotic gifts the Department had received from around the world.

Mounted in its old frame, alongside George Washington's commission, the Declaration was placed in this main room in a standing case fronted by doors that swung shut at night. Though the scroll was now removed from the general public, it could be seen by distinguished visitors and anyone persistent enough to make their way to the library, as it had been a half century before.

The move did little to preserve the parchment. The Declaration was placed under the skylights of the atrium, and sunlight continued to wear away at it. Worse, the library had an open fireplace, at least somewhat undercutting Fish's justification for moving the scroll from the Patent Office to the safer State Department. The damaging effects of air quality and direct light were still little understood. Covered by a simple pane of glass, the Declaration was as much at risk of deterioration in the fireproof State Department library as it had been in the National Gallery.

In its new setting, the Declaration was separated from other historical objects, but in 1880 it gained a companion artifact. Four years earlier, Thomas Jefferson's granddaughter, Eleonora Randolph Coolidge, had died at the age of eighty. A half century before, her grandfather had given her as a wedding present the very writing desk on which he had drafted the Declaration. Her family now donated the desk to the U.S. Government, and it was decided to put it in the State Department library. Frank Etting would have paid any price to have the desk brought to Independence Hall. Instead, only a few privileged visitors would be able to gaze upon Jefferson's enduring document and the desk on which it was first conceived.[12]

Though the State Department had taken the engrossed Declaration off public display, it compensated for that decision by keeping the document in the public's consciousness. In 1893, the department struck off new copies from the original Stone copperplate and sent them to historical associations around the country. Within two years, the Stone engraving at long last made its way to the masses. On June 30, 1895, the *Chicago Daily Tribune* announced that it would run a full-page reproduction of the Stone engraving in its July Fourth issue and urged that the print "be framed and displayed in every school-room in America," linking civics and commerce like so many before it.[13]

The next day, the *Tribune* recounted the dramatic day of the Declaration's adoption, describing the scene in Independence Hall of "men of all ages, some with wigs, some with powdered hair . . . men in the full vigor of middle life . . . young men in the ardor and flush of lusty patriotism," all leading to the mythical moments when "the bell of the State House rang out the tidings; the Declaration was read to a surging crowd." The *Tribune* then announced that in addition to publishing the Declaration's image in the paper, it would distribute hundreds of thousands of copies to subscribers, proclaiming that "for the first time in the history of the United States over half a million of its inhabitants will be able to see this Declaration of Independence on the Fourth of July."[14]

The *Tribune*'s July Fourth special reprint, taking up an entire page, was soon adopted as an annual tradition by newspapers around the country. It had taken seven decades, but at last, the best copy ever made of the Declaration was now freely available to millions. Though the Stone now became the de facto official version of the document, by the turn of the twentieth century, at least 110 distinct reproductions, prints, and facsimiles of the Declaration had appeared, many with multiple variants, ensuring that images of the Declaration were constantly in public view, even if the actual scroll was kept deep inside the State Department.[15]

Perhaps given their constant exposure to the Declaration, Americans continued to express their social and national aspirations with reference to its lofty promises. One such expression was a mid-1880s cartoon, entitled "A New Declaration of Independence in the Year 1885." Mimicking John Trumbull's famous painting, the cartoon portrayed the new President, Grover Cleveland, presenting to his Cabinet a scroll on which was written, "When, in the course of human events, it becomes necessary for a President to dissolve the political bands which the machinery of his party has imposed upon him, he must speak in unmistakable words . . ." Cleveland was the first Democrat to take the presidency since the Civil War. He had promised reform of the federal civil service, which had been mired in political corruption under both parties. Portraying the reforming president in the guise of a Thomas Jefferson, courageously taking on his own party in one of the most popular political movements of the time, was but one example of the symbolic position the Declaration had come to occupy in the national mind.[16]

Other commemorations in this era were more dignified and enduring. When the Library of Congress opened its massive Beaux Arts building in front of the U.S. Capitol in 1897, elaborate murals, paintings, carvings, and sculpture adorned every surface. In the two-hundred-foot-long, elegantly decorated South Gallery on the second floor, visitors could look up to find delicate stained-glass panels in the ceiling commemorating the fifty-six Signers of the Declaration. Inside perhaps the supreme architectural expression of American national confidence, the patriots responsible

"A New Declaration of Independence in the Year 1885," in *Puck* magazine, portrayed President Grover Cleveland as a new Thomas Jefferson for supporting civil service reform.

for the Declaration were celebrated alongside the greatest thinkers, writers, and artists in history.[17]

In the spring of 1893, a gleaming White City arose on the shores of Lake Michigan. Dozens of graceful neoclassical buildings created a dreamscape on the south side of Chicago. Built for the World's Columbian Exposition to celebrate the four-hundredth anniversary of Christopher Columbus's arrival in what Europeans called the New World, the White City dazzled visitors with its elegance and glowed through the night thanks to the new technology of electrical illumination.

These same visitors may have wondered why, nestled between the whitewashed plaster and wood palaces, was a building seemingly ripped from America's colonial days, its clock tower and spire piercing the sky. The Pennsylvania State Building, located on Fifty-Seventh Street, not far from the spot where the Griffin Museum of Science and Industry stands today, was not an actual colonial structure, but a fanciful reconstruction of Independence Hall. Inside, past the welcoming plaster statue of Benjamin

Franklin, were hundreds of historical artifacts from Pennsylvania's past. In the center hall, crowds surrounded the original Liberty Bell, carefully transported halfway across the country.

Independence Hall was re-created in Chicago for one purpose: to display the engrossed Declaration of Independence at the biggest world's fair in history. The original parchment, however, was nowhere to be found. It had, in fact, disappeared entirely from public view.

For decades, concerns had been mounting over the physical deterioration of the engrossed Declaration. While John Quincy Adams and Daniel Webster had worried about its condition earlier in the century, it was only after the Civil War that the problem really entered the public consciousness. In his 1869 guidebook to Washington, John Ellis warned visitors to the Patent Office that the parchment "is old and yellow, and the ink is fading from the paper," a story picked up the following year in the popular *Historical Magazine*, which noted that the Declaration and Washington's commission "are said to be rapidly fading out, so that, in a few years, only the naked parchments will remain."[18]

The dire state of things forced an official acknowledgment in 1872 by the Commissioner of Patents, Mortimer D. Leggett, in the *Historical Magazine*. "It is true that the writing and the names in . . . the Declaration of Independence are rapidly fading out," Leggett conceded. "Many of the names to the Declaration are already illegible." He went on to reveal for the first time the damage wrought earlier in the century when the first facsimiles were made, explaining that "acid was used that is resulting in the destruction of the original."[19] As he carried the scroll up to Philadelphia for the Centennial Exposition, in the spring of 1876, Alonzo Bell noted that the signatures were "almost faded from sight."[20] Could the parchment be preserved for future generations, or would it perish as had so many of history's priceless documents? The race for an answer started even as the Declaration was displayed in Independence Hall.

Congress became concerned enough to pass a resolution on August 3, 1876, directing that a blue-ribbon commission be formed. The Secretary of the Interior, the Secretary of the Smithsonian Institution, and the Librarian of Congress were "empowered to have resort to such means as will most effectually restore the writing of the original manuscript of the Declaration of Independence."[21] This was wildly ambitious, not to mention risky, for it went beyond simple preservation to untested restoration. The science of archival conservation did not exist in 1876, nor would it for a good many years after that. There were no trained conservators or reliable techniques to repair or preserve fragile documents.

Perhaps for this reason, despite the high-level imprimatur of the commission, it did not even meet until the end of May 1880, four years after it was established, when Secretary of the Interior Carl Schurz called the group together. In good bureaucratic fashion the commission punted the issue. It asked William B. Rogers, president of the National Academy of Sciences, to form a committee of leading scientists to determine how to restore the Declaration. Rogers named the Harvard chemist Oliver Wolcott Gibbs chairman and named four other members. The scientists returned their report in January 1881.

This was a turning point for the Declaration. Had the wrong road been taken, the document very probably would not have survived. Fortunately, the committee adopted a conservative approach and rejected several options that would have permanently altered the parchment. These options ranged from tracing over the original ink to applying a chemical solution to the parchment to adhere to the ink and restore its boldness. The committee wisely reported to the commission that it was "not expedient to attempt to restore the manuscript by chemical means partly because such methods of restoration are at best imperfect and uncertain in their results." It confirmed the claim that the wet process of making copies by William Stone had likely harmed the document and made it clear that "no press copies of any part of it should in future be permitted." In the end, the committee opted for the most conservative route: "it will be best either to cover the present receptacle of the manuscript with an opaque lid or to move the manuscript from its frame and place it in a portfolio, where it may be protected from the action of light."[22]

The report in essence called for the Declaration to be hidden from view. But that would not do anything to restore it. A few years later, Frederic Bancroft and Andrew H. Allen, successive heads of the State Department's Bureau of Rolls and Library, commissioned the first attempts at proper conservation. They turned to private printing firms "for the restoration, mounting, and binding" of the records of the Continental Congress, as well as the papers of Madison, Monroe, and Washington.[23] These early conservators used folded linen or silk hinges with an adhesive solution to bind the fragile papers together into volumes. They sometimes enclosed the records in a transparent silk lining coated with paraffin, in an attempt to prevent exposure to oxygen or insects. These were primitive attempts at long-term preservation, safer than alternatives, but hardly sufficient, especially for a document as priceless as the Declaration.

After several years of experimentation on other documents, fears over the Declaration's condition had reached a fever pitch inside the State Department. To Allen, the department librarian, only one course of action could be taken. "The rapid fading of the text . . . and the deterioration of the parchment upon which it is engrossed," he wrote, "render it impracticable for the Department longer to exhibit or to handle it."[24] On February 12, 1894, Secretary of State Walter Q. Gresham ordered that the scroll be taken out of its standing case. In its place was displayed one of the Stone facsimiles, now paired with Thomas Jefferson's handwritten rough draft. The engrossed Declaration was placed between two "hermetically

The Declaration was put in a steel safe in 1894, and a facsimile was displayed in its place in the State Department Library (photograph circa 1900).

sealed" panes of glass and laid horizontally in a drawer of a steel case in the northwest corner of the library, along with the Constitution. Gresham's extraordinary action, taken on Abraham Lincoln's birthday, consigned the parchment Lincoln so loved to the darkness.[25]

Only rarely was the Declaration's closed drawer opened over the next three decades, and only once for the public's benefit. In 1898, the Declaration was brought out into "the searching effect of the sun's bright rays" where it was photographed for the popular *Ladies' Home Journal.* Though the Stone engraving was now regularly reproduced in newspapers, the *Journal*'s photograph was the first true mass-produced image of the engrossed parchment itself.

The public could see for themselves how badly the document had deteriorated. It was severely wrinkled and creased, its edges worn away and torn, with a sizable hole above the *m* in "America" in the title. The signatures were almost completely gone, but an eagle-eyed observer may have wondered at John Hancock's famous signature. It was almost certain that someone had partially traced over the lower part of the *J.* When this had happened and who did it will forever remain a mystery, yet it showed how badly any attempts to "restore" the Declaration would have turned out.[26]

Nearly a decade after the Declaration was put in its steel cabinet, it was taken out in another attempt to save it. In 1903, Secretary of State John Hay, Abraham Lincoln's old aide, now ill and in the final years of his public service, requested that the National Academy of Sciences convene another committee to better understand "the Condition and Preservation of the Declaration of Independence." Headed by the Columbia University chemist Charles F. Chandler, this panel came to a more draconian conclusion than its predecessors.

Chandler's committee reported back in April that the Declaration "has suffered very seriously from the very harsh treatment to which it was exposed in the earlier years of the Republic." "Folding and rolling have creased and broken the parchment. The wet press-copying operation, to which it was exposed about 1820, for the purpose of producing a facsimile copy, removed a large portion of the ink. Subsequent exposure to the action of light for more than thirty years, while the instrument was placed on exhibition, has resulted in the fading of the ink, particularly in the signatures." Not all was lost, however, as the committee was "pleased to find that no evidence of mould or other disintegrating agents can be discovered upon the parchment . . . nor any evidence that disintegration is now in progress."

The recommendations largely followed those of the 1881 panel: "The committee does not consider it wise to apply any chemicals with a view to restoring the original color of the ink . . . nor does the committee consider it necessary or advisable to apply any solution . . . with a view to strengthening the parchment . . . The committee is of the opinion that the present method of protecting the instrument should be continued . . ." The final recommendation, however, was absolute: the Declaration "should be kept in the dark and as dry as possible, and never placed on exhibition."[27]

Hay followed these recommendations to the letter. But before locking the Declaration away, he ordered it photographed as a record of its condition. This was done by Levin C. Handy, nephew of the famous Civil

This photo from 1912, taken in the State Department Library, is the only known image of the engrossed Declaration between 1903 and 1924. Note the absence of handprints or water stains.

War–era photographer Mathew Brady. Hay then had the parchment's frame checked, to ensure that its French glass seals were airtight, before closing the cabinet permanently.

"Did you ever see the Declaration of Independence—the original manuscript?" asked the *Dallas Morning News*, on July 4, 1897, three years after the scroll was taken down from display. "If you have not, you probably never will," it rather pessimistically concluded. After Hay's decision in 1903, the *Baltimore American* soberly informed its readers that "The Declaration of Independence is to be seen no more by the public [and] will never be exhibited again at any of the great international fairs."[28] Perhaps the most dramatic reaction to the scroll's disappearance was in the New Orleans *Times-Picayune*, whose headline screamed "The Lost Declaration—Jefferson's Immortal Composition Will Soon Cease to Have Material Existence." Readers of that late-October 1903 article were told that "no one can hope . . . to look upon the Declaration of Independence again . . . the time must inevitably arrive when the writing will have practically disappeared."[29] There remained no answer to preserving the document with the science of the time.

For decades, biographies of the Signers had appeared, and the scroll had been celebrated in tales, cartoons, and even song. As an object of scholarly study, however, the Declaration had yet to find a champion. The waning years of the nineteenth century and opening of the twentieth now witnessed the first attempts to scrape away legend and tell the Declaration's true history.

For Mellen Chamberlain, it started with the signatures. He was the head librarian at the Boston Public Library and an avid collector of autographs, among them a rare, complete set of the Signers. Ever since Benjamin Owen Tyler had made his "curiously exact imitation" of the Signers' autographs in 1818, Americans had been fascinated with the signatures, and multiple facsimiles sold in the nineteenth century were only of the names. Chamberlain used his own collection to make a composite reproduction of the Declaration to hang in the Room for Younger Readers in the Library, ingeniously pasting original autographs of the Signers on a copy of the Stone engraving. Praised as a "treasure," the effect was to show a generation of young Bostonians what the Declaration had looked like in 1776.[30]

It was perhaps a short leap for Chamberlain from collecting the signatures to wanting to know how they had come to be on the parchment. He undertook a detailed study of the Declaration's origins, becoming the first scholar known to use Charles Thomson's *Secret Journal.* Chamberlain untangled for a modern audience the difference between the vote for Independence on July 2 and the adoption of the public announcement on July 4, and dove into the controversy over Adams and Jefferson's final quarrel over authorship in 1823. He traced the steps leading up to the "authentication" of the broadside printed by John Dunlap and explained the subsequent order on July 19 to engross the document on parchment. His *Authentication of the Declaration of Independence, July 4, 1776*, first published in the *Proceedings of the Massachusetts Historical Society* in November 1884 and as a book the following year, sparked a new field of Declaration studies.[31] Chamberlain's monograph appeared the same year the American Historical Association was founded, inaugurating the modern historical profession. Within a few years scholars of American history joined legal theorists and political scientists in bringing new, rigorous methods to the study of the Declaration.[32]

In 1891, R. M. Black explored the ethics of the Declaration in the *Annals of the American Academy of Political and Social Science*, considering what the Founding Fathers meant by "equality" and how it should be understood as a modern philosophical concept.[33] Five years later, Moses Coit Tyler of Cornell took to the pages of the *North American Review*, the country's most prominent periodical, to refute the age-old claim that the Declaration was but "a stately patchwork of sweeping propositions of somewhat doubtful validity." Tyler, the first professor of American History in the country, argued that Thomas Jefferson's document accurately reflected the mid-eighteenth-century English understandings of tyranny, and that Jefferson's supposed lack of originality showed him to be "the very mouthpiece and prophet of the people whom he represented, and as such required . . . to gather up into his own soul, as much as possible, whatever was then also in their souls, their very thoughts and passions."[34]

To Tyler, the Declaration was a living philosophy acutely relevant for the dawning twentieth century. This was an argument advanced by Herbert Friedenwald, whose prizewinning PhD dissertation at Johns Hopkins University was published in 1904 as *The Declaration of Independence: An Interpretation and Analysis*. Friedenwald examined the political events that had made Independence a reality in the minds of Americans in the 1770s, complementing a 1900 *Harvard Law Review* article by Massachusetts State Senator William F. Dana on the political sources of the Declaration. In addition to arguing that the Declaration had a profound effect on "the whole fabric of our constitutional legal development," he offered one of the first in-depth explorations of John Locke's influence on the document. Tracing both English thought of the seventeenth century and its reception in eighteenth-century America, Friedenwald noted that it was "Jefferson, to whose metaphysical mind Locke seems to have made an especial appeal."[35]

Few of these early efforts fully exploited the wealth of historical materials available from the Declaration's earliest days. It was up to a thirty-six-year-old New York lawyer to produce the most detailed, and to this day unsurpassed, volume on the origins and drafting of the Declaration. Appearing in 1906, John Hampden Hazelton's *The Declaration of Independence: Its History* minutely re-created the day-by-day debates and decisions related to the Declaration and painstakingly traced its drafting and editing. Using Congress's journals, letters, diaries, pamphlets, books, newspapers, and periodicals, Hazelton provided a detailed portrait of the debates in Congress, gave the first accounts of its reception around the colonies, and briefly followed the fortunes of the parchment after 1776. He dispelled popular myths and apocryphal stories, including Benson Lossing's claim that the Liberty Bell was rung on July Fourth. His hefty volume included foldouts of facsimiles of the most important resolutions of the Congress, the rough draft, and of course the engrossed parchment.

With a sixty-eight-page appendix and 228 pages of notes, Hazelton's opus clocked in at 630 pages, providing a complete, one-volume archive on the Declaration's origins. His research was so thorough that all following books on the Declaration have relied on it as the most complete collection of primary sources related to the document. Other studies would follow, but none would surpass Hazelton's monumental achievement.[36]

Yet not even John Hazelton knew everything there was to know about the Declaration. Now that any American could see actual photographs of the scroll as well as the high-quality Stone engraving, some began to wonder whose hand it was that had engrossed it so memorably.

The mystery was resolved in the July 29, 1916, issue of *The Youth's Companion*, a popular periodical at the time. In an article entitled "The

Penmanship of the Declaration of Independence," Gaillard Hunt, chief of the Library of Congress's Manuscript Division, described for his young readers the detective work that his staff had done comparing the Declaration to other pieces of calligraphy. Hunt then revealed to the world that the long-forgotten Timothy Matlack was the scribe of America's founding document. One hundred and forty years after carrying out his most important commission, Matlack finally took his rightful place in American history.

Chapter 14
The People's Declaration

"Silent Cal" Coolidge may well have been gratified that the ceremony on the second floor of the Great Hall in the Library of Congress was entirely without speeches—or, indeed, words of any kind. The President, First Lady, and distinguished guests watched mutely as two large American flags were drawn back to reveal an elegant marble shrine set in the west wall of the Library. Through the windows, the dome of the U.S. Capitol could be seen across the street.

Herbert Putnam, the Librarian of Congress, hoisted a large glass frame and climbed up a makeshift stand. Now towering above the crowd, the compact, wiry Putnam posed for photographers before swinging open the two bronze doors, inserting the frame into the case, and climbing down. After Putnam similarly installed the Constitution, in a standing case below the shrine, the Library staff sang two stanzas of "America." A guard then took his place next to the shrine. It was February 28, 1924, and with this simple ceremony, the Declaration of Independence was returned to the people.[1]

Officially, the road to the shrine began in April 1920, when Secretary of State Bainbridge Colby appointed a committee to tackle "the question of the display of certain of these documents for the benefit of the patriotic public."[2] Just seventeen years after John Hay had prohibited the parchment from ever being shown again, the changes transforming America had persuaded officials of the importance of displaying the scroll once more.[3]

A surge in immigration from 1880 to 1920 had brought over 20 million newcomers to America, many from Scandinavia and southern and eastern Europe. From a population of 50 million in 1880, the country had shot up to 106 million four decades later. High birth rates combined with waves of immigrants who settled in the new territories and packed into rising metropolises like Chicago, Cleveland, St. Louis, and Kansas City.

With the foreign-born now 15 percent of the population, turning these immigrants into patriotic Americans became a priority for politicians, employers, and educators. Mandatory elementary school and civics classes were designed to imbue them with American values and to teach them about the principles of self-government. Community groups also played a key role. The Educational Alliance, founded in 1889 on East Broadway as one of New York's original settlement houses, gave tens of thousands of Jewish immigrants from Russia and Eastern Europe "that practical understanding of American government, institutions, and ideas which alone can make them real Americans."[4] During World War I, the National Americanization Committee, headed at one point by Thomas Edison and Mrs. Cornelius Vanderbilt, distributed thousands of copies of a forty-eight-page *Citizenship Syllabus* to "train our foreign-born population for good, efficient and devoted American citizenship."[5] In 1922, the Ford Motor Company began advertising educational films on "Civics and Citizenship" aimed at public schools.[6]

Meanwhile, the country's founding documents were translated into immigrants' native languages. While German and French versions of the Declaration had existed since 1776, a veritable Babel of new translations now flooded cities and towns alike. References to the Declaration increasingly popped up in community newspapers, pamphlets, and handbooks for immigrants. In 1880, the large Swedish communities throughout the upper Midwest could find the *Sjelfständighetsförklaring* in a book on American history printed in Chicago. A Yiddish *Erklarung fuun zelbest shtendigkite* appeared on New York's blossoming Lower East Side as early as 1892, and later, in 1920, as the *Aunafhengigkeyt Derklerung*.[7]

The tide of translation picked up in the first decades of the twentieth century. The *Prokyrixis tis anexartisías* appeared in 1917 in Greek, the language of the ancient homeland of democracy, and in 1923, a guide to obtaining American citizenship for Italian immigrants contained *La*

ערקלערונג פון זעלבסט שטענדיגקייט.

DECLARATION OF INDEPENDENCE.

A Declaration by the Representatives of the United States of America, in Congress Assembled.

When, in the course of human events, it becomes necessary for one people to dissolve the political bands which have connected them with another, and to assume, among the powers of the earth, the separate and equal station to which the laws of nature and nature's God entitle them, a decent respect to the opinions of mankind requires that they should declare the causes which impel them to the separation.

We hold these truths to be self-evident—that all men are created equal; that they are endowed by their

Swedish (1880), Yiddish (1892), and Greek (1917) translations of the Declaration were used for civics classes and citizenship education of immigrants.

Dichiarazione d'Indipendenza, reminding the newcomers that the Founders had pledged "le nostre vite, le nostre fortune, il nostro sacro onore" to the cause. James Brown Scott of the Carnegie Endowment of International Peace published a Russian translation of the *Deklaratsiia nezavisimosti* for Slavic immigrants, in 1919, two years after the Bolsheviks had taken power, ending any hopes for democracy in what was soon to become the Soviet Union.[8]

While the Declaration in these decades was reaching millions of immigrants who had never experienced democracy, families who could trace their lineage back to the Revolutionary era began to claim a unique connection to the scroll and its history. On July 4, 1907, at the Jamestown Tercentennial Exposition, over 150 men and women whose forefathers had been delegates to the Continental Congress formed the "Society of Descendants of the Signers of the Declaration of Independence." The minutes from their first meeting noted that the attendees, representing a majority of the Signers, were "filled with patriotic spirit and expressing loyalty to the principles of those who signed that immortal document . . . and full appreciation of their noble achievements."[9] Among the speeches, Hollins N. Randolph, a direct descendant of Thomas Jefferson, spoke on the "great deed wrought by the signers" of the Declaration, his remarks taken down by the Society's secretary, his cousin Thomas Jefferson Randolph. Interest in the Signers had never really abated, but to honor the action of their ancestors, the Society of Descendants took their place alongside members of the Society of the Cincinnati (founded in 1783), the Daughters of the American Revolution (founded in 1890), and other founding-era genealogical organizations that flourished at the time.[10]

Some who had been connected to the land for much longer were also made aware of the Declaration during these years, if unwillingly. On July 4, 1897, a group of Lakota (Sioux) elders, some wearing ceremonial headdress, sat in a circle under the bright sun in an open field on the Rosebud Agency reservation in South Dakota while a dark-suited government agent read out the Declaration.[11] Similar ceremonies were organized on Indian reservations for the Blackfeet in Montana and the Nez Perce in Idaho. We don't know if the agents reading the Declaration on the reservations skipped the document's condemnation of "the merciless Indian Savages, whose known Rule of Warfare, is an undistinguished Destruction, of all Ages, Sexes and Conditions." That line held a tragic irony, given the brutal suppression campaign waged by the U.S. Army against American Indian tribes during the 1860s and 1870s.[12]

Thousands of Indians had been killed in battles and massacres in the Indian Wars of the 1870s, while thousands more perished from disease. The wars crushed their hopes of retaining independence and forced resettlement gave American Indians no choice but to leave their ancestral tribal lands and migrate over long distances to large reservations, which were often on "bad lands" west of the Rockies. Successive administrations now embarked on a campaign to assimilate the Native Americans insofar as possible into the mainstream culture, though they were not yet considered citizens. Government agents set up schools that aimed to instill Western values in Indian youth. Thousands were forced into boarding schools off the reservations.

As part of the government's assimilation campaign, the Declaration was read to Lakota (Sioux) elders on the Rosebud Agency reservation in South Dakota on July 4, 1897.

As part of the project of assimilation, civic documents like the Declaration were brought to their remote homesteads along with the Bible.[13] Some scholars speculate that the Declaration was translated into some Indian languages, like that of the Nez Perce.[14] The Declaration's insistence that a government's legitimacy depended on the consent of the governed fitted uneasily with federal attempts to restrict the autonomy of people on the reservations and to break the power of the tribes by granting land directly to individuals and families. Not until 1924 did the American Indian Citizenship Act give citizenship to those individuals who had not left their reservations or who joined the Armed Forces during World War I.[15] At the same time, the Act allowed Indians to retain their tribal membership, essentially giving them dual citizenship and recognizing the primacy of the tribe in Indian affairs. By the mid-1930s, the last of the boarding schools were closed, having largely failed, and the more overt elements of the assimilation campaign were ended, but the final subjugation of the Indians had left them economically, politically, and socially neglected.[16]

The Declaration was also embroiled in the intense debates over the emergence of the modern American economy in these years. The shift from local agriculture and production to a nationwide managerial industrial system in the decades after the Civil War created dramatically new economic relationships. Tinkerers such as Thomas Edison and Alexander Graham Bell had pushed the boundaries of technology. Corporate titans like John D. Rockefeller, founder of Standard Oil; Andrew Carnegie, who created the modern steel industry; Henry Ford, who made the automobile affordable to the middle class; and Cornelius Vanderbilt, creator of modern shipping and rail lines, forged the first monopolies. Behind them were financiers like J. P. Morgan, who completed the process of trust building, combining these corporations into larger, more powerful entities.[17] When Rockefeller was quoted as saying that "The combination is here to stay. Individualism has gone, never to return," he summed up the view of the new industrialists.[18]

Whether derided as "robber barons" or celebrated as visionary builders, these captains of industry hammered out the modern United States from its prewar agricultural roots.[19] Their efforts increased the standard of living and sparked innovative competition, but also dramatically widened the gap between owners and wage earners, bringing forth inequality and dissension. Such far-reaching changes called into question the relationship between Americans and their state, as social and economic reformers began to see the Declaration as a defense, first and foremost, of individual rights.[20]

Such reformers invoked the Declaration as a symbol of traditional American values, or to express the common aspirations of the laboring class. The more radical, the less effective the effort. The Socialist Labor Party, primarily German in membership, published a "Declaration of Interdependence," on July 4, 1895, in the party's New York organ, *The People*. The manifesto began "When, the course of human progression, the despoiled class of wealth producers becomes fully conscious of it rights and determined to take them, a decent respect to the judgment of posterity requires that it should declare the causes which impel it to change the social order." The party's declaration ended with more Marx than Jefferson, urging "Americans, fall into line! Onward to the Co-operative Commonwealth!" Both hectoring and awkward, such exhortations gained as little traction nationwide as had earlier socialist appeals.[21]

More mainstream reforming voices also leaned on the Declaration. In 1895, the year before he became the Democratic Party nominee for president, Nebraska Representative William Jennings Bryan wrote "Of the self-evident truths set forth in that immortal document, the declaration that 'All men are created equal' is the most important . . . Its application now would solve aright the questions which vex the civilized world . . ." To progressive reformers like Bryan, true fidelity to the promise of the Declaration could help the nation redress economic inequalities and serve to protect the rights of farmers and workers against the concentrations of capital represented by financiers like Morgan and industrialists such as Rockefeller and Carnegie.[22]

Amid such dramatic domestic change, America stepped onto the world stage. When President Woodrow Wilson decided, in April 1917, to bring the United States into World War I, which had been raging in Europe for three years, he justified his action by claiming that "[t]he world must be made safe for democracy." Believing, like Thomas Jefferson, that democracy was a global cause, Wilson proclaimed to Congress on April 6 that "America is privileged to spend her blood and her might for the principles that gave her birth and happiness and the peace which she has treasured." In making his call to arms, Wilson explicitly evoked the language of the Declaration, asserting that to such a task "we can dedicate our lives and our fortunes."[23]

On July 4, 1918, over a hundred representatives of immigrant communities gathered in Philadelphia to sign a "Unanimous Declaration of Men of Many Races in the United States of America" in support of the war. "Publicly affirming our whole-hearted loyalty to these United States," these citizens imitated the Declaration of 1776, asserting that "When later in the course of human history the Nation which thus declared its independence is found in armed resistance to the aggressions of autocracy, and when men of many races stand ready to give their lives that the cause of democracy may prevail, it becomes a duty which they owe alike to themselves and to the world to make known the reasons for their determination."[24] Winston Churchill echoed the sentiment at a July Fourth celebration in England that same day. "A great harmony exists between the spirit and language of the Declaration of Independence and all we are fighting for now," proclaimed Churchill, linking the Declaration with Magna Carta and the English Bill of Rights "as the third great title-deed on which the liberties of the English-speaking people are founded."[25]

While Woodrow Wilson invoked the Declaration in his bid to preserve liberty abroad, at home he took a very different position. Speaking before a large crowd at Independence Hall on July 4, 1914, he dismissed Jefferson's famous preamble that all men are created equal. To understand the document, Wilson argued, one must "pass beyond those preliminary passages which we are accustomed to quote about the rights of men" and focus merely on the specifics of that "vital piece of practical business." Wilson made clear there was nothing timeless or universal about the Declaration in his view, asserting that "[t]here is nothing in it for us unless we can translate it into the terms of our own conditions and of our own lives."[26]

Those conditions for Wilson included dramatically increasing the size and power of the federal government in ways that would have horrified Jefferson, introducing government censorship during wartime, and severely infringing on civil liberties. Perhaps even more dramatically, he reversed decades of modest integration of Black Americans into government service, resegregating government offices, and did little to oppose emerging Jim Crow policies of local segregation and discrimination.[27]

By 1920, the combined effects of urbanization, immigration, industrialization, Progressivism, and the dramatic growth of the federal government threatened to make anachronistic the Declaration's focus on limited central power and individual rights. Yet at the same time, only the Declaration seemed able to inspire a new sense of what it meant to be American that could hold together the now vastly larger and more diverse nation than the thirteen colonies Adams and Jefferson had known.[28]

In May 1920, for the first time in at least eight years the stout safe in the library of the Department of State was opened. A small knot of men gathered around as the top drawer was slid out and the engrossed Declaration emerged into the light. The group had been appointed by President Wilson's Secretary of State, Bainbridge Colby, to reconsider the recommendation of the two previous expert committees that the parchment was too fragile to display. After examining the scroll, the committee reported back that the "parchment is still strong, pliable, and without signs of deterioration." "We believe the fading can go no further," it continued. "We see no reason why the original document should not be exhibited if the parchment be laid between two sheets of glass, hermetically sealed at the edges and exposed only to diffused light."[29]

Colby was out of office before he could finalize any plans. In March 1921, President Warren G. Harding took office and appointed Charles Evans Hughes as Secretary of State. After a few months, Hughes took up the issue of the Declaration. He accepted the recommendation of Colby's committee but then made a decision no one expected. At the urging of Gaillard Hunt, Hughes used a 1903 executive order by Theodore Roosevelt to transfer the Declaration to the Library of Congress, where Hunt was chief of the Manuscripts Division.

Roosevelt's order allowed any executive department to send books, maps, and papers they no longer needed to the Library of Congress. He had directed that the papers of the Continental Congress, as well as those of George Washington, James Madison, Alexander Hamilton, and other Revolutionary-era leaders, be stored at the Library. Hughes now used Roosevelt's precedent to transfer custody of the Declaration, citing both the lack of any departmental need for the document and safety concerns, especially the ever-present fear of fire.

On September 28, 1921, Hughes formally recommended to President Harding that the Declaration and Constitution be transferred to the Library of Congress. Marshalling his argument in the precise style of the Associate Justice of the Supreme Court that he had until recently been, Hughes explained that in the Library, "these muniments will be in the custody of experts skilled in archival preservation, in a building of modern fireproof construction, where they can safely be exhibited to the many visitors who now desire to see them." None of this could be guaranteed in the State Department.[30] The next day Harding issued an executive order calling for the Declaration and Constitution to be sent to the Library of Congress, "to satisfy the laudable wish of patriotic Americans to have an opportunity to see the original fundamental documents upon which rest their independence and their Government." This formally removed the Declaration as a paper of state and reclassified it as part of a nascent national archive.

Hughes then wrote Herbert Putnam, Librarian of Congress since 1899, that he was prepared to turn the documents over whenever Putnam was ready to receive them. While modernizing the Library and expanding its collection, the sixty-year-old Putnam had long argued that the Library of Congress was in effect a national library.[31] To gain custody of the nation's founding documents, to be charged with their preservation and allowed to decide how to bring them back to the American people, was an acknowledgment that the Library of Congress was much more than a repository of books for the legislative branch.

Putnam wasted no time. On September 30, 1921, the day he received Hughes's letter, he grabbed several assistants and showed up before noon

The Declaration of Independence and Constitution being placed into a Ford Model T mail truck for transfer to the Library of Congress, September 30, 1921.

at the looming State, War, and Navy Department, where the safe was opened and the Declaration and Constitution were removed one last time. With no ceremony, the fragile document was carried in its frame of "cheapest oak" to the Library of Congress's Model T mail wagon, where it was placed on a pile of leather U.S. Mail sacks, driven to the Library, and put in yet another safe, this time in the Librarian's office.[32]

Putnam immediately began planning how to display the Declaration. The next year's budget was due, and he quickly added a request for $12,000 to construct a suitable case to protect and display the Declaration. In January 1922, he went before a Congressional appropriations committee to lobby for the funds, enticing the legislators with his vision of a bronze case with a railed enclosure. If he could build it, Putnam assured the congressmen, "you would have something that every visitor to Washington would wish to tell about when he returned and who would regard it . . . with keen interest as a sort of 'shrine.'"[33]

Putnam's appeal was approved, and he quickly turned to the task of bringing the shrine into existence, commissioning Francis H. Bacon, the brother of Henry Bacon, the architect of the almost-completed Lincoln Memorial. Bacon's plan included a back panel made out of marble from

New York, a two-foot-high enclosure of Italian marble, and a floor made of marble from Greece and Vermont. The bronze case, with its gold-plated doors, was set into the wall and a second, larger bronze case, for the Constitution, was installed on the floor in front, behind the low wall. A marble bench would allow people to step up for a closer look. Into the grayish-black back panel was incised and gilded "The Declaration of Independence and the Constitution of the United States."

While the shrine was being prepared, Putnam had received another treasure. Miraculously, Jefferson's original rough draft of the Declaration had survived the passage of years. In 1848, his descendants had sold it to the Department of State, which transferred it to the Library on January 4, 1922. Within a few months, Putnam had obtained the alpha and omega of the Declaration, joining them with a rare volume containing the autographs of all the Signers presented to the Library in 1911 by J. P. Morgan.[34]

By January 1924, Putnam's shrine was ready. He and his staff handled the parchment with the greatest possible care, yet the methods used were only slightly more sophisticated, and potentially as damaging, as those of the previous century. On January 22, two members from the repair shops of the Library's Manuscripts and Prints Divisions took the Declaration out of its old oak frame and glued the fragile parchment to a tissue paper border affixed to a pulpboard mount. When the mount was slipped vertically into the bronze case, out of direct sunlight at last, it would be covered by two panes of glass between which was inserted a special gelatin film designed to diffuse the indirect light inside the Library. Though it was undeniably an advance, this was the extent of the technology available to prevent further deterioration and fading of the Declaration. The next month, Putnam gathered President and Mrs. Coolidge, Secretary of State Hughes, the Speaker of the House of Representatives, and other dignitaries in the Library for the installation ceremony.[35]

Now spotlighted in its elegant shrine, the Declaration of Independence quickly became the Library of Congress's crown jewel and most popular attraction. Over a million visitors a year, from all over the country and the world, passed through the Library's doors, and most, if not all, went to the shrine. An *Atlanta Constitution* article from July 1926 noted that three thousand people entered the marble enclosure each day. Never had so many Americans and other visitors viewed the Declaration. Herbert Putnam had elevated the Declaration to an unparalleled position of prominence, his vision of a marble shrine inspiring a new veneration for

Herbert Putnam, Librarian of Congress, prepares to place the Declaration in its new case during the enshrinement ceremony on February 28, 1924.

the scroll among the "patriotic public." Newspapers reported that some treated the shrine literally, kneeling in prayer on the marble bench beneath the Declaration, and claimed that one woman sobbed while wrapping her arms around the bronze case holding the Constitution.[36]

While Herbert Putnam's shrine was being prepared, a quiet Cornell scholar named Carl Lotus Becker wrote what was to stand for half a century as the definitive interpretation of the document. His *The Declaration of Independence: A Study in the History of Political Ideas*, published in 1922, expanded on Herbert Friedenwald's 1904 book. Becker painstakingly detailed how the primary influence on Jefferson was the seventeenth-century English philosopher John Locke, who claimed that people have natural rights to "life, liberty, and property" that exist beyond the reach of government. Yet Becker's own philosophical views led him to deny any universal, timeless validity to Jefferson's theory, rejecting Abraham Lincoln's understanding of the document as well. "To ask whether the natural rights philosophy of the Declaration of Independence is true or false," Becker concluded, "is essentially a meaningless question," echoing Woodrow Wilson's reinterpretation of the document. Though long influential, Becker's provocative judgment eventually led to strong refutations, including in 1959 by the scholar Harry Jaffa, who reasserted Lincoln's universal interpretation in *The Crisis of the House Divided*, and Garry Wills, who in 1978's *Inventing America* denied that Locke was Jefferson's primary influence, suggesting that other figures in the Scottish Enlightenment were equally if not more important.[37]

Outside of the academic world, the Declaration and its creators remained visible in early-twentieth-century American culture. As an image, the Declaration reached new heights of popularity. Around the turn of the century, the artist Howard Pyle produced a heroic image of Thomas Jefferson drafting the Declaration in his rooms on Market Street, a solitary genius standing by candlelight as he contemplates his creation.[38] A few years later, in one of a series of seventy-eight paintings on American history entitled *The Pageant of a Nation*, the Philadelphia artist J. L. G. Ferris idealized a different scene of the drafting of the Declaration. Jefferson, quill pen in hand, stands over Franklin and Adams, their small table and the floor beneath it strewn with discarded paper, with Independence Hall faintly seen through the window. Reproduced as a postcard by the Foundation Press in 1932, this illustration became one of the most popular representations of the founding document (see insert).

High-minded art aside, mass advertising had first appropriated the Declaration in the late 1800s, and the scroll continued to be good business in the new century. The *National Geographic Magazine* ran an offer in 1930 from the venerable John Hancock Life Insurance Company for a free, "officially approved facsimile parchment" of the Stone engraving, continuing a long tradition of using the scroll as a promotional item. That same company, whose logo since 1862 has been Hancock's famous signature, also distributed thousands of copies of two small pamphlets during the 1920s on the history of the Declaration, one of which reproduced a drawing of the Library of Congress's new shrine and informed readers that they could see the "precious" document there at any time.[39]

Along with mass advertising came mass entertainment to twentieth-century America. As early as 1924, the Yale University Press Film Services released a twenty-four-minute, three-reel silent film entitled *The Declaration of Independence*, aimed at public schools. Based on Carl L. Becker's book *The Eve of Revolution*, and part of a series called *The Chronicles of America*, the historically detailed film portrayed the tumult of the summer of 1776, with Thomas Paine rabble-rousing in the streets while John Adams and Benjamin Franklin maneuvered inside Independence Hall. Yale also published a teaching guide that included a synopsis, lesson aids, and reading list.[40]

Fourteen years later, the Declaration reached the moviegoing masses when the Vitaphone Corporation produced a seventeen-minute colorized movie short of the same events with a decidedly more dramatic flair. Fictionalizing Caesar Rodney's mad dash from Delaware to Philadelphia, the film included a thrilling chase scene that could have been mistaken for a penny Western, with Rodney escaping anti-independence forces to arrive just in time for the vote on July 2, 1776. Despite, or perhaps because of, such liberties with the facts, the film won an Oscar. Also in 1938, famed director Cecil B. DeMille produced *The Buccaneer*, starring well-known actor Frederic March, which included a scene of the burning of Washington in 1814 and Dolley Madison's fanciful rescue of the Declaration from the flames. In its inimitable way, Hollywood was bringing the Declaration to life for millions of moviegoers, but how much was myth few seemed to inquire or care.

On the evening of Monday, July 5, 1926, a crowd estimated at twenty-five thousand gathered in the front of the U.S. Capitol to celebrate the 150th anniversary of American Independence. No events had been scheduled on the actual date, since it fell on a Sunday, but the following day, the massive crowd saw the Capitol Dome brightly lit in different colors for the first time. At the other end of the Mall, the rockets' red glare of fireworks burst over the Washington Monument. After the pyrotechnics, over one thousand performers presented a pageant entitled "The Story of America" on the steps of the Capitol Building.[41] Among its set pieces was a reenactment of the signing of the Declaration of Independence.

It was also the centenary of the deaths of Thomas Jefferson and John Adams. At Monticello, a week's worth of events by the Daughters of the American Revolution, the University of Virginia, and other groups included an interfaith service in honor of Jefferson's promotion of freedom of religion. The week culminated in a ceremony in which ownership of the famed house formally passed from the Levy family to the Thomas Jefferson Memorial Foundation. *The Washington Post* celebrated the hand-over by trumpeting that "Jefferson's House Is Given to Nation as People's Shrine." Up in Massachusetts, a grand procession in Quincy made its way to the tomb of John and Abigail Adams and marched on to the small saltbox cottage in which the elder Adams was born, where his great-great-grandson read the Declaration to the assembled crowd.[42]

Patriotic education was a focus of the Sesquicentennial commemorations, whether in newspapers and periodicals, government pamphlets, or in a new history written for young readers by Mabel Mason Carlton and Henry Fisk Carlton. Well-illustrated and dismissing some of the myths surrounding the document, *The Story of the Declaration of Independence* wrapped up its 113 pages of text by reinforcing for American youth what had come to be the dominant interpretation of the Declaration's importance, as "the living expression of the ideals of true American liberty!"[43]

Not all voices were so celebratory. With segregation deepening and Jim Crow laws multiplying, the reality of inequality was palpable to Black Americans. The Ku Klux Klan had undergone a resurgence since the 1915 premiere of D. W. Griffith's "lost cause" epic *The Birth of a Nation*, which President Wilson had screened at the White House and which was seen by twenty-five million Americans.[44] Racial violence also was increasing. Chicago exploded in a violent riot in the summer of 1919, in which 23 Blacks and 15 Whites were killed, while in 1921, the Tulsa Race Massacre took the lives of as many as 300 Blacks and at least 100 Whites and burned down Oklahoma's second-largest Black neighborhood.[45]

Now, just five years after Tulsa, the National Equal Rights League requested that President Coolidge "fulfill the principles of the Declaration for all regardless of race or color." The League in particular protested the decision to name Southerners to head the government commission planning the Sesquicentennial celebrations, according to *The Chicago Defender*, one of the country's leading Black newspapers.[46] Writing in the same newspaper on the eve of the anniversary, the Reverend Theodore Stevens offered just one of hundreds of criticisms of American society. "Does such a state of affairs as pledged in the American Declaration of Independence obtain in the 48 states of the Union with respect to people of African descent?" Stevens asked. "Men of color know that it does not."[47] A few months later, the National Equal Rights League again asked that President Coolidge "show his loyalty to the Declaration of Independence" by outlawing segregation in the federal workforce.[48] The Declaration had been used to help extirpate slavery and bring about constitutional equality, yet one hundred fifty years after its creation, its promise had yet to be fully realized.

Amid such celebration and criticism, Philadelphia again invited the world to commemorate the anniversary in its streets. Despite attractions including an eighty-foot reproduction of the Liberty Bell, lit by twenty-six thousand electric light bulbs, the Sesquicentennial Exposition was largely a failure, riven by internal dissension and civic opposition, and plagued by bad weather. Heavily in debt, the exposition attracted fewer than five million paying visitors.[49]

If there was a highlight to the exposition, it came on Monday, July 5, 1926, when President Calvin Coolidge gave the keynote address. Though the president was often caricatured as less than talkative, Coolidge's forty-minute speech, entitled "The Inspiration of the Declaration of Independence," offered an interpretation dramatically different from that of scholars like Carl Becker.

Coolidge acknowledged that the Declaration's historical significance was in proposing a new nation based on principles of equality. Yet he found its source not in the Enlightenment philosophy of John Locke but in America's religious soil, particularly its Protestant tradition. Locke's theory of natural right of course depended on the existence of God, but Coolidge saw more power in the sermons of the clergy with their direct focus on revealed truth. "The Declaration was the result of the religious teachings" of the colonial era, Coolidge told his thirty-five thousand listeners. He quoted in particular the Reverend John Wise of Massachusetts, who had fought for the freedom of individual churches from hierarchical religious control. Around the turn of the eighteenth century, Wise had argued that "Every man must be acknowledged equal to every man" and proclaimed that "The end of all government is to cultivate humanity, and promote the happiness of all, and the good of every man in all his rights, his life, liberty, estate, honor, etc."[50]

Coolidge now asserted that Americans owed their freedom not to rational speculation, but to this religious tradition. Not only Wise, Coolidge argued, but the teachings of theologians like Jonathan Edwards and George Whitefield, who brought the Great Awakening to America, ensured an egalitarianism among men while in hierarchical obedience to God. This, Coolidge continued, inspired the country's founding charter. "In its main features the Declaration of Independence is a great spiritual document," Coolidge intoned, in a phrase picked up by national newspapers. He warned his fellow citizens that "unless the faith of the American people in these religious convictions is to endure, the principles of our Declaration will perish."

A plainspoken man of the people, Coolidge offered an interpretation that was more intelligible and congenial to ordinary Americans than the abstract musings of scholars like Carl Becker. Many Americans instinctively tied faith to freedom, something Alexis de Tocqueville had observed as early as 1835, in *Democracy in America*. Americans believe that religion is "necessary to the maintenance of republican institutions," wrote Tocqueville. "It is almost impossible to have them conceive of the one without the other."[51] Instinctively channeling the great French interpreter of America, Coolidge asked only that the citizen continue to live as he always had, faithful to God and to democratic practice alike. "Whatever else we may say of it," concluded the President, "the Declaration of Independence was profoundly American."[52]

Chapter 15

A Secret Journey in the Fight Against Fascism

When he was twenty-six, Archibald MacLeish came under aerial attack as an officer in World War I. "I have heard death overhead and have felt the swiftness of death and seen the hand of death," he wrote at the time. Perhaps he remembered the old fear decades later, as he watched the Declaration of Independence gingerly placed into a series of containers before being sealed in a bronze box, like a Russian *matryoshka* doll. MacLeish, now forty-nine, was the Librarian of Congress, and on the day after Christmas 1941, he was preparing to send the Declaration hundreds of miles away for fear of a new war from the air. The United States was three weeks into the second great global conflict of the twentieth century.[1]

MacLeish had not wanted to head the Library of Congress. He was a successful poet, a man of letters, not papers. Yet President Franklin D. Roosevelt had got his way, as he usually did, after several rounds of cajoling. The Yale alumnus and member of Skull and Bones took the position in October 1939, just weeks after Germany invaded Poland, and he became a wartime administrator. His main concern soon became the threat from the skies. The London Blitz, with its nightly bombings starting in September 1940, had proved that national capitals were largely defenseless against air attack. Both sides were developing even bigger bombers, leading the *New York Times* to comment that "the long-range bombing plane is coming into its own as a weapon of war." The President had warned that Germany had designs on Ireland and the Azores, which would put Washington in reach of new Nazi bombers like the four-engine Focke-Wulf "Kurier."[2]

MacLeish was consumed with the question of how to protect America's priceless literary, artistic, and archival treasures. Under the auspices of the National Resources Planning Board, he had helped form a "Committee on Conservation of Cultural Resources" in 1940. But unlike the heads of other cultural institutions, he faced a unique problem. He had responsibility for America's most important artifacts, the Declaration, Constitution, and Bill of Rights, and had accepted temporary custody from the British of the finest copy of Magna Carta, written in 1215, for safekeeping.[3]

Studies had concluded that the Library of Congress's nineteenth-century masonry would not withstand the bombs Germany was raining down on European cities. Convinced that America would eventually enter the war, MacLeish had written to Roosevelt as early as October of 1939 about the need to prepare "a safe depository for the most valuable books" of the Library. He and his staff had considered storing the most priceless items in a bombproof shelter underneath the Library itself and in a railway tunnel running beneath downtown Washington.[4] By April 1941, they had concluded that only one place could ensure the documents' survival. On April 30, MacLeish wrote Secretary of the Treasury Henry Morgenthau, "to enquire whether space might perhaps be found at Fort Knox . . . in the unlikely event that it becomes necessary to remove them from Washington." Morgenthau quickly replied that he would provide any needed storage at the heavily guarded Bullion Depository, eventually setting aside sixty cubic feet of space.[5]

Even while such plans were afoot, the Library of Congress continued to emphasize the Declaration's importance to Americans' self-identity. On the afternoon of Sunday, May 18, 1941, MacLeish premiered a radio program entitled "Hidden History" on the NBC Blue network. This first episode re-created the debates over the Declaration of Independence, starting with "Tom" and "Frank" wrangling over the draft in Philadelphia before moving to Williamsburg and Coxsackie, New York, where local declarations were written before the one in Philadelphia. In a world where fascism now threatened to crush individual liberty, MacLeish reminded his radio audience that "The people were not only the inspiration but the actual authors of the Declaration of Independence."[6] Seven months later, Japan attacked, and MacLeish immediately made plans to send the Declaration to the rolling green hills of Kentucky, 485 miles inland from Washington.

A week after Pearl Harbor, President Roosevelt went on radio to celebrate the 150th anniversary of the adoption of the Bill of Rights. "The rights to life, liberty, and the pursuit of happiness which seemed to the Founders of the Republic, and which seem to us, inalienable, were, to Hitler and his fellows, empty words which they proposed to cancel forever," he told his listeners. "The truths which were self-evident to Thomas Jefferson—which have been self-evident to the six generations of Americans who followed him—were to these men hateful," the President warned.[7] Now MacLeish moved to protect the parchment upon which those words were written.

On December 23, 1941, the Declaration was removed from the shrine, placed between sheets of acid-free paper, and wrapped in a millboard container. It was then carefully placed in a larger bronze box that had been cleaned and heated to remove any hint of moisture, then stuffed with rag wool insulation. The top container was screwed shut and sealed with a padlock. The same treatment was given to the Constitution, Bill of Rights, and Magna Carta.

On December 26, Attorney General Francis Biddle determined that the Librarian could "without further authority from the Congress or the President take such action as he deems necessary for the proper protection and preservation" of the Declaration and Charters of Freedom. Armed with the necessary authority, MacLeish had the bronze container fastened with wire and a lead seal, and packed it in a heavy metal-bound wood box. Stenciled on the box was the legend "Property Library of Congress." The box was forty inches by thirty-six inches and weighed an astonishing 150 pounds.[8]

That evening, with temperatures in the low forties, the Declaration and other Charters were driven in a truck escorted by armed guards the half-mile from the Library of Congress to Washington's Union Station. No one other than staff member Verner Clapp, who would become Chief Assistant Librarian in 1947, and a pair of armed Secret Service agents accompanying the strange packages knew what was carried into Sleeper Compartment B, in Car A-1 of the Baltimore and Ohio Railroad's *National Limited.* The train left Union Station at 6:30 p.m. and traveled west

Librarian of Congress Archibald MacLeish and Chief Assistant Librarian Verner Clapp sealing the Declaration for its secret transport to Fort Knox, December 26, 1941.

through the dark countryside all night. When he arrived in Louisville, Kentucky, at ten thirty the next morning, the weary Clapp was met by four additional Secret Service agents and a platoon of soldiers from the Thirteenth Armored Division.

The Declaration was loaded onto an Army truck and driven forty miles south. When the convoy reached the squat, gray granite Bullion Depository of Fort Knox, the massive vault was opened and Clapp turned over his precious cargo to Chief Clerk R. J. Van Horne, who placed it in compartment No. 24, about the size of a large living room, in an outer tier of the building on the ground level. The vault was shut just after noon and Verner Clapp was given a receipt for the world's most famous documents.

We could end the story of World War II here, a straightforward tale that wraps up with the Declaration's return to Washington after V-J Day. But the document's relocation to Fort Knox was seized upon as an opportunity for the first serious attempt at repairing the parchment. Those charged with protecting the Declaration could finally bring modern conservation techniques not just to its display, but to its preservation. They were just in time.

When Herbert Putnam set the Declaration in the shrine in 1924, much was made of the new mounting, sealed glass, and gelatin film protecting the scroll from the light. By the time the parchment was moved to Fort Knox, it had been hung vertically for seventy years and laid horizontally for thirty more in various locations. Enormous stress had been put on the document during these decades, and by 1940 the parchment was cracking and buckling from its mounting. A hasty repair sometime that year only made things worse.

A few months before the Declaration was spirited off to Fort Knox in the dead of the night, the Library had arranged for Dr. George L. Stout, its consultant on the care of manuscripts, and Evelyn Ehrlich, both of Harvard University's Fogg Museum of Art, to make any repairs needed. To keep prying eyes from learning that the priceless Declaration was to be removed from its case and repaired, letters going back and forth between the Library and Harvard carefully avoided naming the "certain famous documents" under discussion. The wartime move to Kentucky did not derail the plans, and in mid-May 1942, the two experts traveled with Verner Clapp to Fort Knox to begin a four-day examination and restoration of the Declaration.[9]

On May 13, the Declaration was moved to a specially cleaned workroom inside the vault. While soldiers drilled outside and guards patrolled the enclosure, Clapp and this team of restorers carefully measured the temperature (76 degrees) and humidity (59%) and spent an hour opening the bronze case before examining and photographing the document. What they found was disconcerting. The good news was, there still was no evidence of mold on the document. After that, things went downhill. Immediately noticeable was the continued fading of the script. For a century, observers had noted the disappearance of most of the signatures, but now the main text itself was much less readable. Just why this had happened, when the special glass and filters were supposed to prevent such deterioration, was unclear.

The Bullion Depository in Fort Knox, Kentucky, where the Declaration was brought for safekeeping during World War II. Postcard from the late 1930s.

Other damage soon became evident. At some point, likely 1924, "copious" amounts of glue had been used to affix the Declaration to its mounting of pulpboard, tissue paper, and green velvet, and the glue had spattered other spots. The upper right-hand corner of the parchment had cracked and separated and someone had tried to reattach it with Scotch tape, now discolored to a molasses shade. There were also two holes, one old one above the *m* in *America* in the heading, and a newer one above the *S* in *States*.

Perhaps worse, on the lower left-hand corner of the parchment was a clear handprint, and a fainter handprint could also be seen toward the center of the document. The middle area of the scroll was also marred by a large water stain, referred to as a "tide line." As late as 1912, when the Declaration was briefly taken out and photographed, neither the handprint nor the tide line had appeared, yet both were present in the photos taken in 1942 and remain visible today.

Sometime in those three decades serious damage had occurred, but the experts had no way to pinpoint when. In early 1922, a few months after the Library took custody of the Declaration, Herbert Putnam asked L. C. Handy, who had photographed the document in 1903, to take another photo. The prints and glass negative plates from that shoot disappeared and have never been located. Had they been available, Stout could have seen if the handprint and tide lines were visible in the missing photo.

In a grainy photograph taken of Putnam holding the Declaration at the installation ceremony in February 1924, the handprint and tide line seem to be just discernible. They are even clearer in photos taken some time in the 1920s of the scroll in the shrine. It is possible that when the Declaration was pressed down onto pulpboard during the mounting process in 1924, the oils from the hand that pressed it adhered to the parchment. That hand may have belonged to one of two men whose names Stout discovered written in pencil on the mount under the document: R. T. Anderson and Robt L. Bier, employees in the repair shops of the Library of Congress's Manuscripts Division and Prints Division, respectively. As for the water damage, we will never know how or when it came about.

While neither the handprint nor tide line could be removed, other damage to the body of the parchment could be repaired. On May 14, 1942, the two restorers began their delicate work, removing the Declaration from its mount, a painstaking job that took more than twelve hours. In several places they had to cut the mount away from the parchment and remove the remaining glue, paste, and paper attached to the document. They did this by "slicing and scraping," and by applying a touch of ethyl alcohol. Interestingly, when they chemically tested the ink, they concluded that it was not iron based, as had long been thought, but offered no alternative as to its composition.

On May 15, Stout and Ehrlich turned to the actual repair of the Declaration. Working on the back side of the scroll, they delicately joined the separated pieces and filled in the cracks in a process known as "luting." The material they used was a compound of fibers from Japanese tissue paper moistened with rice paste. Just six months after Pearl Harbor, America's foe was unknowingly providing vital technical assistance to preserve the founding document of the nation it was fighting. Using the rice paste–tissue mix, the upper right-hand corner was reattached, and the holes patched. The process worked so well that the restorers found no need to do it on both sides of the parchment, as the repairs made on the back meshed almost seamlessly on the front. After eight hours of detailed work, they placed the Declaration under glass, weighted down with bags of sand.

The restoration process was finished up the following day. Now cleaned and repaired, the Declaration was photographed by soldiers of the U.S. Army Signal Corps. As the parchment was lit by floodlights for fifteen minutes or so during the photography session, the conservators noticed that it shrank by as much as an eighth of an inch, just as it had "relaxed appreciably" the day before when the rainy weather had raised the humidity inside the bullion vault. After more than a century and a half, the Declaration was still a living scroll.

Once the photo session was finished, Stout and Ehrlich attached the Declaration to a new mount of "all-rag board," warmed overnight to allow moisture to evaporate. To prevent future cracking, fabric hinges designed to let the parchment contract and expand depending on the weather were attached at several places on the upper and lower edges. After this, the Declaration was locked back in its bronze case and replaced in its compartment. Before closing the door, the temperature and humidity were once again measured, and a thermo-hygrograph, to chart fluctuations in temperature and humidity, was installed. The door was then sealed with the personal seal of the Chief Clerk and the bullion vault locked.

Before returning to Cambridge, Stout and Ehrlich wrote up a detailed report on the work they had done and gave it and the journal containing their examination notes to Verner Clapp.[10] Two weeks after Clapp returned to Washington, the U.S. Navy won a crushing victory over the Japanese at Midway. The tide of war was beginning to turn.

Though it was locked away for safekeeping in Fort Knox, the Declaration was far from invisible during the four-year struggle against fascism. In the Library of Congress's shrine, a high-resolution photostat facsimile was installed, an apparently acceptable substitute for the visitors who continued to crowd the building. But the spirit of the Declaration played an even more powerful role during World War II than it had in the Great War. On the first Independence Day of America's involvement in the conflict, in 1942, *New York Times* editorial board member and Pulitzer Prize winner Anne O'Hare McCormick passionately linked the Declaration to the titanic struggle being waged overseas. "Only when we imagine what it would mean to live under another rule, another law," she wrote, "will we ever understand what we are fighting for. To understand that clearly will kindle passion for America as an idea and a Great Possession that will make the words of the Declaration as fresh and thrilling as when they were first written."[11] In the *Christian Science Monitor*, Reuben Markham, a bestselling author who had promoted intervention before Pearl Harbor, asserted that World War II was a continuation of the struggle against tyranny first begun in 1776. "We reverently stand before the very Declaration they signed, and as we read it, paragraph after paragraph, we see that every single right for which they struck is jeopardized by Axis despots."[12]

Yet while invoked, those rights were taken away from one group at home. By Executive Order 9066, signed on February 19, 1942, President Roosevelt mandated the internment of Japanese-American citizens living on the West Coast. This appalling violation of civil rights, later upheld by the Supreme Court, was based on unfounded fears that Americans of Japanese descent would not be loyal in wartime. It appeared motivated solely by racial animus, as German- and Italian-Americans, who were of much larger numbers, were not subject to similar repression and forced to move to isolated, spartan camps in the American West.

Despite this tragic reminder that equality and freedom remained vulnerable to the whims of xenophobia and political expediency, the following year offered a once-in-a-lifetime opportunity to celebrate the "sublime audacity," as Anne McCormick had put it, of the Founding Fathers. To commemorate the bicentennial of Thomas Jefferson's birth, on April 13, 1943, a memorial designed by the great architect John Russell Pope and modeled on the Roman Pantheon was dedicated in his honor. President Roosevelt ordered that the engrossed Declaration be brought back from Fort Knox for the dedication of the memorial on the Tidal Basin. Under tight security, the Declaration was returned in secret to the Library of Congress, where it was transferred to a special steel exhibition case and then moved to the new Jefferson Memorial. Four U.S. Marines struggled to carry the heavy case up to the towering statue of Jefferson, laying it at the base (see insert).

The formal dedication was made by President Roosevelt in a public ceremony. In his inimitable accent, Roosevelt tied the living Declaration to the struggle against fascism, and to his own economic reform policies. He reminded his listeners that Jefferson's "cause was a cause to which we also are committed, not by our words alone but by our sacrifice. The Declaration of Independence and the very purposes of the American Revolution itself, while seeking freedoms, called for the abandonment of privileges." As Abraham Lincoln and Woodrow Wilson had done, FDR sought legitimacy for his policies and to strengthen social unity by appealing to the Declaration's universal principles.[13] That Roosevelt presided over the greatest expansion of the federal government in American history, permanently altering the relationship of citizen and state, something Jefferson would have firmly opposed, went unremarked upon by the President and the press.

The scroll remained in the Memorial for a week after the ceremony, displayed at the base of Jefferson's statue for the crowds that continued to come. At night, it was moved into a side room and guarded by a detachment of Marines. Then, on April 21, under heavy guard, the Declaration returned to the safety of Fort Knox.[14]

Though the parchment was gone, visitors thronged the Memorial, gazing at Jefferson's greatest phrases chiseled into panels in the marble walls. The memorial's commission, which included Jefferson's great-great-grandson Brigadier General Jefferson Randolph Kean, had chosen the inscriptions, which were approved by Roosevelt. The southwest portico contained a quotation from the Declaration, yet no one publicly noted the fact that on this last and greatest of presidential memorials the quotes taken from the Declaration were incorrectly reproduced. In all, there were two words misspelled, five words omitted, and minor changes made in punctuation. Not only was "inalienable" carved into the wall instead of "unalienable," the rest of the Declaration's most famous quote was redacted: "We hold these truths to be self-evident: that all men are created equal, that they are endowed by their creator with certain inalienable rights, ~~that~~ among these are life, liberty and the pursuit of happiness, that to secure these rights governments are instituted among men~~, deriving their just powers from the consent of the governed, that whenever any form of government becomes destructive of these ends it is the right of the people to alter or abolish it~~." The three other panels contained edited quotations from other writings of Jefferson that highlighted his condemnations of slavery but omitted his belief that the races could not live together.[15]

While the commission wrangled over the Declaration inscription for the Jefferson Memorial, a major study appeared that traced just how the document's words were finalized in 1776. To mark the bicentennial of Jefferson's birth, Julian P. Boyd, the editor of the Jefferson Papers and Librarian of Princeton University, published *The Declaration of Independence: The Evolution of a Text* with the Library of Congress. Boyd painstakingly analyzed the changes in the Declaration from rough draft to engrossed parchment, claiming that "In a broad sense the author of the Declaration of Independence was the American people." This reflected Jefferson's own comment that the Declaration represented the mind of the colonists and repeated the judgment of the Library of Congress's "Hidden History" radio broadcast of 1941.[16]

Invoking a united American public in 1776 was a way to maintain solidarity during the brutal combat. For two more years, the American people would "fight for the principles of the Declaration," as the prominent Columbia University historian Henry Steele Commager wrote in a long essay on July 4, 1943. Firmly identifying the struggle overseas with the ultimate triumph of the American ideal at home and abroad, he extolled the ideals of the Declaration as "the common heritage of men." Commager and others returned to this theme repeatedly throughout the war. *The New York Times* reprinted a long speech by the economist and business executive Beardsley Ruml reminding Americans that the "faith for which we fight . . . is stated in the first part of the second paragraph of the Declaration of Independence." The doctrine of the Declaration, continued Ruml, "declares the dignity and holiness of men. The Axis denies it."[17]

On September 19, 1944, Verner Clapp traveled again to Fort Knox, handed over the receipt he had been issued nearly three years previously, and accompanied the Declaration, Constitution, Bill of Rights, and Magna Carta back to Washington, D.C. With the threat of an Axis attack no longer of concern, a solemn reinstallation ceremony took place in the Library of Congress on October 1. A Marine Guard of Honor stood beside the shrine, to be relieved in succeeding weeks by Army and Navy Guards of Honor. Librarian Archibald MacLeish stepped up to the shrine and gave a short, poignant speech. "It is appropriate that these fragile objects which bear so great a weight of meaning to our people," MacLeish said, addressing the Marines, "and indeed to all the peoples of the world, should be entrusted to the guard of men who have themselves seen active service in a war against the enemies of everything this Constitution and this Declaration stand for."[18] The National Anthem played, and the shrine was again open to the people.

Having inspired America through its greatest conflict since the Civil War, the Declaration was sanctified in almost religious terms. The *Evansville Courier*, in Indiana, ran a cartoon entitled "May They Never Have to be Hidden or Kept in the Dark Again," on September 27, 1944, picturing workmen carrying the shrine, from which light radiated like a halo, as the Declaration was brought back into the Library of Congress. America's most popular magazine, *Life*, ran a photo spread in its October 16, 1944, edition, headlined "America's Priceless Documents Reappear." Celebrating their return to the public eye, the article printed behind-the-scenes images of the conservation of the Declaration, though it carefully kept the location of its journey secret. In the waning months of the war, after the surrender of Nazi Germany, the cover cartoon of the June 30, 1945, issue of *The New Yorker* portrayed the silhouettes of a crowd of young women reverentially gazing up at the illuminated shrine, the golden parchment glowing within. Appealed to through the conflict, the Declaration attained an unparalleled position of devotion in the American mind.[19]

World War II was the Good War, and the Declaration had played a key role in promoting patriotism and reinforcing what was rightly understood as a moral crusade, an existential fight against evil. Though the physical scroll was relegated to a remote vault, the Declaration had helped carry the Nation from the darkness to the light. The next decades would see it employed again in a new kind of global struggle, even as a final battle to possess it broke out at home.

Chapter 16
Cold War Icon

On Saturday, April 14, 1945, a somber funeral procession stretched for over a mile through the streets of Washington, D.C., winding through the broad avenues at the metronomic speed of a horse's hoofbeat. Under a bright blue sky half a million people, men and women of all races, old and young, lined up seven-deep along the two-mile route to pay their final respects to President Franklin Delano Roosevelt.

Roosevelt had led his country through the most terrible war in human history, but he did not live to see victory. Felled by a cerebral hemorrhage in Warm Springs, Georgia, at the age of sixty-three, he was brought back to the capital where he had been President for twelve years, longer than any other man. Yet even as he was being laid to rest, while the battle against Nazi Germany and Imperial Japan still raged, the outlines of a new struggle were emerging, one in which the United States would face off against its wartime ally, the Soviet Union, in a contest to determine the fate of the postwar world. In the shadow of what soon would be called the Cold War, the Declaration of Independence was to become an even greater symbol of the American ideal than before.

Despite the hopes of a war-weary world, within two years of the victories of 1945, America's wartime alliance with "Uncle Joe" Stalin was in tatters.

The Soviet Union was rapidly establishing puppet regimes throughout Eastern Europe and expanding its influence in strategic spots like Iran. In March 1947, President Harry Truman, Roosevelt's successor, pledged to help Greece and Turkey fight domestic Communist movements. That June, Secretary of State George Marshall announced an unprecedented aid and economic development plan for Europe. The following month, Congress passed the National Security Act, creating a unified Department of Defense and Central Intelligence Agency. The wartime expansion of government now became permanent as Washington committed the country to a global battle for hearts and minds, pitting the promise of openness and democracy against Communist oppression.[1]

The Declaration was a powerful tool in the new struggle. The political and territorial competition was mirrored by an ideological clash between America and the Soviet Union. At the heart of the struggle lay very different definitions of the words at the heart of the Declaration: liberty, equality, and consent of the governed. The Communist Party claimed that it had created a more equal society, leveling elites and empowering the masses. It argued that opportunity was best assured by central economic planning and the elimination of political and economic competition. Yet the reality of daily life in the Soviet Union was a far cry from these ideals. The dictator Joseph Stalin ensured that Russians suffered endless repression and had no freedom. To most Americans, equality without real liberty was meaningless. Soviet citizens were all theoretically equal, but they were most certainly not free. The Declaration understood equality as a God-given natural right that existed independent of government, not one dependent on the sufferance of the state, especially a coercive one. Soviet "equality" was something to be opposed no matter the cost.

The Declaration's postwar global influence was undeniable, thanks to its long heritage of inspiring rebellion against oppression, at a time when former colonies of the British, French, and Dutch empires were fighting for independence, but also due to America's overwhelming victory in World War II. Peoples struggling to forge nations in the wake of the conflict invoked the Declaration, yet emulating the American philosophy required a commitment to representative and participatory democracy, not just achieving sovereignty. In September 1945, a fifty-five-year-old revolutionary named Ho Chi Minh invoked Jefferson's phrases in his declaration of independence of the Democratic Republic of Vietnam. "All men are created equal," Ho began, demanding the end of French rule. "They are endowed by their Creator with certain inalienable rights, among them are Life, Liberty, and the pursuit of Happiness. This immortal statement was made in the Declaration of Independence of the United States of America in 1776. In a broader sense, this means: All the peoples on the earth are equal from birth, all the peoples have a right to live, to be happy and free." Yet Ho was more committed to a leveling revolution than to protecting individual rights.[2]

Ho was part of a larger global movement of decolonization after World War II, many of whose leaders were inspired by socialist ideals. No fewer than twenty-eight declarations of independence were promulgated over the next thirty years as colonial empires disintegrated.[3] Even during the war, Roosevelt's administration made clear it would not support its European allies in recovering their colonies, a position that incensed Winston Churchill. In the postwar period, Washington initially supported many of the independence movements as proof that self-determination was universal. Eleanor Roosevelt, whose public role increased after her husband's death, hoped that the Declaration's principles would erase centuries of conflict and competition between nations and lead to a new era of global cooperation. She lent her considerable influence to crafting and then promoting the United Nations' 1948 "Universal Declaration of Human Rights," whose first article began "All human beings are born free and equal in dignity and rights."[4]

The hopes of those who saw revolutionaries like Ho as democrats and the UN as a transcendent force in world politics would soon be dashed as it became clear that honoring the spirit of the Declaration was more important than parroting its phrases. By 1950, the Cold War had turned hot in Korea, and a new war in Europe seemed inevitable. Some felt the Declaration should be used as a symbolic tool in the battle between the two irreconcilable systems. One plan, floated in February 1951 by Republican Representative Paul Shafer of Michigan, called for "constantly pouring out the message of Americanism" by distributing the Declaration of Independence over the world in "all languages."[5] Such would be the focus of activity of the U.S. Information Agency and the Voice of America, which during these years used speakers, publications, and broadcasts to promote American ideals.[6]

Hidden from public view, the Central Intelligence Agency covertly sponsored groups like the Congress for Cultural Freedom, which countered Soviet propaganda by promoting the Declaration's values of consent of the governed and liberty. Within a decade, however, Washington would turn against left-leaning self-determination movements. The CIA organized coups to overthrow nationalist and socialist leaders in Iran and Guatemala, began a fruitless attempt to oust Fidel Castro in Cuba, and conspired to assassinate former Congolese prime minister Patrice Lumumba. Power politics in the Cold War soon revealed the limits of Washington's fealty to the spirit of the Declaration.[7]

If Washington opposed socialist liberation movements, it gave full support to those now struggling to oppose Communism in their conquered lands. In February 1951 the National Committee for a Free Europe hosted over two hundred Eastern European exiles at Independence Hall to release a "Declaration of the Aims and Principles of Liberation" for their Communist-controlled nations.[8] American legislators further promoted such ideas. A few years later, eleven House Democrats offered their own plan for the peaceful liberation of Eastern Europe "based on the revolutionary principles of the American Declaration of Independence." In both cases, the hope was not matched by any realistic plan, but keeping hope alive had its own value in the war of ideas.[9]

While the Declaration was passionately invoked by freedom fighters on the right and revolutionaries on the left hoping to topple oppressive regimes abroad, it was used at home to strengthen patriotism in the new struggle. Civic leaders feared that Americans ready for normalcy after four years of war might not be quite so devoted to another battle to export America's values. As Tom Clark, Truman's Attorney General, lamented in 1947, there was a need to reawaken "in the mind and heart of the American people a greater appreciation of our American heritage."[10]

Amid growing fears over Soviet propaganda and Communist sympathizers at home undermining liberal values, a plan was soon hatched for just such a reawakening. While viewing the exhibits at the National Archives on a lunch break, a Justice Department official named William Coblenz came up with the idea of sending America's greatest treasures on the road. The Freedom Train of 1947–1949 would become one of the most memorable patriotic campaigns during the early Cold War. It was sponsored by the American Heritage Foundation, with cooperation from the National Archives, major corporations, and the motion picture industry.[11] Pulled by a white engine emblazoned with the logo "Spirit of 1776," the Streamliner train's seven carriages detailed in red, white, and blue featured three exhibit cars with 126 priceless items, ranging from England's Magna Carta to the flag raised over Iwo Jima. The train was guarded by a detachment of U.S. Marines and (in the comics) by the superhero Captain Marvel.

The Freedom Train started in Philadelphia on September 17, 1947, the 160th anniversary of the signing of the Constitution, and finished in Washington, D.C., on January 22, 1949, traveling thirty-seven thousand miles and visiting 322 cities in all forty-eight states. Not all went smoothly. The train skipped Birmingham, Alabama, and Memphis, Tennessee, as both cities insisted on racially segregated entrances, a reminder that the equality extolled by the exhibits on display, including Abraham Lincoln's handwritten Emancipation Proclamation, remained in many places an elusive ideal.[12]

Over three million Americans viewed Thomas Jefferson's handwritten Rough Draft of the Declaration between 1947 and 1949 as it traveled across the country on the Freedom Train. The Declaration was protected by bulletproof glass.

Americans of all races and creeds gathered to view the Freedom Train's treasures. Over three and a half million people boarded the train during its journey, often after queuing for hours in all weather. In pride of place among the exhibits was Thomas Jefferson's handwritten rough draft of the Declaration of Independence, on loan from the Library of Congress, safe in a steel case behind green-tinted, bulletproof glass. *The New York Times* noted that many visitors lingered in front of Jefferson's draft, the first time in its history that so many had seen it. Visitors were encouraged to sign a "Freedom Scroll," which ultimately contained over three million names. In all, organizers estimated that one-third of the country, some fifty million people, participated in some form of Freedom Train activity.[13]

As the Cold War heated up, the Declaration became more visible than ever. It could be physically held, a single (if large) sheet of paper, reminding Americans of their birthright and challenging Communist claims. How judicious was its moderate eighteenth-century radicalism, when compared to the brutal Soviet experiment to reshape man. Government, business, and the educational system all in their own ways sought to keep Americans conscious of that contrast.

As a cultural object, the Declaration was everywhere. A mere reprint of the scroll could hardly guarantee a greater appreciation of America's ideals, but keeping the founding document in front of the eyes of Americans was presumed to have a value of its own. In 1951, the Stone engraving at last became available for public purchase when the National Archives, holder of the original copperplate, printed full-size facsimiles that sold for just thirty cents. For those who could not visit the Archives in person, copies were advertised nationally and shipped around the country. When the Archives published an oversize booklet entitled *Charters of Freedom* the following year, the engrossed Declaration was deemed to be too faded to reproduce, so the Stone engraving was printed instead, along with images of the actual Constitution and Bill of Rights. In reviewing the booklet, Millicent Taylor, education editor of the *Christian Science Monitor* and former literary assistant to the poet and biographer Carl Sandburg, exclaimed in print that every school and home needed at least one copy of it, containing as it did "our precious heritage of freedom."[14]

Taylor's wish seemed fulfilled. Luther Evans, Archibald MacLeish's successor as the Librarian of Congress, noted that by midcentury, thousands of copies of the Stone engraving had been printed, so that "the Declaration hanging on the classroom wall is known to every boy and girl in school."[15] Local leaders contributed to the effort. In Chicago, Sol Polk, head of the country's largest retailer of brand-name appliances, Polk Brothers, gave away fifty thousand framed copies of the Stone engraving in 1956 to schools, churches, civic groups, and newly naturalized citizens, encouraging all to "renew the pledge that these United States must ever be free."[16]

One reproduction stood above all others, and it came about as the result of an accident. Back in the mid-1920s, a chemist named Charles Promislo had spilled a solution on some papers in his laboratory, which crinkled overnight and turned a golden brown. Promislo eventually turned the accident into the Historical Documents Company, "antiquing" famous American records. By the 1950s, the company's antiqued Declaration, using the Stone engraving's image, became ubiquitous through direct sales and promotions with major companies such as Domino Sugar. For millions of Americans this reproduction, with its unique feel and odor, became the very image of the Declaration. Whether it was kept in a drawer or hung on the wall in bedrooms throughout the country, it remained a perennial bestseller at museums and historical sites nationwide.[17]

At the same time, more direct messaging was invoked in the ideological battle against Communism. Books on the lives of the Signers had sold well for over a century, but now long essays highlighting their sacrifices ran in popular periodicals, reaching even more Americans. One such article, in the July 5, 1947, issue of *The Saturday Evening Post*, dramatically entitled "They Signed Away Their Lives for You," recounted how the Signers were "hunted, shot, captured, robbed, and subjected to every conceivable hardship and abuse," while fighting for freedom. The message was unmistakable: the inheritors of the Signers' gift must prepare themselves to defend those ideals against a new enemy.[18]

Mass entertainment brought the Declaration to millions more. The 1940s was the decade of radio, and listeners tuning into the March 21 and July 4, 1948, episodes of the popular CBS Radio series *You Are There* heard a dramatization of the events in Independence Hall in the summer of 1776. The show moved to television in 1953, and on April 26 of that year, CBS newsman Walter Cronkite introduced the same episode, re-creating the debate over the adoption of the Declaration and climaxing in the dramatic vote for Independence. If the Declaration had been presented to moviegoers in the 1920s and 1930s as historical melodrama, Cold War radio and television now brought the story directly into Americans' living rooms with messages designed to instill patriotism and promote good citizenship.[19]

Such productions were often joint efforts between the media and leading intellectuals, part of a midcentury ethos that delivered Mortimer Adler's Great Books and Lionel Trilling's Readers' Subscription Book Club to middle-class Americans.[20] One notable effort was a thirteen-part radio series entitled *The Jeffersonian Heritage*, produced by the National Association of Educational Broadcasters (NAEB) with the assistance of Dumas Malone, the eminent Jefferson scholar at Columbia University. Starring the famous actor Claude Rains as Jefferson, the series premiered on September 14, 1952, with "The Living Declaration," highlighting fictional debates between Jefferson and John Dickinson. An unmistakable Cold War message was hammered home when a balladeer sang Jefferson's famous (and much later) statement "I have sworn upon the altar of God, eternal hostility against every form of tyranny over the mind of man." "This is the meaning of the Declaration," Jefferson then intones, linking the founding to the current struggle.[21] The NAEB also produced a thirty-minute television show, "The Independent Mr. Jefferson," broadcast on NBC the following year. Reflecting a growing national debate over civil rights, this episode dramatized the weeks in which Jefferson wrote his rough draft in Philadelphia in the summer of 1776, focusing on his wrestling with the question of the slave trade.

On July 4, 1951, the Declaration celebrated another milestone anniversary. *Demisemiseptcentennial* was one of the least-used words in the English language, all the more so as Americans were getting used to new terms like *megaton* and *fallout*.[22] Nor was it a locution likely to find favor with the plainspoken president from Missouri who stepped before a crowd of 175,000 at the base of the Washington Monument for the 175th anniversary of the Declaration of Independence.

President Harry Truman spoke in a pure American idiom as he told his audience that, just six short years after the great victory in World War

II, the challenges facing the United States at home and abroad were as daunting as any that had come before. With American troops now fighting in Korea, segregation at home, and the threat of global Communism growing, Truman argued that America's founding ideals remained both aspirational and eternal. "The principles of the Declaration of Independence are the right principles," said Truman. "They are sound enough to guide us through this crisis as they have guided us through other crises of the past." In this new, strange Cold War that had already turned hot, Truman cast the Declaration as a beacon guiding not just the United States, but countries around the world.[23]

Though he had spoken with optimism, the sense of urgency Truman and his counselors felt was reflected in an executive order he signed declaring the 175th anniversary to be "a national 'Year of Rededication' to the principles of the Declaration of Independence." A commission headed by the Chief Justice of the Supreme Court and supported by groups like the American Heritage Foundation planned events and an advertising campaign to instill a greater reverence for the Declaration and commitment to its values through "active personal participation in the affairs of our country."[24] This was a call to action spread by public intellectuals like Henry Steele Commager, who wrote in *The New York Times* that "each generation must not only familiarize itself anew with the philosophy of the Declaration, it must justify and vindicate that philosophy anew." Commager's plea was an implicit acknowledgment that, no matter how many Stone engravings hung on how many walls, the citizenry of a mammoth, centralized, industrialized superpower would not without some effort feel the same connection to their nation or to its founding document as those who had fought for freedom in 1776.[25]

Dumas Malone attempted to help forge that connection three years later, in his *The Story of the Declaration of Independence*. This was perhaps the first modern general history of the document, retelling the adventures of the scroll and the lives of the Signers in a well-illustrated, large-format volume. "In the middle of the twentieth century," wrote Malone, "the weight of tyranny—political, economic, and social—is still heavy on the shoulders of men . . . The great Declaration still issues its ringing challenge to the tyrants who would ride mankind, and it still proclaims the undying faith in human beings which has permeated and glorified the history of America."[26]

As the Cold War lengthened into a decades-long competition, it also seemed vital to forge a connection between the next generation of Americans and the country's founding principles. In 1958, Commager, the prolific Columbia professor, published a new volume for middle-school libraries. Filled with documents from the Revolutionary era, *The Great Declaration: A Book for Young Readers* was written to ensure that those who would be called upon to defend American values would understand that "the most important document in modern history" was as universal as it was American, and was "the possession of all mankind."[27]

Chapter 17

The Final Battle to Control the Declaration

In the summer of 1951, a month after the Declaration celebrated its 175th anniversary, an unmarked panel truck pulled into the basement of the Library of Congress. Once loaded, it drove to the National Bureau of Standards, the government's primary scientific facility. There the Declaration of Independence and Constitution were placed in the care of Gordon M. Kline, chief of the Plastics Section. Kline and his team had one focus: to create the most technologically sophisticated cases that science could envision to preserve these delicate parchments for posterity.

Kline's mission had started before World War II. In 1940 Archibald MacLeish had charged the National Bureau of Standards with determining the best way to conserve the Declaration and Constitution. The war pulled the Bureau away from these efforts, but once peace returned, Kline and his scientists had gone back to work.

By 1951, Kline's team had run years of tests. They had examined different sealing materials and analyzed a range of inert gases. They had explored optimal humidity levels: too much and the document would lose strength, too little and it would become brittle. They had experimented with different types of glass, created new paper backing, and designed special sensors so that the environment surrounding the document could be constantly monitored. At last, they were ready, and the Declaration was taken out of the shrine in the Library of Congress to be delivered to the scientists.

In a carefully cleaned laboratory room whose air quality was monitored, the aged scroll was removed from the glass case into which George Stout and Evelyn Ehrlich had placed it at Fort Knox and carefully separated from its rag board backing. Gingerly, the parchment was laid on a new moisture-absorbing cellulose backing custom-made in the Bureau's own experimental paper mill and then covered with a thin plate of tempered glass held by brass brackets. This inner cradle was enclosed between thicker, quarter-inch panes of Thermopane glass specially made by the Libbey-Owens-Ford Glass Company. The case was hermetically sealed with a metal border and lead. When completed, the new enclosure weighed seventy pounds.

After being tested for airtightness, helium was pumped into the glass enclosure through thin tubes inserted into the lead lining, to protect the document from corrosive oxygen and parasites. The humidity was calibrated at 25 to 35 percent, and an ingenious leak detector and platinum

National Bureau of Standards chemist E. Carroll Creitz testing the new encasement on a copy of the parchment in 1951.

wire sensor were designed to measure humidity and temperature levels. Past efforts at protecting the Declaration paled in comparison to the full power of modern science brought to bear for the first time to preserve the timeworn parchment. A similar treatment was given to the Constitution.[1]

On September 17, Constitution Day, the newly encased Declaration and Constitution were brought back to the shrine at the Library of Congress. President Truman and Chief Justice Fred Vinson participated in the ceremonies to reinstall the documents in their viewing cases. The marble altar was now fronted by specially designed laminated glass with a filter of yellow-orange acetate film produced by the Eastman Kodak Corporation, designed to block light radiation. Yet as impressive as the scientific efforts were, Librarian of Congress Luther Evans went to some length to remind his audience that science was secondary to the documents' philosophy. "Only the most deluded," he intoned, "could attach more importance to their physical well-being than to the preservation of the principles for which they stand."[2] The new technology and impressive ceremony seemed to make clear that the Declaration had returned to its permanent home.

A month or so after the engrossed Declaration was returned to the Library of Congress, two men huddled over a table in the dining room of the exclusive Cosmos Club, then located across Lafayette Square from the White House. Luther Evans hosted Wayne Grover, the Archivist of the United States, in a bid to settle one of the strangest, and longest-simmering, custody disputes in government history.[3]

The dispute's origins could be traced back to 1926, when Congress had passed a "Public Buildings Act" that included plans for an official archives. Up to then, the untold millions of government documents had lain in various locations, from the Library of Congress and State Department to local government offices, the Patent Office, and private collections. To begin the process of recording, collecting, and preserving these documents was a gargantuan undertaking. Above all, it needed a headquarters.

Plans for the building continued through the Great Depression, and in 1930, Herbert Hoover's Secretary of the Treasury, Andrew Mellon, settled on both site and architect. The National Archives were to be the symbolic center of the new Federal Triangle reshaping Washington's center.[4] The site, wedged between Constitution and Pennsylvania Avenues at the midpoint of the National Mall, was halfway between the U.S. Capitol and the White House. Mellon commissioned John Russell Pope, who a decade later would design the Jefferson Memorial, for the task. Pope created a striking neoclassical plan for the building. Its 118-foot-wide pediments would be the largest in Washington and its seventy-two Corinthian columns were each over 53 feet high and weighed 95 tons. The sliding bronze doors, at 38 feet high, were the largest in the world.[5]

On February 20, 1933, a bitterly cold winter day, President Hoover had laid the cornerstone of the new archives. In his speech, Hoover paid homage to Pope's design, calling the building a "temple of our history." More significantly, he indicated that this temple would also be a treasure house, informing the assembled dignitaries that "there will be aggregated here the most sacred documents of our history, the originals of the Declaration of Independence and of the Constitution of the United States."[6]

There was just one problem with Hoover's announcement. Washington's other Herbert, then–Librarian of Congress Herbert Putnam, refused to surrender the engrossed Declaration. As had happened when the Patent Office and the State Department had briefly tussled over control of the Declaration back in the 1870s, the question of custody was a thorny one. As another Librarian of Congress later noted, "A threat had been proclaimed. The period of uncertainty had begun."[7] Putnam considered the transfer from the State Department to the Library to be the final one, referring to Congress's 1922 appropriation for a "permanent repository." It would take another act of Congress, Putnam believed, for him to give it up. Facing such an obstacle, neither Hoover nor his successor, Franklin D. Roosevelt, pushed the issue. Putnam's successor, Archibald MacLeish, was more sympathetic to a transfer, but had been forced by World War II to focus on protecting the Declaration. Now in peacetime and with a new set of actors, the time had come to bury the hatchet and settle the issue between them.[8]

A stout, avuncular Texan with a ribald sense of humor, Luther Evans took over the Library of Congress from MacLeish in 1945, when he was only forty-three years old. A committed New Dealer, he had directed the Historical Records Survey of the Works Progress Administration in the 1930s, making him more of an archivist than a librarian.[9] Within a few years of succeeding MacLeish, he had come to believe that a new era required a new approach to the Declaration. A political scientist with a PhD from Stanford University on the topic of international diplomacy, Evans told Grover over lunch at the Cosmos Club that he was concerned about the security of the founding documents in view of the "international situation," a guarded reference to the danger of atomic warfare.[10] From an archival standpoint, Evans also worried about the long-term effects of keeping the Declaration housed against an exterior wall, where temperature fluctuations were more extreme. Evans considered it unseemly that the great Rotunda of the National Archives remained empty more than a decade after its completion. In short, he was ready to give up the Declaration. But he knew he would need political cover to hand over the scroll.

Wayne Grover, at thirty-nine, was only the third Archivist of the United States and had been one of its first staffers when the National Archives had opened in 1935. Known for his genial wit, Grover had joined the Office of Strategic Services during World War II before returning to head the Archives in 1948.[11] In his quest to gain custody of the scroll, Grover felt he had the weight of presidential support behind him. Hoover, Roosevelt, and Truman had all three indicated that they believed the Declaration should be relocated to the National Archives, and the new Federal Records Act of 1950 seemed to give Grover authority to request any document for the National Archives. After so many years of acrimony and uncertainty, Grover and Evans settled the issue amicably over lunch. If Congress agreed, the issue of custody would be decided once and for all.

With President Truman's support, on April 30, 1952, Evans was unanimously directed by Congress's Joint Committee on the Library to transfer the Declaration and Constitution to Grover. It was a bitter blow to many at the Library of Congress who had so conscientiously guarded and cared for the founding documents. David C. Mearns, Chief of the Manuscripts Division, expressed the feelings of many in an article entitled "Forever Is Twenty-Eight Years": "From the time they came to the Library in 1921 the well-being of the Declaration and the Constitution has ever been of paramount concern to us . . . To have been host to these imperishable records even for a few decades has been an extraordinary privilege."[12]

At 11 a.m. on December 13, 1952, the shrine in the Library of Congress was opened one last time. Library officials turned the Declaration and Constitution over to the commanding general of the U.S. Air Force Headquarters

Command.[13] In the winter morning sunshine, two tanks and an armored personnel carrier moved slowly down Constitution Avenue, accompanied by troops carrying submachine guns, while soldiers, sailors, airmen, and Marines lined the street. The Declaration and each page of the Constitution had been packed in cases and ceremoniously carried down the steps of the Library between a cordon of eighty-eight uniformed servicewomen, and each case placed in a Marine Corps personnel carrier. Escorted by a color guard and motorcycle squadron, the impressive procession moved slowly toward the National Archives Building, crowds lining the streets to watch. There, surrounded by armed soldiers, the founding documents were reverentially carried up the thirty-nine steps, passing through another cordon of servicewomen. The procession continued under the portico of the neoclassical building and through the bronze doors.

Inside, the Declaration was carried through twelve-foot-high bronze gates, topped by spearpoints and eagles, into the magnificent Rotunda. Under the seventy-five-foot dome, Archivist Wayne Grover took formal

The Declaration and Constitution being carried up the steps of the National Archives under armed guard during their transfer from the Library of Congress, December 13, 1952.

custody of the Declaration. No more honor was paid to Presidents on their inauguration than to the founding charters on that morning.[14]

Two days later, the Declaration and Constitution were formally enshrined, joining the Bill of Rights at last in the space built so long ago to house them. Appropriately enough, December 15 was Bill of Rights Day. At 10:15 a.m., in front of a crowd of dignitaries including the President and Chief Justice, Grover and Evans together drew back a large curtain to reveal the new shrine.

Three leaves of the Constitution and the single sheet of the Bill of Rights lay horizontally in a marble and bronze casement elevated three feet off the floor. On the wall behind was the shrine's central altar, bronze doors open on either side. The altar was flanked by two twelve-foot-high columns of green marble topped by Corinthian capitals supporting a larger, curved pediment, next to which were two oversize American flags set into floor stands. Above the altar the names of the three documents had been chiseled into a large gray marble panel and then gilded. On either side, two massive marble columns soared twenty feet up, topped by huge stone eagles. High up on the curving walls to either side were large murals painted in the 1930s by the artist Barry Faulkner portraying Thomas Jefferson handing the Declaration to John Hancock and James Madison submitting the Constitution to George Washington.[15]

At the center of it all, perfectly aligned with the flags, columns, architraves, and pediments, was the engrossed Declaration in its altar, surmounted by a bronze eagle. The flawless symmetry automatically drew one's eyes toward the faded scroll, safe in its helium-filled, hermetically sealed casement. For those in the Rotunda that December day, and for tens of millions of visitors over the next half century, the overwhelming power of the Declaration as symbol and relic was manifest (see insert).

Perhaps the setting was too majestic. To many, the Declaration appeared like a secular version of the Ten Commandments, an almost religious testament from the Founding Fathers to the People. President Truman, aware of the danger of mindless veneration, warned in his dedicatory remarks that the Declaration and Constitution should not become "idols whose worship would be a grim mockery of the true faith." To others, who may have dismissed the shrine as antirepublican or antithetical to the spirit of democracy, Truman admonished that American freedom would be lost "if the time ever comes when these documents are regarded not as the supreme expression of our profound belief, but merely as curiosities in glass cases." Despite its grandeur, Truman went on, the new setting was designed to deepen visitors' attachment to the democratic ideal and "our faith in human liberty."[16]

While visitors in the Rotunda lifted their eyes up to the Declaration, some also looked down, aware that twenty feet below them lay a massive concrete and steel vault. Built by the Mosler Safe Company in Ohio, the vault's doors opened upward, activated by two massive counterweights that swung down at the press of a button. In just forty seconds, the inner cases could be carried down on a scissors-jack platform into the fifty-ton vault, where the reinforced doors would shut tight, protecting the priceless parchments from atomic attack. Every night, the Declaration and its companion documents were to be lowered into the vault for safekeeping, "as safe from destruction as anything that the wit of modern man could devise," Truman noted at the enshrinement ceremony. In a world living in the shadow of the mushroom cloud, the vault was a grim reminder that after nearly two hundred years, the American experiment needed to be defended.[17]

The vault was necessary now that Soviet spies had stolen plans for the atomic bomb. The open society Truman praised was also vulnerable to organized penetration by Communist agents who sought to use the very freedoms celebrated in the Rotunda to undermine the United States. This led to a bitter and partisan struggle over the right balance between protecting civil liberties, respecting individual beliefs, and defending the U.S. Government and other areas of civil society from subversive Communist activity. FBI investigations had uncovered the presence of Communist sympathizers, spies, and fellow travelers among civil servants but also hounded innocent people whose politics were left of center. What would become known as the "Red Scare," and the subsequent blacklisting of academics, artists, entertainers, and others, raised difficult questions about the "profound belief" in liberty Truman had alluded to.[18]

Most Americans, however, were not touched by the shadow of great power games or the political and legal struggles playing out on Capitol Hill. Year after year, they continued to pour into the National Archives. "We do not know much of what is in the minds of Americans as they file past the altar," acknowledged the *Christian Science Monitor* in 1953. Yet their presence, day after day in never-ending lines, seemed proof that the enshrined scroll was the most powerfully symbolic document in the world. One comes away from the altar, noted a correspondent for *The*

New York Times, "with an increased faith that this nation, having hoped so much and achieved so much, having endured so much, cannot, in Lincoln's own words, perish from the earth."[19] The magnetic pull of the engrossed parchment in its new altar in the National Archives sent a powerful message that American exceptionalism, American identity, and the Nation's purpose were centered on Jefferson's inspiring promises of liberty and equality, both achieved and achievable.

Chapter 18

The Promise of the Declaration in the Civil Rights Era

Just before ten thirty on the morning of Sunday, September 15, 1963, a blast blew out the windows and shattered the inside of the Sixteenth Street Baptist Church in Birmingham, Alabama. When the bomb went off, it could be heard for over a mile. Four young girls preparing for Sunday services—Addie Mae Collins, Cynthia Wesley, and Carole Robertson, all fourteen, and eleven-year-old Carol Denise McNair—were killed in the attack. It was one of the most tragic assaults against Black Americans in an era of racial strife.[1]

That it happened in Birmingham was no accident. Back in 1947, the Freedom Train, with its exhibit of Thomas Jefferson's rough draft of the Declaration of Independence, had chosen to bypass Birmingham when city officials, led by Commissioner of Public Safety Theophilus "Bull" Connor, had insisted on racially segregating the viewing lines. As one of the most segregated States in the South, Alabama had become a focus of efforts to force integration. Five months before the bombing, the Reverend Dr. Martin Luther King, Jr., had come to Birmingham with other civil rights leaders to lead a campaign of economic boycotts and public pressure. After his arrest, King wrote his "Letter from a Birmingham Jail," in which he explained that the struggle for equality was a crusade to carry America "back to the great wells of democracy which were dug deep by the founding fathers in the formulation of the Constitution and the Declaration of Independence."[2]

In just over a decade, America would celebrate its Bicentennial, but Jefferson's great promise had yet fully to be realized. A century after Abraham Lincoln had justified the sacrifices of the Civil War by invoking the Declaration, many Black Americans were denied the full equality mandated by the Thirteenth and Fourteenth Amendments. The irony—many would say hypocrisy—of leading a global struggle against Communism in the name of freedom while segregation was rampant at home could not be ignored. A sense of shame that the country still allowed such blatant racial discrimination, and racially motivated violence, propelled a religiously, racially, and politically diverse coalition to band together in an effort to make the country live up to the Declaration's promises.[3]

When Harry Truman praised the Declaration at the National Archives in December 1952, the fulsome press accounts portrayed a national unity that was as fictional as it was real. Of patriotism there was no doubt, in a country that saw its sacrifice in men and materiel in World War II as justified by high principles and a new role on the world stage. Truman understood that inequality at home was both morally wrong and a weakness in the Cold War. In his remarks on the 175th anniversary of the Declaration, Truman had made it clear that "Anyone who undertakes to abridge the right of any American to life, liberty, or the pursuit of happiness commits three great wrongs. He wrongs the individual first, but in addition, he wrongs his country, and he betrays the hopes of mankind . . . It is for this reason that persecution of minorities, which is wrong anywhere, is worse in America."[4]

As States in the South maintained Jim Crow laws and discrimination remained the norm throughout the country, Truman sought to deflect more radical demands for reform at home and to deny the Soviets this potent weapon in the propaganda war. He formed a special Committee on Civil Rights, composed of civic leaders and headed by Charles E. Wilson, the CEO of General Motors. The Committee's 1947 report was entitled "To Secure These Rights," a direct reference to the Declaration.

The Committee's conclusions were deemed important enough to be released as a book by Simon & Schuster, a major publishing house founded in 1924. Quoting Jefferson's passage on inalienable rights, the report carefully explained the proper relationship contained within America's "basic moral principle: all men are created equal as well as free." Equality, though given by God, is expressed in the political sphere as "equality of opportunity," without which "freedom becomes an illusion." The Jeffersonian influence was evident in the Committee's conclusion that "the only aristocracy that is consistent with the free way of life is an aristocracy of talent and achievement," extending this thought to include race and religion as well as social status at birth. Building social institutions that would ensure this form of equality was thus the political prerequisite of a just society. The report concluded with over twenty pages of recommendations, including proposals to give suffrage to American Indians in the Southwest, establish civil rights offices in the Federal Government, and end segregation in the Armed Forces. Truman acted on this last recommendation the following year.[5]

What many had hoped would be the final struggle to fulfill the Declaration's promise of equality was ignited after Truman left office, during the early years of the Eisenhower Administration. In 1954, the landmark *Brown v. Board of Education of Topeka* Supreme Court decision overturned the "separate but equal" standard justifying the segregation of public schools adopted in 1896, yet many believed that substantive change remained all too slow. Schools, stores, restaurants, hotels, and other public accommodations in the South remained segregated, as did many in the North. A particularly appealing target for protest was public transportation. A veteran activist named Rosa Parks became the face of the Civil Rights Movement when she was arrested in December 1955 for refusing to give up her seat on a segregated bus in Montgomery, Alabama. Parks and other activists organized a bus boycott that led to more violence but ultimately forced another Supreme Court decision, in 1956, striking down segregated seating on public buses.

Enforcement, however, remained the real test, and the federal government carefully began to intervene. President Dwight D. Eisenhower sent U.S. troops to Little Rock Central High School, in Arkansas, in September 1957 to enforce the Supreme Court's school desegregation order. In a national speech explaining his decision and denouncing "the call of extremists to violence," he directly linked the struggle at home with the broader Cold War battle for global opinion. "At a time when we face grave situations abroad because of the hatred that Communism bears toward a system of government based on human rights," Eisenhower intoned, "it would be difficult to exaggerate the harm that is being done to the prestige and influence, and indeed the safety, of our nation and the world" by continued discrimination.[6]

A prominent intellectual who believed that Thomas Jefferson would not have supported the calls for equal rights was William F. Buckley, Jr., father of the modern conservative movement and founder of the magazine *National Review*. In 1957, at the height of the school integration controversy, Buckley wrote an article entitled "Why the South Must Prevail." In it, he asked "whether the White community in the South is entitled to take such measures as are necessary to prevail, politically and culturally, in areas in which it does not predominate numerically? The sobering answer is *Yes*—the White community is so entitled because, for the time being, it is the advanced race." Buckley recalled that Jefferson believed in "reasonable limitations on the vote" and concluded that "the problem in the South is not how to get the vote for the Negro, but how to equip the Negro—and a great many Whites—to cast an enlightened and responsible vote." Yet he also warned that exclusion could not be an end in itself: "[The South] must not exploit the fact of Negro backwardness to preserve the Negro as a servile class." While he would later distance himself from this position, Buckley's call for upholding segregation was lauded by Southern anti-integrationists but deplored by those who saw the Declaration's assertion of equality in unequivocal terms.[7]

As Martin Luther King, Jr., rose to national prominence by calling for nonviolent resistance and leading the Southern Christian Leadership Conference, President Eisenhower's successor, John F. Kennedy, and his successor, Lyndon Baines Johnson, embraced the cause, yet the movement was a grassroots one, with activists forming networks and organizing protests in their own streets. It was a tumultuous contest that sparked fierce state resistance, whose intransigence was best captured by Alabama Governor George Wallace's infamous 1963 declaration, "segregation now, segregation tomorrow, segregation forever."[8]

No document, or set of beliefs, was invoked more often than the Declaration during the civil rights struggle. Hundreds of newspaper editorials urged Americans to act on its promises. When Blacks were prevented from attending the Memphis Automobile Show in January 1960, the *Tri-State Defender* bluntly told city commissioners to reread the preamble of the Declaration.[9] Some of these appeals made it seem as though the document was a magic fairy dust that simply needed to be sprinkled over the nation's social and political ferment. "A civil rights bill doesn't need to be any stronger than the Declaration of Independence," offered *The Boston Globe* hopefully in 1963. The *Los Angeles Times* suggested that same year that in the Declaration's self-evident truths "lies the prescription for the cure of America's current racial problem: granting to all its citizens the 'unalienable rights' to which each is constitutionally entitled."[10]

The reality was far more complicated, as street violence and Senate filibusters revealed. In 1961, a group of Black and White activists protested the continuation of segregated seating on buses in the South by riding together from Washington, D.C., down to Florida. Calling themselves "Freedom Riders" in a nod to the birth of America, they were beaten, arrested, and forced to appeal their convictions all the way to the Supreme Court, with little support from the Kennedy Administration. In March 1963, Birmingham police used water cannons against nonviolent demonstrators protesting segregation in the city. Pictures of Black high school students huddling against the powerful streams of water shocked the nation.

The summer of 1963 was a time of great peril, with regular bombings and violence in Birmingham. On June 11, just hours after President Kennedy had delivered a nationally televised address on long-delayed civil rights legislation, the activist Medgar Evers was gunned down in front of his home in Jackson, Mississippi. That Independence Day, Vice President Lyndon B. Johnson spoke in front of Independence Hall, saying that America would not be a just society until "every citizen receives the benefits of the Declaration of Independence . . . They need to be implemented, for all Americans."[11] Some explained the entire Civil Rights Movement in terms of the Declaration. In *The Washington Post*, prominent columnist Joseph Alsop directly linked the movement to the founding document: "On July 4, 1776, when a number of the boldest leaders signed the Declaration of Independence, the American Revolution began in deadly earnest . . . something like a second revolution has begun here in America." Alsop pointed to the murdered Evers as the symbolic figure of the new revolution.[12]

In early August, Alfred Duckett lent his voice to that spirit of revolution in *The Chicago Defender*, reminding his readers that a century had passed since the signing of the Emancipation Proclamation. "I am ashamed that—in this one hundredth anniversary year of what was supposed to be the freeing of the Negro people—we still have with us the issue of being accorded our freedom. I am ashamed—not only for my own sake—but because I am an American and I do not see my country living up to the affirmations of the Declaration of Independence," scolded Duckett before calling on others to join him for a highly anticipated March on Washington.[13]

A quarter of a million people crammed in front of the Lincoln Memorial on August 28, 1963, despite afternoon temperatures in the mideighties. The "March on Washington for Jobs and Freedom" was sponsored by a coalition of civil, religious, labor, and student organizations to show support for the civil rights legislation that the Kennedy Administration was at last pushing in Congress.[14] Guarded by police and troopers, a constellation of speakers addressed the sweltering crowd that day. The young Georgia activist and future congressman John Lewis was told by organizers to tone down his fiery rhetoric, but he still exhorted those present to stay in the streets "until the revolution of 1776 is complete."[15]

Soaring above the rest was the speech of Martin Luther King, Jr. On the centenary of the Emancipation Proclamation, King lamented that "When the architects of our great republic wrote the magnificent words of the Constitution and the Declaration of Independence, they were signing a promissory note to which every American was to fall heir . . . Instead of honoring this sacred obligation, America has given its colored people a bad check." Yet King, like Frederick Douglass before him, refused to abandon all hope, directly invoking Thomas Jefferson and inviting Americans to join in his vision of a more just future. Tying the moment to the concept of the American Dream and to the Declaration, King thundered, "I have a dream that one day this nation will rise up and live out the true meaning of its creed: 'We hold these truths to be self-evident, that all men are created equal.'" Concluding with the words of an old spiritual, King made the crucial link between equality and liberty, declaiming "Free at last, free at last, thank God Almighty we are free at last."[16]

No rhetoric, however powerful, could guarantee the success of the Civil Rights Movement. A month after the March on Washington, the Sixteenth Street Baptist Church was bombed and in November, President Kennedy was assassinated in Dallas. These tragedies gave the final impetus for Kennedy's successor, Lyndon Johnson, to push the Civil Rights Act through Congress in the face of powerful resistance from his fellow

Dr. Martin Luther King, Jr., quoted the Declaration in his "I Have a Dream" speech at the Lincoln Memorial during the March on Washington on August 28, 1963.

Southern Democrats. After months of maneuvering, Johnson signed the bill into law on July 2, 1964, the anniversary of the Continental Congress's vote on Independence. The Act prohibited intentional discrimination in federally funded programs, in public accommodations and employment, and in stores, theaters, and restaurants, giving hope that America would begin to act as a colorblind society.

In his remarks to the nation on the passing of the 1964 law, Johnson made clear his belief that in correcting the abuses of the past, the Civil Rights Act would bring America at last into conformity with the philosophy of the Declaration:

> We believe that all men are created equal. Yet many are denied equal treatment. We believe that all men have certain unalienable rights. Yet many Americans do not enjoy those rights. We believe that all men are entitled to the blessings of liberty. Yet millions are being deprived of those blessings—not because of their own failures, but because of the color of their skin.

Living up to the principles of the Declaration was the only way to "make our Nation whole," Johnson concluded, equating the health of

America, in all its complexity and vastness, with fidelity to its founding document.[17]

Johnson was not finished after the Civil Rights Act. In 1965, in a commencement address at Howard University, in Washington, D.C., he outlined the "next and the more profound stage of the battle for civil rights." "We seek not just freedom but opportunity," announced Johnson, "not just equality as a right and a theory but equality as a fact and equality as a result."[18] To many, this hint that the government wanted not just equal opportunity, but equal outcomes went far beyond the contours of the Civil Rights Act. It further alarmed those who believed that Eisenhower's decision to force school integration in the 1950s, Kennedy's executive orders on affirmative action in federal contracting, and Johnson's flurry of civil rights legislation had trampled their rights, especially that of free association, and foreshadowed ever more intrusive attempts to ensure compliance.[19] The meaning of "equality" and "freedom" remained at the center of America's political debates. The struggle between different interpretations of these concepts was not settled by the Civil Rights Movement and would roil American society over the coming decades.

As the push to complete the revolution that had begun in the streets, given official support by the Kennedy and Johnson Administrations, and codified into law by the Civil Rights Act, continued, the Declaration remained the touchstone for political and civic leaders pushing for change, who appealed to it both as justification and exemplar. In a speech on Independence Day in 1965 urging more antidiscrimination legislation, King reminded his audience of the uniqueness of the Declaration. "Very seldom, if ever, in the history of the world," he reflected in what became known as the "American Dream" speech, "has a sociopolitical document expressed in such profound, eloquent, and unequivocal language the dignity and the worth of human personality."[20]

The next month, President Johnson signed the Voting Rights Act, designed to ensure that illegal efforts to prevent people from casting ballots based on the color of their skin could be prosecuted at the federal level. Passage of the act was influenced by the January 1964 murders of civil rights workers James Chaney, Andrew Goodman, and Michael Schwerner. Goodman and Schwerner had traveled from New York to join Chaney, a fellow member of the Congress of Racial Equality, to register locals to vote in rural Mississippi. After a group of locals that included Ku Klux Klan members and local police followed them out of the county seat, ironically named Philadelphia, the three were pulled over on a rural road, shot, and dumped in a shallow grave, and their car was burned. Whereas previous killings of civil rights activists had garnered little attention, this became national news. Attorney General Robert F. Kennedy ordered FBI Director J. Edgar Hoover to have the Bureau take over the investigation, which eventually resulted in federal conviction of seven defendants for "conspiring to deny the civil rights" of the victims.[21]

The passage of the Voting Rights Act did not mark the end of racial violence or usher in the peace some had hoped it would. A few days after Johnson signed the act, the Watts section of Los Angeles erupted in riots after a Black driver pulled over for drunken driving was beaten by the police. Similar use of force against Blacks had led to riots in Harlem, Philadelphia, and other cities in previous years, but the scale of the Watts riots shocked the nation. Over six days of chaos, thirty-four people died and a large part of the area was set on fire. Only the dispatch of over fourteen thousand National Guardsmen allowed the authorities to regain control.[22]

After having started out committed to nonviolent protest, the Black community now split into competing factions. On one side, King moved toward a democratic socialism that identified injustice at home with militarism abroad, while on the other side, more radical elements emerged. In October 1966, the Black Panther Party for Self-Defense was formed in Oakland, California. The Panthers' Ten-Point Platform and Program began by demanding "We want freedom. We want power to determine the destiny of our black community" and culminated by reprinting verbatim the first two paragraphs of the Declaration of Independence.[23] As the colonists had separated from England, so must Black America from White, in the view of the Panthers.

With their emphasis on separation of the races, the Black Panthers rejected the vision of colorblind integration that Martin Luther King had offered at the Lincoln Memorial. Within a year, the Panthers' militant rhetoric inspired an armed incursion into the California State Capitol and violent clashes with police, including the deaths of several officers, all portrayed as a legitimate resistance to state oppression. When the Black Panther platform was reprinted in the movement's newspaper on July 5, 1969, the nod to the Declaration could only be seen as an attempt to justify armed resistance by recalling America's origins.

Such tactics gained headlines but not many adherents. *Newsweek* magazine commissioned a major poll by Louis Harris & Associates in August 1966, just before the Black Panthers organized. The poll revealed that by overwhelming margins, Black people supported integration and only 15 percent said they would join violent riots. Yet the same poll showed the vast gulf between Blacks and Whites on the question of equality. Though 61 percent of Whites polled by Harris acknowledged that discrimination remained, fully 70 percent thought that Blacks "were trying to move too fast," compared to just 4 percent of Blacks who thought so.[24] Though a majority of Whites, who made up 84 percent of the population, desired more gradual integration, Johnson and federal officials believed that living up to the Declaration meant no further delay. It was an attitude eventually adopted even by those who initially opposed forced integration. "I once believed we could evolve our way up from Jim Crow," William F. Buckley, Jr., the staunch advocate of smaller government, told *Time* magazine in 2004. "I was wrong. Federal intervention was necessary."[25]

Despite hardened racial views and endemic violence, the government continued to push through new legislation. On April 11, 1968, Johnson signed a Fair Housing Act, designed to eradicate the de facto segregation that had developed in the real estate market after the Civil Rights Act with "redlining" and the continuing use of restrictive covenants.[26] Tragically, Martin Luther King did not live to see its signing. He was assassinated one week earlier in Memphis, Tennessee, where he had come to demonstrate in support of striking sanitation workers in a commitment to linking racial and economic justice. As word spread of King's murder, riots broke out across the country, including in the nation's capital. Acrid smoke from the fires set along Fourteenth Street wafted down to the National Archives, where the Declaration hung in its shrine, while more than thirteen thousand National Guard forces took over the streets at the order of President Johnson to stop the lootings and destruction.[27]

King's assassination was grim proof of the survival of racial hatred. Neither federal legislation nor reciting the Declaration fully resolved America's social issues, as struggles over school integration and housing remained, leading to new types of informal segregation. Yet the successes of the grassroots Civil Rights Movement, which had finally forced the government's hand, and the constant invocation of the Declaration as its lodestar, represented a watershed in American history. It had given hope to a new generation struggling to make the country live up to its founding principles. While deep-seated problems remained, appeals to the country's founding document had helped dismantle an immoral system and create a fairer society. Though it was invoked by Black militants as a justification for secession from a country they considered irredeemable, for most Americans the Declaration served as a beacon guiding the ship of state through some of the roughest seas since the Civil War.

Chapter 19
Bicentennial

On July 6, the British Sovereign, ruler of the Dominions beyond the Seas and Defender of the Faith, landed in Philadelphia. Descending the gangplank of the royal vessel *Britannia*, the monarch proceeded directly to Independence Hall. But it was too late. Independence had been declared two days—and two hundred years—previously.

The visit of Queen Elizabeth II for America's Bicentennial in 1976 was a masterstroke of diplomacy. "God bless Elizabeth II, the queen of England," raved the *Boston Globe*, the leading newspaper of the cradle of the Revolution.[1] The Queen presented Philadelphia with a massive "Bicentennial Bell" in honor of the special transatlantic relationship and spoke at Independence Hall before traveling to Washington, D.C., where she met President Gerald R. Ford and partook in more festivities to honor a document her ancestor George III had dismissed as treasonous. Stoutly republican Americans cheered the Queen wherever she went. The *Christian Science Monitor* praised her "quiet dignity and competence" at a time when many Americans looked at their leaders with disdain.[2]

America's two-hundredth anniversary came either at the worst possible moment or just in time. The previous thirteen years had been among the most disruptive since the Great Depression, possibly even the Civil War.

The upheavals of the Civil Rights Movement had been punctuated by the tragic assassinations of John F. Kennedy, Martin Luther King, Jr., and Robert F. Kennedy. America's postwar consensus had spectacularly disintegrated barely two decades after the resounding victory in World War II.

The pivotal year was 1968. Student protests erupted on college campuses and the Chicago Police Department beat and arrested scores of protesters at the Democratic National Convention, all televised throughout the country. While domestic terror groups like the Weather Underground and Black Panthers murdered innocents in violent crimes and bombings, the country was embroiled in a divisive and seemingly unwinnable war in far-off Vietnam. Hippies and flower children smoked marijuana in public and seemed to reject all tradition and social norms, celebrating the "counterculture."[3] On Independence Day, California Governor Ronald Reagan observed that though America was born in revolution, "today's domestic revolutionaries" sought only to tear down and not to build up. Reagan, who earlier that decade had narrated the Declaration on a record album for the *Living American Stories* series, warned of the protesters, "Their cause is not freedom, it is anarchy."[4]

Richard Nixon was elected president in 1968 on the promise of peace and stability, and reelected in 1972 by the largest majority in history, but his administration was consumed by the Watergate scandal and ended up expanding the war in Southeast Asia into Cambodia. After his resignation in 1974, not wanting to be impeached over Watergate, his successor, Gerald Ford, struggled with a crippling inflation that dragged down the economy and oversaw a chaotic withdrawal of American troops from Saigon in a televised catastrophe.

To many, America had fundamentally changed. After the assassinations and riots, and the lies of Vietnam and Watergate, it seemed the country had become more cynical and distrusting of government, the elites, and big business. As a *Boston Globe* columnist wrote, the great issue in the 1976 presidential campaign would be "to restore confidence of the American people in their government and themselves," short of which he feared the country would remain "purposeless, rudderless, powerless."[5]

Some saw America's brash and unrestrained self-interest as part of the problem. Working with the World Affairs Council of Philadelphia, the irrepressible Henry Steele Commager continued in the long tradition of adapting the Declaration to contemporary causes, drafting "A Declaration of Interdependence" in October 1975, calling for a new world order of compassion, peace, and justice. "When in the course of history the threat of extinction confronts mankind," his declaration began, "it is necessary for the people of the United States to declare their interdependence with the people of all nations and to embrace those principles and build those institutions which will enable mankind to survive and civilization to flourish." His declaration was signed by dozens of members of Congress and nongovernmental organizations as well as by a bevy of public intellectuals, including former Librarian of Congress Archibald MacLeish.[6]

In a country at once exhausted and divided, it could well be questioned whether Americans would celebrate or jeer the Bicentennial of the Declaration of Independence.[7] Overwhelmingly, they celebrated, perhaps precisely because of the upheavals.

Even in the chaotic years leading up to the Bicentennial, there had been signs that things were not as bleak as appeared in the news and on television. An irrepressible interest in the approaching jubilee of the founding document and its era bubbled up even in what seemed the worst of times. In March 1969, less than a year after King's assassination and the subsequent riots, and at the height of Vietnam, Broadway's Forty-Sixth Street Theater debuted a new musical on the unlikeliest theme: the signing of the Declaration of Independence. *The New York Times*'s British-born theater critic described *1776*, written by Sherman Edwards and starring William Daniels, as "a musical with style, humanity, wit and passion."[8]

1776 won the Tony Award for Best Musical and was celebrated for bringing the Signers to life, especially the acerbic John Adams and avuncular Ben Franklin. "Yours, Yours, Yours," a romantic duet between Adams and Abigail, captured the passion between the two in a way the Revolutionary generation had rarely been portrayed:

ABIGAIL:

Write to me with sentimental effusion
Let me revel in romantic illusion

ADAMS:

Do you still smell of vanilla and spring air?
And is my favorite lover's pillar still firm and fair?

Yet such lightness was dispelled by the musical's climax, the dramatic Congressional debate over Jefferson's draft Declaration and his condemnation of the slave trade. The country's dark past was summoned by the haunting lyrics of "Molasses to Rum," laying bare the brutality and hypocrisy of slavery:

> Molasses to rum to slaves
> 'Tisn't morals, 'tis money that saves
> Shall we dance to the sound of a profitable pound
> In molasses and rum and slaves.

It was no surprise that *1776* sacrificed historical accuracy for theatrical effect, especially in the final scene, which portrayed the triumphant signing of the Declaration as taking place on July Fourth. So popular was the musical that on George Washington's birthday in 1970, *1776* became the first full-length Broadway show ever presented at the White House, hosted by President Nixon.[9] In 1972 it was turned into a popular film and soon became a staple for high school productions. A surprise hit, *1776* gave a retro-hipness to patriotic feeling in an America divided by war and politics.

While the main character in *1776* was John Adams, giving the often-overlooked Founder his due at last, Thomas Jefferson's irreplaceable role was also highlighted in the buildup to the Bicentennial. On April 24, 1975, the Library of Congress opened a major exhibit entitled "To Set a Country Free." Among the dignitaries at the opening was Lady Bird Johnson, widow of President Lyndon Johnson. The exhibit, which celebrated the Library's 175th anniversary by focusing on the lead-up to Independence, displayed as its centerpiece Thomas Jefferson's handwritten rough draft of the Declaration. This was the first time the priceless document had been displayed since it had joined the Freedom Train nearly three decades earlier.[10]

At the same time, up in Philadelphia, the National Park Service was completing a unique multiyear reconstruction project on the corner of Seventh and Market Streets. Thoughtlessly torn down in 1883, the narrow Jacob Graff house once again rose on its original site, re-creating the premises in which Jefferson had penned his draft. The $1 million project faithfully rebuilt the structure, with its exterior Flemish bond brickwork in a distinctive checkerboard pattern, and installed period furniture and a replica of his famous writing desk.[11] It was a project worthy of Frank Etting.

Lady Bird Johnson views Jefferson's Rough Draft of the Declaration at the Library of Congress's 175th anniversary celebration, April 24, 1975.

As the jubilee approached, Bicentennial fever swept the country. Over 12,566 towns and cities participated in the Bicentennial Communities project, renovating parks and historic buildings or building new community centers. A new Freedom Train was rolling through the country, filled with cultural and historical artifacts. The train left Wilmington, Delaware, on April 1, 1975, and drew seven million visitors before ending its run on December 31, 1976.[12] In honor of the jubilee, a new Air and Space Museum of the Smithsonian Institution was officially opened on July 1, 1976, while 212 million miles away, the *Viking 1* spacecraft was in orbit around Mars, waiting for a July 4 landing that ultimately would be postponed for two weeks. The Bicentennial was turning into both the greatest patriotic celebration and the greatest sales event in American history, with hats, shirts, flags, medallions, coins, mini–Liberty Bells, commemorative booklets, posters, pillow covers, bed linens, and pewter engravings marketed as keepsakes.[13] While most of the festivities centered on the two-hundred-year history of the United States as a nation, there was a surge of interest in the Declaration.

Opinion pieces and magazine articles on the Declaration poured off the presses. Over a year before the Bicentennial, the Daughters of the American Revolution kicked off their commemorations in the spirit of Abigail Adams's remonstrance to her husband not to forget the ladies. The DAR's magazine for January 1975 published an article entitled "Women Behind the Men," recounting the sacrifices and heroism of the wives of the Signers of the Declaration and noting that they should be remembered, "not as footnotes, but as women who committed themselves and acquitted themselves bravely during the signing of the Declaration of Independence and Revolutionary War."[14] On the Bicentennial itself Henry Steele Commager wrote a paean on "Jefferson and the Great Declaration" for *The Boston Globe*, praising the document for ushering in an "empire of reason" and giving the pursuit of happiness as a birthright to Americans, but delicately ignoring social issues such as recent tension over forced busing in Boston.[15]

The eminent Black historian John Hope Franklin was less laudatory, writing that "the Founding Fathers set the stage for every succeeding generation of Americans to apologize, compromise, and temporize on those principles of liberty." The Texas-based Black periodical *Sepia* more optimistically reminded its readers that "With or even without the anti-slavery passage in the Declaration, America's black population . . . [saw] in the Declaration's talk of freedom a vision of their own, too." *The Chicago Defender*'s Ethel Payne took a middle ground, writing that those "mature enough to absorb the meaning of the day" understood that the partially completed journey to realize the Declaration's philosophy remained the "legacy and the challenge" unique to America.[16]

Another challenge that had been playing out received special attention during the Bicentennial. The Equal Rights Amendment (ERA), passed by the Senate in 1972, had been ratified by thirty-four States, but remained four short of the required three-fourths majority to become a constitutional amendment. "This should be the year the Equal Rights Amendment becomes the law of the land," editorialized the *Los Angeles Times*. The editorial went on optimistically to quote a National Organization for Women speaker: "The bicentennial celebrations, bringing as they will a rededication to the basic rights of the individual to develop his or her own potential, may provide the necessary impetus."[17] Phyllis Schlafly, a prominent conservative opponent to the ERA, countered that the proposed amendment "gives you no right, no benefit, no opportunity that you don't have right now." "There is absolutely nothing it will do," Schlafly warned, adding "there is no end to the mischief and the nonsense" of the measure.[18] Disgusted at the state of affairs, Letty Cottin Pogrebin, the prominent activist and co-founder of *Ms.* magazine, wrote, "Maybe women should use 1976 to challenge the American Dream, not celebrate it."[19]

Some of the country's most powerful women embraced the Bicentennial in an attempt to promote the ERA. On June 29, Pilgrim Hall in Plymouth, Massachusetts, opened an exhibit on women in the Revolutionary Era, appropriately entitled "Remember the Ladies." The ribbon was cut by First Lady Betty Ford, who was joined by Joan Kennedy, wife of Senator Edward Kennedy; Nancy Kissinger, wife of the Secretary of State; and Kitty Dukakis, whose husband, Michael, was Governor of Massachusetts. "We're here to honor the unsung women who helped to win our national revolution," said Ford, "and to focus attention on the unfinished business of our revolution for full freedom and justice for women."[20] Such high-level support failed to push the amendment over the line, and it fell short of the required number of States before the deadline for ratification passed.[21]

These political and social debates played out in the background of months of celebration. Over 1.2 million people viewed the scroll at the National Archives over the course of 1976, while up to 10 million tourists were expected to tour Independence Hall and see the Liberty Bell in Philadelphia.[22] Sales of Declaration facsimiles and reprints ran at record levels. The Post Office released a special 13-cent stamp series and after a lapse of a decade the U.S. Treasury issued $2 bills, both featuring John Trumbull's iconic painting of Jefferson presenting the Declaration to the Continental Congress.[23] For the first time in nearly a century, William Stone's original 1823 copperplate was put into service. At the government's Bureau of Engraving and Printing, master printer Angelo LoVecchio received the copperplate from the National Archives, carefully peeled off the protective wax, and gingerly cleaned the surface before inking the plate and running off six new copies. In a nod to Frank Etting's vision for the Centennial, one sheet was sent to Independence Hall, bringing as authentic a copy of the Declaration as possible back to its birthplace.[24]

The National Archives published an engaging and well-illustrated forty-three-page history for the millions of visitors expected in Washington, D.C., entitled *Declaration of Independence: The Adventures of a Document.* Up in Philadelphia, the American Philosophical Society released a booklet in honor of the fifteen members of the society who had been

Signers, reproducing four different versions of the Declaration, all from 1776; these included the society's copy of Jefferson's draft, the Dunlap broadside, the first newspaper printing, and the unique Dunlap copy printed on parchment. For those not traveling to either city, the Jefferson scholar Dumas Malone released a special Bicentennial edition of his *Story of the Declaration of Independence*, first published in 1954.[25]

Even after two hundred years, science continued to reveal new facts about the Declaration. While Bicentennial fever raged, Frederick Goff, the Library of Congress's former Chief of the Rare Book Division, gathered a veritable treasure deep inside the Library: seventeen of the twenty-one known copies of the Dunlap broadside. Using calibrated light boxes, paper-micrometers, and beta-radiology, Goff painstakingly compared the minute differences of each sheet and later examined in person the remaining copies. For the first time, the intricacies of how Dunlap printed the Declaration on the night of July 4, 1776, were understood, from layout and pressing to the types of paper used to inform the world about Independence.

To commemorate the Bicentennial the Library published Goff's results in a volume entitled *The John Dunlap Broadside*, one of the most important scholarly studies of the Declaration done since Carl Becker's work a half-century earlier. In addition to Goff's scientific analysis, the volume included handsomely reproduced, full-page images of each of the twenty-one known surviving Dunlap copies, giving Americans a sense of what their forebears might have seen and read in the days and weeks after Independence was declared.[26]

On July 2, 1976, President Gerald Ford stood in front of the shrine in the Rotunda of the National Archives. Flanked by the Speaker of the House of Representatives and the Chief Justice of the Supreme Court, Ford addressed a crowd of dignitaries to officially kick off the national commemoration of the Bicentennial. Noting the layout of the shrine, with the Declaration at its center and the Constitution below, Ford observed that the physical arrangement put the Declaration "properly central and above all." That composition mirrored the Declaration's unique position in American history as "the Polaris of our political order—the fixed star of freedom. It is impervious to change because it states moral truths that are eternal." The Archives then opened its doors for a marathon seventy-six-hour "vigil,"

President Gerald Ford called the Declaration the "Polaris of our political order" in his Bicentennial remarks on July 2, 1976. To the left, Speaker of the House of Representatives Carl Albert; to the right, Chief Justice Warren Burger.

during which over ten thousand visitors stood in lines more than three hours long to gaze up at the parchment.[27]

Though Ford had acknowledged in the Rotunda that July 2 was the day the Continental Congress had voted for Independence, the apex of national celebrations took place, as usual, on the Fourth. Ford asked that Americans honor the day through a "renewed dedication to the principles embodied in our Declaration of Independence," just as Harry Truman had done in 1951. But celebration more than rededication took place around the country on the 200th anniversary.

At 9 a.m. in front of a crowd in Manhattan's Battery Park, the famed composer Leonard Bernstein read the entire Declaration, prefacing his recitation with a speech in which he recounted how for years he had been reading the document on the Fourth, "each year marveling anew at its precision of rhetoric, its visionary hopes, its solemn legal diction, its stubborn adherence to facts, and its barely contained rage."[28] Sixteen tall ships and over a hundred smaller vessels sailed into New York Harbor before visiting ports along the Atlantic Coast. In Washington, a street party took over Constitution Avenue in front of the National Archives, as eight thousand people gathered for a reading of the Declaration, heard patriotic songs, and then joined in the cutting of a six-foot-tall, multilayered birthday cake.[29]

President Ford had flown that morning by helicopter to Philadelphia, where more than a hundred thousand people were crammed into the park between Independence Hall and the Liberty Bell. There, he gave his official remarks, noting how both Thomas Jefferson and John Adams had lived long enough to see the "Declaration's clear call for human liberty and equality arouse the hopes of all mankind," a message that resonated in the depths of the Cold War. At 2 p.m. Eastern Time, bells rang out across the nation for two minutes, from church steeples, town halls, and firehouses,

Over eight thousand people watched as James Rhoads, Archivist of the United States, cut the Bicentennial birthday cake in front of the National Archives on July 4, 1976.

to millions of hands. Parades large and small snaked through Main Streets across the nation as people celebrated with barbecues, sports activities, and bands. The evening of July Fourth was the climax of the festivities as over a million people packed the National Mall and lined the Potomac to witness a gigantic pyrotechnics display depicting eras in America's past.[30]

Other groups held their own, less celebratory, events. Under a large banner reading "Independence from Big Business," several thousand protesters organized by the Peoples Bicentennial Commission (PBC) gathered near the U.S. Capitol on July 4. Formed in 1971 as an outgrowth of the New Left movements of students, activists, and radicals by a young socialist named Jeremy Rifkin, the commission had sought to disrupt previous events, such as Ford's speech at the 200th anniversary of Lexington and Concord in April 1975. After the PBC's antics in Massachusetts, former California Governor Ronald Reagan lambasted the group in his newspaper column as a bunch of "self-appointed political radicals" happy to take government grants to spread its anticapitalist message. "The PBC doesn't represent the people," Reagan warned, and "isn't interested in celebrating the Bicentennial."[31] Decrying the commercialization of the Bicentennial by profit-seeking corporations, the government-supported PBC called for a new revolutionary attitude on the part of the American people, justifying opposition to the late-twentieth-century capitalist system by appealing to the patriots of 1776.[32] As with other attempts at socialist-aligned, anticapitalist reform, they saw little return on their investment.

For a while, the festivities seemed to unite the country. As the *Washington Post* summed up a few months later, the Bicentennial was widely hailed as a monthslong respite from pressing economic problems, social divisions, and Cold War fears. "Small towns that were marked only by prairie grass when the Declaration of Independence was signed," noted the *Post*, "brought out the bands, the flags, the boy scouts, the beauty queens and all the heartfelt sentiment that John Adams could have wished for."[33]

Throughout the year, the Declaration inspired speeches, books, exhibits, and community celebration, though the president of the American Historical Association lamented the absence of a national debate on "our value system, the Revolution's relevance to our own day and of how its values can be preserved in our own day." Yet even he was forced to admit that the celebrations achieved "the kind of harmony and unity that we haven't seen in decades."[34] In retrospect, the *Tri-State Defender* may well have been speaking for Americans of all races when it wrote the year before that "this land is the only land that we have to live in, and most importantly, few black Americans want to leave it for some other place."[35]

If there was any dissatisfaction at the Bicentennial extravaganzas, it may have been felt in Philadelphia. Though the city had the honor of hosting the President for his official address, what it really wanted was the Declaration. It had brought the scroll back in 1876, and wanted to do the same a century later. More than seven hundred thousand Philadelphians, including Mayor Frank Rizzo, signed a petition asking President Ford to return the engrossed Declaration to Independence Hall for the festivities. Some old salt in government may have remembered how the City of Brotherly Love had tried to keep the Declaration the last time Washington had loaned it and nixed the idea, but the real reason was more likely the fragile condition of the parchment and the higher risk of damage in a country so recently roiled by riots and violence.[36] The Declaration stayed put in the National Archives, where it was viewed by millions.

In a cynical era, it was perhaps naive to believe the Declaration still answered the aspirations of Americans, and yet how else to explain the tens of millions who celebrated it? No republic had lasted as long as the United States, and there was little doubt that much of the reason for the survival of the world's oldest democracy was the philosophy embedded in its founding document. Though many felt the country needed to do more to live up to its promise, the Bicentennial reminded Americans how much was worthy of being conserved to protect the Declaration's goal of individual liberty. Despite the anger and distrust of government and other institutions, an opinion poll taken by the Gallup Organization in June 1976 found that 77 percent of respondents felt that "we had succeeded over these 200 years in achieving the ideals for which this country was founded."[37]

The Declaration appeared to have an even greater resonance amid the fear of national division and decline as citizens by the tens of millions honored the scroll and their independence. Through civil unrest, social change, and cultural shifts, the Declaration remained the "Polaris" of the Union, rising above political disputes.

Chapter 20
The Declaration in a New Millennium

The morning of September 11, 2001, dawned with a clear blue sky over most of the East Coast. As Washingtonians filed into their offices, their morning routine was shattered by news of first one, then two airplanes hitting the World Trade Center in Manhattan. Then, less than an hour after the first reports came in, American Airlines Flight 77 was flown by five terrorist hijackers into the west side of the Pentagon, killing 184 innocent passengers and military personnel in the building.

Suddenly, people streamed out of the White House complex and Capitol Building as Secret Service and Capitol police shouted at staff and civilians to run. Another plane bound to San Francisco was reported to be heading toward Washington. Two unarmed D.C. Air National Guard F-16s roared into the sky to intercept the Boeing 757. Their pilots, Colonel Marc Sasseville and Lieutenant Heather "Lucky" Penney, were determined to bring down the hijacked jet by ramming it in their own suicide mission.[1] Rumors were circulating that bombs had exploded at the State Department. For the first time since the Civil War, Washington was under attack.

Amid the chaos, with no firm information about how many planes had been taken over by whom or why and reports of bombs going off around the District, the head of the National Archives would have pressed the button to lower the Declaration into its indestructible bombproof vault below the Rotunda. Except that on that tragic morning, the shrine and the vault were both empty. While America was propelled into a new global war on Islamist terror, the Declaration, Constitution, and Bill of Rights were in a different vault ten miles away in suburban Maryland. Just two months previously, on July 5, 2001, the founding documents had been removed under heavy guard and taken to the sprawling National Archives and Records Administration (NARA) facility in College Park, Maryland, known as Archives II. Half a century after they were fitted into their new cases in the Rotunda, the priceless parchments needed new protection.

For over a decade, NARA had monitored the condition of the Declaration and its case with space-age detection technology designed by NASA's Jet Propulsion Laboratory. The Charters Monitoring System used an overhead camera to scan one-inch squares of the parchment and make digital files that could be compared to earlier images. By 1996, after more than 125 scans, the verdict was clear: the documents were holding up, but their cases were not.[2]

In fact, all the cases containing the Charters of Freedom were starting to break down. Tiny cracks had appeared, and minute crystals and microdroplets were forming inside. That meant humidity inside the cases was building up. Over time, as the irregularities grew, the likelihood of damage would increase. Of particular concern was that the pane of glass that lay directly on the Declaration, to keep it flat, could wind up attaching itself to the document or abrading the parchment's surface as it traveled up and down the lift into its vault every night.

In a dust-free, temperature and humidity–controlled lab, Mary Lynn Ritzenthaler, Chief of NARA's Document Conservation Laboratory, experienced "awe and kind of amazement," as she and her partner, senior conservator Catherine "Kitty" Nicholson, became the first people in half a century to touch the Declaration of Independence. After testing the interior atmosphere of the case, the two carefully opened the frame. Nicholson, who said it was "nerve wracking," used a small blade to slice through the soft lead sealing the two sheets of glass that the National Bureau of Standards had pumped full of helium back in 1951.[3]

When they lifted the interior pane, Ritzenthaler and Nicholson were relieved to find that no flake of ink had stuck to the glass. Now the conservators could examine the scroll and photograph it. To their further relief, microscopes showed no spots where the Declaration's writing was lifting or flaking. The Constitution had suffered from just such damage in a few spots, requiring careful readhesion of the ink. Ritzenthaler and Nicholson gently cleaned away the dirt and grime from the Declaration and removed the remaining adhesive from the parchment. Finally, minor repairs were made using special Japanese paper, as in 1942.[4] It was now time to fit the Declaration into its new holder.

A team of scientists, engineers, and technicians from the National Institute of Standards and Technology (NIST), NARA, NASA, and the engineering firm Heery International had spent four years and $5 million designing and constructing new cases.[5] The specifications read like something from a James Bond novel.[6] Ritzenthaler and Nicholson laid the Declaration on a cushion of handmade cellulose paper designed to absorb and release moisture. They secured the parchment with polyester tabs to a thin, detachable platform made of high-grade aluminum with holes to provide moisture transfer, nestled in a custom-made base of solid aluminum alloy with nickel plating on the exterior and a black anodized interior finish. The parchment was covered by ⅜-inch laminated, tempered float glass with an antireflective coating made (as in 1951) by Libbey-Owens-Ford, but this time it would not touch the document. The whole was framed by a casing of pure titanium with its aluminum base, covered with nickel gold plating, and secured by seventy steel bolts spaced slightly less than two inches apart. NIST had decided that argon maintained consistent humidity levels better than helium, so the sealed case was filled with that inert gas. The seal was plated, machined smooth with a diamond tool, and nickel plated again before a final polishing.[7]

The aluminum base included openings to supply and purge the argon gas, a humidity sensor, two pressure sensors, and a pressure relief device. Temperature sensors outside the encasement measured heat changes. Light beams were shot through two small sapphire windows placed on one edge of the encasement. Their reflection off interior mirrors made it possible for conservators to measure the relative humidity and oxygen content inside the case, where the temperature was kept at a constant 67 degrees Fahrenheit and the relative humidity at 40 percent. Similar encasements were made for the Constitution and Bill of Rights.

The Declaration's new case was much larger than the old encasement at 39¼" tall by 33⅝" wide, which meant it would not fit into the old altar in the shrine. The changes that were about to sweep the National Archives Building went far beyond simple glass and metal coverings.

While the scientists pored over the parchment at Archives II, construction workers were busy dismantling the shrine and altar in the Rotunda. When the dust had cleared, a dramatically new layout would take their place. After seventy years, the 1930s Archives Building desperately needed mechanical and safety upgrading. Yet in bringing the neoclassical building up to modern specifications, the entire visitor experience would dramatically change.

For decades, the public had entered the Archives by walking up thirty-nine grand but steep steps on Constitution Avenue to the massive bronze doors. Now, a new street-level entrance was created under the staircase, giving onto a lobby with elevators and interior staircases leading up to the Rotunda level. While far less impressive, this new entrance complied with the provisions of the 1990 Americans with Disabilities Act and the 1984 Uniform Federal Accessibility Standards requirements. It offered easier access for the entire public, including weary children, and better security screening in a post-9/11 capital.[8] But the biggest change was yet to come.

Inside, the old shrine dominated the Rotunda. It could only be approached by climbing up marble steps, though a wheelchair ramp had been added. The elevated altar that held the Declaration, while emotionally powerful, did not provide the best angle to view the parchment. Gazing up at the scroll may have instilled a proper reverence, but it made for a less-than-ideal experience. Perhaps more importantly to conservators like Mary Lynn Ritzenthaler, the stress put on the Declaration from this vertical position was becoming dangerous. In addition, given the constraint on space, only the first and final sheets of the Constitution had been on continous display since 1952. A renovated exhibit space would allow for the permanent display of the remaining two leaves, along with the Declaration and Bill of Rights.

And so, the imposing shrine and altar were removed. In their place were built three large floor cases designed to hold the documents in high-tech individual encasements. Each floor case was twenty-nine inches high at the front, sloping up to forty-four inches at the rear, easily viewable by small children and visitors in wheelchairs. The Constitution, in a four-bay case, now took the central spot, between the grand Corinthian columns. In a separate case to the left was the Declaration, with the Bill of Rights flanking the Constitution on the opposite side. The new layout required an entirely new security and vault system for the three new floor cases, a task given to the Diebold Safe Company, of Canton, Ohio, which donated a million dollars' worth of material and labor.

The original plan to renovate the Rotunda was intended to take three years. But finding matching limestone from Georgia and Indiana and marble from Maryland and Missouri almost seventy years after the building was first constructed took time, ingenuity, and luck. The dome of the Rotunda was to be rewired for fiber-optic lighting to protect the documents. Even the massive Barry Faulkner murals of the presentation of the Declaration and Constitution were cut free from their mounts and literally rolled up for cleaning and restoration, before being remounted on new aluminum backing plates.

The Smithsonian Institution suggested that the Declaration and Constitution be put on display in a new exhibition space in the National Museum of American History while the Archives was under reconstruction. But having successfully gained custody of the founding documents from the Library of Congress in 1952, the Archives was not about to lose control of its most valuable documents. The Rotunda project was sped up, some renovations were simplified or dropped, and the time frame was shortened to just over two years. Completing the renovations and upgrades would cost $135 million and require support from the National Endowment for the Arts and the National Park Service. Millions of dollars in donations were received from groups including the John S. and James L. Knight Foundation, while the William G. McGowan Charitable Fund gave a gift to build a new 294-seat theater.[9]

When completed, the new flow along the Rotunda's curving wall was intended to bring visitors first to the Declaration, then the Constitution, and finally the Bill of Rights, re-creating their chronological order and giving an intellectual coherence to the display (see insert). The Archives tried to minimize the aesthetic changes, pointing out that the Rotunda remained "an enormous and awe-inspiring place," in the words of one senior curator.[10] Yet there was no ignoring the fact that the new arrangement dethroned the Declaration. The scroll now was more accessible, trading power for an unexpected intimacy.

On September 17, 2003, Constitution Day, the Rotunda reopened to the public. Addressing the gathered dignitaries, President George W. Bush spoke to a nation awash in anxiety. The collapse of the Soviet Union in 1991 proved the strength of both the American system and the country's ideals as much as it did Russian weakness, ushering in a decade of American dominance. Yet the end of the Cold War offered little respite from both domestic and foreign challenges. The half century since Pearl Harbor had permanently transformed the country and government, with a massive bureaucracy now involved in nearly every aspect of national life, while America's overseas commitments seemed only to grow with the demise of the Soviets.[11] The 9/11 terror attacks forced America into its second war in the Middle East in a decade while social and economic problems festered at home.

These worries exacerbated a critical and often dismissive view of the country's past that had crystallized in the decades after Vietnam and Watergate, especially among the intellectual class. A larger culture war dividing the political left and right fueled endemic partisanship. Bush opened his National Archives speech by rejecting the new relativism that dismissed America's achievements and values. "The ideals of our founders were stronger than any flaws of the founders," he said, countering fashionable critiques that sought to delegitimize their achievements on the grounds of their failure to address slavery, racism, and sexual inequality in the eighteenth century.

Speaking to a far more racially and ethnically diverse society than in 1976, Bush sought to link the Declaration to the nation's enduring aspirations while stressing its universal validity. "America owns the Declaration of Independence and the Constitution, but the ideals they proclaim belong to all mankind," he stated, a reminder of the ongoing wars against Islamic extremism. "Free people everywhere remain in their debt," Bush concluded, in terms so often repeated during the Cold War.[12] Criticisms that Bush had used the Declaration's call for liberty to justify launching wars in Iraq and Afghanistan, and that his government had abused civil liberties in the war on terror, replayed similar debates reaching back to the

Civil War, and World Wars I and II, revealing once more the perennial debate over government power versus individual freedom.

A decade later, Barack Obama would give his second inaugural address to an even more cynical and weary country, one still at war in the Middle East and now recovering from the traumatic 2008 global financial crisis and recession. A skilled orator, he tied the concept of American exceptionalism to an allegiance to the Declaration's self-evident truths on equality. Obama, the nation's first biracial president, acknowledged Jefferson's and Locke's natural rights theory, stating that freedom was a gift from God, before reminding his listeners that the Founders entrusted "each generation to keep safe our founding creed."[13]

Not all Americans agreed with either Bush's or Obama's conception of liberty. In the previous decades, the Declaration's ideals had also been part of the inspiration for a homegrown militia movement that was violently opposed to the actions of the federal government. In 1995, a veteran of the first Gulf War named Timothy McVeigh had conspired with a group of like-minded separatists to blow up the Alfred P. Murrah Federal Building in Oklahoma City, killing 168 people in the worst case of domestic terrorism in U.S. history. McVeigh was radicalized by government clashes with the Weaver family at Ruby Ridge, Idaho, and the Branch Davidians, a religious group stockpiling weapons in anticipation of the end of time in Waco, Texas. Part of a militia movement with networks across the American West, McVeigh regularly quoted the Declaration to justify resistance to the federal government, which he believed to be infringing on the basic rights of American citizens.[14] When McVeigh was arrested, officials searching his truck found a copy of the Declaration among other writings on liberty.

McVeigh's trial brought to national attention this web of militia members alienated from modern American society and government. His lawyer argued that McVeigh was one of the "community of people who follow the revolutionary rule and its antecedents."[15] Yet, as prosecutor Joseph Hartzler argued in his opening statement in the trial, "McVeigh isolated and took these statements out of context, and he did that to justify his anti-government violence . . . the statements of our forefathers can never be televised to justify warfare against innocent children. Our forefathers didn't fight British women and children. They fought other soldiers."[16] Now a topic of widespread debate, the link between the Declaration and the militias made its way into popular culture. In a 1997 episode of the popular television series *J.A.G.*, the scroll was kidnapped by disgruntled former soldiers under the sway of a charismatic officer committed to a new American revolution based on the Declaration's call for opposition to tyranny, before being rescued by heroic military lawyers.

McVeigh was executed for his crime less than three weeks before September 11, 2001, maintaining that the Declaration justified violent resistance to a tyrannical federal government. Yet this view, as unsettling and persistent among extremists as it had been among Black Panthers a generation earlier, remained distinctly in the minority. For the vast majority of Americans, the Declaration represented the foundation of a system of government that defended their liberty. As Archivist of the United States John Carlin reminded the audience at the rededication of the Rotunda in 2003, "Every day we celebrate the freedom first declared in the Declaration of Independence."[17]

In a darkened room somewhere in the suburbs of Washington, D.C., a couple bends over an ancient scroll. After swabbing the parchment with lemon juice and heating it with their breath, a long-hidden key to a fabulous treasure emerges. The scroll is no less than the engrossed Declaration of Independence, stolen from its impregnable fortress inside the National Archives. Pursued by a gang of bloodthirsty thieves as well as by the FBI, the couple and their two colleagues find an unimaginable golden hoard dating back to the Knights Templar, before safely returning the Declaration to government officials.

This thrilling story was the plot of *National Treasure*, an adventure movie released in November 2004. Starring Nicolas Cage and directed by Jon Turteltaub, the film became a smash hit, earning well over $347 million and spawning an equally popular sequel. With a starring role for the National Archives Building and the Declaration, *National Treasure* spurred a cult following of amateur treasure hunters and sparked interest in a fictional American past where the Signers of the Declaration were Freemasons as obsessed with ciphers and underground vaults as they were with establishing a new country. Thanks to *National Treasure*, the engrossed Declaration became a bona fide pop culture icon. Families, school groups, and tourists from around the country and world poured into the renovated Archives, nearly eight hundred thousand alone in 2004, the first full year after the reopening.[18]

The same month *National Treasure* premiered, another fabulous hoard was revealed. For more than half a century, Albert H. Small, a native Washingtonian and major real estate developer, had amassed the country's largest private collection of Declaration artifacts. Small bequeathed the collection to his alma mater, the University of Virginia, nestled near the Shenandoah Valley just two and a half hours away from the National Archives. Among the more than 350 rarities in the Small Collection were a nearly pristine Dunlap broadside believed to have been sent to Mount Vernon; the Marquis de Lafayette's personal copy of the Stone engraving, which had hung in his bedroom; a complete set of autographs of the Signers, most dating from 1776; rare letters, including Caesar Rodney's famous "thunder and rain" note; and equally scarce broadsides and newspaper printings of the Declaration. To house and display the items, Small funded the construction of a new special collections building, which opened in November 2004.[19]

For those inspired by Nicolas Cage or Albert Small to hunt their own treasure, it was the Dunlap broadside they were after. Rare but lucky finds had happened for decades, sending document hunters into a tizzy. In 1968, staff clearing out the venerable Leary's Book Store in Philadelphia opened a crate in the storage room that had been sealed since 1911; inside, they found a Dunlap broadside among the musty papers. Its sale the next year at auction for $404,000 (nearly $3.6 million in 2025 dollars) made the front page of *The New York Times.* Nearly two decades later, up in Exeter, New Hampshire, renovations to a Revolutionary-era home owned by the Society of the Cincinnati brought to light a nearly perfect Dunlap in the attic. During the Revolution, the house had belonged to the Gilman family, whose son had read from that very copy to the local townsfolk on July 16, 1776. The New Hampshire Cincinnati turned the home into a public museum where their Dunlap is put on annual display. Such happy accidents enticed Americans with visions of finding their own personal link to the Signers.[20]

Perhaps the best treasure story began in 1989, when a man browsing in a flea market in Adamstown, Pennsylvania, paid four dollars for a torn painting, buying it for the picture frame. When he removed the painting, he discovered a nearly pristine Dunlap broadside stuffed in the back. Two years later, that copy was auctioned for a record $2.4 million. That mark was smashed in 2000, when television producer and political activist Norman Lear bought the same broadside for $8.1 million (over $15 million in 2025 dollars) in the first major internet auction held by Sotheby's. Far from keeping his Dunlap as a hidden trophy accessible only to a privileged few, on July 4, 2001, Lear loaded it into a specially outfitted semitractor trailer and sent it off on a three-and-a-half-year tour, where it visited roughly one hundred towns and cities in all fifty States, harking back to the Freedom Trains of the twentieth century.[21]

Just as Norman Lear's nationwide Dunlap broadside tour was winding down, *National Treasure* hit the big screen at the end of 2004. The Archives embraced the surge of interest in the Declaration, opening new exhibits to bring in even more visitors. Over one million people filed through the renovated Rotunda in 2005, increasing to 1,075,000 in 2006. The national media took notice of the Declaration's new popularity, with the *Washington Post* punning that thanks to the movie, "the National Archives are on the map."[22]

Even the normally staid Supreme Court was swept up in Declaration fever. Around 2000, Matthew Hofstedt, then an assistant curator at the Court, started hunting for a Stone engraving. He had come across an old record noting that one of the original 1823 Stone facsimiles had been moved from the U.S. Capitol to the Court's new building in 1935, the same year the National Archives opened. By the turn of the twenty-first century, no one knew anything about it, and the trail had gone cold. In 2003, Hofstedt stumbled on a photograph of the Declaration on the wall in the Clerk's office prior to a renovation that had taken place in 1996. He and the Supreme Court staff now searched in earnest. Tucked behind an automated filing cabinet they found a large, sealed garbage bag. Inside was the Stone, where it had been placed during the renovations and promptly forgotten. Reframed in a custom case, the facsimile went on public display in the Court in 2005, eventually attracting media attention about the "lost" Declaration. In 2008, it was placed in the chambers of Chief Justice John Roberts, where it has hung since.[23]

While the National Archives broke physical attendance records, the Declaration also entered the digital era. New technologies now made the scroll instantly accessible to anyone anywhere. When the parchment had been removed for cleaning during the renovation, NARA had taken the opportunity to do the first high-resolution digital scans. These were uploaded to the internet in conjunction with the reopening of the Rotunda.

Americans who might never make it to Washington could now take a detailed look at the Declaration and even view the now-famous reverse side of the parchment, straining to make out any faint treasure maps or book ciphers. Uploading such detailed images was the final stage of a process that had brought the Declaration to the public starting back in 1818 with the release of the first decorative reproduction by Benjamin Owen Tyler, followed by that of John Binns, and finally the definitive facsimile of the Stone engraving. This was just the beginning of a new digital life for the scroll.

Over the next decades, as storage capacity and resolution technology increased, the entire history of the Declaration emerged from the vaults of the National Archives and Library of Congress and entered the virtual world. From Richard Henry Lee's June 7, 1776, resolution calling for Independence to the actual tally of the July 2 vote, documents never before seen by the public could now be accessed by anyone at a school, library, or home. Soon, a veritable flood of data was unleashed. Not just historical artifacts, but detailed oral histories by those who had cared for the Declaration were scanned and put online. NARA and the Library of Congress scanned and uploaded thousands of photographs and recordings related to the Declaration, from images of its Victorian-era case in the State Department library to pictures of the Library of Congress's famous first shrine. Also available were a rare video recording of the transfer to the National Archives in 1952 and pictures of the building of the Mosler Vault underneath the Rotunda. At the same time, NARA teamed up with presidential libraries and other websites, making it possible for students of history to hear Harry Truman's Demisemiseptcentennial address from 1951 and his remarks at the transfer to the National Archives the following year, Lyndon Johnson's comments at the signing of the Civil Rights Act, and Martin Luther King's "American Dream" address from 1965, all of which captured the unparalleled influence of the Declaration on American history.

Despite this digital opportunity and an endless stream of reproductions, seeing the engrossed Declaration in person remains a unique experience. On spring days, when busloads of school groups descend on the nation's capital, or during summer vacation, when families trek to a steamy

Washington, the lines outside the National Archives regularly stretch along Constitution Avenue and around the corner, onto Ninth Street.

No longer snaking up the imposing steps to John Russell Pope's magnificent portico, tourists patiently wait to enter the neoclassical building, often snacking on pretzels or hot dogs from the food trucks intrusively parked on Constitution Avenue, or buying Washington souvenir caps from the ubiquitous street vendors. The lines have been there now for over seven decades, slowly wending their way into the great Rotunda, hushed and expectant as they draw near. Standing quietly in front of the Declaration, consternation at the condition of the faded document battles with a sense of awe at encountering the very parchment that John Hancock, Thomas Jefferson, John Adams, and Benjamin Franklin signed: the one that turned a dispute into a revolution, that inspired Frederick Douglass and Susan B. Anthony, that Abraham Lincoln defended and Martin Luther King, Jr., quoted, and that set in motion a democratic upheaval throughout the world. It had enticed to these shores tens of millions of people yearning for a better life and guided generations governing themselves based on shared principles and a commitment to living in a free society.

And then, having seen the Declaration, trooping past the Constitution and Bill of Rights, the groups head to the bookstore, where more often than not they purchase crinkly paper copies of the parchment, making it an object of their own. At last, they walk back out into the sunshine, remembering its eternal phrases, and hopefully recommitted to playing their part in its pageant.

EPILOGUE

There is no ending to this history of the Declaration of Independence. New generations will continue to excavate its past. Scholars will continue to argue over which thinkers most influenced Thomas Jefferson and what role other hands played in its drafting. Battles over whether the Declaration or the Constitution is more central to the spirit of the Republic will flare up. Demands that we live up to the Declaration's promises will never cease. Treasure hunters will dream of finding unknown copies of the Dunlap broadside or original Stone engravings hidden in old country attics or stuffed in the pages of dusty volumes.

And yet, for all we know about the Declaration, and for all the terabytes of information now available, much of the document's past remains tantalizingly lost. No records of the debates over its adoption or editing of the draft are likely to turn up. No contemporary print or engraving of the Declaration in its original exhibit case in the Old Patent Office has yet come to light. No record, if one ever existed, of the order transferring the Declaration to the old State Department building in July 1861 during the Civil War is among the millions of pages of digitized government papers. No trace has been unearthed of the 1922 photos of the Declaration taken by L. C. Handy when the Library of Congress took custody of the scroll, nor of the detailed examination undertaken by Librarian Herbert Putnam at the same time, which could tell us when the parchment was further damaged. And above all, the official "fair copy" of the Declaration adopted by the Continental Congress on July 4, 1776, and taken to John Dunlap's print shop—the holy grail—almost certainly no longer exists.

Clearing up these mysteries would add to our understanding of the fragile parchment that has now survived for a quarter of a millennium. But it would not fundamentally change our relationship to our founding document. Our connection to this most precious of inheritances is both material and intellectual, emotional and logical. We care about, and are fascinated by, the Declaration's physical survival because its existence connects us in a tangible way with our common past and our shared principles. The parchment, and the prints and facsimiles and knickknacks, connects us to those who created our Nation and those who struggled to honor its promises.

For that physical link we are indebted to the generations of Americans who protected and preserved the Declaration, from Charles Thomson to Stephen Pleasonton, from Herbert Putnam and Archibald MacLeish to Mary Lynn Ritzenthaler and Catherine Nicholson, along with hundreds of other conservators, custodians, scientists, and technicians. And we are in the debt of those who brought the Declaration to the people in innumerable, small, and personal ways, from John Binns and William J. Stone to John Trumbull and Frank Etting, and in the twentieth century, entrepreneurs like Charles Promislo and businesses like the John Hancock Mutual Life Insurance Company.

The engrossed Declaration may one day crumble into dust, though not without legions of scientists and conservators fighting to preserve it. If that happens, something priceless will be lost, but its philosophy will live on. Americans like to believe that the Declaration has inspired the world, and in many ways, it is right to think so. As Thomas Jefferson believed and Abraham Lincoln asserted, the desire for freedom and opportunity is a universal one. The same could be said about American constitutionalism, which has similarly influenced the development of governments around the globe.

Yet after 250 years, the Declaration—both parchment and symbol—uniquely animates the "American Dream." The historian James Truslow Adams coined that famous phrase in his 1932 history, *The Epic of America.* It is, he wrote, "that dream of a land in which life should be better and richer and fuller for every man, with opportunity for each according to his ability or achievement."[1] The promise of the Declaration heartened settlers who created towns and cities out of the wilderness and inspired immigrants who braved the ocean hoping for a better, freer life. It gave hope to those fighting for freedom at home and abroad while its Judeo-Christian underpinnings shaped American society. Because the Declaration still survives both physically and symbolically, it links us to this past. It is no magic wand for solving our problems, but it ties us to one another in all our messy, shortsighted, self-interested, often vicious, but also inspiring attempts to maintain a self-governing constitutional republic. And it gives hope that our children and grandchildren will enjoy the same bounty and freedom, with the same opportunities, that we and our ancestors did.

As long as the country exists, the scroll will be invoked by those demanding equity even more than equality and by those who see the federal government as oppressive and favor violence in pursuit of their vision of liberty. For the majority of us, however, the Declaration of Independence is a reminder of the values and principles that bind us together, validating our individual aspirations even as it calls on our sacrifice and sets up the foundation of our civil society.

The Declaration is not an abstract idea, but the expression of a living political community. It grew out of a British cultural and political tradition that believed in the importance of both protecting and tempering our individualism. It expects us to keep faith with those traditions and also with our unfulfilled possibilities.[2] Both its secular philosophy and its belief in a divine providence allow us to come together as equals in a social compact, inviting each American to commit himself or herself to its principles and defend that fragile system. It requires, as George Washington memorably wrote of our democratic system in 1790, "only that they who live under its protection should demean themselves as good citizens."[3] The Declaration of Independence makes us one Nation, uniting us in a still-radical experiment in republican self-government.

This is the power of a parchment that has been, and will continue to be, the purest expression of what it means to be American, a true national treasure.

ACKNOWLEDGMENTS

In his 1837 seminal address "The American Scholar," Ralph Waldo Emerson noted, "Each age must write its own books, or rather, each generation for the next succeeding. The books of an older period will not fit this." This might be the only valid justification for being ambitious or foolhardy enough to offer a new history of America's most famous founding document. I can only hope the result vindicates the effort to write a comprehensive history for this generation.

For this book especially I am indebted to a great number of people. Condoleezza Rice, director of the Hoover Institution, allowed me to begin a new chapter in my scholarly career, and for that, I am deeply grateful. Without Jessie Kratz, Historian of the National Archives, this book would never have left the ground. She provided enormous amounts of material and cheerfully answered the most obscure questions; our email chain alone is almost as long as this book. Coffee with Colleen Shogan, then Archivist of the United States, unexpectedly kicked off this project. My sincere thanks to Kevin Butterfield, director of the Library of Congress's John W. Kluge Center, who arranged a Distinguished Visiting Scholar position in 2025, giving me access to the Library's unparalleled resources and allowing me to finish the book, and the opportunity to join a community of extraordinary scholars. At the Library of Congress, the staffs of the Manuscripts Division, Rare Book and Special Collections Division, Prints and Photographs Division, European Division, Newspaper and Current Periodical Reading Room, American Folklife Center, Recorded Sound Research Center, and the Moving Image Research Center all provided expert assistance with requests ranging from rare documents to old films. At the Society of the Cincinnati's American Revolution Institute, Andy Morse and Thomas Lannon provided a very welcome research fellowship to use its excellent collection and especially their rare pamphlets.

Others who gave generously of their time or answered requests for assistance include David Langbart and Sarah LeRoy at the National Archives, Matthew Hofstedt and Katie Byerly at the Supreme Court, Keeley Tulio at Founding Forward in Philadelphia, Randy Hammond and Hugh Robinson of the New Hampshire Society of the Cincinnati, Joy O'Donnell at the National Society of the Daughters of the American Revolution, Lindsay Dupertuis at the Cosmos Club, Ruby Landau-Pincus of the YIVO Institute for Jewish Research, Samatha Majhor at the Newberry Library, Katie Kelaidis of the National Hellenic Museum, Emily Herron at Manulife (John Hancock Mutual Life Insurance), Akhil Reed Amar and Ned Blackhawk at Yale, Darmouth's Colin Calloway, and Alan Weiss of the Historical Documents Company. I would also like to thank Bianca Coronado, Chris Dauer, Steve Davis, Chris Marino, Amanda Robb, Kaoru Ueda, and Eric Wakin, at the Hoover Institution; as well as Stanford's Department of Special Collections and Josh Capitanio at Stanford's East Asia Library. Jessie Kratz, Ralph Eshelman, Deborah Lehr, Laura Grutzeck, and Alexandra Lane provided great help with images and permissions. Seth Kaller not only helped with images but also shared some of his vast knowledge of prints of the Declaration. At various stages, Evan and Oscie Thomas offered much needed encouragement and assistance as well as wonderful lunches at their home. In addition, my thanks for their kind help to Jane Aikin, Douglas Bradburn, John Y. Cole, Steve Darnall, Chris DeMuth, Michael Douma, Joyce Goodfriend, David Grossman, Maarten Kooij, Josiah Osgood, Megan Romney, Aryman Singh, and Berel Wolvovsky. My thanks, as well, to Keith Edwards for permission to use the lyrics from *1776*. Special appreciation to Ted Bromund for his orthographic and grammatical advice. My apologies to anyone I inadvertently left out.

History comes alive for me when I can tangibly encounter it. Connecting to the Declaration was made a reality thanks to Chief Justice John Roberts, who kindly allowed me into his private chambers at the Supreme Court to view a rare copy of the Stone engraving; Jessie Kratz, who brought me into the vault at the National Archives (not *that* one) to show me Charles Thomson's original journals, resolutions, and tally sheets of the Continental Congress; Patrick Spero, who opened up the priceless holdings of the American Philosophical Society, including its unique parchment Dunlap; Anne Bentley, who set before me John Adams's handwritten copy of Jefferson's draft at the Massachusetts Historical Society; Cary Hutto and Anthony DiGiovanni, of the Historical Society of Pennsylvania, who let me see their unique Dunlap "proof" copy with its famous "errant *a*" (and made sure I saw James Wilson's handwritten first draft of the Constitution, for balance); Krystal Appiah and Anne Causey at the University of Virginia's Albert H. Small Declaration of Independence Collection, who showed me Mr. Small's collection of Signers' autographs and Benjamin Owen Tyler's subscription book; the Manuscript and Rare Books Divisions of the Library of Congress, which brought out Dunlap and Goddard broadsides and Binns and Tyler facsimiles; Karie Diethorn at Independence National Historic Park, who brought the summer of 1776 alive during a fascinating walk around Independence Hall; Steven Livengood at the Capitol Historical Society, who took me on a memorable tour of the Capitol to view Trumbull's masterpiece and numerous Declaration-related images; and Christine Brennan, who graciously allowed me into her beautiful home, Rokeby Mansion, and Rocky Robinson, who took me down to Rokeby's vault where the engrossed Declaration was hidden in 1814.

Special thanks go to those distinguished scholars who generously responded to an interloper into their academic community and kindly read draft chapters, often during summer vacation. Peter Berkowitz, Kevin Butterfield, James Campbell, Lindsay Chervinsky, Frank Cogliano, Matt Costello, Jane Kamensky, David Kennedy, Chandra Manning, Peter Onuf, Jack Rakove, Daniel Sargent, Adam Smith, Steven Smith, and Patrick Spero all gave valuable and insightful feedback that greatly helped me improve the manuscript and saved me from numerous mistakes. Even an all-star bench of experts can only do so much; needless to say, any remaining errors of fact or interpretation remain mine alone.

I also appreciate the efforts of my research assistants, Nina Michele Burik, Emelia Richling, Diana Smith, Yasha Van Praagh, and especially Lucas Warren for his indefatigable research at the Library of Congress.

My agent, Emma Parry, at Janklow Nesbit, saw what this book could be and, along with Jessica Gitre, guided me with good cheer and needed encouragement through a publishing world very different from that which I had known. Thanks to Joy de Menil, my editor at Simon & Schuster's Avid Reader Press, I now can empathize with Thomas Jefferson, who gnashed his teeth at the "mutilations" done to his draft of the Declaration by the Continental Congress. Joy passionately believed in this project, which explains why she left literally no line of the manuscript unscathed;

and though we'll never agree on the correct use of commas, she dragged me, often unwillingly if not uncomprehendingly, into the completely new style of writing needed to make this book come alive. Megan Noes and Alexandra Silvas at Avid Reader Press also helped cheerfully with the production process; Laurie McGee and Annalea Manalili expertly copyedited the manuscript, saving me from numerous (and embarrassing) errors; and Alison Forner and Jim Tierney did an outstanding job with the cover.

I dedicated this book to Max Shulman and Bella Revson, Max Mazur and Rose Wolkow, and Morris Eauslinsky and Rose Hecht, all of whom left the world they knew to start a new life in a promised land. Each became a proud American, feeling themselves for the first time part of a larger national community. They respected, honored, and tried to maintain their new country's customs and beliefs while observing their own traditions, and eventually sent their sons off to fight for the freedom they now enjoyed. Their example inspired me to tell this story to the best of my ability, and while doing so, my own family gave unstintingly of their love and support. My brother, Dan, read the entire manuscript twice with a discerning (and arch) eye. Ginko and Benjamin were again my most trusted advisors and confidants, and with good cheer they listened for months to stories about the Declaration or heard about "discoveries" I made in archives, online, or at historic sites. If only we had found a Dunlap together.

APPENDIX

In Congress, July 4, 1776

The unanimous Declaration of the thirteen united States of America, When in the Course of human events, it becomes necessary for one people to dissolve the political bands which have connected them with another, and to assume among the powers of the earth, the separate and equal station to which the Laws of Nature and of Nature's God entitle them, a decent respect to the opinions of mankind requires that they should declare the causes which impel them to the separation.

We hold these truths to be self-evident, that all men are created equal, that they are endowed by their Creator with certain unalienable Rights, that among these are Life, Liberty and the pursuit of Happiness. --That to secure these rights, Governments are instituted among Men, deriving their just powers from the consent of the governed, --That whenever any Form of Government becomes destructive of these ends, it is the Right of the People to alter or to abolish it, and to institute new Government, laying its foundation on such principles and organizing its powers in such form, as to them shall seem most likely to effect their Safety and Happiness. Prudence, indeed, will dictate that Governments long established should not be changed for light and transient causes; and accordingly all experience hath shewn, that mankind are more disposed to suffer, while evils are sufferable, than to right themselves by abolishing the forms to which they are accustomed. But when a long train of abuses and usurpations, pursuing invariably the same Object evinces a design to reduce them under absolute Despotism, it is their right, it is their duty, to throw off such Government, and to provide new Guards for their future security. --Such has been the patient sufferance of these Colonies; and such is now the necessity which constrains them to alter their former Systems of Government. The history of the present King of Great Britain is a history of repeated injuries and usurpations, all having in direct object the establishment of an absolute Tyranny over these States. To prove this, let Facts be submitted to a candid world.

He has refused his Assent to Laws, the most wholesome and necessary for the public good.

He has forbidden his Governors to pass Laws of immediate and pressing importance, unless suspended in their operation till his Assent should be obtained; and when so suspended, he has utterly neglected to attend to them.

He has refused to pass other Laws for the accommodation of large districts of people, unless those people would relinquish the right of Representation in the Legislature, a right inestimable to them and formidable to tyrants only.

He has called together legislative bodies at places unusual, uncomfortable, and distant from the depository of their public Records, for the sole purpose of fatiguing them into compliance with his measures.

He has dissolved Representative Houses repeatedly, for opposing with manly firmness his invasions on the rights of the people.

He has refused for a long time, after such dissolutions, to cause others to be elected; whereby the Legislative powers, incapable of Annihilation, have returned to the People at large for their exercise; the State remaining in the mean time exposed to all the dangers of invasion from without, and convulsions within.

He has endeavoured to prevent the population of these States; for that purpose obstructing the Laws for Naturalization of Foreigners; refusing to pass others to encourage their migrations hither, and raising the conditions of new Appropriations of Lands.

He has obstructed the Administration of Justice, by refusing his Assent to Laws for establishing Judiciary powers.

He has made Judges dependent on his Will alone, for the tenure of their offices, and the amount and payment of their salaries.

He has erected a multitude of New Offices, and sent hither swarms of Officers to harrass our people, and eat out their substance.

He has kept among us, in times of peace, Standing Armies without the Consent of our legislatures.

He has affected to render the Military independent of and superior to the Civil power.

He has combined with others to subject us to a jurisdiction foreign to our constitution, and unacknowledged by our laws; giving his Assent to their Acts of pretended Legislation:

For Quartering large bodies of armed troops among us:

For protecting them, by a mock Trial, from punishment for any Murders which they should commit on the Inhabitants of these States:

For cutting off our Trade with all parts of the world:

For imposing Taxes on us without our Consent:

For depriving us in many cases, of the benefits of Trial by Jury:

For transporting us beyond Seas to be tried for pretended offences:

For abolishing the free System of English Laws in a neighbouring Province, establishing therein an Arbitrary government, and enlarging its Boundaries so as to render it at once an example and fit instrument for introducing the same absolute rule into these Colonies:

For taking away our Charters, abolishing our most valuable Laws, and altering fundamentally the Forms of our Governments:

For suspending our own Legislatures, and declaring themselves invested with power to legislate for us in all cases whatsoever.

He has abdicated Government here, by declaring us out of his Protection and waging War against us.

He has plundered our seas, ravaged our Coasts, burnt our towns, and destroyed the lives of our people.

He is at this time transporting large Armies of foreign Mercenaries to compleat the works of death, desolation and tyranny, already begun with circumstances of Cruelty & perfidy scarcely paralleled in the most barbarous ages, and totally unworthy the Head of a civilized nation.

He has constrained our fellow Citizens taken Captive on the high Seas to bear Arms against their Country, to become the executioners of their friends and Brethren, or to fall themselves by their Hands.

He has excited domestic insurrections amongst us, and has endeavoured to bring on the inhabitants of our frontiers, the merciless Indian Savages, whose known rule of warfare, is an undistinguished destruction of all ages, sexes and conditions.

In every stage of these Oppressions We have Petitioned for Redress in the most humble terms: Our repeated Petitions have been answered only by repeated injury. A Prince, whose character is thus marked by every act which may define a Tyrant, is unfit to be the ruler of a free people.

Nor have We been wanting in attentions to our Brittish brethren. We have warned them from time to time of attempts by their legislature to extend an unwarrantable jurisdiction over us. We have reminded them of the circumstances of our emigration and settlement here. We have appealed to their native justice and magnanimity, and we have conjured them by the ties of our common kindred to disavow these usurpations, which, would inevitably interrupt our connections and correspondence. They too have been deaf to the voice of justice and of consanguinity. We must, therefore, acquiesce in the necessity, which denounces our Separation, and hold them, as we hold the rest of mankind, Enemies in War, in Peace Friends.

We, therefore, the Representatives of the united States of America, in General Congress, Assembled, appealing to the Supreme Judge of the world for the rectitude of our intentions, do, in the Name, and by Authority of the good People of these Colonies, solemnly publish and declare, That these United Colonies are, and of Right ought to be Free and Independent States; that they are Absolved from all Allegiance to the British Crown, and that all political connection between them and the State of

Great Britain, is and ought to be totally dissolved; and that as Free and Independent States, they have full Power to levy War, conclude Peace, contract Alliances, establish Commerce, and to do all other Acts and Things which Independent States may of right do. And for the support of this Declaration, with a firm reliance on the protection of divine Providence, we mutually pledge to each other our Lives, our Fortunes and our sacred Honor.

John Hancock

Georgia
Button Gwinnett
Lyman Hall
George Walton

North Carolina
William Hooper
Joseph Hewes
John Penn

South Carolina
Edward Rutledge
Thomas Heyward, Jr.
Thomas Lynch, Jr.
Arthur Middleton

Maryland
Samuel Chase
William Paca
Thomas Stone
Charles Carroll of Carrollton

Virginia
George Wythe
Richard Henry Lee
Thomas Jefferson
Benjamin Harrison
Thomas Nelson, Jr.
Francis Lightfoot Lee
Carter Braxton

Pennsylvania
Robert Morris
Benjamin Rush
Benjamin Franklin
John Morton
George Clymer
James Smith
George Taylor
James Wilson
George Ross

Delaware
Caesar Rodney
George Read
Thomas McKean

New York
William Floyd
Philip Livingston
Francis Lewis
Lewis Morris

New Jersey
Richard Stockton
John Witherspoon
Francis Hopkinson
John Hart
Abraham Clark

New Hampshire
Josiah Bartlett
William Whipple
Matthew Thornton

Massachusetts
Samuel Adams
John Adams
Robert Treat Paine
Elbridge Gerry

Rhode Island
Stephen Hopkins
William Ellery

Connecticut
Roger Sherman
Samuel Huntington
William Williams
Oliver Wolcott

Note: The text above is a transcription of the Stone Engraving of the Declaration, taken from the National Archives' website. The spelling and punctuation reflects the original parchment.

NOTES

Abbreviations

AP: AFC L. H. Butterfield, ed., *The Adams Papers: Adams Family Correspondence* (Cambridge, MA: Harvard University Press, 1963)

AP: DAJA L. H. Butterfield, ed., *The Adams Papers: Diary and Autobiography of John Adams*, vol. 3, *Diary, 1782–1804; Autobiography, Part One to October 1776* (Cambridge, MA: Harvard University Press, 1961)

AP: PJA Robert J. Taylor, ed., *The Adams Papers: Papers of John Adams*, vol. 4, *February–August 1776* (Cambridge, MA: Harvard University Press, 1979)

BID John Bidwell, *The Declaration in Print and Script: A Visual History of America's Founding Document* (University Park, PA: The Pennsylvania State University Press, 2024)

DLC Library of Congress, Washington, D.C.

DSoc. Society of the Cincinnati Library, Anderson House, Washington, D.C.

JCC W. C. Ford, et al., eds., *Journals of the Continental Congress* (Washington: Government Printing Office, 1906)

JHH John H. Hazelton, *The Declaration of Independence: Its History* (New York: Dodd, Mead and Company, 1906)

LSS Lincoln: Selected Speeches and Writings (New York: The Library of America, 1992)

PMHB The Pennsylvania Magazine of History and Biography

PP: GRF Public Papers of the Presidents of the United States: Gerald R. Ford (Washington: United States Government Printing Office, 1979)

PP: HST Public Papers of the Presidents of the United States: Harry S. Truman (Washington: United States Government Printing Office, 1965, 1966)

PP: LBJ Public Papers of the Presidents of the United States: Lyndon Baines Johnson (Washington: United States Government Printing Office, 1965, 1966)

PQHN ProQuest Historical Newspapers online archive

PTJ Julian P. Boyd, ed., *The Papers of Thomas Jefferson* (Princeton, NJ: Princeton University Press, 1950–55)

PTJR J. Jefferson Looney, ed., *The Papers of Thomas Jefferson, Retirement Series* (Princeton, NJ: Princeton University Press, 2016, 2019)

PWC W. W. Abbot and Dorothy Twohig, eds., *The Papers of George Washington, Colonial Series* (Charlottesville: University Press of Virginia, 1990)
PWR Philander D. Chase, et al., ed., *The Papers of George Washington, Revolutionary War Series* (Charlottesville: University Press of Virginia, 1993, 1997)
RAHN Readex: America's Historical Newspapers online archive
WJA Charles Francis Adams, ed., *The Works of John Adams, Second President of the United States: with a Life of the Author* (Boston, 1850–1856); 10 vols.

All uniform resource locators (URLs) listed in the Notes were accessible as of the time of publication.

INTRODUCTION

1. Pauline Maier, *American Scripture: Making the Declaration of Independence* (New York: Vintage, 1997); Danielle Allen, *Our Declaration: A Reading of the Declaration of Independence in Defense of Equality* (New York: Liveright, 2015); Harry V. Jaffa, *Crisis of the House Divided: An Interpretation of the Issues in the Lincoln-Douglas Debates* (Garden City, NY: Doubleday & Company, 1959); and Gordon S. Wood, *The Radicalism of the American Revolution* (New York: Knopf, 1992).

PROLOGUE: Declaration

1. "John Adams to Abigail Adams, 3 July 1776," *AP: AFC* II: 29–33.
2. Kenneth R. Bowling, "Good-by 'Charle': The Lee-Adams Interest and the Political Demise of Charles Thomson, Secretary of Congress, 1774–1789," in *PMHB* 100, no. 3 (July 1976): 314–335.
3. "Thomas Jefferson's Anecdotes of Benjamin Franklin, [ca. 4 December 1818]," *PTJR* XIII: 462–465. On Congress's role in amending the document, see Danielle Allen, *Our Declaration: A Reading of the Declaration of Independence in Defense of Equality* (New York: Liveright, 2015), 72–78; Pauline Maier, *American Scripture: Making the Declaration of Independence* (New York: Vintage, 1997), 123–133; Garry Wills, *Inventing America: Jefferson's Declaration of Independence* (New York: Vintage, 1978), 310–319; and Julian P. Boyd, *The Declaration of Independence: The Evolution of the Text* (Washington, DC: Library of Congress, 1943, 1999), 25–37.
4. Paul H. Smith, "Time and Temperature: Philadelphia, July 4, 1776," *The Quarterly Journal of the Library of Congress* 33, no. 4 (October 1976): 294–299. Original "Rough Journal of the Continental Congress" (no volume number, unpaginated), held in the National Archives. The only accurate reprinting of the *Rough Journal*'s entry for July 4 is in JHH, 170. The officially printed *Journals of the Continental Congress* (Washington, DC: Government Printing Office, 1906) misleadingly include the text in V: 510–515, as do earlier commissioned printings of the Journals, the first by R. Aitken, in 1777.
5. JHH, 222; John Clement Fitzpatrick, *The Spirit of the Revolution: New Light from Some*

of the Sources of American History (Boston: Houghton Mifflin Company, 1924), 15. Clement was the assistant chief of the Manuscript Division in the Library of Congress.

6. Dumas Malone, *Jefferson and His Times, Volume 1: Jefferson the Virginian* (Charlottesville: University of Virginia Press, 1948, 2006), 229.

CHAPTER 1: The Road to July Fourth

1. Brendan Simms, *Three Victories and a Defeat: The Rise and Fall of the First British Empire* (New York: Basic Books, 2007), 388–396, 423–428, 504–506. For a general history, see Walter R. Borneman, *The French and Indian War: Deciding the Fate of North America* (New York: Harper Perennial, 2007).
2. The standard political treatment of the road to Revolution remains Robert Middlekauff, *The Glorious Cause: The American Revolution, 1763–1789* (New York: Oxford University Press, 1982), Chs. 1–11. For a discussion of the French and Indian War's aftermath on the western frontier, see Patrick Spero, *Frontier Rebels: The Fight for Independence in the American West, 1765–1776* (New York: W. W. Norton & Company, 2018).
3. The deep-seated fear of a "conspiracy of power against liberty" is emphasized by Bernard Bailyn, *The Ideological Origins of the American Revolution* (Cambridge, MA: Harvard University Press, 1967, 2017), esp. Ch. 4. See also Carl J. Richard, *Greeks & Romans Bearing Gifts: How the Ancients Inspired the Founding Fathers* (Lanham, MD: Rowman and Littlefield, 2008), 158–159.
4. On tensions in Boston, see Eric Hinderaker, *Boston's Massacre* (Cambridge, MA: Harvard University Press, 2019).
5. William Dalrymple, *The Anarchy: The Relentless Rise of the East India Company* (London: Bloomsbury Publishing, 2019), 229–231.
6. Mark Peterson, *The City-State of Boston: The Rise and Fall of an Atlantic Power, 1630–1865* (Princeton, NJ: Princeton University Press, 2019), 341–342.
7. Jonathan Levy, *Ages of American Capitalism: A History of the United States* (New York: Random House, 2021), Ch. 1.
8. Figures on slavery from Ira Berlin, *Generations of Captivity: A History of African-American Slaves* (Cambridge, MA: Harvard University Press, 2003), 271–275.
9. See Billy G. Smith, ed., *Down and Out in Early America* (University Park: The Pennsylvania State University Press, 2004).
10. For an overview, see Peter H. Wood, *Strange New Land: Africans in Colonial America* (New York: Oxford University Press, 2003), and Berlin, *Generations of Captivity*.
11. David Hackett Fischer, *Albion's Seed: Four British Folkways in America* (New York: Oxford University Press, 1989).
12. For the leadup to the Revolutionary War and its course, see Jill Lepore, *These Truths: A History of the United States* (New York: W. W. Norton and Company, 2018), Ch. 3. For a compelling revisionist take on George, see Andrew Roberts, *The Last King of America: The Misunderstood Reign of George III* (New York: Viking, 2021).
13. Elisha Fish, A.M., *A Discourse Delivered at Worcester, March, 28th, 1775*... (Worcester, MA: Printed by Isaiah Thomas, 1775), p. 3. DSoc.

14. Rick Atkinson, *The British Are Coming: The War for America, Lexington to Princeton, 1775–1777* (New York: Henry Holt and Co., 2019), 35–82.
15. H.W. Brands, *Our First Civil War: Patriots and Loyalists in the First American Revolution* (New York: Vintage, 2022), and Maya Jasanoff, *Liberty's Exiles: American Loyalists in the Revolutionary World* (New York: Vintage, 2012) discuss the Loyalists. On the number of exiles, Gordon Wood gives the figure of 80,000 in *The Radicalism of the American Revolution* (New York: Knopf, 1992), 176, while Jasanoff gives 60,000 plus 15,000 slaves, in "The Other Side of Revolution: Loyalists in the British Empire," in Denver Brunsman and David J. Silverman, eds., *The American Revolution Reader* (New York: Routledge, 2014), 416.
16. See Stacy Schiff, *The Revolutionary: Samuel Adams* (New York: Back Bay Books, 2023).
17. See Harlow Giles Unger, *Thomas Paine and the Clarion Call for American Independence* (Boston: Da Capo Press, 2019).
18. "Wednesday May 15. 1776," *AP: DAJA* III: 385–386. "From John Adams to James Warren, 15 May 1776," *AP: PJA* IV: 186–187.
19. The eight in favor of Independence were New Hampshire, Massachusetts, Connecticut, Rhode Island, Virginia, North Carolina, South Carolina, and Georgia. These weeks are discussed in William Hogeland, *Declaration: The Nine Tumultuous Weeks When America Became Independent, May 1–July 4, 1776* (New York: Simon & Schuster, 2010), 73–149.
20. *JCC* V: 425.
21. "Notes of Proceedings in the Continental Congress, 7 June–1 August 1776," *PTJ* I: 299–329.
22. George Dangerfield, *Chancellor Robert R. Livingston of New York, 1746–1813* (New York: Harcourt Brace and Company, 1960), 76–79.
23. Walter Isaacson, *Benjamin Franklin: An American Life* (New York: Simon & Schuster, 2003), 309–313.
24. November 9, 1775, *Secret Journals of the Acts and Proceedings of Congress* (Boston: Thomas S. Wait, 1821), I: 34.
25. *JCC* V: 430; John R. Wunder, "'Merciless Indian Savages' and the Declaration of Independence: Native Americans Translate the Ecunnaunuxulgee Document," 25, no. 1 (2000): 70.
26. "From John Adams to Samuel Chase, 24 June 1776," *AP: PJA* IV: 333–335. Quote on Hancock in JHH, 135–136.
27. *JCC* V: 504. Jefferson's notes can be found at "Notes of Proceedings in the Continental Congress, 7 June–1 August 1776," *PTJ* I: 299–329.
28. *Ibid.*; see also JHH, 162, 113. Adams's letter to Chase quoted in *JCC* V: 505.
29. *JCC* V: 505.
30. For these years, see Woody Holton, *Abigail Adams* (New York: Free Press, 2009), 78–121.
31. Adams wrote two letters to Abigail that day. "John Adams to Abigail Adams, 3 July 1776," *AP: AFC* II: 27–29 and "John Adams to Abigail Adams, 3 July 1776," *ibid.*, 29–33.
32. *The Pennsylvania Evening Post*, July 2, 1776, 4 (Newspaper and Current Periodical Reading Room–DLC).

CHAPTER 2: "Our Lives, Our Fortunes, and Our Sacred Honor"

1. "From Adams to Pickering, 6 August 1822."
2. "From John Adams to Timothy Pickering, 6 August 1822," *WJA* II, 514n (hereafter,

"From Adams to Pickering, 6 August 1822"). "From Thomas Jefferson to James Madison, 30 August 1823," *PTJR* XX: 123–125 (hereafter, "Jefferson to Madison, 30 August 1823").

3. The Graff House was demolished in 1883 and reconstructed by the National Park Service in 1975. Jefferson's desk is now in the Smithsonian's National Museum of American History.
4. "Jefferson to Madison, 30 August 1823."
5. "From Adams to Pickering, 6 August 1822."
6. "Jefferson to Madison, 30 August 1823."
7. "From Thomas Jefferson to Henry Lee, 8 May 1825," *Founders Online,* National Archives, https://founders.archives.gov/documents/Jefferson/98-01-02-5212.
8. On religious influences on the Founders, see Carl J. Richard, *The Founders and the Bible* (Lanham, MD: Rowman & Littlefield Publishers, 2016), and Barry Alan Shain, *The Myth of American Individualism: The Protestant Origins of American Political Thought* (Princeton, NJ: Princeton University Press, 1994), esp. Ch. 6.
9. "A Summary View of the Rights of British America," in *Thomas Jefferson: Writings* (New York: The Library of America, 1984), 105.
10. See Garry Wills, *Inventing America: Jefferson's Declaration of Independence* (New York: Vintage, 1978), and his reconsideration of his dismissal of Locke in the introduction to the 2002 Mariner edition (pp. v–viii), in part in response to Ronald Hamowy, "Jefferson and the Scottish Enlightenment: A Critique of Garry Wills's *Inventing America: Jefferson's Declaration of Independence*," *The William and Mary Quarterly* 36, no. 4 (October 1979): 503–523.
11. The "Declarations and Resolves" can be found at *JCC* I: 67. The Boston Pamphlet was formally titled *The Votes and Proceedings of the Freeholders and other Inhabitants of the Town of Boston, in Town Meeting Assembled*; it can be found online at the Massachusetts Historical Society, https://www.masshist.org/database/viewer.php?pid=2&old=1&mode=nav&ft=Coming%20of%20the%20American%20Revolution&item_id=649.
12. The Virginia Declaration of Rights is online at https://www.archives.gov/founding-docs/virginia-declaration-of-rights. For a more recent take on Jefferson's intellectual world, see Gordon S. Wood, *Revolutionary Characters: What Made the Founders Different* (New York: Penguin, 2006), 91–118; see also Joseph J. Ellis, *American Sphinx: The Character of Thomas Jefferson* (New York: Vintage, 1998).
13. On local declarations, see Pauline Maier, *American Scripture: Making the Declaration of Independence* (New York: Vintage, 1997), esp. Ch. 2. See also Jay Fliegelman's *Declaring Independence: Jefferson, Natural Language and the Culture of Performance* (Stanford: Stanford University Press, 1993). For further discussion, see Danielle Allen, *Our Declaration: A Reading of the Declaration of Independence in Defense of Equality* (New York: Liveright, 2015); see also Myron Magnet, "The Founders' Priceless Legacy," in *The New Criterion* 39, no. 3 (November 2020), pp. 4–11.
14. A detailed reading of each of the Declaration's passages is the focus of Allen, *Our Declaration.*
15. Jefferson's draft contained the word *inalienable*, but it was changed to *unalienable* at the first printing on July 4, 1776. On the crafting of this phrase, see Walter Isaacson, *The Greatest Sentence Ever Written* (New York: Simon & Schuster, 2025).

16. David Armitage, *The Declaration of Independence: A Global History* (Cambridge, MA: Harvard University Press, 2007), 22. See also Eliga Gould, *Among the Powers of the Earth: The American Revolution and the Making of a New World Empire* (Cambridge, MA: Harvard University Press, 2012).
17. [Thomas Jefferson to Benjamin Franklin, June 1776], Mss.B.F85, XLII, 73, Benjamin Franklin Papers, American Philosophical Society.
18. "From Jefferson to Madison, 30 August 1823."
19. On Jefferson and the Committee, see Maier, *American Scripture*, 123–143; and Julian P. Boyd, *The Declaration of Independence: The Evolution of the Text* (Washington, DC: The Library of Congress, 1945, 1999), 27–32. On Franklin, see John Clement Fitzpatrick, *The Spirit of the Revolution: New Light from Some of the Sources of American History* (Boston: Houghton Mifflin Company, 1924), 12. The John Adams quote is in Andrew Roberts, *The Last King of America: The Misunderstood Reign of George III* (New York: Viking, 2021), 306.
20. Boyd, *Evolution*, 26.
21. In all, there are seven copies of drafts of the declaration written out in Jefferson's hand, the others sent to political allies. The various drafts and versions are thoroughly discussed in Boyd, *Evolution.*
22. Wilfred J. Ritz, "From the *Here* of Jefferson's Handwritten Rough Draft of the Declaration of Independence to the *There* of the Printed Dunlap Broadside," *PMHB* 116, no. 4 (October 1992), 499–512.
23. The most detailed exposition of the revision process in Congress is in Maier, *American Scripture*, 143–50; see also Boyd, *Evolution*, 32–35; and Carl Lotus Becker, *The Declaration of Independence: A Study in the History of Political Ideas* (New York: Harcourt, Brace, and Company, 1922), Ch. 4.
24. Later, in his *Notes on the State of Virginia*, written in 1795, Jefferson would express his belief that Blacks were inferior intellectually to Whites; for a discussion, see Jeffrey Rosen, *The Pursuit of Happiness: How Classical Writers on Virtue Inspired the Lives of the Founders and Defined America* (New York: Simon & Schuster, 2024), 131–136.
25. Maier, *American Scripture*, 34–36.
26. Eran Shalev, *American Zion: The Old Testament as a Political Text from the Revolution to the Civil War* (New Haven, CT: Yale University Press, 2013), 23–25.
27. "From John Adams to Mercy Otis Warren, 30 July 1807," *Collections of the Massachusetts Historical Society, Volume 4, Fifth Series* (Boston, 1878), 394.
28. See Carl J. Richard, *The Founders and the Classics: Greece, Rome, and the American Enlightenment* (Cambridge, MA: Harvard University Press, 1995); Rosen, *Pursuit of Happiness*; and Thomas E. Ricks, *First Principles: What America's Founders Learned from the Greeks and Romans and How That Shaped Our Country* (New York: Harper Perennial, 2021).
29. "In virtue of his nature" is used by Harry Jaffa, in *The Crisis of the House Divided*, 50th anniversary ed. (Chicago: University of Chicago Press, 2009), 318.
30. Allen, *Our Declaration*, esp. 171–182.
31. Gordon S. Wood, *Revolutionary Characters: What Made the Founders Different* (New York: Penguin, 2006), 100.
32. John Adams, *Thoughts on Government* (1776), in Adrienne Koch and William Peden, eds., *The Selected Writings of John and John Quincy Adams* (New York: Alfred A. Knopf,

1946), 52. The pamphlet began life as a letter to George Wyeth of Virginia, an eminent jurist and Signer of the Declaration.

33. Gordon S. Wood, "Thomas Jefferson, Equality, and the Creation of a Civil Society," *Fordham Law Review* 64, no. 5 (April 1996): 2133–2148.
34. See notes to "To George Washington from George Mason, 23 December 1765," *PWC*, 424–425. See also Richard, *Founders and the Classics*, 95–97.
35. Thomas Jefferson, *Writings*, 115. Among the many writings on Jefferson and slavery, see Annette Gordon-Reed, *Thomas Jefferson and Sally Hemings: An American Controversy* (Charlottesville: University of Virginia Press, 1997). See also John P. Diggins, "Slavery, Race, and Equality: Jefferson and the Pathos of the Enlightenment," in *American Quarterly* 28, no. 2, "Special Issue: An American Enlightenment" (Summer 1976): 206–228; Wills, *Inventing America*, esp. Ch. 15.
36. Quoted in Bernard Bailyn, *The Ideological Origins of the American Revolution* (Cambridge, MA: Harvard University Press, 1967, 2017), 236.
37. *JCC* IV: 258.
38. "Taxation No Tyranny: An Answer to the Resolutions and Address of the American Congress" (1775), quoted in Kaplan, "'Domestic Insurrections,'" 253.
39. "Abigail Adams to John Adams, 31 March 1776," *AP: AFC* I: 369–371.
40. For one treatment of legal and social issues related to women in this period, see Elizabeth Cobbs, *Fearless Women: Feminist Patriots from Abigail Adams to Beyonce* (Cambridge, MA: Harvard University Press, 2023), Ch. 1. On the broader questions of citizenship, see Douglas Bradburn, *The Citizenship Revolution: Politics and the Creation of the American Union, 1774–1804* (Charlottesville: University of Virginia Press, 2014), Ch. 1.
41. Roberts's point-by-point disputation of the Declaration is in Roberts, *Last King of America,* 294–307. Different scholars count the charges/indictments in different ways. Danielle Allen counts eighteen, with charge number 13 having nine subparts; see Allen, *Our Declaration*, pp. 204–206. On the controversial question of slave revolts, see Sidney Kaplan, "The 'Domestic Insurrections' of the Declaration of Independence," *The Journal of Negro History* 61, no. 3 (July 1976): 243–255.
42. "Freedoms envisioned but never lost sight of" paraphrases John Burt, "Lincoln, Calhoun, and Cultural Politics," *Raritan Quarterly* 23, no. 2 (Fall 2003): 153.
43. Bailyn, *Ideological Origins*, p. 232.
44. "Letter from Robert Morris to Joseph Reed," July 20, 1776; Peter Force, *American Archives: Fifth Series: Containing a Documentary History of the United States of America from the Declaration of Independence, July 4, 1776 to the Definitive Treaty of Peace with Great Britain, September 3, 1783* (Washington, DC: 1848), I: 467. Morris ultimately would sign the Declaration for unanimity's sake.
45. JHH, 231.

CHAPTER 3: Bringing the Declaration to the People

1. "From John Adams to James Lloyd, 28 January 1815," *WJA* X: 110–111.
2. *JCC* V: 516.

3. Julian P. Boyd, "The Declaration of Independence: The Mystery of the Lost Original," *PMHB* 100, no. 4 (October 1976): 438–467.
4. On Jefferson's diacritical marks and performative rhetoric, see Jay Fliegelman's *Declaring Independence: Jefferson, Natural Language and the Culture of Performance* (Stanford: Stanford University Press, 1993), 5–21.
5. Dunlap also has been criticized for changing Jefferson's "inalienable" to "unalienable." However, John Adams's handwritten copy of Jefferson's draft also included "unalienable," and the two words were considered largely interchangeable.
6. Carl Lotus Becker, *The Declaration of Independence: A Study in the History of Political Ideas* (New York: Harcourt, Brace, and Company, 1922), 185. For a dissenting view, see Richard Wendorf, "Declaring, Drafting, and Composing American Independence," *The Papers of the Bibliographic Society of America* 108, no. 3 (September 2014): 307–324.
7. A thorough study is found in Frederick R. Goff, *The John Dunlap Broadside: The First Printing of the Declaration of Independence* (Washington, DC: Library of Congress, 1976). An image of the parchment Dunlap can be found in Whitfield J. Bell Jr., *The Declaration of Independence: Four 1776 Versions* (Philadelphia: The American Philosophical Society, 1976), n.p. My thanks to Dr. Patrick Spero, executive director of the American Philosophical Society, for showing me the Society's unique Dunlap copy.
8. It is possible that a German-language broadside may have appeared even earlier, on July 6. "German Settlement in Pennsylvania: An Overview," https://hsp.org/sites/default/files/legacy_files/migrated/germanstudentreading.pdf; Karl T. J. Arndt, "The First Translation and Printing in German of the American Declaration of Independence," *Monatshefte* 77, no. 2 (Summer 1985): 138–142.
9. *The Pennsylvania Evening Post* II, no. 228, 6 July 1776: 335. Michael J. Walsh, "Contemporary Broadside Editions of the Declaration of Independence," *Harvard Library Bulletin* (Harvard University Library) III, no. 1 (Winter 1949): 33–34; also "First Newspaper Printing of the Declaration of Independence," Museum of the American Revolution (https://www.amrevmuseum.org/collection/first-newspaper-printing-of-the-declaration-of-independence).
10. Walsh, "Contemporary Broadside Editions," 35–41.
11. The proof copy in the Historical Society of Philadelphia comes from the family of Col. John Nixon.
12. "John Adams to Samuel Chase," July 9, 1776, *AP: PJA* IV: 372–373.
13. William Duane, ed., *Extracts from the Diary of Christopher Marshall: Kept in Philadelphia and Lancaster, During the American Revolution, 1774–1781* (Albany: Joel Munsell, 1877), 82. I am indebted to Dr. Patrick Spero, executive director of the American Philosophical Society, for telling me about Marshall's diary.
14. JHH, 137.
15. *PWR* V: 258–261.
16. *PWR* V: 191–194.
17. "John Adams to Abigail Adams," July 7, 1776, *AP: AFC* II: 37–38.
18. "From George Washington to John Hancock, 10 July 1776," *PWR* V: 258–261.
19. "1774 Aug. 20. Saturday." *AP: DAJA* II: 103. George Washington, "General Orders, 10 July 1776," *PWR* V: 256–257.
20. "Abigail Adams to John Adams, 21 July 1776," *AP: AFC* II: 55–57.

21. The sequence of local proclamations is traced in JHH, 273–281.
22. The Watertown treaty is at https://web.archive.org/web/20060206132437/http://www.watertowntreaty.org/treatytext.htm.
23. On Indian–American relations during the Revolution, see Ned Blackhawk, *The Rediscovery of America: Native Peoples and the Unmaking of U.S. History* (New Haven, CT: Yale University Press, 2023), 179–181.
24. Daniel N. Paul, *We Were Not the Savages: A Mi'kmaq Perspective on the Collision Between European and Native American Civilizations* (Halifax, N.S.: Fernwood, 2000), 168–170. In a 1987 address to the Massachusetts House of Representatives, Mi'kmaq Grand Captain Alex Denny stated that the tribe never broke its treaty with the Americans; see https://web.archive.org/web/20060109100839/http://www.watertowntreaty.org/. For a transcript of the treaty conference, see http://historicalsocietyofwatertownma.org/HSW/HSWdocs/treatyminutes.pdf. See also Ernest Clarke, *The Siege of Fort Cumberland, 1776* (Montreal: McGill Queens University Press, 1995).
25. "Account of the Proceedings of the American Colonists, since the passing of the Boston port-bill," *The Gentleman's Magazine: and Historical Chronicle* 46 (August 1776): 377–381.
26. John Lind, *An Answer to the Declaration of the American Congress* (London: T. Cadell in the Strand, 1776), 7. James MacPherson, *The Rights of Great Britain Asserted against the Claims of America: Being an Answer to the Declaration of the General Congress* (London: T. Caddell, 1776).
27. See Bernard Bailyn, *The Ordeal of Thomas Hutchinson* (Cambridge, MA: Harvard University Press, 1974).
28. Quoted in Andrew Roberts, *The Last King of America: The Misunderstood Reign of George III* (New York: Viking, 2021), 295.
29. Quoted in Mary Beth Norton, *The British-Americans: The Loyalist Exiles in England, 1774–1789* (Boston: Little Brown & Company, 1972), 48.
30. JHH, 234; Roberts, *Last King of America*, 307.
31. JHH, 234. On William Lee in London, see Paul C. Nagle, *The Lees of Virginia: Seven Generations of an American Family* (New York: Oxford University Press, 1990), 105–110.
32. F. P. Lock, *Edmund Burke, Volume I, 1730–1784* (Oxford: The Clarendon Press, 1988), 399. On British responses generally, see Roberts, *Last King of America*, Ch. 13; Howard H. Peckham, "Independence: The View from Britain," *Proceedings of the American Antiquarian Society* 85, part 2 (October 1975): 387–403.

CHAPTER 4: The Signing

1. *JCC* V: 590–591, 626.
2. "Notes of Proceedings in the Continental Congress, 7 June–1 August 1776," *PTJ* I: 299–329. "To John Adams from Benjamin Rush, 20 July 1811," *Founders Online,* National Archives, https://founders.archives.gov/documents/Adams/99-02-02-5659.
3. See the detailed discussion appended to Jefferson's "Notes," at *Founders Online,* National Archives, https://founders.archives.gov/documents/Jefferson/01-01-02-0160.
4. See Wilfred J. Ritz, "The Authentication of the Engrossed Declaration of Independence on July 4, 1776," in *Law and History Review* 4, no. 1 (Spring 1986): 179–204.

5. An excellent discussion is by Mary Lynn Ritzenthaler and Catherine Nicholson, "The Declaration of Independence and The Hand of Time," *Prologue Magazine* 48, no. 3 (Fall 2016), https://www.archives.gov/publications/prologue/2016/fall/declaration.
6. Ritzenthaler and Nicholson, "Hand of Time."
7. Verner Clapp, "The Declaration of Independence: A Case Study in Preservation," *Special Libraries* 62, no. 12 (December 1971): 503; Julian P. Boyd, "The Declaration of Independence: The Mystery of the Lost Original," *PMHB* 100, no. 4 (October 1976): 464.
8. For a debunking of the myth, see Brooke Barbier, *King Hancock: The Radical Influence of a Moderate Founding Father* (Cambridge, MA: Harvard University Press, 2023), 2–3.
9. For McKean's account, see "Enclosure: Thomas McKean to Caesar A. Rodney, 22 [September] 1813," *PTJR* IX: 470–472.
10. George Dangerfield, *Chancellor Robert R. Livingston of New York, 1746–1813* (New York: Harcourt Brace and Company, 1960), 80.

CHAPTER 5: Success and Neglect

1. "From George Washington to John Hancock, 12 December 1776," *PWR* VII: 309–312. On the event, see David Hackett Fischer, *Washington's Crossing* (New York: Oxford University Press, 2004).
2. *JCC* VII: 48. On the battles of Trenton and Princeton, see Rick Atkinson, *The British Are Coming: The War for America, Lexington to Princeton, 1775–1777* (New York: Henry Holt and Co., 2019), 512–554.
3. Little has been written on Goddard, but see https://www.smithsonianmag.com/history/mary-katharine-goddard-woman-whose-name-appears-declaration-independence-180970816/, and https://msa.maryland.gov/msa/educ/exhibits/womenshallfame/html/goddard.html.
4. Reprinted in *The Declaration of Independence: Four 1776 Versions* (Philadelphia: American Philosophical Society, 1976) (unpaginated).
5. "To John Adams from Thomas McKean, January 1814," *WJA* X: 88.
6. If July 4 fell on a Sunday, commemorations were held the following day, a practice that continued through the first quarter of the twentieth century. "John Adams to Abigail Adams 2d, 5 July 1777," *AP: AFC* II: 274–275. *Pennsylvania Packet*, July 4, 1778, 1 (RAHN); "General Orders, 3 July 1778," PWR XVI: 15. On early celebrations, see Len Travers, *Celebrating the Fourth: Independence Day and the Rites of Nationalism in the Early Republic* (Amherst: University of Massachusetts Press, 1997), and David Waldstreicher, *In the Midst of Perpetual Fetes: The Making of American Nationalism, 1776–1820* (Chapel Hill: The Omohundro Institute of Early American History and Culture and the University of North Carolina Press, 1997).
7. "Mr. and Mrs. Richard Bennett Lloyd to Franklin and John Adams, [2 July? 1778]," *The Papers of Benjamin Franklin,* XXVII, *July 1 through October 31, 1778*, ed. Claude A. Lopez (New Haven, CT, and London: Yale University Press, 1988), 21. On Franklin in Paris, see Walter Isaacson, *Benjamin Franklin: An American Life* (New York: Simon & Schuster, 2003), 325–349; for Adams, see David McCullough, *John Adams* (New York: Simon & Schuster, 2001), 188–210.

8. The continuity of Congress is a point stressed by Jack Rakove, *The Beginnings of National Politics: An Interpretive History of the Continental Congress* (New York: Alfred Knopf, 1979; reprint: Baltimore: Johns Hopkins University Press, 1982).
9. Travers, *Celebrating the Fourth*, 35–37.
10. *New York Packet*, July 4, 1788; accessible at *Documentary History of the Ratification of the Constitution* (Digital Edition), https://rotunda-upress-virginia-edu.stanford.idm.oclc.org/founders/default.xqy?keys=RNCN-search-1-9&expandNote=on#match1.
11. John Brooks, "An Oration Delivered to the Society of the Cincinnati in the Commonwealth of Massachusetts, July 4th 1787" (Boston: Edmund Freeman, 1787), 6. DSoc.
12. "The United States elevated to Glory and Honor" (1783), reprinted in *The Pulpit of the American Revolution: or, The Political Sermons of the Period 1776. With a Historical Introduction, Notes and Illustrations by John Wingate Thornton* (Boston: Gould and Lincoln, 1860), 453–454.
13. On failures of the Articles of Confederation, see Pauline Maier, *Ratification: The People Debate the Constitution, 1787–1788* (New York: Simon & Schuster, 2010), 11–17.
14. Leonard L. Richards, *Shays's Rebellion: The American Revolution's Final Battle* (Philadelphia: University of Pennsylvania Press, 2003).
15. Joseph Ellis, *His Excellency: George Washington* (New York: Vintage Books, 2004), 172.
16. Quoted in Gordon S. Wood, *The Creation of the American Republic, 1776–1787* (Chapel Hill: University of North Carolina Press, 1969), 398.
17. See Wood, *Creation*, 396–413, 430–438. See also Jack Rakove, *Original Meanings: Politics and Ideas in the Making of the Constitution* (New York: Vintage, 1997).
18. The standard treatment is Maier, *Ratification*. On Hamilton during this period, see Richard Brookhiser, *Alexander Hamilton, American* (New York: Simon & Schuster Paperbacks, 2015), 61–68, and Ron Chernow, *Alexander Hamilton* (New York: Penguin, 2005), 222–243. On Madison's thought, see Jack Rakove, *A Politician Thinking: The Creative Mind of James Madison* (Norman: University of Oklahoma Press, 2017). Madison's notes on the Convention give the best account of the process; see Edward J. Larson and Michael P. Winship, eds., *The Constitutional Convention: A Narrative History from the Notes of James Madison* (New York: Random House, 2005).
19. See Federalist No. 40 (Madison), in *The Federalist Papers* (New York: New American Library, 1961), 253.
20. George Mason, "Objections to the Constitution," *Virginia Journal*, November 22, 1787; reprinted in Robert J. Allison and Bernard Bailyn, eds., *The Essential Debate on the Constitution: Federalist and Anti-Federalist Speeches and Writings* (New York: Library of America, 2018), 111–115.
21. Dumas Malone, *Jefferson and His Time, Volume 2: Jefferson and the Rights of Man* (Charlottesville: University of Virginia Press, 1951), pp. 161–164.
22. *PTJ* 12: 355–357.
23. "An act to provide for the safe keeping of the acts, records, and seal of the United States, and for other purpose," First Congress, Session 1 (1789); accessible at https://maint.loc.gov/law/help/statutes-at-large/1st-congress/session-1/c1s1ch14.pdf.
24. Kenneth R. Bowling, "Good-by 'Charle': The Lee-Adams Interest and the Political

Demise of Charles Thomson, Secretary of Congress, 1774–1789," *PMHB* 100, no. 3 (July 1976): 314–335.

25. See William Howard Adams, *The Paris Years of Thomas Jefferson* (New Haven, CT: Yale University Press, 1997), Ch. 8.
26. The best recent treatments of the French Revolution are Peter McPhee, *Liberty or Death: The French Revolution* (New Haven, CT: Yale University Press, 2016) and Jeremy D. Popkin, *A New World Begins: The History of the French Revolution* (New York: Basic Books, 2019).
27. Elise Marienstras and Naomi Wulf, "French Translations and Reception of the Declaration of Independence," *The Journal of American History* 85, no. 4 (March 1999): 1299–1324.
28. The text of the Declaration of the Rights of Man can be found at https://www.elysee.fr/en/french-presidency/the-declaration-of-the-rights-of-man-and-of-the-citizen.
29. Gordon S. Wood, *Empire of Liberty: A History of the Early Republic, 1789–1815* (New York: Oxford University Press, 2009) is the best recent treatment. See also Lindsay M. Chervinsky, *The Cabinet: George Washington and the Creation of an American Institution* (Cambridge, MA: Harvard University Press, 2020).
30. The Twelfth Amendment to the Constitution, ratified on June 15, 1804, changed the manner in which the Vice President was elected, requiring the Electoral College to vote for President and Vice President separately, thereby ensuring that they almost certainly would be from the same party.
31. On domestic politics in this era, see Francis J. Cogliano, *A Revolutionary Friendship: Washington, Jefferson, and the American Republic* (Cambridge, MA: Harvard University Press, 2024). For John Adams's presidency, see Lindsay M. Chervinsky, *Making the Presidency: John Adams and the Precedents That Forged the Republic* (New York: Oxford University Press, 2024).
32. Tom Lewis, *Washington: A History of Our National City* (New York: Basic Books, 2015), Ch. 1.
33. See Adam Costanzo, *George Washington's Washington: Visions for the National Capital in the Early American Republic* (Athens: The University of Georgia Press, 2018).
34. Jessie Kratz, "'P.S.: You Had Better Remove the Records': Early Federal Archives and the Burning of Washington during the War of 1812," *Prologue* 46, no. 2 (Summer 2014), 36–44.
35. Charles Warren, "Fourth of July Myths," *The William and Mary Quarterly* 2, no. 3 (July 1945): 264–266. See also Travers, *Celebrating the Fourth*, pp. 155–190.
36. Mercy Otis Warren, *History of the Rise, Progress and Termination of the American Revolution* (Boston: Manning and Loring, 1805), I: 309, II: 307–308.

CHAPTER 6: The Declaration Escapes the Flames

1. Benson J. Lossing, *The Pictorial Field-Book of 1812* (New York: Harper & Brothers, 1869), 936.
2. Jeremy Popkin, *A New World Begins: The History of the French Revolution* (New York: Basic Books, 2019), 318–320.

3. Lindsay M. Chervinsky, *Making the Presidency: John Adams and the Precedents That Forged the Republic* (New York: Oxford University Press, 2024), 265–272.
4. Walter R. Borneman, *1812: The War That Forged a Nation* (New York: Harper Perennial, 2005), 7–55.
5. James Sterling Young, *The Washington Community, 1800–1828* (New York: Harcourt Brace Jovanovich, 1966), 183–186.
6. Walter Lord, *The Dawn's Early Light* (Baltimore: The Johns Hopkins University Press, 1972), 73.
7. See Anthony S. Pitch, *The Burning of Washington: The British Invasion of 1812* (Annapolis, MD: Naval Institute Press, 1998), 42–48.
8. Jessie Kratz, "'P.S.: You Had Better Remove the Records': Early Federal Archives and the Burning of Washington during the War of 1812," *Prologue* 46, no. 2 (Summer 2014): 36–44.
9. Pleasonton's letter of August 7, 1848, to William Winder, as cited in Edward Duncan Ingraham, *A Sketch of the Events Which Preceded the Capture of Washington by the British on the Twenty-Fourth of August, 1814* (Philadelphia: Carey and Hart, 1849), 47–49.
10. Jane Aikin, *The Library of Congress: From Jefferson's Vision to the Digital Age* (Washington, DC: Georgetown University Press, 2025), 12–13.
11. William Seale, *The President's House: A History* (Washington, DC: White House Historical Association, 2008), I: 127–135.
12. John S. Williams, *History of the Invasion and Capture of Washington, and the Events Which Preceded and Followed* (New York: Harper and Brothers, 1857), 274.
13. See Peter S. Onuf, *Statehood and Union: A History of the Northwest Ordinance* (South Bend, IN: University of Notre Dame Press, 2019).
14. Jon Kukla, *A Wilderness So Immense: The Louisiana Purchase and the Destiny of America* (New York: Alfred A. Knopf, 2003). For America in this era, see Daniel Walker Howe, *What Hath God Wrought: The Transformation of America, 1815–1848* (New York: Oxford University Press, 2009), esp. Chs. 1–2.
15. See Len Travers, *Celebrating the Fourth: Independence Day and the Rites of Nationalism in the Early Republic* (Amherst: University of Massachusetts Press, 1997). "Thirty-Ninth Anniversary," *National Intelligencer*, July 6, 1815. *Nineteenth Century U.S. Newspapers*, link.gale.com/apps/doc/GT3017473121/NCNP?u=stan90222&sid=bookmark-NCNP&xid=f7ea7a94.
16. *The Albany Register* (Albany, New York), July 4, 1815 (RAHN).
17. "Themistocles and Bonaparte," *Weekly Aurora* (Philadelphia) VI, no. 29, October 10, 1815, 226 (RAHN). "Thursday, October 8, 1818. Trumbull's Independence," *New-York Daily Advertiser* (New York, New York) II, no. 466, October 8, 1818, 2 (RAHN).
18. On the varieties of Enlightenment, see Gertrude Himmelfarb, *The Roads to Modernity: The British, French, and American Enlightenments* (New York: Knopf, 2004).
19. David Armitage, *The Declaration of Independence: A Global History* (Cambridge, MA: Harvard University Press, 2007), 108.
20. Elise Marienstras and Naomi Wulf, "French Translations and Reception of the Declaration of Independence," *The Journal of American History* 85, no. 4 (March 1999): 1307.

21. Josefina Zoraida Vazquez, "The Mexican Declaration of Independence," *Journal of American History* 85, no. 4 (March 1999): 1362–1369.
22. On other foreign declarations of independence, see Armitage, *Global History*. For a brief discussion of American relations with Latin America in this period, see Bradford Perkins, *The Cambridge History of American Foreign Relations*, Vol. 1, *The Creation of a Republican Empire, 1776–1865* (New York: Cambridge University Press, 1993), Ch. 6.
23. On Bulfinch, see Harold Kirker, *The Architecture of Charles Bulfinch* (Cambridge, MA: Harvard University Press, 1998).
24. Lee H. Burke, *Homes of the Department of State, 1774–1976: The Buildings Occupied by the Department of State and Its Predecessors* (Washington, DC: Department of State, 1976), 33–34.

CHAPTER 7: Seeing the Declaration At Last

1. "Advertisement," *Democratic Press (*Philadelphia, Pennsylvania) IX, no. 2399, March 26, 1816, 3 (RAHN).
2. "Advertisement," *Democratic Press* (Philadelphia, Pennsylvania) I, no. 2, March 30, 1807, 1 (RAHN).
3. The collection was entitled *Observations on the American Revolution*. "Advertisement," *American Journal and General Advertiser* (Providence, Rhode Island) II, no. 63, May 24, 1780, 4 (RAHN).
4. *Essex Register,* July 19, 1815, 4 (RAHN).
5. BID, 38–39.
6. "Advertisement," *Salem Gazette* (Salem, Massachusetts) XXX, no. 51, June 25, 1816, 3 (RAHN).
7. *Ibid.*
8. "Advertisement," *Vermont Republican* (Windsor, Vermont), April 6, 1818, 3 (RAHN).
9. John Clement Fitzpatrick, *The Spirit of the Revolution: New Light from Some of the Sources of American History* (Boston: Houghton Mifflin Company, 1924), 17. For a detailed discussion of reproductions of the Declaration during this period, see BID.
10. "Manuscript Subscription Book" (1815–1818), MSS 12143, Albert H. Small Declaration of Independence Collection, Albert and Shirley Small Special Collections Library, University of Virginia.
11. *City of Washington Gazette*, April 2, 1818, 2 (RAHN).
12. Irma B. Jaffe, *Trumbull: The Declaration of Independence* (New York: The Viking Press, 1976), 61–65.
13. See Richard Brookhiser, *Glorious Lessons: John Trumbull, Painter of the American Revolution* (New Haven, CT: Yale University Press, 2024).
14. Malcolm Goldstein, *Landscape with Figures: A History of Art Dealing in the United States* (New York: Oxford University Press, 2000), Ch. 1. "Thursday, October 8, 1818. Trumbull's Independence," *New-York Daily Advertiser* II, no. 466, October 8, 1818, 2 (RAHN).
15. John H. Hazelton, "The Historical Value of Trumbull's 'Declaration of Independence,'" *PMHB* 31, no. 1 (1907): 35.

16. Quoted in BID, 72.
17. "Advertisement," *Evening Post* (New York, New York), no. 6622, September 23, 1823, 1 (RAHN).
18. "John Sanderson to Thomas Jefferson, 19 August 1820," *PTJR* XVI: 213–214.
19. "Thomas Jefferson to Peter S. DuPonceau, 28 December 1820," MSS 12613-a, Albert H. Small Declaration of Independence Collection (University of Virginia).
20. Rev. Charles A. Goodrich, *Lives of the Signers to the Declaration of Independence* (New York: W. Reed & Co., 1829); Nathaniel Dwight, *Sketches of the Lives of the Signers of the Declaration of Independence, Intended Principally for the Use of Schools* (New York: J. & J. Harper, 1830); Benson J. Lossing, *Biographical Sketches of the Signers of the Declaration of American Independence: The Declaration Historically Considered* (New York: G. F. Cooledge & Brother, 1848).
21. The last major collection of Signers' biographies was by David Freeman Hawke, *Honorable Treason: The Declaration of Independence and the Men Who Signed It* (New York: Viking, 1976). Other late volumes include John and Katherine Bakeless, *Signers of the Declaration* (Boston: Houghton Mifflin, 1969), and David C. Whitney, *Founders of Freedom in America; Lives of the Men Who Signed the Declaration of Independence and So Helped to Establish the United States of America* (Chicago: J. G. Ferguson Pub. Co., 1964; reissued 1971). Brief sketches continued to appear in newspapers and periodicals.
22. "Fourth of July," *Daily National Intelligencer* (Washington (DC), District of Columbia) IX, no. 2645, July 4, 1821, 3 (RAHN).
23. John Quincy Adams, *An Address Delivered at the Request of a Committee of the Citizens of Washington; on the Occasion of Reading the Declaration of Independence on the Fourth of July, 1821* (Washington, DC: Davis and Force, 1821).
24. *American Mercury* (Hartford, CT), July 17, 1821, 3 (RAHN). On Matlack's life, see Chris Coelho, *Timothy Matlack: Scribe of the Declaration of Independence* (Jefferson, NC: McFarland & Company, Inc., Publishers, 2013).
25. "For the Aurora to the Public," *Weekly Aurora* (Philadelphia, Pennsylvania) IX, no. IX, April 20, 1818, 65 (RAHN).
26. On Adams, see James Traub, *John Quincy Adams: Militant Spirit* (New York: Basic Books, 2017), and Fred Kaplan, *John Quincy Adams: American Visionary* (New York: Harper Perennial, 2015).
27. Catherine Nicholson, "The Stone Engraving: Icon of the Declaration," *Prologue* 35, no. 3 (Fall 2003).
28. "To John Adams from John Quincy Adams, 24 June 1824," *Founders Online*, National Archives, https://founders.archives.gov/documents/Adams/99-03-02-4419.
29. Catherine Nicholson, "Finding the Stones," *Prologue* 44, no. 2 (Summer 2012), https://www.archives.gov/publications/prologue/2012/summer/stone.html.

CHAPTER 8: Semicentennial

1. "9 July 1826," Diary of John Quincy Adams, John Quincy Adams Digital Diary, https://www.primarysourcecoop.org/publications/jqa/document/jqadiaries-v35-1826-07-p323--entry9?doci=undefined. On the passing of Adams and Jefferson, see

David McCullough, *John Adams* (New York: Simon & Schuster, 2002), 611–618; Joseph J. Ellis, *American Sphinx: The Character of Thomas Jefferson* (New York: Vintage, 1998), 345–347.

2. "Adams & Jefferson," *Newburyport Herald* (Massachusetts), July 14, 1826, 2 (RAHN).
3. *The Great Orations and Senatorial Speech of Daniel Webster* (Rochester, NY: Wilbur M. Hayward, 1853), 3–24.
4. Christian Wolmar, *The Great Railroad Revolution: The History of Trains in America* (New York: Public Affairs, 2012), 23.
5. *Ibid.*, 1.
6. BID, 4–5.
7. Daniel Walker Howe, *What Hath God Wrought: The Transformation of America, 1815–1848* (New York: Oxford University Press, 2007), Chs. 6–7, 14. Ralph Waldo Emerson, "Self-Reliance," in Carl Bode, ed., *The Portable Emerson* (New York: Penguin, 1981), 138–164.
8. Alexander Bölöni Farkas, *Journey in North America*, trans. and ed. by Theodore and Helen Benedek Schoenman (Philadelphia: The American Philosophical Society, 1977), 85.
9. James Truslow Adams, *The Epic of America* (Boston: Little, Brown, and Company, 1931), 161. "Oration," *Edwardsville Spectator*, August 17, 1822, 1 (RAHN).
10. Adams, *The Epic of America*, p. 161. "Declaration of Independence," *Edwardsville Spectator*, June 26, 1821, 1 (RAHN).
11. "Alton; Capt. Charles Gear; Mr. H. H. Snow; Alton," *Edwardsville Spectator* (Edwardsville, Illinois) III, no. 109, July 10, 1821, 2 (RAHN).
12. Abraham Lincoln, "Address to the Young Men's Lyceum of Springfield" (January 27, 1838), *LSS*, 17.
13. On the Adams-Jefferson relationship, see Gordon S. Wood, *Friends Divided: John Adams and Thomas Jefferson* (New York: Penguin, 2017). For their famed correspondence, see Lester J. Cappon, ed., *The Adams-Jefferson Letters: The Complete Correspondence Between Thomas Jefferson and Abigail and John Adams*, reprint (Chapel Hill, NC: Omohundro Institute, The University of North Carolina Press, 1987).
14. "From John Adams to Timothy Pickering, 6 August 1822," *WJA* II: 512n.
15. "From Thomas Jefferson to James Madison, 30 August 1823," *PTJR* XX: 123–125.
16. "To Roger C. Weightman," June 24, 1826, in Merrill D. Peterson, *Thomas Jefferson: Writings* (New York: The Library of America, 1984), 1516–1517. On July Fourth commemorations during these years, up to 1826, see Len Travers, *Celebrating the Fourth: Independence Day and the Rites of Nationalism in the Early Republic* (Amherst: University of Massachusetts Press, 1997).
17. Josiah Quincy, *An Oration Delivered on the Fourth of July, 1826, It Being the Fiftieth Anniversary of American Independence . . .* (Boston: True and Greene, 1826).
18. "Oration Containing a Declaration of Mental Independence," in *Selected Works of Robert Owen*, ed. by Gregory Claeys (London: W. Pickering, 1993), II: 48–55. On Owens, see Anne Taylor, *Visions of Harmony: A Study in Nineteenth-Century Millenarianism* (New York: Oxford University Press, 1987), and Brian Thompson, *Devastating Eden: The Search for Utopia in America* (London: Harper Collins, 2004).

19. A collection of such declarations can be found in Philip S. Foner, *We, the Other People: Alternative Declarations of Independence by Labor Groups, Farmers, Woman's Rights Advocates, Socialists, and Blacks, 1829–1975* (Urbana: University of Illinois Press, 1976).
20. Foner, *We, the Other People,* 64–70.
21. "A Riproarious Fight on the Mississippi River," in B. A. Botkin, ed., *A Treasure of American Folklore* (New York: Crown Publishers, 1944), 23.
22. On the temperance movement, see Jack S. Blocker, Jr., *American Temperance Movements: Cycles of Reform* (Boston: Twayne Publishers, 1989). On the role of women, see Holly Berkley Fletcher, *Gender and the American Temperance Movement of the Nineteenth Century* (New York: Routledge, 2008), and Scott C. Martin, *Devil of the Domestic Sphere: Temperance, Gender, and Middle-Class Ideology, 1800–1860* (DeKalb: Northern Illinois University Press, 2008).
23. *A Second Declaration of Independence; or, The Manifesto of All the Washington Total Abstinence Societies of the United States of America. Prepared For, and Delivered at the Temperance and Union Celebration of the 4th of July in Worcester, Mass. A.D. 1841, by Jesse W. Goodrich* (Worcester: Spooner and Howland, 1841).
24. Harriet Sigerman, *Elizabeth Cady Stanton: The Right Is Ours* (New York: Oxford University Press, 2001); Lori D. Ginzburg, *Elizabeth Cady Stanton: An American Life* (New York: Hill and Wang, 2009).
25. "Declaration of Sentiments," in Elizabeth Cady Stanton, *A History of Woman Suffrage* (Rochester, NY: Fowler and Wells, 1889), I: 70–71. See also Sigerman, *Elizabeth Cady Stanton,* 44–53.
26. Text of the Texians' Declaration of Independence, https://www.tsl.texas.gov/treasures/republic/declaration.html.
27. Stephen L. Hardin, *Texan Iliad: A Military History of the Texas Revolution, 1835–1836* (Austin: University of Texas Press, 1994).

CHAPTER 9: Into the Light

1. "[Charles Carroll; Carrollton; Washington]," *Alexandria Gazette* (Alexandria, Virginia), November 16, 1832, 3 (RAHN).
2. The most recent biography is Bradley J. Birzer, *American Cicero: The Life of Charles Carroll* (Wilmington, DE: ISI Books, 2010).
3. "Advertisement," *Charleston Courier* (Charleston, South Carolina), April 14, 1830, 4 (RAHN). On the other Jefferson drafts, see JHH, 347–348; Julian P. Boyd, *The Declaration of Independence: The Evolution of the Text* (Washington, DC: Library of Congress, 1943, 1999), 25, 79.
4. Daniel Webster, "Second Reply to Hayne," in Lindsay Swift, ed., *The Great Debate Between Hayne and Webster; The Speech of Daniel Webster in Reply to Robert Young Hayne* (New York: Houghton, Mifflin, 1898), 217.
5. "South Carolina Convention," *Charleston Courier,* November 28, 1832, 2 (RAHN).
6. "Memorial of John Ross, Geo. Lowrey, Major Ridge, and Elijah Hicks, delegates from the Cherokee Nation of Indians : April 16, 1824 : read, and referred to a committee of

the whole House on the state of the Union" (Washington, DC: Gales and Seaton, 1824), Amherst College Archives and Special Collections, https://acdc.amherst.edu/view/NativeLiterature/E99-C5_C46_1824#mode/1up.

7. See Ned Blackhawk, *The Rediscovery of America: Native Peoples and the Unmaking of U.S. History* (New Haven, CT: Yale University Press, 2023), 243–246.
8. JHH, 290.
9. The classic studies are by Arthur Schlesinger, Jr., *The Age of Jackson* (Boston: Little, Brown and Company, 1946), and Robert V. Remini, *The Life of Andrew Jackson* (New York: Harper and Row, 1988). For a more recent treatment, see David Walker Howe, *What Hath God Wrought: The Transformation of America, 1815–1848* (New York: Oxford University Press, 2007), esp. Ch. 9.
10. In 1850, the United States Census reported almost 23,200,000; Great Britain had 20 million, while France had 36 million. https://www.census.gov/library/publications/1853/dec/1850a.html.
11. On the Wilkes expedition, see Nathaniel Philbrick, *Sea of Glory: America's Voyage of Discovery: The U.S. Exploring Expedition, 1838–1842* (New York: Viking, 2003).
12. For a history of the Patent Office Building, see Charles J. Robertson, *Temple of Invention: History of a National Landmark* (Washington, DC: Smithsonian, 2006).
13. George Brown Goode, "The Genesis of the United States National Museum," in *A Memorial of George Brown Goode . . .* (Washington, DC: Government Printing Office, 1901), 118.
14. "Robbery," *The Sun* (Baltimore, MD), December 21, 1841, 2 (RAHN).
15. *A Popular Catalogue of the Extraordinary Curiosities of the National Institute* (Washington, DC: Alfred Hunter, 1855), 31–35; "The New Patent Office," *Jamestown Journal* (Jamestown, New York) XVI, no. 804, November 25, 1841, 2 (RAHN).
16. "The New Patent Office," *Jamestown Journal.*
17. John F. Stover, *History of the Baltimore and Ohio Railroad* (West Lafayette, IN: Purdue University Press, 1987), 41, 83.
18. William Q. Force, *Picture of Washington and Its Vicinity* (Washington, DC, 1845), 59.
19. William M. Morrison, *Morrison's Stranger's Guide to the City of Washington and Its Vicinity* (Washington, DC, 1852), 52–53, 78.
20. On Levy, see Marc Leepson, *Saving Monticello: The Levy Family's Epic Quest to Rescue the House that Jefferson Built* (Charlottesville: University of Virginia Press, 2003).
21. William Q. Force, *Picture of Washington*, 76–77. The Jefferson statue was moved back to the U.S. Capitol in the 1870s, and since 1900 has again stood in the Rotunda, next to John Trumbull's painting.
22. For the Amistad Affair, see Marcus Rediker, *The Amistad Rebellion: An Atlantic Odyssey of Slavery and Freedom* (New York: Penguin Books, 2013).
23. See, for example, Robin Blackburn, "Why the Second Slavery?" in Dale Tomich, ed., *Slavery and Historical Capitalism During the Nineteenth Century* (Lanham, MD: Lexington Books, 2017), 1–35; Anthony E. Kaye, "The Second Slavery: Modernity in the Nineteenth-Century South and the Atlantic World," in *The Journal of Southern History* 75, no. 3 (August 2009): 627–650.

24. Charles Dickens, *American Notes for General Circulation* (1842) (Middlesex, England: Penguin Books, 1972), 166.
25. "A Fac Simile of the Original Rough Draft of the Declaration of Independence" (1848), Albert H. Small Declaration of Independence Collection (University of Virginia).
26. On American culture during these years, see Michael Kammen, *Mystic Chords of Memory: The Transformation of Tradition in American Culture* (New York: Vintage, 1991), 62–90.
27. "Part I: Peopling St. Louis," *Stlouis*, www.stlouis-mo.gov/government/departments/planning/cultural-resources/preservation-plan/Part-I-Peopling-St-Louis.cfm.
28. See H. W. Brands, *The Age of Gold: The California Gold Rush and the New American Dream* (New York: Anchor Books, 2008). Census figures from California Department of Finance, https://dof.ca.gov/wp-content/uploads/sites/352/Reports/Demographic_Reports/Census_2010/documents/California-HistoricalPop-Seats1850-2010.pdf.
29. Malcolm J. Rohrbough, *Days of Gold: The California Gold Rush and the American Nation* (Berkeley and Los Angeles: University of California Press, 1998).
30. *Daily Alta California*, July 2, 1850, 2 (RAHN).
31. *Sacramento Transcript*, December 28, 1850, 4 (RAHN).
32. *Deseret News* (Salt Lake City), July 9, 1853, 2 (RAHN).
33. *Daily Missouri Republican* (St. Louis), June 6, 1851, 1 (RAHN).
34. Benson J. Lossing, *Biographical Sketches of the Signers of the Declaration of American Independence: The Declaration Historically Considered; And a Sketch of the Leading Events Connected with the Adoption of the Articles of Confederation and of the Federal Constitution* (New York: George F. Cooledge & Brother, 1848), 12.
35. See Kammen, *Mystic Chords*, 69–75.
36. See list of reproductions in BID, 130–187.

CHAPTER 10: The "Apple of Gold" and the Coming of the Civil War

1. Image in *Declaring Independence: The Origin and Influence of America's Founding Document* (Charlottesville: University of Virginia Library, 2008), xviii.
2. I am indebted to Frank Cogliano for this insight.
3. See Wendy Warren, *New England Bound: Slavery and Colonization in Early America* (New York: Liveright, 2017). Quote from John Jay Chapman, *William Lloyd Garrison*, 2nd ed. (Boston: Atlantic Monthly Press, 1921), 9.
4. On the profitability of slavery, see Edward E. Baptist, *The Half Has Never Been Told: Slavery and the Making of American Capitalism* (New York: Basic Books, 2014), and more briefly, Anthony E. Kaye, "The Second Slavery: Modernity in the Nineteenth-Century South and the Atlantic World," in *The Journal of Southern History* 75, no. 3 (August 2009): 627–650. Figures on export earnings and acreage from Robin Blackburn, "Why the Second Slavery?" in Dale Tomich, ed., *Slavery and Historical Capitalism During the Nineteenth Century* (Lanham, MD: Lexington Books, 2017), 24. On the triumph of cotton in general, see Giorgio Riello, *Cotton: The Fabric that Made*

the Modern World (New York: Cambridge University Press, 2013), and Sven Beckert, *Empire of Cotton: A Global History* (New York: Knopf, 2014). For economic figures, see Peter H. Lindert and Jeffrey G. Williamson, "American Incomes, 1774–1860," in *NBER Working Paper Series*, Working Paper 18396, National Bureau of Economic Research (September 2012), http://www.nber.org/papers/w18396.

5. Among broader treatments of slavery are Edmund Morgan, *American Slavery, American Freedom* (New York: W. W. Norton & Co., 2003), and Ira Berlin, *Many Thousands Gone: The First Two Centuries of Slavery in North America* (Cambridge, MA: Harvard University Press, 2000).
6. A thorough discussion is in Sean Wilentz, *No Property in Man: Slavery and Antislavery at the Nation's Founding* (Cambridge, MA: Harvard University Press, 2018).
7. On the domestic slave trade, see Joshua D. Rothman, *The Ledger and the Chain: How Domestic Slave Traders Shaped America* (New York: Basic Books, 2021).
8. See Peter S. Onuf, *Statehood and Union: A History of the Northwest Ordinance* (South Bend, IN: University of Notre Dame Press, 2019), Ch. 6, and Bernadette Meyer, "Between the States and the Signers: The Politics of the Declaration of Independence Before the Civil War," *Southern California Law Review* 89, no. 54 (2016): 541–573.
9. Quoted in Robert Pierce Forbes, *The Missouri Compromise and Its Aftermath: Slavery and the Meaning of America* (Chapel Hill: The University of North Carolina Press, 2007), 38–39.
10. On expansion and Southern influence see, for example, Matthew Karp, *This Vast Southern Empire: Slaveholders at the Helm of American Foreign Policy* (Cambridge, MA: Harvard University Press, 2016). Also, Brian Schoen, *The Fragile Fabric of Union: Cotton, Federal Politics, and the Global Origins of the Civil War* (Baltimore: The Johns Hopkins University Press, 2009). The classic account is David M. Potter, *The Impending Crisis: America Before the Civil War, 1848–1861* (New York: Harper & Row, 1976).
11. James Forten, "From 'Letters from a Man of Colour on a Late Bill Before the Senate of Pennsylvania,'" in James G. Basker, *American Antislavery Writings: Colonial Beginnings to Emancipation* (New York: The Library of America, 2012), 211.
12. David Walker, *An Appeal to the Colored Citizens of the World* (Boston, 1829), 74.
13. Not much has been written lately on Garrison, but see Henry Mayer, *All on Fire: William Lloyd Garrison and the Abolition of Slavery* (New York: St. Martin's Press, 1998), and James Brewer Stewart, ed., *William Lloyd Garrison at Two Hundred* (New Haven, CT: Yale University Press, 2008), a collection of essays.
14. The text of the 1833 Declaration of Sentiments is available at https://teachingamericanhistory.org/document/declaration-of-the-national-anti-slavery-convention/.
15. John C. Calhoun, "On the Oregon Bill," June 27, 1848, in Richard Kenner Cralle, ed., *The Works of John C. Calhoun*, Vol. 4 (New York: D. Appleton & Co., 1888), 503–512. Petit quoted in Jeremy Tewell, *A Self-Evident Lie: Southern Slavery and the Threat to American Freedom* (Kent, OH: Kent State University Press, 2013), 24.
16. Fred. A. Ross, *Slavery as Ordained by God* (Philadelphia: J. B. Lippincott & Co., 1857).
17. On Douglass's life see David W. Blight, *Frederick Douglass: Prophet of Freedom* (New York: Simon & Schuster, 2018).

18. Blight, *Frederick Douglass,* 274–282. The speech is at *Oration, Delivered in Corinthian Hall, Rochester, by Frederick Douglass, July 5th 1852* (Rochester, NY: Lee, Mann & Co., 1852).
19. William Lloyd Garrison to Rev. Samuel J. May, July 17, 1845, in Walter M. Merrill, ed., *The Letters of William Lloyd Garrison* (Cambridge, MA: Harvard University Press, 1973), III: 303.
20. More has been written on Lincoln than any figure in American history. The best place to start is probably David Herbert Donald, *Lincoln* (New York: Simon & Schuster, 1995).
21. Allen C. Guelzo, *Abraham Lincoln: Redeemer President* (Grand Rapids, MI: Wm. B. Eerdmans Pub. Co., 1999); see also Allen Jayne, *Lincoln and the American Manifesto* (Amherst, NY: Prometheus Books, 2007).
22. "Speech on the Kansas-Nebraska Act, at Peoria, Illinois," in *LSS*, 98–99. For a detailed study of the background to the speech, see Lewis E. Lehrman, *Lincoln at Peoria: The Turning Point* (Mechanicsburg, PA: Stackpole Books, 2008).
23. See Earl M. Maltz, *Dred Scott and the Politics of Slavery* (Lawrence: University of Kansas Press, 2007).
24. "Speech on the Dred Scott Decision," *LSS*, 118–121.
25. The classic account of the Lincoln-Douglas Debates is Harry V. Jaffa, *Crisis of the House Divided: An Interpretation of the Issues in the Lincoln-Douglas Debates* (Garden City, NY: Doubleday & Company, 1959).
26. "Speech at Chicago, Illinois," July 10, 1858, *LSS*, 145–146.
27. "Address at Cooper Institute," February 27, 1860, *LSS*, 240–251.
28. On the 1860 Convention, see Edward Achorn, *The Lincoln Miracle: Inside the Republican Convention that Changed History* (New York: Atlantic Monthly Press, 2023). On the campaign, see Michael F. Holt, *The Election of 1860: 'A Campaign Fraught with Consequences'* (Lawrence: University of Kansas Press, 2017).
29. See Harold Holzer, *Lincoln President-Elect: Abraham Lincoln and the Great Secession Winter, 1860–1861* (New York: Simon & Schuster, 2008).
30. "Declaration of the Immediate Causes Which Induce and Justify the Secession of South Carolina from the Federal Union," https://avalon.law.yale.edu/19th_century/csa_scarsec.asp.
31. "The Right of Peaceable Succession," *Cincinnati Daily Press*, November 21, 1860, 2; https://lccn.loc.gov/sn84028745.
32. "Farewell Speech," *The Papers of Jefferson Davis,* Vol. 7 (Baton Rouge and London: Louisiana State University Press, 1992), 18–23.
33. Stephens's Cornerstone Speech is in H. Cleveland, *Alexander H. Stephens, in Public and Private: With Letter and Speeches, Before, During and Since the War* (Philadelphia: National Publishing, 1866), 717–729.
34. For these months, see William J. Cooper, Jr., *We Have the War Upon Us: The Onset of the Civil War, November 1860–April 1861* (New York: Alfred A. Knopf, 2012).
35. The Cherokee Declaration was promulgated on October 28, 1861. The text can be found in *The War of the Rebellion: A Compilation of the Official Records of the Union and Confederate Armies* (Washington, DC: Government Printing Office, 1885), 1: XIII, 503–505. I am indebted to Jane Kamensky for bringing this document to my attention.

36. This and the following quotes from "Speech at Independence Hall" (February 22, 1861), *LSS*, 282.
37. "Fragment on the Constitution and Union," Paul M. Angle, compiler, *New Letters and Papers of Lincoln* (Boston: Houghton Mifflin Company, 1930), 240–241.

CHAPTER 11: The Last Civil War Mystery

1. "Virginia News," *Alexandria Gazette*, April 22, 1861, 2 (RAHN). A recent narrative is Erik Larsen, *The Demon of Unrest: A Saga of Hubris, Heartbreak, and Heroism at the Dawn of the Civil War* (New York: Crown, 2024).
2. Quote from John Lockwood and Charles Lockwood, *The Siege of Washington: The Untold Story of the Twelve Days That Shook the Union* (New York: Oxford University Press, 2011), xiv. Among the thousands of books on the Civil War, those dealing with Washington include, in addition to Lockwood, Benjamin Franklin Cooling III, *Symbol, Sword, and Shield: Defending Washington During the Civil War* (Shippensburg, PA: White Mane Publishing Company, 1991); Marc Leepson, *Desperate Engagement: How a Little-Known Civil War Battle Saved Washington, DC, and Changed American History* (New York: St. Martin's Griffin, 2007); Ernest B. Furgurson, *Freedom Rising: Washington in the Civil War* (New York: Vintage Books, 2004); and Kenneth J. Winkle, *Lincoln's Citadel: The Civil War in Washington, DC* (New York: W. W. Norton, 2013).
3. George Brown Goode, "The Genesis of the United States National Museum," in *A Memorial of George Brown Goode . . .* (Washington, DC: Government Printing Office, 1901), 142.
4. "Army and Navy Sketches," *Evening Post* (New York), December 16, 1861, 1 (RAHN). Burnside's facial hair was the inspiration for the term "sideburns," originally called "burnsides."
5. *The New York Herald*, April 16, 1861, 3 (RAHN).
6. Winkle, *Lincoln's Citadel*, 163–164.
7. "Military Demonstration, Necessity of Discipline," *New-York Tribune*, July 8, 1861, 6 (RAHN).
8. "Stephens' Last Speech," *The Philadelphia Inquirer*, May 8, 1861, 2 (RAHN).
9. "Letter from our Washington House," *The Scientific American* 4 (May 1861): 374.
10. Quoted in Charles J. Robertson, *Temple of Invention: History of a National Landmark* (Washington, DC: Smithsonian, 2006), 50–51.
11. Cooling, *Symbol, Sword, and Shield*, 20–21.
12. Furgurson, *Freedom Rising*, 20–40; on spies and plotters, see Ann Blackman, *Wild Rose: Rose O'Neale Greenhow, Civil War Spy* (New York: Random House, 2006), and James L. Swanson, *Manhunt: The 12-Day Chase for Lincoln's Killer* (New York: William Morrow, 2007).
13. "Letter from the First Regiment," *Providence Evening Press*, June 22, 1861, 2 (RAHN).
14. "Why Washington Is Not Taken," *Daily National Intelligencer*, July 12, 1861, 3 (RAHN).

15. On the battle, see Edward G. Longacre, *The Early Morning of War: Bull Run, 1861* (Norman: University of Oklahoma Press, 2014).
16. Quoted in Cooling, *Symbol, Sword, and Shield*, 56.
17. "Is Washington Safe?" *The Boston Post*, July 29, 1861, 1 (RAHN); "Startling Revelations—Apprehended Attack upon Washington," *The New York Herald*, July 28, 1861, 4 (RAHN).
18. William H. Michael, *The Declaration of Independence: Illustrated Story of Its Adoption* (Washington, DC: Government Printing Office, 1904); Dumas Malone, *The Story of the Declaration of Independence* (New York: Oxford University Press, 1954); *Declaration of Independence: The Adventures of a Document* (Washington, DC: National Archives and Record Service, 1976).
19. "Why Washington Is Not Taken," *Daily National Intelligencer*, July 12, 1861, 3 (RAHN).
20. "The Original Declaration of Independence," *Wood's Household Magazine*, July 1, 1873, 16–20.
21. "Soldier's Letter," *Jamestown* (NY) *Journal*, August 9, 1861, 1 (RAHN).
22. *Daily Evening Bulletin* (San Francisco), August 23, 1861, 1; *Newport Mercury*, August 10, 1861, 2 (RAHN).
23. William F. Richstein, *Strangers' Guide-Book to Washington City* (Washington, DC: 1864), 31.
24. "From Washington," *Commercial Advertiser*, March 8, 1861, 2 (RAHN).
25. Furgurson, *Freedom Rising*, 245.
26. John E. Wilson, Composer, and John E. Wilson, Lyricist, Declaration of independence, of the United States (Baltimore: John E. Wilson, 1861). Civil War Music collection, Music Division–DLC; https://www.loc.gov/item/2023784216/.
27. "Independence Monument," *Philadelphia Enquirer*, June 19, 1861, 8 (RAHN); *Commercial Advertiser*, June 21, 1861, 2 (RAHN). I am grateful to Keeley Tulio, of Founding Forward, for arranging for me to view the Rothermel painting in the Union League Club of Philadelphia.
28. For insightful takes on the Gettysburg Address, see Steven B. Smith, "How Lincoln Created Democracy," *Liberties* 5, no. 1 (Autumn 2024): 228–250, and Leon R. Kass, "Abraham Lincoln's Re-Founding of the Nation" (2007), https://www.whatsoproudlywehail.org/curriculum/the-meaning-of-america/abraham-lincolns-re-founding-of-the-nation/. It is the subject of Garry Wills, *Lincoln at Gettysburg: The Words That Remade America* (New York: Simon & Schuster, 1992).
29. *Complete Works of Ralph Waldo Emerson*, X: *Lectures and Biographical Sketches* (Boston: Houghton Mifflin, 1904), 530.
30. "Speech at Richmond," *The Papers of Jefferson Davis* (Baton Rouge and London: Louisiana State University Press, 1997) IX: 10–16.
31. *The Jewish Messenger* (New York), February 3, 1865, 36 (RAHN).
32. "Speech on Reconstruction, Washington, DC," in *LSS*, 456–458.
33. Lincoln as restorer and reformer of the Union is argued in Ralph Lerner, "Lincoln's Declaration—and Ours," in Steven B. Smith, ed., *The Writings of Abraham Lincoln* (New Haven, CT: Yale University Press, 2012), 449–460.

CHAPTER 12: Centennial

1. Akhil Reed Amar, *Born Equal: Remaking America's Constitution, 1840–1920* (New York: Basic Books, 2025), Ch. 15.
2. See Bernadette Cahill, *No Vote for Women: The Denial of Suffrage in Reconstruction America* (Jefferson, NC: McFarland & Company, Publishers, 2019).
3. See Joel Achenbach, *The Grand Idea: George Washington's Potomac and the Race to the West* (New York: Simon & Schuster, 2004).
4. Christian Wolmar, *The Great Railroad Revolution: The History of Trains in America* (New York: Public Affairs, 2012), Chs. 1–8.
5. "Thoughts and Facts," *The Press*, May 25, 1868, 4 (RAHN).
6. See Richard White, *The Republic for Which It Stands: The United States During Reconstruction and the Gilded Age, 1865–1896* (New York: Oxford University Press, 2017); H.W. Brands, *American Colossus: The Triumph of Capitalism, 1865–1900* (New York: Anchor Books, 2011); John Steele Gordon, *An Empire of Wealth* (New York: Harper Perennial, 2004), Chs. 11–14. On social and cultural history, see Daniel E. Sutherland, *The Expansion of Everyday Life, 1860–1876* (New York: Harper & Row, 1989), and Thomas J. Schlereth, *Victorian America: Transformations of Everyday Life, 1876–1915* (New York: Harper Perennial, 1991).
7. "Ring Out the Old Century and Ring in the New," *The Cincinnati Daily Enquirer*, January 1, 1876, 4 (RAHN).
8. "July Fourth," *Quincy Daily Whig*, June 29, 1868, 4 (RAHN).
9. James Truslow Adams, *The Epic of America* (Boston: Little, Brown, and Company, 1931), 306.
10. "Republican. Opening of the Campaign," *Cincinnati Daily Gazette*, August 6, 1867, 1 (RAHN).
11. John F. Ellis, *Guide to Washington City and Vicinity* (Washington, DC: 1868), 72.
12. "Independence Bell July 4, 1776," in G. S. Hillard, ed., *The Franklin Fifth Reader* (New York: Taintor Bro's, Merrill & Co., 1878), 81–84.
13. A good account is Stephen W. Stathis, "Returning the Declaration of Independence to Philadelphia: An Exercise in Centennial Politics," in *PMHB* 102, no. 2 (April 1978): 167–183.
14. On Levy, see Marc Leepson, *Saving Monticello: The Levy Family's Epic Quest to Rescue the House that Jefferson Built* (Charlottesville: University of Virginia Press, 2003); on Mount Vernon, see Carol Borchert Cadou, *Stewards of Memory: The Past, Present, and Future of Historic Conservation at George Washington's Mount Vernon* (Charlottesville: University of Virginia Press, 2018), and Lydia Mattice Brandt, *First in the Homes of His Countrymen: George Washington's Mount Vernon in the American Imagination* (Charlottesville: University of Virginia Press, 2016).
15. "Hancock's chair" was likely a replacement for the one present during 1776, though it was used by George Washington during the Constitutional Convention.
16. "A Historic Inkstand," *American Stationer*, June 23, 1875, 28. The inkstand is still held by the National Park Service, though now in storage.
17. An account of the restoration of Independence Hall can be found in Edward M. Riley,

Independence National Historical Park, Philadelphia, Pa. (Washington, DC: National Park Service Historical Handbook Series, No. 17, 1956), 41–45.

18. Frank M. Etting, *An Historical Account of the Old State House of Pennsylvania Now Known as the Hall of Independence* (Boston: James R. Osgood and Company, 1876), "Preface."
19. Etting's letter in Gaillard Hunt, *Department of State: Its History and Functions* (New Haven, CT: Yale University Press, 1914), 301–302. See also Stathis, "Returning the Declaration," 167–183.
20. "To-Day—To-Morrow," *New-York Daily Tribune*, May 11, 1876, 4 (RAHN).
21. "Centennial Year," *The Inter Ocean*, January 1, 1876, 4 (RAHN).
22. See Bruno Giberti, *Designing the Centennial: A History of the 1876 International Exhibition in Philadelphia* (Lexington: The University Press of Kentucky, 2002); Faith K. Pizor, "Preparations for the Centennial Exhibition of 1876," *PMHB* 94, no. 2 (April 1970): 213–232; S. Edgar Trout, *The Story of the Centennial of 1876: Golden Anniversary* (n.p., 1929), 145–147.
23. "The Centennial," *The Madison Journal* (Delta, Louisiana), May 23, 1876, 1 (RAHN).
24. *Trenton State Gazette*, June 4, 1866, 1 (RAHN).
25. Trout, *Story of the Centennial*, 47.
26. JHH, 152–153. The National Park Service reconstructed the house in 1975, for the Bicentennial.
27. "Senator Ferry's Speech," in *Cincinnati Commercial Tribune*, July 5, 1876, 2 (RAHN).
28. *Ibid.*
29. *Philadelphia Inquirer*, July 6, 1876, 3 (RAHN).
30. Trout, *Story of the Centennial*, 137–145; Pizor, "Preparations for the Centennial Exhibition," 31, 39; *Public Ledger*, July 5, 1876, quoted in *Declaration of Independence: The Adventures of a Document* (Washington, DC: National Archives and Record Service, 1976), 20.
31. *Woodhull and Claflin's Weekly*, January 2, 1871.
32. *United States of America v. Susan B. Anthony: Closing Arguments* (1873), quoted in Ann D. Gordon, *The Trial of Susan B. Anthony* (Federal Judicial Center: Federal Judiciary History Office, 2005), 46.
33. "Woman's Suffrage," *Philadelphia Inquirer*, July 5, 1876, 7 (RAHN). The "Declaration of Rights of the Women of the United States - July 4, 1876," Printed Ephemera Collection; Portfolio 160, Folder 3, Rare Book and Special Collections Division–DLC.
34. Alexander Tsesis, *For Liberty and Equality: The Life and Times of the Declaration of Independence* (New York: Oxford University Press, 2012), Ch. 12.
35. BID, 105–115; copies of the B&O Railroad and R. J. Baker editions of the McBride facsimile can be found in the Manuscripts Division (hereafter MSS)–DLC, "Declaration of Independence collection, 1776–1942," Box OV 5.
36. The best account of the Centennial printings is by BID, Ch. 5.
37. Images available from the Prints and Photographs Division, Library of Congress (hereafter, PP–DLC), PGA - Currier & Ives–Declaration committee (B size); PP–DLC, PGA - Currier & Ives–John Hancock's . . . (A size); PP–DLC, Unprocessed in PR 13 CN 1975:071, p. 039.

38. *Cincinnati Daily Times*, May 5, 1876, 4 (RAHN).
39. BID, 182; *Portland Daily Press*, March 27, 1876, 1 (RAHN).
40. "A Centennial Memento," *Albany Evening Journal*, July 1, 1876, 3 (RAHN).
41. See BID, 174–177; *Commercial Advertiser* (New York, NY), January 4, 1876, 3 (RAHN).

CHAPTER 13: The Gilded Age

1. *North American* (Philadelphia, PA), February 14, 1877, 1 (RAHN).
2. Quoted in Gaillard Hunt, *The Department of State of the United States: Its History and Functions* (New Haven, CT: Yale University Press, 1914), 308–309.
3. JHH, 291.
4. Hunt, *The Department of State*, 305–306.
5. *Ibid.*, 309–310.
6. *Ibid.*, 308–309.
7. JHH, 292.
8. Charles J. Robertson, *Temple of Invention: History of a National Landmark* (Washington, DC: Smithsonian, 2006), 67–70.
9. Lee H. Burke, *Homes of the Department of State, 1774–1976: The Buildings Occupied by the Department of State and Its Predecessors* (Washington, DC: Department of State, 1976), 43.
10. Quote from "Unsafe Buildings," *New-York Tribune*, October 13, 1877, 1 (RAHN). On the building, see Burke, *Homes of the Department of State*, 43–47. The best study of the building is by Thomas E. Luebke, *Palace of State: The Eisenhower Executive Office Building* (Washington, DC: Commission of Fine Arts, 2018).
11. "The Nation's Books. The Libraries of the Capital - A Grand Collection of Volumes," *San Francisco Bulletin*, October 17, 1877, 4 (RAHN).
12. "Jefferson's Desk," *Boston Journal*, April 19, 1880, 4 (RAHN). The desk can be seen in the Smithsonian Institution's National Museum of American History.
13. "Get in Your Fourth of July Orders," *Chicago Daily Tribune*, June 30, 1895, 7 (PQHN).
14. "Revival of Independence Day," *Chicago Daily Tribune*, July 1, 1895, 2 (PQHN). The facsimile was printed on July 4 as a supplement; "Other 22 — no Title," *Chicago Daily Tribune*, July 4, 1895, 13 (PQHN).
15. BID, 141–142. See Bidwell's checklist of prints and reproductions in his Appendix.
16. PP–DLC, Illus. in AP101.P7 1885 (Case X). On Cleveland, see Troy Senik, *A Man of Iron: The Turbulent Life and Improbable Presidency of Grover Cleveland* (New York: Threshold Editions, 2023).
17. The panels are still there, spanning an exhibition space and part of the European Reading Room.
18. Dr. John B. Ellis, *Sights and Secrets of the National Capital* (1869), 347–348; *Historical Magazine*, ser. 3, vol. 8 (October 1870): 252.
19. *Historical Magazine*, May 1, 1872, 306.
20. BID, 118.
21. Hunt, *Department of State*, 297–298.

22. *Ibid.*, 299–300. See also *Annual Report of the Librarian of Congress for the fiscal year ending June 30, 1949* (Washington, DC: Government Printing Office, 1950), 38–40.
23. James L. Gear, "The Repair of Documents—American Beginnings," in *The American Archivist* 26, no. 4 (October 1963), 469–475.
24. Andrew H. Allen, "The Historical Archives of the Department of State," in *Annual Report of the American Historical Association 1894* (Washington, DC: Government Printing Office, 1895), 295.
25. "To Be Viewed by the Public No More," *New-York Tribune*, February 13, 1894, 5 (RAHN). The paper erroneously reported that the Declaration was rolled up and stored in the cabinet.
26. The overdrawn *J* is clearly visible today on the engrossed Declaration, and National Archives conservators have determined that the *H* in Hancock was similarly overwritten, though that is much harder to see with the naked eye.
27. Charles F. Chandler to John Hay, "Report of a Committee of the National Academy of Sciences on the Condition and Preservation of the Declaration of Independence," April 24, 1903, Entry A1–578: Memorandums of the Bureau of Rolls and Library, 1888–1918, RG 59: General Records of the Department of State, National Archives and Records Administration.
28. "Can Not See the 'Declaration,'" *Dallas Morning News*, July 4, 1897, 11 (RAHN); "Declaration Will Be Seen No More," *Baltimore American*, April 25, 1903, 4 (RAHN).
29. "The Lost Declaration," *Times-Picayune* (New Orleans), October 25, 1903, 38 (RAHN).
30. "Treasures in a Library," *Irish American Weekly* (New York), July 29, 1895, 3 (RAHN); BID, 122.
31. Mellen Chamberlain, *The Authentication of the Declaration of Independence: July 4, 1776* (Cambridge: John Wilson and Son, 1885).
32. On the history of professional American historians, see Peter Novick, *That Noble Dream: The 'Objectivity Question' and the American Historical Profession* (New York: Cambridge University Press, 1988).
33. R. M. Black, "The Ethics of the Declaration of Independence," *Annals of the American Academy of Political and Social Science* II (July 1891): 138–144; reprinted in Robert Ginsberg, *A Casebook on the Declaration of Independence* (New York: Thomas Y. Crowell Company, 1967), 78–82. This is a question Danielle Allen would return to a century later, in *Our Declaration.*
34. Moses Coit Tyler, "The Declaration of Independence in the Light of Modern Criticism," in *The North American Review* 163, no. 476 (July 1896): 1–16. The second quote was taken from Tyler's discussion of the pre–Civil War era but reflected his judgment on the Declaration's then-contemporary relevance.
35. William F. Dana, "The Declaration of Independence," in *Harvard Law Review* 13, no. 5 (January 1900): 319–343; Herbert Friedenwald, *The Declaration of Independence: An Interpretation and Analysis* (New York: The MacMillan Company, 1904), 197, 205.
36. John H. Hazelton, *The Declaration of Independence: Its History* (New York: Dodd, Mead and Company, 1906). Like others before me, I relied heavily on Hazelton for the early chapters of this book, though I used his comprehensive quotations to guide me

to the original sources, many of which are now digitized through the National Archives *Founders Online* site and the Readex American Historical Newspapers archive.

CHAPTER 14: The People's Declaration

1. "Documents Noting Birth of U.S. Laid in Last Shrine," *The Washington Post*, February 29, 1924, 4 (PQHN).
2. *Annual Report of the Librarian of Congress for the Fiscal Year Ending June 30, 1949* (Washington, DC: Library of Congress, 1950), 42.
3. See Jackson Lears, *Rebirth of a Nation: The Making of Modern America, 1877–1920* (New York: Harper Perennial, 2010); Robert Wiebe, *The Search for Order, 1877–1920* (New York: Hill and Wang, 1967); and Thomas J. Schlereth, *Victorian America: Transformations of Everyday Life, 1876–1915* (New York: Harper Perennial, 1991).
4. "Splendid Work Accomplished by the Educational Alliance," *The New York Times*, February 3, 1907, SM4 (PQHN).
5. "Citizenship Syllabus Now Being Distributed," *The New York Times*, April 2, 1916, X4 (PQHN).
6. "Ford Educational Library" [advertisement], *Moving Picture Age* V, no. 10 (October 1922), n.p.
7. See, for example, A. H. Laidlaw Jr., trans., *The Constitution of the United States and the Declaration of Independence in German, French and English in parallel columns* (New York: Laidlaw Bros. & Co., 1888); Joh. A. Enander, trans., *Förenta Staternas historia* (The history of the United States) (Chicago: Enander and Bohmans Förlag, 1880), 381; *Ḳonsṭiṭushon fun di Fereyṇigṭe Shṭaaṭen un di Deḳlereyshon of Indipendens: iberzeṭtsṭ in rayn Yidish-Dayṭsh und der Englisher ṭeḳst derbay* (New York: Sarasohn & Son, 1892); Reuben Fink, trans., *Di Amerikaner ḳonsṭiṭutsion un di Unaphengigḳeyṭ derḳlerung* (New York: Max N. Maisel Publisher, 1920).
8. *To kleidi tou Hellēnos en Amerikē* (New York: The Ennosis Publishing Company, 1917), p. 29; *L'Indispensabile Manuale Degli Italiani D'America* (Brooklyn: F. Sparacino, 1923), 81–89; James Brown Scott, *Deklaratsiia nezavisimosti, stat'i konfederatsii, konstitutsiia Soedinennykh Shtatov* (New York: Charles Scribner's Sons, 1919); the first Russian translation did not appear until 1863 and an accurate one did not appear until 1897; see Nikolai N. Bolkhovitinov, "The Declaration of Independence: A View from Russia," *The Journal of American History* 84, no. 4 (March 1999): 1389–1398.
9. "Minutes" from the 1907 meeting, available at https://www.dsdi1776.com/historical-minutes-scanned-from-the-societys-minute-books/.
10. "Minutes" at https://www.dsdi1776.com/historical-minutes-scanned-from-the-societys-minute-books/. The Descendants of the Signers of the Declaration of Independence remains an active organization with annual meetings; their website is at https://www.dsdi1776.com.
11. Reading the Declaration of Independence [White man to Lakota (Brule) assemblage] Rosebud Agency, S.D. (July 4, 1897), PP–DLC, Lot 3328.
12. Peter Cozzens, *The Earth Is Weeping: The Epic Story of the Indian Wars for the American*

West (New York: Alfred A. Knopf, 2016), and Bill Yenne, *Indian Wars: The Campaign for the American West* (Yardley, PA: Westholme Publishing, 2005).

13. Ned Blackhawk, *The Rediscovery of America: Native Peoples and the Unmaking of U.S. History* (New Haven, CT: Yale University Press, 2023), 334–357.
14. John R. Wunder, "'Merciless Indian Savages' and the Declaration of Independence: Native Americans Translate the Ecunnaunuxulgee Document," *American Indian Law Review* 25, no. 1 (2000): 65–92.
15. Thomas Grillot, *First Americans: U.S. Patriotism in Indian Country After World War I* (New Haven, CT: Yale University Press, 2018).
16. David Wallace Adams, *Education for Extinction: American Indians and the Boarding School Experience: 1875–1928*, 2nd ed. (Lawrence: University Press of Kansas, 2020).
17. See Ron Chernow, *The House of Morgan: An American Banking Dynasty and the Rise of Modern Finance* (New York: Atlantic Monthly Press, 1990), and Ron Chernow, *Titan: The Life of John D. Rockefeller, Sr.* (New York: Random House, 1998).
18. Quoted in Allan Nevins and Henry Steele Commager, *A Short History of the United States* (New York: The Modern Library, 1945), 306.
19. See Richard White, *The Republic for Which It Stands: The United States During Reconstruction and the Gilded Age, 1865–1896* (New York: Oxford University Press, 2017), and H.W. Brands, *American Colossus: The Triumph of Capitalism, 1865–1900* (New York: Anchor Books, 2011).
20. See Samuel P. Hays, *The Response to Industrialism, 1885–1914*, 2nd ed. (Chicago: The University of Chicago Press, 1995). See also John Steele Gordon, *An Empire of Wealth* (New York: Harper Perennial, 2004), 240–310.
21. Philip S. Foner, *We, the Other People: Alternative Declarations of Independence by Labor Groups, Farmers, Woman's Rights Advocates, Socialists, and Blacks, 1829–1975* (Urbana: University of Illinois Press, 1976), 142–149.
22. William Jennings Bryan to I. J. Dunn, January 4, 1895, https://www.gilderlehrman.org/history-resources/spotlight-primary-source/william-jennings-bryan-and-ideals-declaration. See also Alexander Tsesis, *For Liberty and Equality: The Life and Times of the Declaration of Independence* (New York: Oxford University Press, 2012), Ch. 13.
23. "President Wilson's Joint Address to Congress, April 2, 1917," Record Group 46, Records of the U.S. Senate, NARA, National Archives Identifier 2668825. Washington's Farewell Address can be accessed at https://avalon.law.yale.edu/18th_century/washing.asp; a classic analysis is Felix Gilbert, *To the Farewell Address: Ideas of Early American Foreign Policy* (Princeton, NJ: Princeton University Press, 1961).
24. "Unanimous Declaration of Men of Many Races in the United States of America," July 4, 1918, Balch Institute Broadsides (Collection 3213), NB1 75-184, The Historical Society of Pennsylvania, Philadelphia.
25. "The Third Great Title-Deed of Anglo-American Liberties," July 4, 1918, in *Winston Churchill: His Complete Speeches 1897–1963*, edited by Robert Rhodes James, 8 vols. (London: Chelsea House Publishers, 1974), III: 2614.
26. "A Fourth of July Address," July 4, 1914, *The Papers of Woodrow Wilson Digital Edition* (Charlottesville: University of Virginia Press, Rotunda, 2017), https://rotunda-upress-virginia-edu.stanford.idm.oclc.org/founders/WILS-01-30-02-0253.

27. See Adam Hochschild, *American Midnight: The Great War, a Violent Peace, and Democracy's Forgotten Crisis* (New York: Mariner Books, 2022), 59–70, and Chris Myers Asch and George Derek Musgrove, *Chocolate City: A History of Race and Democracy in the Nation's Capital* (Chapel Hill: The North Carolina University Press, 2017), 217–236. An older article is by Kathleen L. Wolgemuth, "Woodrow Wilson and Federal Segregation," *The Journal of Negro History* 44, no. 2 (April 1959): 158–173.
28. On America in these years, see David M. Kennedy, *Over Here: The First World War and American Society* (New York: Oxford University Press, 2004).
29. *Annual Report of the Librarian 1949,* 42.
30. *Ibid.*, 44. Hughes would later become Chief Justice of the Supreme Court.
31. On Putnam, see Jane Aikin Rosenberg, *The Nation's Great Library: Herbert Putnam and the Library of Congress, 1899–1939* (Urbana: University of Illinois Press, 1993).
32. *Annual Report of the Librarian 1949*, 44–45, 46.
33. *Ibid.*, 46.
34. "Thomas Jefferson Papers, 1606–1943," *Index to the Thomas Jefferson Papers* (Washington, DC: Library of Congress, 1976), vii–xvii. "Taft Thanks J. P. Morgan," *The Washington Post*, November 22, 1912, 6.
35. Verner Clapp, "The Declaration of Independence: A Case Study in Preservation," *Special Libraries* 62, no. 12 (December 1971): 503–508.
36. Attendance figures from *Annual Reports*, DLC, 1925 through 1930. "Declaration of Independence—Copy Still in Good Condition—Viewed by Thousands Daily," *Atlanta Constitution*, July 2, 1926, 4 (PQHN); "1,000 a Day Visit Shrine of U.S. Constitution—Some to Kneel in Prayer," *Washington Post,* September 13, 1936, B2 (PQHN).
37. Carl Lotus Becker, *The Declaration of Independence: A Study in the History of Political Ideas* (New York: Harcourt, Brace, and Company, 1922), 277. Becker's arguments were challenged on different grounds by Harry Jaffa, *The Crisis of the House Divided: An Interpretation of the Issues in the Lincoln-Douglas Debates* (Chicago: University of Chicago Press, 1959), and Garry Wills, *Inventing America: Jefferson's Declaration of Independence* (New York: Vintage, 1978).
38. The Pyle portrait is in the Delaware Art Museum, and can be accessed at https://emuseum.delart.org/objects/3965/thomas-jefferson-writing-the-declaration-of-independence?ctx=408b6dc7d47d6c1839dbf30ca086ad1d4d565144&idx=13; the illustration for "The Story of the Revolution," by Henry Cabot Lodge, in *Scribner's Magazine*, March 1898. The Ferris painting can be accessed (in monochrome), LOT 4412-LV, PP–DLC.
39. Ads in *The National Geographic Magazine*, June 1923, n.p., and March 1930, n.p.
40. *The Chronicles of America Photoplays* (New Haven, CT: Yale University Press Film Service, n.d.); a revised guide was published in 1959, attesting to the films' continuing popularity. Chronicles of America Photoplays papers, Box A-0170, Moving Image Research Center, National Audio-Visual Conservation Center–DLC. The filming script can be accessed at https://tile.loc.gov/storage-services/service/mbrs/cdmmi/s1/22/91/20/18/4/s1229120184/s1229120184.pdf.
41. "Fireworks Display and Pageant to End City's Celebration," *The Washington Post*, July 5, 1926, 1 (PQHN).

42. "Jefferson Praised for Free Religion at His Old Home," *The Washington Post*, July 5, 1926, 1 (PQHN); "Jefferson's Home Is Given to Nation as People's Shrine," *The Washington Post*, July 6, 1926 (PQHN), 1; "Quincy Parade Ends at Birthplace of John Adams Where Great-Great-Grandson Reads Declaration," *Boston Daily Globe*, July 6, 1926, 15 (PQHN).
43. James C. Boykin, *The Story of the Declaration of Independence* (Washington, DC: Government Printing Office, 1926); Mabel Mason Carlton and Henry Fisk Carlton, *The Story of the Declaration of Independence* (New York: Charles Scribner's Sons, 1926), 113.
44. Dick Lehr, *The Birth of a Nation: How a Legendary Filmmaker and a Crusading Editor Reignited America's Civil War* (New York: Public Affairs, 2014).
45. Janet L. Abu-Lughod, *Race, Space, and Riots in Chicago, New York and Los Angeles* (New York: Oxford University Press, 2007), Ch. 2; Tim Madigan, *The Burning: Massacre, Destruction, and the Tulsa Race Riot of 1921* (New York: Thomas Dunne Books, 2001).
46. "Protest Plans for Independence Week," *The Chicago Defender*, June 12, 1926, A1 (PQHN).
47. Theodore Stevens, "The World's Great Documents," in *The Chicago Defender*, July 3, 1926, 4 (PQHN).
48. "Nation Must Pray Against Segregation," *Afro-American* (Baltimore), October 30, 1926, 5 (PQHN).
49. An informative, if brief, article on the exposition is accessible at https://philadelphiaencyclopedia.org/essays/sesquicentennial-international-exposition/.
50. Relatively little has been written on Wise, but see Perry Miller, *The New England Mind: From Colony to Province* (Cambridge, MA: The Belknap Press, 1953), 288–302; and Clinton L. Rossiter, "John Wise: Colonial Democrat," in *The New England Quarterly* 22, no. 1 (March 1949): 3–32.
51. Alexis de Tocqueville, *Democracy in America*, ed. Harvey C. Mansfield and Delba Winthrop (Chicago: The University of Chicago Press, 2000), 280–281.
52. "The Inspiration of the Declaration of Independence," in Amity Shlaes, ed., *The Autobiography of Calvin Coolidge* (Wilmington, DE: ISI Books, 2021), 217–231. Coolidge's sesquicentennial speech has been ignored by all the main recent interpreters of the Declaration: Bernard Bailyn, Garry Wills, Pauline Maier, and Danielle Allen, all of whom focus to one degree or another on the Enlightenment, rationalist origins of the document, though Bailyn acknowledges the important role of sermons (reprinted as pamphlets).

CHAPTER 15: A Secret Journey in the Fight Against Fascism

1. Quoted in Scott Donaldson, *Archibald MacLeish: An American Life* (New York: Houghton Mifflin, 1992), p. 93.
2. "The Long-Range Bombers," *The New York Times*, November 6, 1940, 22 (PQHN); "Roosevelt Pictures Ireland Under Reich," *The New York Times*, December 30, 1940, 7 (PQHN); "Goering's Latest Long-Range Bomber," *The New York Times*, January 18, 1941, 3 (PQHN).

3. Jane Aikin, "Preparing for a National Emergency: The Committee on Conservation of Cultural Resources, 1939–1944," *The Library Quarterly* 77, no. 3 (July 2007): 257–285.
4. Aikin, "Preparing," 259–260; Stephen Puleo, *American Treasures: The Secret Efforts to Save the Declaration of Independence, the Constitution, and the Gettysburg Address* (New York: Picador, 2016), 9–11.
5. Robert Penn Warren, "The War and the National Muniments," *Quarterly Journal of Current Acquisitions* 2, no. 1 (November 1944): 65.
6. "Hidden History: The Declaration of Independence," Book No. 4¼, Radio Research Project manuscript collection (1942, 1941). Manuscript/Mixed Material. Box 2, MS 023. American Folklife Center–DLC.
7. "Radio Speech of the President. Bill of Rights Day," December 15, 1941, Franklin D. Roosevelt Presidential Library. The following account relies heavily on David C. Mearns's essay in the *Annual Report of the Librarian 1949*, 47–51.
8. *Annual Report of the Librarian 1949*, 48.
9. See, for example, Luther H. Evans to George Stout, January 22, 1942, "Declaration File LC NARA 1940–1975," miscellaneous files, National Archives and Records Administration; PDF file provided by NARA to author.
10. George L. Stout and Evelyn Ehrlich, "The Declaration of Independence - Notes on Examination and Treatment," June 20, 1942. Also, Verner Clapp, "Restorative Treatment of the Declaration of Independence," May 18, 1942, which includes the journal that Stout made while working with Ehrlich on the Declaration. Box 786, Central File (MacLeish-Evans), MSS–DLC.
11. Anne O'Hare McCormick, "The Heritage for Which We Fight," *The New York Times*, July 5, 1942, SM3 (PQHN).
12. R. H. Markham, "Independence Declared Anew," *The Christian Science Monitor*, July 3, 1942, WM1 (PQHN).
13. Henry Steele Commager, "'We Hold These Truths'—Now as in 1776," *The New York Times*, July 4, 1943, SM6 (PQHN).
14. Franklin D. Roosevelt, "Address at the Dedication of the Thomas Jefferson Memorial, Washington, DC," April 13, 1945, *The Public Papers and Addresses of Franklin D. Roosevelt: 1943, The Tide Turns* (New York: Random House, 1950), 162–164.
15. Frank Whitson Fetter, "The Revision of the Declaration of Independence in 1941," *The William and Mary Quarterly* 31, no. 1 (January 1974): 133–138. As this book went to press claims emerged that the Jefferson Memorial Commission sought to whitewash Jefferson's slaveholding and instead portray him as a champion of abolition; see Michael Kranish, "How Jefferson's Words Were Doctored in His Memorial," *The Washington Post*, November 2, 2025, https://wapo.st/47TnMH2.
16. Julian P. Boyd, *The Declaration of Independence: The Evolution of the Text* (Washington, DC: The Library of Congress, 1943; rev. ed. 1999), 15. This would be the conclusion half a century later of Pauline Maier, in *American Scripture: Making the Declaration of Independence.*
17. Beardsley Ruml, "Fighting Creed for America," *The New York Times*, June 20, 1943, SM8 (PQHN).
18. *Annual Report of the Librarian 1949*, 51.

19. The *Evansville Courier* cartoon can be accessed at https://www.visitthecapitol.gov/artifact/may-they-never-have-be-hidden-or-kept-dark-again-drawing-karl-kae-knecht-evansville; "America's Priceless Documents Reappear," *Life* Magazine 17, no. 16 (October 16, 1944): 43–46; *The New Yorker*, June 30, 1945.

CHAPTER 16: Cold War Icon

1. See Michael J. Hogan, *A Cross of Iron: Harry S. Truman and the Origins of the National Security State, 1945–1954* (Cambridge: Cambridge University Press, 1998); Douglas T. Stewart, *Creating the National Security State: A History of the Law That Transformed America* (Princeton, NJ: Princeton University Press, 2008); and Odd Arne Westad, *The Cold War: A World History* (New York: Penguin 2017), 71–127.
2. Text of Vietnamese Declaration of Independence can be accessed at https://historymatters.gmu.edu/d/5139/. On Ho's use of Jefferson, see Mark Moyar, *Triumph Forsaken: The Vietnam War, 1954–1965* (Cambridge: Cambridge University Press, 2006), 1–3, 17. More briefly see also Ronald Spector, *In the Ruins of Empire: The Japanese Surrender and the Battle for Postwar Asia* (New York: Random House, 2007), 107–108; David Armitage, *The Declaration of Independence: A Global History* (Cambridge, MA: Harvard University Press, 2007), 134–135.
3. See list in Armitage, *Global History*, 152–153.
4. "Universal Declaration of Human Rights," United Nations, December 10, 1948; https://www.un.org/en/about-us/universal-declaration-of-human-rights.
5. Walter Trohan, "Calls on U.S. to Step Up Its War of Ideas," *Chicago Daily Tribune*, February 25, 1953, 21 (PQHN).
6. On the VOA, see David F. Krugler, *The Voice of America and the Domestic Propaganda Battles, 1945–1953* (Columbia: University of Missouri Press, 2000). On the cultural Cold War, see Louis Menand, *The Free World: Art and Thought in the Cold War* (New York: Picador, 2021), and David Caute, *The Dancer Defects: The Struggle for Cultural Supremacy During the Cold War* (Oxford: Oxford University Press, 2003).
7. On the CCF, see Peter Coleman, *The Liberal Conspiracy: The Congress for Cultural Freedom and the Struggle for the Mind of Postwar Europe* (New York: The Free Press, 1989). The CIA also was in contact with the plotters of a coup to assassinate Dominican Republic dictator Rafael Trujillo, in May 1961.
8. "Aims and Principles of Liberation of the Central and Eastern European Peoples, Independence Hall," Philadelphia, February 11, 1951, Stanislaw Mikolajczyk Papers, Box 76, Folder 12, The Hoover Institution Library and Archives, Stanford University.
9. "President Offered Plan to Free Red Satellites," *Los Angeles Times*, December 30, 1956, 12 (PQHN).
10. "Clark Explains Funds for 'Freedom Train,'" *The New York Times*, June 19, 1947, 44 (PQHN).
11. There has been no full-scale study of the Freedom Train, but for a positive review, see James Gregory Bradsher, "Taking America's Heritage to the People: The Freedom Train Story," *Prologue* 17, no. 4 (Winter 1985): 228–245, and for a more skeptical take, Stuart J. Little, "The Freedom Train: Citizenship and Postwar Political Culture, 1946–1949,"

American Studies 34, no. 1 (Spring 1993): 35–67. See also Stephen Puleo, *American Treasures: The Secret Efforts to Save the Declaration of Independence, the Constitution, and the Gettysburg Address* (New York: Picador, 2016), 336–339.

12. "Freedom Train Tours America," *National Geographic* 96, no. 4 (October 1949), 529–542. On segregation during the tour, see John White, "Civil Rights in Conflict: The 'Birmingham Plan' and the Freedom Train, 1947," *Alabama Review* 52, no. 2 (April 1999): 121–141.
13. "'Melting Pot' Sees the Freedom Train," *The New York Times*, September 26, 1947, 25 (PQHN); Little, "The Freedom Train," 35.
14. Millicent Taylor, "Owning Great Documents in Facsimile," *The Christian Science Monitor*, April 11, 1953, 10 (PQHN).
15. Robert L. Moora, "Preserving America's Immortal Parchment," *New-York Tribune*, July 2, 1950, A3 (PQHN).
16. "Patriot Plugs Declaration of Independence," *Chicago Tribune*, June 11, 1956, A8 (PQHN).
17. Promislo, a Ukrainian Jewish immigrant, discovered the antiquing process by accident in the 1920s and began selling treated Declarations at the 1939 New York World's Fair, according to his grandson, Alan Weiss. The company's real growth started in the post-war period, with commercial promotions. The Historical Documents Company is still the country's largest wholesaler of antiqued records.
18. Roger Butterfield, "They Signed Away Their Lives for You," *The Saturday Evening Post*, July 5, 1947, 39–43.
19. CBS Radio News Theater, "You Are There—July 4, 1776," available at https://youtu.be/sgQkJ50crIE?feature=shared; a transcript is accessible at https://www.genericradio.com/show/FHHY0HBOFDL. The CBS "You Are There" television episode on the Declaration is available at https://youtu.be/-wAO2gAz9qc?feature=shared.
20. Midcentury public educational efforts include Mortimer J. Adler and Charles Van Doren, *How to Read a Book: The Classic Guide to Intelligent Reading*, rev. ed. (New York: Touchstone Books, 2011), first published in 1940, and Arthur Krystal, ed., *A Company of Readers: Uncollected Writings of W. H. Auden, Jacques Barzun, and Lionel Trilling from the Readers' Subscription and Mid-Century Book Clubs* (New York: The Free Press, 2001).
21. "The Jeffersonian Heritage; The Living Declaration," University of Maryland, American Archive of Public Broadcasting (WGBH Boston and DLC, Washington, DC), http://americanarchive.org/catalog/cpb-aacip-500-mg7fw579. Promotional materials for "The Jeffersonian Heritage" are accessible at https://www.unlockingtheairwaves.org/document/naeb-b072-f03/#5. All the scripts were published, with an introduction, in Dumas Malone, ed., *The Jeffersonian Heritage* (Boston: Beacon Press, 1953).
22. *Demisemiseptcentennial* literally means half of half of seven hundred. I am indebted to Jessie Kratz, Historian of the National Archives, for bringing to my attention the term *demisemiseptcentennial.*
23. "Address at the Ceremonies Commemorating the 175th Anniversary of the Declaration of Independence," July 4, 1951, *PP: HST 1951*, 370–374. See also Jessie Kratz, "July 4, 1951: Celebrating America's Demisemiseptcentennial," *Prologue*, July 1, 2024;

https://prologue.blogs.archives.gov/2024/07/01/july-4-1951-celebrating-americas-demisemiseptcentennial/.

24. "U.S. Freedom Drive to Start on July 4," *The New York Times*, June 13, 1951, 15 (PQHN).
25. Henry Steele Commager, "The Declaration Is for Today!," *The New York Times*, July 1, 1951, 113 (PQHN).
26. Dumas Malone, *The Story of the Declaration of Independence* (New York: Oxford University Press, 1954), 267–268.
27. Henry Steele Commager, *The Great Declaration: A Book for Young Readers* (New York: Macmillan and Company, 1958), 11, 107.

CHAPTER 17: The Final Battle to Control the Declaration

1. The account of the resealing of the Declaration is taken from *Preservation of the Declaration of Independence and the Constitution of the United States*, National Bureau of Standards Circular 505 (Washington, DC: National Bureau of Standards, 1950), and Elio Passaglia, *A Unique Institution: The National Bureau of Standards, 1950–1969* (Gaithersburg, MD: U.S. Department of Commerce, 1999), 47–53.
2. "Introduction," *Annual Report of the Librarian of Congress for the Fiscal Year Ending June 30, 1952* (Washington, DC: The Library of Congress, 1952), xvii.
3. This account draws on Milton O. Gustafson, "The Empty Shrine: The Transfer of the Declaration of Independence and the Constitution to the National Archives," *American Archivist* 39, no. 3 (July 1976): 271–286, which remains the best examination of the transfer.
4. Sally Kress Tompkins, *A Quest for Grandeur: Charles Moore and the Federal Triangle* (Washington, DC: Smithsonian Institution Press, 1993).
5. *First Annual Report of the Archivist of the United States* (Washington, DC: Government Printing Office, 1936), 5–8.
6. "Remarks Upon Laying the Cornerstone of the National Archives Building," February 20, 1933, *Public Papers of the Presidents of the United States: Herbert Hoover, 1932–1933* (Washington, DC: United States Government Printing Office, 1977), 1002.
7. "Introduction," *Report of the Librarian of Congress* (1952), xiv.
8. Wayne C. Grover to Luther Evans, April 28, 1952, "Negotiations with Library of Congress for Transfer of Constitution, etc.," National Archives and Records Service, Transaction 052–114, May 20, 1952.
9. William J. Sittig, "Luther Evans: Man for a New Age," *The Quarterly Journal of the Library of Congress* 33, no. 3 (July 1976): 250–267.
10. On Washington and the threat of atomic attack, see David F. Krugler, *This Is Only a Test: How Washington, DC, Prepared for Nuclear War* (New York: Palgrave Macmillan, 2006).
11. Greg Bradsher, "Wayne Grover: Shaping the National Archives," *Prologue* 41, no. 4 (Winter 2009): 24–31.
12. Gustafson, "The Empty Shrine," 284–285. David C. Mearns, "Forever Is Twenty-Eight Years. Concerning the transfer of the Declaration of Independence and the Constitution of the United States to the National Archives," August 14, 1952, Box 100, David C. Mearns Papers, MSS–DLC.

13. This section relies on Jessie Kratz, "Carting the Charters," *Prologue*, December 12, 2014, https://prologue.blogs.archives.gov/2014/12/12/carting-the-charters/, and Gustafson, "The Empty Shrine."
14. For a discussion of the National Archives Building see Steven McLeod Bedford, *John Russell Pope: Architect of Empire* (New York: Rizzoli, 1998), 143–155.
15. The murals measure thirty-seven and a half feet wide and fourteen feet high and were painted by Barry Faulkner in 1935–36.
16. "Address at the National Archives Dedicating the New Shrine for the Declaration of Independence, the Constitution, and the Bill of Rights," December 15, 1952; *PP: HST 1952–1953*, 1077–1079.
17. "Address at the National Archives," 1077–1079. On the vault, see Jessie Kratz, "Protecting the Bill of Rights: the Mosler Vault," *Prologue*, December 17, 2015, https://prologue.blogs.archives.gov/2015/12/17/protecting-the-bill-of-rights-the-mosler-vault/.
18. The "Red Scare" remains a controversial topic, though most historians now accept that amid innocent victims, Communist agents did exist and subversive networks were established. A recent study is Clay Risen, *Red Scare: Blacklists, McCarthyism, and the Making of Modern America* (New York: Scribner, 2025). See also John Earl Haynes and Harvey Klehr, *Venona: Decoding Soviet Espionage in America* (New Haven, CT: Yale University Press, 2000). The classic text from an insider is Whittaker Chambers, *Witness* (Washington, DC: Regnery History, 2014).
19. Roland Sawyer, "A Visit to the Archives of the United States Gives You a Look at Historic Documents and What Freedom Means," *The Christian Science Monitor*, July 3, 1953, 13 (PQHN); R. L. Duffus, "Thoughts at One of Freedom's Shrines," *The New York Times*, July 4, 1954, SM3 (PQHN).

CHAPTER 18: The Promise of the Declaration in the Civil Rights Era

1. For an account of the attack, see Taylor Branch, *Parting the Waters: America in the King Years, 1954–1963* (New York: Simon & Schuster, 1989), 889–896. For a personal account, see Condoleezza Rice, *Extraordinary, Ordinary People: A Memoir of Family* (New York: Three Rivers Press, 2010), esp. Chs. 10–11. On Birmingham in general, see Diane McWhorter, *Carry Me Home: Birmingham, Alabama: The Climactic Battle of the Civil Rights Revolution* (New York: Simon & Schuster, 2001).
2. Martin Luther King, Jr., "Letter from a Birmingham Jail," https://www.africa.upenn.edu/Articles_Gen/Letter_Birmingham.html.
3. The Thirteenth Amendment was ratified December 6, 1865, and the Fourteenth on July 9, 1868.
4. "Address at the Ceremonies Commemorating the 175th Anniversary of the Declaration of Independence," July 4, 1951, *PP: HST 1951*, 370–374.
5. *To Secure These Rights: The Report of the President's Committee on Civil Rights* (New York: Simon & Schuster, 1947), 4, 151–173.
6. Dwight D. Eisenhower, "Radio and Television Address to the American People on

the Situation in Little Rock," September 24, 1957; *Public Papers of the Presidents of the United States: Dwight D. Eisenhower, 1957* (Washington, DC: Government Printing Office, 1958), 689–694.

7. William F. Buckley, Jr., "Why the South Must Prevail," *National Review* 4, no. 7 (August 24, 1957): 148–149.
8. On the Civil Rights Movement generally, see Branch, *Parting the Waters*, and Juan Williams, *Eyes on the Prize: America's Civil Rights Years, 1954–1965* (New York: Penguin Books, 2013); on King, see David J. Garrow, *Bearing the Cross: Martin Luther King, Jr., and the Southern Christian Leadership Conference* (New York: William Morrow, 1986).
9. "We Hold These Truths . . . ," *Tri-State Defender* (Memphis), January 16, 1960, 1 (PQHN). See also the examples given in Alexander Tsesis, *For Liberty and Equality: The Life and Times of the Declaration of Independence* (New York: Oxford University Press, 2012), 283–311.
10. "Editorial Points," *The Boston Globe*, October 26, 1963, p. 4; "Civil Rights in Los Angeles," *Los Angeles Tribune*, June 23, 1963, K6 (PQHN).
11. "'Implement the Declaration of Independence,' Johnson Urges," *The Chicago Defender*, July 6, 1963, 2 (PQHN).
12. Joseph Alsop, "Matter of Fact . . . ; A New Revolution," *The Washington Post, Times Herald*, July 3, 1963, A15 (PQHN).
13. Alfred Duckett, "Impatient, Want Freedom Now," *The Chicago Defender*, August 3, 1963, 8 (PQHN).
14. For a positive view of the Kennedy Administration, see Patricia Sullivan, *Justice Rising: Robert Kennedy's America in Black and White* (Cambridge, MA: Harvard University Press, 2021).
15. John Lewis, "Speech at the March on Washington," August 28, 1963, http://voicesofdemocracy.umd.edu/lewis-speech-at-the-march-on-washington-speech-text/.
16. The speech can be found in Clayborne Carson and Kris Shepard, eds., *A Call to Conscience: The Landmark Speeches of Dr. Martin Luther King, Jr.* (New York: Grand Central Publishing, 2002), 75–88.
17. Lyndon B. Johnson, "Radio and Television Remarks Upon Signing the Civil Rights Bill," July 2, 1964, *PP: LBJ 1963–1964,* II: 842–844. On the Act, see Todd S. Purdum, *An Idea Whose Time Has Come: Two Presidents, Two Parties, and the Battle for the Civil Rights Act of 1964* (New York: Picador, 2015); on its legacy, see Christopher Caldwell, *The Age of Entitlement: America Since the Sixties* (New York: Simon & Schuster Paperbacks, 2020), 19–23.
18. "Commencement Address at Howard University: 'To Fulfill These Rights,'" June 4, 1965, *PP: LBJ 1965* II: 635–640.
19. Fears of what opponents described as an ever-expanding civil rights regime were furthered by the 1978 *Regents of the University of California v. Bakke* case, in which the Supreme Court found racial quotas for admission to university programs to be unconstitutional, but allowed the use of race as a deciding factor. The following decades would see claims of "systemic racism" pitted against charges of "reverse discrimination" in the workplace, educational system, and throughout society, with both sides claiming that equality was being undermined. In a pair of cases in 2023, the Supreme Court

overturned several prior decisions that had upheld affirmative action in college admissions processes, determining they were unconstitutional.

20. King's "American Dream" speech can be found at https://www.rev.com/transcripts/the-american-dream-july-4th-speech-transcript-martin-luther-king-jr.
21. Bruce Watson, *Freedom Summer: The Savage Season of 1964 That Made Mississippi Burn and Made America a Democracy* (New York: Penguin, 2011).
22. Gerald Horne, *The Fire This Time: The Watts Uprising and the 1960s* (Charlottesville: University of Virginia Press, 1995).
23. The Black Panther Party Platform and Program can be found in Judith Clavir Albert and Stewart Edward Albert, eds., *The Sixties Papers: Documents of a Rebellious Decade* (New York: Praeger, 1984), 159–64.
24. "Crisis of Color, '66," *Newsweek*, August 22, 1966, 20–23.
25. Alvin Felzenberg, "How William F. Buckley, Jr., Changed His Mind on Civil Rights," *Politico*, May 13, 2017, https://www.politico.com/magazine/story/2017/05/13/william-f-buckley-civil-rights-215129/.
26. See Richard Rothstein, *The Color of Law: A Forgotten History of How Our Government Segregated America* (New York: Liveright, 2018).
27. See Chris Myers Asch and George Derek Musgrove, *Chocolate City: A History of Race and Democracy in the Nation's Capital* (Chapel Hill: The North Carolina University Press, 2017), 355–359; J. Samuel Walker, *Most of 14th Street Is Gone: The Washington, DC Riots of 1968* (New York: Oxford University Press, 2018).

CHAPTER 19: Bicentennial

1. David Wilson, "God Bless Elizabeth II, the Queen of England," *The Boston Globe*, July 11, 1976, A5 (PQHN).
2. "Well done, Your Majesty," *The Christian Science Monitor*, July 13, 1976, 28 (PQHN).
3. Among the many studies, see Mark Kurlansky, *1968: The Year That Rocked the World* (New York: Random House Trade Paperbacks, 2004).
4. "The Declaration of Independence, narrated by Ronald Reagan" [LP sound disc], Martin Anderson papers, Box 360, Folder 7, Hoover Institution Library & Archives, Stanford University. "Reagan Calls Tyranny of Mob Threat to America," *The New York Times*, July 5, 1968, 14 (PQHN).
5. Herbert Brucker, "Voter Cynicism the Big Issue for '76," *The Boston Globe*, February 17, 1976, 12 (PQHN).
6. "A Declaration of Interdependence," reprinted in Philip S. Foner, ed., *We, the Other People: Alternative Declarations of Independence by Labor Groups, Farmers, Woman's Rights Advocates, Socialists, and Blacks* (Urbana: University of Illinois Press, 1975), 202–205. See also see Daniel Sargent, *A Superpower Transformed: The Remaking of American Foreign Relations in the 1970s* (New York: Oxford University Press, 2015), 165.
7. For these tumultuous years, see James T. Patterson, *Grand Expectations: The United States, 1945–1974* (New York: Oxford University Press, 1996), 524–790; Sargent, *A Superpower Transformed*, 1–228.

8. Clive Barnes, "Spirited '1776': Founding Fathers' Tale is a Happy Musical," *The New York Times*, March 17, 1969, 46 (PQHN).
9. Nan Robertson, "White House Is Host to '1776,' Its First Full-Length Broadway Show," *The New York Times*, February 23, 1970, 1 (PQHN).
10. *To Set a Country Free; An Account Derived from the Exhibition in the Library of Congress Commemorating the 200th Anniversary of American Independence* (Washington, DC: The Library of Congress, 1975).
11. On the reconstruction, see John D. R. Platt, *Historic Structure Report: Graff House, Historical Data Section* (Philadelphia: Independence National Historical Park, 1972).
12. John Brannon Albright, "Major Bicentennial Celebrations," *Chicago Tribune*, June 27, 1976, C4. The only significant amount of information on the 1975–1976 Freedom Train is online, accessible at https://www.freedomtrain.org/american-freedom-train-home.htm.
13. Tammy S. Gordon, *The Spirit of 1976: Commerce, Community, and the Politics of Commemoration* (Amherst: University of Massachusetts Press, 2013), Chs. 2–3.
14. Nan Carroll, "Women Behind the Men," *The Daughters of the American Revolution Magazine* 109, no. 1 (January 1975): 23–25.
15. Henry Steele Commager, "Jefferson and the Great Declaration," *The Boston Globe*, July 4, 1976, G6 (PQHN).
16. John Hope Franklin, "The Moral Legacy of the Founding Fathers," *Chicago Tribune*, October 5, 1975, M8 (PQHN); Ted Stewart, "Black Patriots in the American Revolution," *Sepia* (July 1976), 49; Ethel L. Payne, "Beyond Bicentennial," *The Chicago Defender*, July 3, 1976, 6 (PQHN).
17. "Rights and the Spirit of '76," *Los Angeles Times*, January 8, 1976, C6 (PQHN).
18. "ERA Does Nothing for Women, Says Schlafly," *The Boston Globe*, October 18, 1976, 4 (PQHN).
19. Letty Cottin Pogrebin, "Sexism Rampant," *The New York Times*, March 19, 1976, 32 (PQHN).
20. Judy Klemesrud, "Mrs. Ford Helps 'Remember the Ladies' of the Revolutionary Era," *The New York Times*, June 30, 1976, 43 (PQHN).
21. The original deadline for ratification was 1979; that was later extended to 1982, but the measure still failed to gain the three-fourths of States required for adoption.
22. "General Services Administration 1976 Annual Report" (Washington, DC: U.S. Government Printing Office, 1977), 12.
23. F. R. Bruns, Jr., "'Declaration Stamps,'" *The Washington Post*, May 16, 1976, 15 (PQHN); Suzanne J. Stone, "The $2 Bill Returns," *Economic Reviews* 62, no. 2 (March/April 1976), n.p. (PQHN).
24. Catherine Nicholson, "Finding the Stones," *Prologue* 44, no. 2 (Summer 2012), https://www.archives.gov/publications/prologue/2012/summer/stone.html. The other copies struck in 1976 were stored at the National Archives.
25. *Declaration of Independence: The Adventures of a Document* (Washington, DC: National Archives and Records Service, 1976); Whitfield J. Bell, Jr., *The Declaration of Independence: Four 1776 Versions* (Philadelphia: The American Philosophical Society, 1976).

26. Frederick R. Goff, *The John Dunlap Broadside: The First Printing of the Declaration of Independence* (Washington, DC: Library of Congress, 1976). Five more Dunlap Broadsides were discovered after 1976.
27. Gerald R. Ford, "Remarks at a Bicentennial Ceremony at the National Archives," July 2, 1976, *PP: GRF 1976,* II: 1954–1957. *General Services Administration 1976 Annual Report* (Washington, DC: Government Printing Office, 1977), 10; Lawrence Meyer, "America Joyfully Toasts Birth of a Nation," *The Washington Post,* July 5, 1976, A1 (PQHN).
28. John Rockwell, "Music: Philharmonic Plays to 50,000," *The New York Times,* July 5, 1976, 6 (PQHN); excerpts from Bernstein's speech at https://www.overgrownpath.com/2008/07/bernstein-on-declaration-of.html.
29. "President's Proclamation," *The New York Times,* July 4, 1976, 25 (PQHN); *General Services Administration 1976 Annual Report,* 2.
30. "Remarks of Gerald R. Ford, in Philadelphia, Pennsylvania," July 4, 1976, *PP: GRF 1976,* II: 1966–1971; Meyer, "America Joyfully Toasts Birth of Nation."
31. Ronald Reagan, "It Isn't the Way It Looks," *San Francisco Examiner,* September 5, 1975, 26 (PQHN).
32. "People's Bicentennial," *The New York Times,* July 5, 1976, 14 (PQHN). On the PBC, see Christoper Culig, "America Can Never Be Revolutionized Until Its Revolutionaries Become Americanized: The Peoples Bicentennial Commission and the United States Bicentennial, 1971–1976," M.A. Thesis, George Washington University, 2009.
33. Lynn Darling, "Bicentennial Hailed for Its Legacies," *The Washington Post,* January 1, 1977, A1 (PQHN).
34. *Ibid.*
35. Horace C. Savage, "This Is Our Country; Why Boycott Its Anniversary?," *Tri-State Defender,* July 19, 1975 (PQHN).
36. Stephen W. Stathis, "Returning the Declaration of Independence to Philadelphia: An Exercise in Centennial Politics," in *PMHB* 102, no. 2 (April 1978): 168.
37. Potomac Associates, *State of the Nation, 1976,* 1976 [Dataset]. Roper #31096399, Version 2. Gallup Organization (Cornell University, Ithaca, NY: Roper Center for Public Opinion Research, 1976). doi:10.25940/ROPER-31096399.

CHAPTER 20: The Declaration in a New Millennium

1. The final plane was United Flight 93, which crashed into a field in rural Pennsylvania when a group of its passengers heroically charged the cockpit in an attempt to regain control of the plane. Steve Hendrix, "F-16 Pilot Was Ready to Give Her Life on Sept. 11: A Pilot Reflects on One of the Lesser-Told Tales Of Sept. 11: How the First Counterpunch the U.S. Military Prepared to Throw at the Attackers Was Effectively a Suicide Mission," *The Washington Post* (Online), August 26, 2011. For an account of September 11, see Garrett Graff, *The Only Plane in the Sky: An Oral History of* 9/11 (New York: Avid Reader Press/Simon & Schuster, 2020).
2. Mary Lynn Ritzenthaler and Catherine Nicholson, "A New Era Begins for the Charters of Freedom," *Prologue* 35, no. 3 (Fall 2003), https://www.archives.gov/publications/prologue/2003/fall/charters-new-era.html.

3. Victoria Blue, "The Last Hands to Touch the Declaration of Independence," *Prologue* (June 30, 2016), https://prologue.blogs.archives.gov/2016/06/30/the-last-hands-to-touch-the-declaration-of-independence/; James Dao, "Self-Evident Truths, Now More Evident," *The New York Times*, September 17, 2003, E2 (PQHN).
4. See also "Transcript of National Archives History Office Oral History Interview" with Mary Lynn Ritzenthaler, June 27, 2016, https://www.archives.gov/files/about/history/mary-lynn-ritzenthaler-final.pdf.
5. NIST was the successor to the National Bureau of Standards, which had carried out the 1951 encasement.
6. The following is taken from "Press Kits: Charters of Freedom Re-encasement Project," National Archives; accessible at https://www.archives.gov/press/press-kits/charters.html#pressrelease1; Ritzenthaler, "A New Era Begins."
7. See "Preserving Our Nation's Watchwords: The Charters of Freedom Encasements," National Institute of Standards and Technology, https://www.nist.gov/nist-time-capsule/making-nist-case-preservation/preserving-our-nations-watchwords-charters-freedom.
8. For a technical discussion of the renovations, see "Oral History Interview Package" of Patrick Alexander, Project Manager, National Archives Building Renovation, conducted December 14, 2006, https://www.archives.gov/files/about/history/pat-alexander-oral-history.pdf. See also "Transcript of National Archives History Office Oral History Interview" of Marvin Pinkert, conducted June 27, 2017, p. 2 (unpaginated), https://www.archives.gov/files/about/history/sources/pinkert-marvin-transcript-final.pdf.
9. Richard Blondo, "A Top-to-Bottom Renovation for the National Archives Building," *Prologue* 35, no. 3 (Fall 2003), https://www.archives.gov/publications/prologue/2003/fall/building-renovation.html.
10. Monte Reel, "A New Showcase for Historic Words," *The Washington Post*, September 17, 2003, MDB1 (PQHN).
11. See James T. Patterson, *Restless Giant: The United States from Watergate to Bush v. Gore* (New York: Oxford University Press), Chs. 7–12, and Christopher Caldwell, *The Age of Entitlement: America Since the Sixties* (New York: Simon & Schuster Paperbacks, 2020).
12. George W. Bush, "Remarks by the President at the Rededication of the National Archives," Washington, DC, September 17, 2003, *Public Papers of the Presidents of the United States, George W. Bush, Book, 2003, II—July 1 to December 31, 2003* (Washington, DC: United States Government Printing Office, 2006), 1175–1176.
13. Barack Obama, "Inaugural Address," Washington, DC, January 21, 2013, *Public Papers of the Presidents of the United States, Barack Obama, 2013, I—January 1 to June 30, 2013* (Washington, DC: United States Government Publishing Office, 2018), 45.
14. See Jeffrey Toobin, *Homegrown: Timothy McVeigh and the Rise of Right-Wing Extremism* (New York: Simon & Schuster, 2023), esp. 3–4, 91, 146.
15. Transcript of McVeigh defense's opening statement, https://law2.umkc.edu/faculty/projects/ftrials/mcveigh/defenseopen.html.
16. Transcript of McVeigh prosecution's opening statement, https://law2.umkc.edu/faculty/projects/ftrials/mcveigh/prosecutionopen.html.

17. "The Rotunda for the Charters of Freedom Reopens at the National Archives," *Prologue* 35, no. 4 (Winter 2003), https://www.archives.gov/publications/prologue/2003/winter/rededication.html.
18. "Performance and Accountability Report," National Archives and Records Administration, FY 2004, p. 22, https://www.archives.gov/files/about/plans-reports/performance-accountability/2004/nara-2004-par-complete.pdf.
19. Christian Y. Dupont, "The Albert H. Small Declaration of Independence Collection," in Christian Y. Dupont and Peter S. Onuf, eds., *Declaring Independence: The Origin and Influence of America's Founding Document* (Charlottesville: University of Virginia Library, 200), 73–80.
20. Sanka Knox, "$404,000 Paid for Early Copy of Declaration of Independence," *The New York Times*, May 8, 1969, 1 (PQHN); Jessica Lepler, "Exeter's Declaration of Independence," *Commonplace* 18, no. 1 (Winter 2018), https://commonplace.online/article/vol-18-no-1-lepler/.
21. The price was equal to $15.26 million in 2025 dollars. Suzanne Muchnic, "Declaration Sold Online for $7.4 Million," *The Washington Post*, June 30, 2000, C3 (PQHN). With Sotheby's commission, the total price came to $8.1 million. On the traveling exhibit, see, https://www.normanlear.com/declaration-of-independence-road-trip.
22. "Performance and Accountability Report, 2006," National Archives and Records Administration, https://www.archives.gov/files/about/plans-reports/performance-accountability/2007/nara-2007-par-summary.pdf; Janice L. Kaplan, "At the Archives, Real National Treasures," *The Washington Post*, December 3, 2004, I67 (PQHN).
23. Steve Chawkins, "Founding Document, Found Again," *Los Angeles Times*, January 19, 2008, A12 (PQHN). I am indebted to Chief Justice Roberts and Matthew Hofstedt, Curator at the Supreme Court, for allowing me to see the Court's copy of the Stone facsimile.

Epilogue

1. James Truslow Adams, *The Epic of America* (Boston: Little, Brown, and Company, 1931), 404.
2. I modify the distinction between Burkean traditions and Jeffersonian possibilities discussed in John Burt, "Lincoln, Calhoun, and Cultural Politics," *Raritan Quarterly* 23, no. 2 (Fall 2003), 142–162, in a review of Harry V. Jaffa, *A New Birth of Freedom: Abraham Lincoln and the Coming of the Civil War* (Lanham, MD: Rowman & Littlefield Publishers, 2000).
3. "George Washington to the Hebrew Congregation in Newport, Rhode Island, 18 August 1790," *The Papers of George Washington, Presidential Series*, VI, *1 July 1790–30 November 1790*, ed. Mark A. Mastromarino (Charlottesville: University Press of Virginia, 1996): 284–286.

IMAGE CREDITS

Insert, image number:

1, 9
Courtesy of the Library of Congress

2, 3
Courtesy of the National Portrait Gallery

4, 5, 7, 11, 13
Courtesy of the National Archives and Records Administration

6
Courtesy of the Yale University Art Gallery

8
Courtesy of the Union League Club, Philadelphia

10
Courtesy of the National Park Service

12
Courtesy of the National Archives

Text, page number:

18
Courtesy of the National Gallery of Art

19, 222, 233, 243, 256
Courtesy of the National Archives and Records Administration

37
Historical Society of Pennsylvania

40, 43, 55, 112, 117, 137, 148, 164, 166, 168, 169, 179, 182, 184, 193, 198, 200, 209, 252
Courtesy of the Library of Congress

75
Courtesy of Dr. Ralph Eshelman

76
White House Historical Association

85, 87
Courtesy of the National Archives

107
Courtesy of Texas State Library Archives Commission

129, 165
Courtesy of the National Portrait Gallery

134
Courtesy of Albert H. Small Declaration of Independence Collection, University of Virginia

191
Courtesy of the Library of Congress and Hathi Trust

211
Courtesy of the U.S. Army

229
Courtesy of the National Institute of Standards and Technology

257
Associated Press

INDEX

Page numbers in *italics* refer to illustrations.
Page numbers after 287 refer to endnotes.

ABOUT THE AUTHOR

Michael Auslin is the Payson J. Treat Distinguished Research Fellow at Stanford University's Hoover Institution. Previously an associate professor of history at Yale, he wrote *National Treasure* as a Distinguished Visiting Scholar at the Library of Congress's John W. Kluge Center and an American Heritage Partners Fellow at the Society of the Cincinnati's American Revolution Institute. He writes a Substack, *The Patowmack Packet*, on Washington, D.C., past and present, and lives in Virginia.